SWIMMING WITH CROCODILES

INTERNATIONAL CENTER FOR ALCOHOL POLICIES

Series on Alcohol in Society

SWIMMING WITH CROCODILES

The Culture of Extreme Drinking

Marjana Martinic and Fiona Measham

Routledge
Taylor & Francis Group
New York   London

Routledge
Taylor & Francis Group
270 Madison Avenue
New York, NY 10016

Routledge
Taylor & Francis Group
2 Park Square
Milton Park, Abingdon
Oxon OX14 4RN

© 2008 by International Center for Alcohol Policies
Routledge is an imprint of Taylor & Francis Group, an Informa business

Printed in the United States of America on acid-free paper
10 9 8 7 6 5 4 3 2 1

International Standard Book Number-13: 978-0-415-95548-5 (Hardcover)

Library of Congress Cataloging-in-Publication Data

Swimming with crocodiles : the culture of extreme drinking / edited by Marjana
  Martinic and Fiona Measham.
       p. ; cm. -- (ICAP series on alcohol in society)
  Includes bibliographical references and index.
  ISBN 978-0-415-95548-5 (hardbound : alk. paper)
  1. Youth--Alcohol use--Cross-cultural studies. 2. Drinking of alcoholic
beverages--Social aspects. 3. Drinking of alcoholic beverages--Cross-cultural studies.
4. Drinking customs--Cross-cultural studies. 5. Alcoholism--Cross-cultural studies. I.
Martinic, Marjana. II. Measham, Fiona, 1963- III. Series: Series on alcohol in society.
  [DNLM: 1. Alcohol-Related Disorders--Case Reports. 2. Adolescent. 3.
Cross-Cultural Comparison--Case Reports. WM 274 S977 2008]

HV5135.S95 2008
362.2920835--dc22   2007049821

Visit the Taylor & Francis Web site at
http://www.taylorandfrancis.com

and the Routledge Web site at
http://www.routledge.com

"When I get drunk, I go swimming…. This is a stupid thing to do because there are crocodiles and hippos in the river, but you feel like you are invincible when you are drunk, so you do it. I do it."

(Male participant, ICAP Focus Group, South Africa)

Contents

Editors

Dr. Marjana Martinic is Vice President for Public Health at the International Center for Alcohol Policies (ICAP). Her work focuses on the nexus between the scientific evidence base and international alcohol policy development. Prior to joining ICAP in 1996, she worked in developmental neuroscience research at the University of Virginia Medical School and at the National Institutes of Health in the United States. She has published extensively in the fields of neuroscience and alcohol policy. Her previous book (co-authored with Barbara Leigh), *Reasonable Risk: Alcohol in Perspective* (2004), is volume 7 in the ICAP book series, Alcohol in Society.

Dr. Fiona Measham was appointed to Lancaster University in 2000 and is now Senior Lecturer in Criminology in the Department of Applied Social Science. Dr. Measham is a nationally renowned researcher with 20 years of experience in the fields of drug and alcohol use, gender, licensed leisure, and cultural criminology. She is co-author of *Illegal Leisure* (1998) and *Dancing on Drugs* (2001), based on two large-scale studies of young people's drug and alcohol use, for both of which she was lead researcher. Her theoretical interests span cultural criminology, gender studies, and the sociology of intoxication, with a particular interest in the boundaries of transgression, the criminalization of leisure, and the problematic-recreational interface in leisure-time consumption.

Contributors

Ademola Ajuwon, University of Ibadan, Nigeria

Barton Alexander, Molson Coors Brewing Company, USA

Afolabi Bamgboye, University of Ibadan, Nigeria

Andrés Bascones Pérez-Fragero, Fundación Alcohol y Sociedad (Alcohol and Society Foundation), Spain

Marie Choquet, Institut National de la Santé et de la Recherche Médicale (French National Institute for Health and Medical Research, INSERM), France

Vera Da Ros, Informação Responsável Sobre Drogas e Afins (Reliable Information about Drugs and Related Issues, DINAMO), Brazil

Keith Evans, Drug and Alcohol Services, Australia

Mônica Gorgulho, Informação Responsável Sobre Drogas e Afins (Reliable Information about Drugs and Related Issues, DINAMO), Brazil

Jason Kilmer, Evergreen State University, USA

Eugenia A. Koshkina, National Research Center on Addictions, Russia

Mary Larimer, University of Washington, USA

Christine Lee, University of Washington, USA

Barbara Leigh, University of Washington, USA

Mark Leverton, Diageo, UK

Chan Makan, (Former Director), Industry Association for Responsible Alcohol Use (ARA), South Africa

Victor Makanjuola, University of Ibadan, Nigeria

Steve March, Alcohol Focus Scotland (AFS), UK

Marjana Martinic, International Center for Alcohol Policies (ICAP), USA

Fiona Measham, University of Lancaster, UK

Véronique Nahoum-Grappe, L'école des Hautes Études en Sciences Sociales (School of Higher Studies in Social Sciences, EHESS) and Le Centre National de la Recherche Scientifique (National Center for Scientific Research, CNRS), France

Ian Newman, University of Nebraska-Lincoln, USA

Olabisi Odejide, University of Ibadan, Nigeria

Olayinka Omigbodun, University of Ibadan, Nigeria

Frederick Oshiname, University of Ibadan, Nigeria

Daniya Tamendarova, International Center for Alcohol Policies (ICAP), USA

Enrico Tempesta, Osservatorio Permanente sui Giovani e L'alcool (Permanent Observatory on Youth and Alcohol), Italy

Disclaimer

The opinions expressed in this book are those of the individual authors and do not necessarily reflect the views of the International Center for Alcohol Policies (ICAP) or its sponsoring companies.[*]

---

[*] ICAP is dedicated to promoting understanding of the role of alcohol in society and to helping reduce the abuse of alcohol worldwide through dialogue and partnerships involving the beverage alcohol industry, the public health community, and others with an interest in alcohol policy. ICAP is a not-for-profit organization supported by major international beverage alcohol companies: Asahi Breweries, LTD; Bacardi-Martini; Beam Global Spirits and Wine; Brown-Forman Corporation; Diageo PLC; Heineken N.V.; InBev; Molson Coors Brewing Company; Pernod Ricard; SABMiller PLC; Scottish & Newcastle.

Chapter 1

Extreme Drinking

Marjana Martinic and Fiona Measham

Concern regarding certain drinking behaviors among youth and young adults transcends countries, cultures, and social classes and has for some time moved to the forefront of alcohol policy and prevention. Whether or not young people are legally permitted to consume alcohol, their drinking often puts them at risk for harm; the toll from accidents and injuries is high. However, it seems to be the visibility of young people's drinking and the potential threat this poses to public order that particularly galvanize communities to call for action to reduce problems of public drunkenness, threats to safety, and instances of public disturbance in general.

Research into the drinking behaviors of young people has kept stride with public health and criminological concerns in an effort to examine drinking patterns that are considered particularly egregious. The outcomes of such patterns have been described and analyzed, and attempts have been made to identify effective approaches to minimize any potential harm. Despite these efforts, a satisfactory definition that encapsulates the full cluster of the behaviors in question has not yet been found. Heavy (or at least excessive) drinking is certainly involved. Nevertheless, the presence of heavy alcohol consumption alone is not sufficient to define these behaviors. More often than not, they are accompanied by intoxication, injury, social disturbance, violence, and even (in extreme instances) death. These outcomes fail to be considered within existing definitions. At the same time, despite this grim picture, such drinking behaviors among young people are driven by an element of risk-taking, excitement, and the pursuit of pleasure.

We propose that the term *extreme drinking* satisfies the need for a new definition of a drinking pattern that has many dimensions. The term takes into account the underlying motivations for heavy, excessive, and unrestrained

1

behaviors associated with drinking for many young people. It also acknowledges the drinking process itself and accommodates greater focus on outcomes that are likely to follow. In many ways, extreme drinking is not so far removed from other extreme behaviors, such as extreme sports, which also offer a challenge; their pursuit is motivated by an expectation of pleasure; and they are, by design, not without risk to those who engage in them, others around them, and society as a whole.

INTOXICATION, DRUNKENNESS, AND THE INADEQUACIES OF "BINGE DRINKING"

Much of the concern around young people's extreme drinking is related to the intoxication that marks it. Clearly, drinking to intoxication is a necessary element in what has variously been described as "binge," "heavy episodic," "excessive," "harmful," and "hazardous" drinking, influencing the outcomes of such behavior. However, none of these terms and their various definitions have succeeded in offering a satisfactory umbrella for the collective of "extreme drinking."

The Pharmacology of Intoxication

The World Health Organization (WHO) defines "intoxication" as poisoning from any one of a wide range of substances. These include narcotics, caffeine, inhalants, and "other substances, [such as] nutmeg, morning glory seeds, catnip, betel nut, kava, and certain over-the-counter and prescription drugs" (World Health Organization [WHO], 1992). Alcohol is certainly included among these intoxicants, all pharmacologically active substances with a direct effect on the central nervous system. Yet, alcohol also differs from other intoxicants because its action on the brain is nonspecific. The action of alcohol on the central nervous system is not confined to any single brain region or neurochemical pathway. Rather, it affects the dopaminergic, GABAergic, and serotonergic systems. As a result of this interaction, alcohol has a primary short-term depressant effect, followed by a more persistent stimulatory effect. The onset of these two effects is dose-dependent.

Intoxication from alcohol can be identified on the basis of its symptoms, as outlined in the American Psychiatric Association's *Diagnostic and Statistical Manual of Mental Disorders* (DSM-IV-TR, 2000). However, the lack of specificity of alcohol for a single neurochemical system and the variety of associated behaviors often make it difficult to define intoxication clearly on the basis of symptoms alone. The presence of different symptoms at different levels of blood alcohol concentration (BAC) may confound attempts to define or identify an exact point of intoxication. Table 1.1 describes the relationship between BAC and physiological symptoms for the "typical" person, although it should

TABLE 1.1 BAC Levels and Their Effects for a "Typical" Person

BAC Levels (mg/ml)	Effects
0.2–0.3	• mental functions begin to be impaired
0.3–0.5	• attention and visual field are reduced, cerebral control relaxes, and there is a sensation of calm and wellbeing
0.5–0.8	• reflexes become retarded • difficulty of adapting vision to luminosity differences • overestimation of performance abilities • aggressive tendency
0.8–1.0	• difficulty in driving/controlling vehicles (for alcohol-impaired pedestrians, in walking along the road) • impairment of neuromuscular coordination
1.0–1.9	• lack of coordination • inability to correctly interpret what is happening • poor judgment • difficulty in walking and standing steadily
2.0–2.9	• nausea • vomiting
3.0–3.9	• serious intoxication • lowered body temperature • partial amnesia ("blackout") likely
≥4.00	• alcohol poisoning • coma • risk of death (about 50% of people who have a BAC ≥4.00 will die of alcohol poisoning)

Sources: International Center for Alcohol Policies (2005), Lang (1992), and Melcop (2003).

be noted that height, weight, gender, and, especially for young people, experience may change the levels at which these symptoms are evident.

Social Dimensions of Drunkenness

While intoxication describes a physiological state arising from heavy drinking, its equivalent in everyday parlance is what we conventionally refer to as "drunkenness." The disinhibition displayed by individuals who become loud and boisterous after drinking is attributable to the action of alcohol on the dopaminergic system, the same neurochemical pathways that elicit emotions such as pleasure and euphoria. However, this is only part of the story. Drunkenness is also very much a social phenomenon, shaped by local attitudes toward alcohol and its effects. The WHO Lexicon of Alcohol and Drug Terms (1994) notes: "[Alcohol] is taken in order to achieve a desired degree of intoxication. The expression of a given level of intoxication is strongly influenced by cultural and personal expectations about the effects of the drug" (see "intoxication" in WHO, 1994).

In their classic review of drunken behavior, MacAndrew and Edgerton (1969/2003) describe "why people's comportment so frequently changes when they have made their bodies alcoholed." The prism of culture sheds an interesting light on why disinhibited behavior often goes hand in hand with intoxication in some societies, whereas in others these disinhibiting effects, despite the heavy drinking that is observed, are nowhere to be seen. Culture also answers questions regarding "appropriate-to-the-occasion" behavior that may be seen with intoxication under some circumstances but not others. It is therefore the combination of intoxication and cultural mores and expectancies about alcohol-related behavior that makes up the complete picture of "drunkenness."

The historical and cultural distinctions of drinking and drunkenness are explored broadly in chapters 2, 3, and 4, but it is the focus groups from a range of different cultures, the results of which are laid out in chapter 5, that make the cultural differences in what is acceptable and what is not come alive. These are

> the learned relations that exist among men living together in a society. More specifically,…the way people comport themselves when they are drunk is determined not by alcohol's toxic assault upon the seat of moral judgment, conscience, or the like, but by what their society makes of and imparts to them concerning the state of drunkenness. (MacAndrew & Edgerton, 1969/2003, p. 165)[1]

The Hijacking of the "Binge"

The literature about binge drinking represents the most comprehensive attempt to describe those drinking behaviors (particularly among young people) that are marked by heavy alcohol consumption, intoxication, and predominantly negative outcomes. A growing number of definitions and meanings of the word *binge* exist, notable not only for their lack of consensus regarding definition and measurement, but also their lack of consideration of outcomes and cultural sensitivity.

The "Bender"

Originating in the literature of social and clinical sciences, the term *binge* has also made its way into popular parlance. The traditional popular concept of a binge conjures up an image of a solitary activity, an unbridled and potentially self-destructive drinking bout lasting up to several days, a "bender" when the drinker becomes "soaked in alcohol." It is perhaps most vividly captured by the portrayals of drinking binges as sustained periods of uncontrolled self-indulgence in novels and films such as the classic *The Lost Weekend* (Jackson, 1944; Wilder & Brackett, 1945) or the more recent film *Leaving Las Vegas* (Figgs, 1995). In the clinical literature, the term is applied particularly in

---

[1] Copyright by Percheron Press/Eliot Werner Publications, 2003.

relation to alcohol dependence; a binge in this context is associated with "loss of control" (e.g., Cloninger, 1987). Clinical definitions describe a binge as continuous, dependent drinking over a period of a day or more until the drinker is unconscious (Newburn & Shiner, 2001, p. 7; see also WHO, 1994). In an attempt to reassert this traditional clinical definition of binge drinking in the face of the more recent unit-based and subjective definitions discussed below, some alcohol researchers have again advocated this concept:[2]

> [A] "binge" describes an extended period of time (often operationalized as at least 2 days) during which a person repeatedly administers a substance to the point of intoxication, and gives up his/her usual activities and obligations in order to use the substance. It is the combination of prolonged use and the giving up of usual activities that forms the core of the definition of a "binge." (Schuckit, 1998, p.123; in response to Wechsler & Austin, 1998)

Quantitative Definitions

A more recent and increasingly used notion of the word *binge* relies on an objective quantitative definition of alcohol consumption in a single drinking session. In an attempt to formally quantify the binge, particularly in the epidemiological literature, a group of researchers from the United States set their definition at five or more drinks for men and four or more for women on a given occasion in the past two weeks (see Wechsler, Davenport, Dowdall, Moeykens, & Castillo, 1994; Wechsler & Nelson, 2006).[3] In the United Kingdom, a binge has been defined as either drinking more than half the recommended weekly maximum intake or (more usually) more than double the recommended daily maximum in a single session (e.g., Gill, 2002; Prime Minister's Strategy Unit, 2004; Department of Health, Home Office, Department for Education and Skills, & Department for Culture, Media and Sport, 2007). Translated into quantitative terms, in the United States, a "bingeing" man would need to consume five drinks (70 grams of alcohol) at a sitting, and four drinks (56 grams) would suffice for a woman to be classified as "binge drinking"; meanwhile, in the United Kingdom, a man consuming beyond eight units (64 grams) and a woman consuming more than six units (48 grams) would be classified as "binge drinking."

At least three key aspects of contemporary unit-based definitions of the term *binge* are problematic. In the first instance, a "binge," by its current definition, focuses on the quantity of alcohol consumed in an unspecified drinking session and sets no requirement for the time interval during which drinking takes place. Binge drinking could thus be concentrated into a short time period, or protracted over a longer one until the specified number of drinks

---

[2] Reprinted with permission from the *Journal of Studies on Alcohol*, vol. 59, pp. 123–124, 1998. Copyright by Alcohol Research Documentation, Inc., Rutgers Center of Alcohol Studies, Piscataway, NJ 08854.

[3] Wechsler and colleagues also used the term *heavy episodic drinking* in a *Journal of Studies on Alcohol* article, but kept the five/four definition (Wechsler, Nelson, Lee, et al., 2003).

is reached or exceeded. Second, formal quantitative definitions of a "binge" neither address nor specifically *require* intoxication as an outcome. Combined with the lack of a specified time period for the drinking session, this means that an individual can potentially be classified as a "binge drinker" without ever reaching altered states of intoxication. For example, under the current definition by Wechsler and colleagues, a man consuming—over a course of four hours—a cocktail before dinner, three glasses of wine or beer with his meal, followed by a liqueur would be classified as a "binge" drinker just like a young woman downing four drinks in half an hour at the bar on a Saturday night. Clearly, neither the behaviors nor their potential consequences are the same in these two cases. Indeed, none of the possible outcomes, whether positive or negative, are even considered.

Third, there are enormous cross-cultural variations in both the definition of a "drink" (or unit) and how many drinks it takes to have "binged." Given the existing discrepancies in unit or standard drink size—for example, one U.S. drink is equivalent to 1.6 units in the United Kingdom—drinking five standard U.K. units would result in the consumption of 40 grams of alcohol, whereas drinking five standard U.S. drinks would equate to 70 grams of alcohol (International Center for Alcohol Policies [ICAP], 2007; see also "Module 20: Standard Drinks" in ICAP, 2005). Alternatively, the application of a universally applicable, objective unit-based measurement of binge drinking based on physiological harm raises the problems of where to draw the line to measure binge drinking, along with the potential usefulness of having a dichotomous variable with a "cut-off" point for harm, and even the potential for disagreement about how such cut-off points are interpreted (e.g., Kolvin, 2005; McAlaney & McMahon, 2006). If it is predominantly based on acute medical outcomes, the definition could include so many drinkers as to lack credibility in the general population. In the U.K., for example, a unit-based definition of binge drinking is widely used and advocated in public health campaigns involving sensible recommended drinking levels. Yet, concerns have been raised about the "credibility gulf" between recommended and actual levels of sessional alcohol consumption by young people, alongside the increased availability and popularity of higher-strength alcohol beverages and larger serving measures, suggesting that academic and public health measures of "standard" drinks are out of step with contemporary serving and drinking practices (Hammersley & Ditton, 2005; Jefferis, Power, & Manor, 2005; Measham, 2006). In some cultures, as illustrated in the focus group study from China in chapter 5, the notion of a single serving may well be irrelevant, as a sign of a good host (both at home and in a public setting) is keeping glasses and drinking vessels topped up at all times. Finally, single unit-based measures not only fail to account for variations in height, weight, gender, alcohol tolerance, and experience, but also disregard the social and cultural contexts of consumption.

These efforts have diluted the earlier complexities inherent in a "binge" as a "bender," stripping it down to a single dimension of drinking to a specified level at a single sitting. As a result, the term *binge* has all but lost its currency.

Subjective Definitions

Aside from the quantitative, unit-based definition described above, other, less widely used definitions exist that rely on self-reported frequency of drunkenness rather than quantity of alcohol consumed. For example, Richardson and Budd's (2003) study of alcohol, crime, and disorder among young people favors a subjective definition of "binge" drinkers to include those respondents who reported feeling "very drunk" at least once a month in the preceding 12 months. Furthermore, Midanik (1999) found that subjective measures of frequency of drunkenness were better predictors of harmful outcomes than unit-based measures, while others have emphasized the importance of considering the rate, social context, and outcomes of consumption along with the quantity consumed (e.g., Goodhart, Lederman, Stewart, & Laitman, 2003; Hammersley & Ditton, 2005; Wright, 2006).

There are several key problems with subjective notions of drunkenness based on the views of drinkers themselves. These include the social and cultural distinctions linked to behavioral components of drunkenness and the enormous variations in attitudes to "being drunk." Such differences in the degree of social acceptance and sanctioning of intoxication and drunkenness, as well as young people's own definitions of drinking patterns and "negative" or "positive" outcomes can be seen in the focus group discussions presented in chapter 5 (see also chapter 4). It is apparent that within certain cultural contexts, as in the U.K., drunkenness is seen as pleasurable, a state to be striven toward, and, indeed, regularly achieved by some drinkers—described elsewhere by Measham as "determined drunkenness" (Measham, 2006; Measham & Brain, 2005). In other cultures, for example, the "typical" Mediterranean scenario, drunkenness is a negative state, to be avoided and generally occurring only occasionally. Thus such cross-cultural disparity in views and attitudes around drunkenness results in major limitations as to consistent measures for such subjective definitions.

Blood Alcohol Concentration

In an attempt to find acceptable middle ground while maintaining objectivity, the U.S. National Institute on Alcohol Abuse and Alcoholism (NIAAA) has attempted a new definition of a "binge" as "a pattern of drinking alcohol that brings blood alcohol concentration...to 0.08 gram percent or above. For the typical adult, this pattern corresponds to consuming 5 or more drinks (male), or 4 or more drinks (female), in about 2 hours" (National Institute on Alcohol Abuse and Alcoholism, 2004, p. 3).[4] Intoxication is implicit in this measure by virtue of the BAC threshold chosen, even though it is not specifically addressed. Once again, however, it is the state of intoxication itself, rather than the outcomes or the process of drinking, that is reflected in the definition.

---

[4] This definition translates into 70 grams (five drinks) and 56 grams (four drinks) of pure ethanol over two hours. A single "standard" U.S. drink contains 14 grams of ethanol.

8

SWIMMING WITH CROCODILES

TOWARD A NEW CONSTRUCT

In view of the inadequacies of current terminology, and the disagreements surrounding it, a new construct is needed to adequately describe the behaviors and outcomes of what we are attempting to examine. We propose that the term *extreme drinking* fits the bill. It involves more than simply heavy drinking; it cannot be constrained by measures of quantity, frequency, or intoxication; and it draws heavily on cultural definitions. Moreover, while excessive consumption is certainly involved, the motivation driving it is key, both during the process of drinking and for the final outcomes, both positive and negative. Although an element of unpredictability seems to be present in extreme drinking (which may indeed be a part of its appeal), there are also aspects of determination in the pursuit of this pattern of consumption. At the same time, despite its quest for disinhibition, extreme drinking hinges upon the ability to manage outcomes in the face of the possible elements of unpredictability.

Defining Extreme Drinking

Trying to define extreme drinking poses a challenge. It encompasses more than just intoxication and more than simply heavy, excessive, and "binge" drinking. Extreme drinking includes a behavioral component: It is concerned not simply with consumption levels but also with the processes and patterns of consumption, as well as their positive and negative outcomes. Extreme drinking extends beyond simply drunkenness, which is often culturally so context-specific and variable in definition and social meaning that it cannot be considered a useful term for international comparative research in this field.

The intensity involved in extreme drinking is not an absolute but, rather, exists on a scale; it is largely defined by the culture within which it occurs and that culture's views on drinking. There are, however, five key criteria around the definition of extreme drinking that need to be satisfied: intoxication, motivation, process, outcomes, and alcohol experience.

To begin with, extreme drinking requires *intoxication*. It includes excessive or heavy drinking and the physiological effects described in Table 1.1 above. Together, the quantity, frequency, and time interval of consumption result in a sustained period of intoxication as measured by a raised BAC level, concentrated in time and intensity.

In addition to intoxication, the *motivation* behind extreme drinking needs to be considered. The consumption pattern addressed here is clearly driven by intent and a directed quest for some degree of loss of control. There is an important caveat, however. What distinguishes extreme from heavy pathological drinking is that it is neither unbridled nor limitless. Rather, extreme drinking is a form of calculated hedonism (see chapter 2) and a desire to achieve a "controlled loss of control" (Measham, 2002). It should be noted that extreme drinking is not always planned. Indeed it may sometimes be "accidental." The key point to bear in mind, however, is that some element of hedonism is always involved in the initial reason for drinking. There may be an element of risk-taking or sensation-seeking, or a desire to push the boundaries of consumption beyond usual or acceptable social levels.

Extreme drinking is also defined by the *process* involved in reaching the desired state. At least from the perspective of the drinker, this process is itself a positive experience, in which the pursuit of pleasure and enjoyment goes beyond the boundaries of the usual social drinking levels. Extreme drinking is, by and large, a social activity, enabled and encouraged by others, usually friends and peers, who share the experience and the broadly positive attitudes to this pattern of consumption.

As already discussed, the definition of extreme drinking involves attention to the *outcomes*. Drunkenness is certainly one of these, whether it is arrived at accidentally or on purpose, and largely determined by culture and the social acceptability of drunken behavior (see chapters 3 and 5). However, beyond the impact of high levels of alcohol on the body, extreme drinking need not by definition be harmful to the individual or society. Indeed, a key aspect of extreme drinking is that it can have both positive and negative outcomes; clearly, for the drinker, extreme drinking and its outcomes may be desirable and viewed as positive on a subjective level. Objectively, however, extreme drinking may have a negative impact on finances, personal relationships, and productivity in work or studies, and will increase the risk for acute health outcomes as a result of accidents and injuries, as well as raise the risk of involvement in crime as both offenders and victims (e.g., Nichols, Kershaw, & Walker, 2007). For society at large, even where there is a high degree of acceptance of extreme drinking, the outcomes are often negative, relating to social order and public disturbance, as well as to the social cost associated with harm.

Yet, for many young people who engage in extreme drinking, the element of controlled loss of control is paramount throughout the experience. Although keen to engage in the process and to reach intoxication, most young people who drink to extremes also want to end the evening safely. The ability to walk the fine line depends on the fifth and final element, the so-called level of *alcohol maturity*. The ability to "handle one's drink" and achieve an acceptable balance between harmful and nonharmful outcomes is influenced by previous *life experiences* with alcohol. It is for this reason that extreme drinking is a pattern of consumption that is usually, although not exclusively, associated with youth and young adults.

OVERVIEW OF THE BOOK

This book and its effort to define in a comprehensive and useful way the term *extreme drinking* grew out of a combined sense of concern about the saliency of certain patterns of drinking among young people and frustration at the inadequacies of existing terminology, which have tended to cloud rather than clarify the issue. Much media attention and political debate across the developed and developing world center on drinking behaviors that result in negative health and social outcomes. However, there has been little comparative research to shed light on these developments. The focus groups which form the basis for the empirical research in this book take a step in this direction. They also represent an effort to examine extreme drinking and identify the elements that are consistent across disparate cultures.

Chapter 2 considers the historical context of intoxication and the changing attitudes surrounding it. Focusing on the United Kingdom in particular, it examines how social and cultural changes have contributed to the variations in whether or not heavy drinking—and ultimately extreme drinking—is thought of as a normative behavior. In the author's view, the changing role of young people in society and the concept of extended adolescence, along with the changing nature of leisure-time consumption, are major factors in prevailing drinking patterns.

Exploring what it means to be young, the culture of youth, and its quest for the extreme, chapter 3 attempts to position extreme drinking within a sociocultural context (speaking primarily from the French perspective), the testing of limits, and the desire for instant gratification. Chapter 4 then reviews the sociological and psychological literature on young people's drinking and discusses the important role of expectancies and social norms that provide the motivation for this behavior.

The key empirical research included in the book tests the "real-life" validity of some of the premises laid out in the preceding chapters. Chapter 5 describes a series of focus groups held in countries around the world. The prevailing cultural views on alcohol, drinking, and young people in the countries selected are quite disparate, allowing both the commonalities and differences in extreme drinking to be considered.

The last part of the book attempts to offer a way forward in addressing the harm that extreme drinking may pose to individuals and society. To do this, it focuses on the roles of different social players in addressing extreme drinking (chapter 6), the policy measures that can be reasonably and realistically implemented (chapter 7), and the prevention efforts that can be specifically applied to extreme drinking (chapter 8).

We argue that there is a need for a new term to describe young people's drinking that encapsulates a specific behavior and its outcomes. It is our hope that *extreme drinking* captures its essence, shifting the focus to what really matters from a public health, criminological, and policy perspective. This hedonistic pursuit of "intense intoxication" (Hayward & Hobbs, 2007) appears to be increasingly favored by youth and young adults in many countries. By sidestepping the moribund debate on definitions and measurements of "binge" drinking, it is hoped that research can refocus on those areas of particular concern with regard to motivations, processes, and acute outcomes identified above. Important changes are under way in relation to drinking patterns worldwide, and this book aims to address some of these emerging issues.

REFERENCES

American Psychiatric Association. (2000). *Diagnostic and statistical manual of mental disorders* (4th ed., text revision). Washington, D.C.: Author.

Cloninger, C. R. (1987). Neurogenetic adaptive mechanisms in alcoholism. *Science, 236*, 410–416.

Department of Health, Home Office, Department for Education and Skills, & Department for Culture, Media and Sport. (2007). *Safe. Sensible. Social. The next steps in the National Alcohol Strategy*. London: Department of Health & Home Office.

Figgs, M. (Director/Screenplay). (1995). *Leaving Las Vegas* [Motion picture]. United States: MGM.

Gill, J. S. (2002). Reported levels of alcohol consumption and binge drinking within the U.K. undergraduate student population over the last 25 years. *Alcohol and Alcoholism, 37*, 109–120.

Goodhart, F. W., Lederman, L. C., Stewart, L. P., & Laitman, L. (2003). Binge drinking: Not the word of choice. *Journal of American College Health, 52*, 44–46.

Hammersley, R., & Ditton, J. (2005). Binge or bout? Quantity and rate of drinking by young people in the evening in licensed premises. *Drugs: Education, Prevention and Policy, 12*, 493–500.

Hayward, K., & Hobbs, D. (2007). Beyond the binge in "Booze Britain": Market-led liminalization and the spectacle of binge drinking. *British Journal of Sociology, 58*, 437–456.

International Center for Alcohol Policies (ICAP). (2005). *ICAP Blue Book: Practical guides for alcohol policy and prevention approaches*. Retrieved October 10, 2007, from http://www.icap.org/Publication/ICAPBlueBook/tabid/148/Default.aspx.

International Center for Alcohol Policies (ICAP). (2007). *Table: Standard alcohol units*. Retrieved August 30, 2007, from http://icap.org/PolicyIssues/DrinkingGuidelines/StandardUnitsTable/tabid/253/Default.aspx.

Jackson, C. (1944). *The lost weekend*. New York: Farrar, Strauss and Cudahy.

Jefferis, B. J. M. H., Power, C., & Manor, O. (2005). Adolescent drinking level and adult binge drinking in a national birth cohort. *Addiction, 100*, 543–549.

Kolvin, P. (2005). *Licensed premises: Law and practice*. Haywards Heath, U.K.: Tottel.

Lang, A. (1992). Alcohol: Teenage drinking. In S. H. Snyder (Series Ed.), *Encyclopedia of psychoactive drugs* (2nd ed., Vol. 3). New York: Chelsea House.

MacAndrew, C., & Edgerton, R. E. (2003). *Drunken comportment: A social explanation*. Clinton Corners, NY: Percheron Press/Eliot Werner Publications. (Original work published 1969)

McAlaney, J., & McMahon, J. (2006). Establishing the rates of binge drinking in the U.K.: Anomalies in the data. *Alcohol and Alcoholism, 41*, 355–357.

Measham, F. (2002). "Doing gender"—"doing drugs": Conceptualising the gendering of drugs cultures. *Contemporary Drug Problems, 29*, 335–373.

Measham, F. (2006). The new policy mix: Alcohol, harm minimisation and determined drunkenness in contemporary society. *International Journal of Drug Policy, 17*, 258–268.

Measham, F., & Brain, K. (2005). "Binge" drinking, British alcohol policy and the new culture of intoxication. *Crime, Media, Culture: An International Journal, 1*, 263–284.

Melcop, A. G. (2003). Stop here and now: The challenges of approaching harm reduction in traffic violence. In E. Buning, M. Gorgulho, A. G. Melcop, & P. O'Hare (Eds.), *Alcohol and harm reduction: An innovative approach for countries in transition* (pp. 87–105). Amsterdam, Netherlands: International Coalition on Alcohol and Harm Reduction.

Midanik, L. T. (1999). Drunkenness, feeling the effects and 5+ measures. *Addiction*, *94*, 887–897.

National Institute on Alcohol Abuse and Alcoholism (NIAAA). (2004, Winter). NIAAA Council approves definition of binge drinking. *NIAAA Newsletter*, *3*, 3.

Newburn, T., & Shiner, M. (2001). *Teenage kicks? Young people and alcohol: A review of the literature*. York, U.K.: Joseph Rowntree Foundation.

Nichols, S., Kershaw, C., & Walker, A. (2007). *Crime in England and Wales 2006/07*. London: Home Office Research Development and Statistics Directorate.

Prime Minister's Strategy Unit. (2004). *Alcohol harm reduction strategy for England*. London: Cabinet Office, Her Majesty's Stationery Office.

Richardson, A., & Budd, T. (2003). *Alcohol, crime, and disorder: A study of young adults*. Home Office Research Study 263. London: Home Office Communication Development Unit.

Schuckit, M. A. (1998). Binge drinking: The five/four measure [Letter]. *Journal of Studies on Alcohol*, *59*, 123–124.

Wechsler, H., & Austin, S. (1998). Binge drinking: The five/four measure [Letter]. *Journal of Studies on Alcohol*, *59*, 122–123.

Wechsler, H., Davenport, A., Dowdall, G., Moeykens, B., & Castillo, S. (1994). Health and behavioral consequences of binge drinking in college: A national survey of students at 140 campuses. *Journal of the American Medical Association*, *272*, 1672–1677.

Wechsler, H., & Nelson, T. F. (2006). Relationship between level of consumption and harms in assessing drink cut-points for alcohol research: Commentary on "Many college freshmen drink at levels far beyond the binge threshold" by White et al. *Alcoholism: Clinical and Experimental Research*, *30*, 922–927.

Wechsler, H., Nelson, T. F., Lee, J., Seibring, M., Lewis, C., & Keeling, R. (2003). Perception and reality: A national evaluation of social norms marketing interventions to reduce college students' heavy alcohol use. *Journal of Studies on Alcohol*, *64*, 484–494.

Wilder, B. (Director/Screenplay), & Brackett, C. (Screenplay/Producer). (1945). *The lost weekend* [Motion picture]. United States: Paramount/C. Brackett.

World Health Organization (WHO). (1992). *The ICD-10 classification of mental and behavioural disorders: Clinical descriptions and diagnostic guidelines*. Geneva, Switzerland: Author.

World Health Organization (WHO). (1994). *Lexicon of alcohol and drug terms*. Retrieved May 8, 2007, from http://www.who.int/substance_abuse/terminology/who_ladt/en/index.html.

Wright, N. R. (2006). A day at the cricket: The breath alcohol consequences of a type of very English binge drinking. *Addiction Research and Theory*, *14*, 133–137.

Chapter 2

A History of Intoxication
Changing Attitudes to Drunkenness and Excess in the United Kingdom

Fiona Measham

It has been suggested that "the pursuit of intoxication [is] a practice which seems universal within human communities" (Dean, 1997, p. 156). However, attitudes toward intoxication are historically and socioculturally specific, ranging from facilitation and celebration to condemnation and criminalization. Indeed, the notion of intoxication as a distinct condition can itself be considered a recent construct (Walton, 2001).[1] This chapter considers the changing social views on drunkenness and excess, exemplified in the processes of regulation, stigmatization, and criminalization, focusing specifically on excessive alcohol consumption in the United Kingdom (U.K.). The U.K. is used as the subject of a case study in order to explore the international reputation of the British for alleged extreme drinking both at home and abroad—to the extent that the pattern of "binge and brawl" behavior has sometimes been characterized as the "British disease" (e.g., former British Prime Minister Tony Blair quoted in "Alcohol the 'New British Disease,'" 2004). The focus on the U.K. also allows us to explore what is often perceived as the extreme end of the spectrum of drinking behavior by young people.

---

[1] The notion of a simple causal relationship between alcohol and intoxication is relatively new. Earlier interpretations of the effects of alcohol are mediated by historically and culturally specific expectations as part of "society's contradictory and muddled relationship with intoxication" (Bancroft, 2008).

The changing representations of intoxication through media such as the press, television documentaries, and feature films are considered, alongside the roles of gender, ethnicity, religion, and socioeconomic class in molding attitudes to intoxication. While recognizing both continuity and change in drink-related attitudes and behavior, this chapter suggests that attitudes to intoxication have been shaped by and can be symbolic of the anxieties of others toward certain marginal, repressed, or "problematic" sociodemographic groups and provide a substantive illustration of the relationship between social change, social control, and self-control.

Attitudes to intoxication are indicative of the role of alcohol within the changing worlds of work, leisure, and pleasure, where it is variously seen as challenging, facilitating, and mediating contemporary life. Although public drunkenness and associated disorder have long been associated with British drinking culture, there have also been significant changes to British drinking patterns—and, as Hayward and Hobbs discuss (2007, p. 444), many of these recent changes can be considered a reflection rather than a rebellion against the social norms and behaviors engendered by contemporary consumer society: "Despite the sirens, vomiting and inevitable hand wringing... , the cumulative behaviour of the young drunk population..." on Britain's high streets "constitute, 'not inversions of the social order but mirrors of it'" (see also Schechner, 1993, p. 48).

RELIGION, RESPECTABILITY, AND CLASS

"Two great European narcotics—alcohol and Christianity." (Mike "The Streets" Skinner, album *The Hardest Way to Make an Easy Living*)

The relationship between religion and intoxication is deeply interwoven. Alcohol is a part of spiritual services and experiences in many religions, including Christianity, Hinduism, Sikhism, and Judaism, as has been ably explored by Rudgley (1993), Weiss (2001), and others (see chapters 3 and 4). It has been used to facilitate or enhance the search for enlightenment, transcendence, creativity, and self-exploration; for example, the writer Jay McInernay has noted his own hope that the "road of excess" would lead to the "palace of wisdom" (2006, para. 2). The diverse reaches of alcohol are indicated here in the role that drinking and, indeed, intoxication have had from the highest realms of religious and spiritual life to the leisure time of the lowest socioeconomic groups, with religion being cited as both a reason to drink and a reason to abstain (Heath, 1995, 2000).

The relationship between festivals, carnivals, and excess has been embedded in all societies—from the polytheistic Dionysian and Bacchanalian festivals of ancient Egypt, Greece, and Rome onward—alongside equally persistent attempts to limit such intemperance (Edwards, 2000). However, even though most societies have used psychoactive substances in both spiritual and secular contexts, it has been suggested that "few societies pursue intoxication in the arbitrary and hedonistic fashion prevalent in the modern West" (Rudgley,

1993, p. 144). Determined attempts to limit excessive alcohol consumption in the U.K. date back to the eighth century, and concerted efforts have been particularly evident since the 1500s (Edwards, 2000; Gusfield, 1991; Warner, 1997). It has been argued that the move to official condemnation of excessive drinking was linked to religious developments in the Middle Ages, when such behavior was associated with excessive eating and both were considered to be indicators of personal weakness. Disapproval of excessive drinking came primarily from the clergy, who associated it with one of the seven deadly sins, gluttony (Bennett, 1991, p. 176; Warner, 1997, p. 99). As such, drunkenness was considered immoral in religious terms. Researchers have related the timing of this growing religious censure to the power struggle between pre-Christian and pagan carnivals on the one hand, and Protestant and Counter-Reformation Catholic festivals and holy days on the other, in an attempt by the Church to disassociate itself from the rowdiness and excess of carnival (Gusfield, 1991; Presdee, 2000).

In Western Christian countries, the balance between carnival and Lent has been characterized as that between popular culture and "high" culture, indulgence and austerity. Socioeconomic and structural divisions within society are linked to apparently oppositional lifestyles and values, reflected in the advocacy of either moderation or indulgence—not only in drinking but also eating, working, sexual relations, aggression, and even spending habits. This juxtaposition of intoxication with sobriety and weekday restraint with weekend excess can be traced from preindustrial times to the Protestant, Puritan, and northern European contemporary drinking cultures, as socioeconomic developments (notably industrialization and urbanization) led to an increasing differentiation between work and leisure, weekday and weekend, home and the workplace (Presdee, 2000; see also chapters 3 and 5). Overall, as sobriety and restraint became distinctive features of festivals for higher socioeconomic groups, so rowdiness and excess were increasingly associated primarily with lower socioeconomic strata during festivals and holidays.[2]

Importantly, however, British historians have suggested that in the early and mid-19th century the distinctions between different sections of the working classes could be as significant as the unifying features within them.[3] One

---

[2] See also Thompson (1963/1988) on "polite culture" and "plebeian culture," as well as Stedman Jones (1971) on the development of working-class popular culture in the 1890s and the "rough–respectable" divide.

[3] This distinction within the lower classes has led some historians to dispute that there *was* a working class, distinct in itself in terms of objective features and subjective identity. While Thompson suggested that "from 1830 onwards a more clearly defined class consciousness, in the customary Marxist sense, was maturing, in which working people were aware of continuing both old and new battles on their own" (1963/1988, p. 782), this dating of the origins of the working class has been disputed. Historians such as Stedman Jones have argued that, although there may have been a first formative phase in the making of the English working classes up to the 1830s, a more convincing dating would be from the 1870s onward. Of significance to the discussion in this chapter, Stedman Jones (1983) identified a second formative phase or "remaking" of the working class as occurring between the 1870s and the 1900s, when the working-class identity, attitudes, and culture we would recognize today were formed.

characteristic distinction across the English working classes at that time was the "rough–respectable" divide, which has been discussed in terms of employment, criminal behavior, strategies for poverty relief, and (of relevance here) use of leisure time.[4] The "respectable" working classes—the skilled artisans or "labour aristocracy" as they were known—were often members of craft unions or mechanics' institutes and identified as striving toward middle-class leisure patterns and values, which included at that period temperance, thrift, non-Conformist church attendance, self-education, social ambition, and political and religious involvement.

The increasing legitimization and assimilation of "respectable" working-class culture was evident in the Victorian promotion of "rational recreation," illustrated by the establishment and use of public parks, public libraries, museums, and churches, along with the codification of sporting rules, increased licensing restrictions on public house and beer house trading hours, and the development of the temperance movement. In a related move, there was a proliferation of tea houses, railway excursions, and seaside holiday resorts (e.g., the first seaside trip was organized by the temperance travel agent Thomas Cook in July 1841). These recreational patterns of the respectable upper-working-class individuals led to their characterization by Harrison as "heroes of abstinence," rather than "heroes of consumption" (1971, p. 26). For the rising middle-class industrialists and upper-working-class artisans, distancing themselves from the features of popular culture and the lower classes was part of their self-definition and aspirational motivation, which resulted in further marginalization of the features of proletarian life.

So what was this "rough" lower-working-class leisure, so discouraged by the broader society, and what were the attempts to suppress it? For the unskilled working classes and the unemployed, a range of recreational activities was associated with fairs, carnivals, races, wakes, beer houses, street gambling, brothels, and brutal sports. In an effort to control behaviors associated with such activities, legislation was introduced that criminalized the more excessive aspects of "rough" lower-class culture, such as animal fighting, bare-knuckle fighting, and street gambling. This was followed over the subsequent 150 years by gradual marginalization and increased social disapproval of elements not outlawed, such as traditional traveling fairs, carnivals, festivals, and—of interest here—rougher drinking establishments that caused anxiety to the respectable classes: the gin palaces, beer houses, alehouses, and music halls of 18th and 19th century Britain.

It must be noted that, in their drinking, gambling, fighting, sports, sexual license, and lack of respect for the law, the lowest classes were sometimes portrayed as more closely allied to the Anglican upper class than the non-Conformist upper working class. However, although excessive drinking was

---

[4] The notion of "deserving" and "undeserving" poor can be traced from the workhouses and the poor laws of 18th and early 19th century England to the late Victorian treatment of the poor (e.g., Stedman Jones, 1971).

a characteristic of both the highest and lowest socioeconomic classes in 19th century England, the behavior was in response to very different socioeconomic circumstances. As Walvin noted (1978, p. 39), "the customs of eating and drinking among the rich and the poor were starkly different. The one represented a display of prosperity and recreation; the other a more familiar and traditional struggle to stay alive."

Both alcohol and drinking establishments had historically specific, central roles in the lives of the working classes in the early and mid-19th century. Alcohol consumption was widespread at this time partly because there were few safe, reasonably priced alternative beverages.[5] However, alcohol was not seen solely as a safe, cheap drink: It was also considered to provide energy and agility for a wide range of manual and professional occupations, and alcohol-based remedies were frequently used for many ailments at a time of limited medical knowledge. Up to the 19th century, drinking alcohol was considered to have stimulating and health-giving properties, by contrast to our contemporary emphasis on its depressant and health-damaging potential.[6] Alcoholic drinks also held symbolic significance: For example, a drink exchanged between two people could seal a commercial bargain or agreement and was considered by a young couple as a betrothal pledge. Moreover, if a single woman entered a 19th century drinking establishment with a single man during an annual feast or holiday, this indicated that she had publicly declared her allegiance to that man and planned to marry him (Harrison, 1971).

The significance of drinking to the general population at this time is illustrated by the sheer number of licensed premises. Between the 1820s and the 1870s, the ratio of pubs to people in England and Wales was relatively high. According to official records, there was one licensed premise per 168 people in 1831, and the number of premises continued to increase with the expansion of the general population until the 1870s (Wilson, *Annual Abstract of Statistics*, quoted in Harrison, 1971, p. 313). However, the ratio is likely to have been even higher in reality, given that informal and unlicensed drinking venues run from private homes and temporary buildings, home brewing, illicit distilling, and smuggling were widespread at that time. Thus, there may have been a drinking place for every hundred or so people in mid-19th century

---

[5] In early 19th century London, for example, it was standard practice for hospitals to give alcohol beverages to patients. Milk was dangerous when fresh, possibly adulterated or contaminated, and cost twice the price of beer. Although cordials, ginger beer, and lemonade were starting to be commercially produced by the 1850s and tea consumption was also spreading, mains-supplied water was still intermittent even in upper-class households, so drinking water remained unsafe and scarce across the country (Harrison, 1971).

[6] See chapter 5 for a discussion of the relationship between age and the effects of alcohol. Evidence from Brazil suggests that a generational difference may exist in motivations to drink and expectations of its effects, with some younger drinkers courting the potentially *stimulating* properties of the social consumption of alcohol, and older drinkers prioritizing its potentially *relaxing* qualities as a depressant.

England and Wales. And since the geographical location of pubs reflected their working-class customer base, Victorian pubs have been aptly described as "omnipresent institutions" (Walvin, 1978, p. 41), "a masculine republic in every street" (Harrison, 1971, as quoted in Hey, 1986, p. 15).

Alongside rapid social change, increasing socioeconomic class gradation, and growing class consciousness, there was a substantial decline in shared recreation between the classes. Unlike in earlier centuries, by the 1830s, professional and tradespeople drank alcohol in their own, increasingly comfortable homes rather than in drinking establishments, with the consequence of "private as opposed to public drinking…becoming a mark of respectability" (Harrison, 1971, p. 45). As a British statistician and economist, G. R. Porter, demonstrated in 1852, "In this country…no person, above the rank of a labouring man or artisan, would venture to go into a public-house to purchase anything to drink" (quoted in Harrison, 1971, p. 319). While upper-class men continued to drink in private clubs, "among the emergent middle class, the cult of domesticity seduced more and more men from public drinking places" (Walvin, 1978, p. 38).

Lower-working-class homes, by comparison, remained dark, dirty, cold, and overcrowded, emphasizing for this group the appeal of drinking establishments as the antithesis of the home environment. Just as with the 16th century alehouse, the 19th century pub offered "many comforts absent from the poor man's home. Light, heat, cooking facilities, furniture, newspapers, and sociability were then obtained by the poor only at the drinking place" (Harrison, 1971, p. 47).

Thus, during the mid-19th century, drinking places became more and more differentiated by socioeconomic class: "It is a significant insight into the growing awareness and strength of Victorian class divisions that the English working class was left to drink by itself" (Walvin, 1978, p. 38). Furthermore, a mere presence in the lower-quality drinking establishments could cast a dark shadow over one's respectability. So by the 19th century, public drinking and public drunkenness became associated with lower socioeconomic groups and a lack of respectability, and the pleasure-seeking of the lower classes was increasingly perceived by broader society as problematic (O'Malley & Valverde, 2004).

INTOXICATION AND THE REGULATION OF LEISURE IN POSTINDUSTRIAL BRITAIN

The key point in this discussion is that attitudes to intoxication are differentiated by class, culture, and religion, with drinking in some contexts portrayed as oppositional to work in industrial and postindustrial societies, as compared to agricultural and developing economies. Thus, the regulation of drinking and drunkenness has been historically targeted at specific forms of alcohol consumption within popular culture (Gusfield, 1991). It has been suggested that the rationalization of daily routines necessary for the development of the capitalist factory system led to "a new industrial morality that prescribed a more routinized and disciplined use of time" (Gusfield, 1991, p. 405) and, with it, the increased control of leisure and leisure-time drinking. The regulation of intoxication and the constraints on excessive drinking are seen to be driven by a presumption that decreased alcohol consumption would result in increased industrial productivity, thereby using alcohol control as a proxy for social and economic control. However, various researchers have challenged this perspective. Gusfield, for example, discussed a range of studies that raised questions about the presumed relationship between alcohol, social control, and industrialization. The underlying assumption that workers would otherwise resist the increased routine and discipline of the new factory system is not always evident, and methods of controlling absenteeism and slackness at work by means beyond alcohol controls were used, such as competition from migrant Irish labor. Furthermore, in some cases it was the upper working classes who were the most receptive to temperance and active in trade union movements, but resistant to increased controls and decreased autonomy within the workplace.

Bell (1976) described the cultural contradictions of capitalism that combine the Protestant Puritan work ethic (notably its emphasis on control and restraint) with the hedonistic consumerist ethic, based on conspicuous consumption and instant gratification. Others, however, have emphasized the complementary rather than contradictory nature of this dualism (e.g., Campbell, 1987). Rather than seeing excessive drinking as a challenge to the working week, this analysis considers it as a pressure valve or release that can counterbalance or even facilitate periods of restraint and application to work. With the development of late modern capitalist consumer society, other commentators have argued that periods of excess—the British "binge and brawl" drinking culture—may not only facilitate periods of economic activity, but are an integral part of (rather than a reaction against) contemporary society.

As Hayward and Hobbs (2007) argue in their consideration of the spectacle of British "binge" drinking,

> It is vital...that the specialization of British high streets into liminal zones should not be misread as spontaneous manifestations of the carnivalesque. Rather, it constitutes...a distinctly corporate manifestation of marketised forms of distinction that serve to reinforce, rather than eliminate the normative order. (p. 443)

Indeed, in late modern consumer culture, as Hayward and Hobbs note (2007) in their discussion of social theorists Baudrillard, Bauman, and Lury, "insatiable desire is now not only normal but essential for the continuance of the socio-economic order...a central feature of [the night-time economy], therefore, is the production of subjects who are constantly on the look out for new commodities and alternative experiences" (p. 444). This idea has been summed up by *The Guardian's* economics editor as the "because I'm worth it" generation, a reference to the popular TV advertising slogan:

Successful advertising slogans are the ones that capture a mood.... This is the "because I'm worth it" generation. Our culture is steeped in a value system that celebrates instant gratification, hedonism and selfishness. It is a get-rich-quick, live-now-pay-later zeitgeist where pampering yourself in the present is a necessity and thinking about the future a bolt-on luxury. (Elliott, 2007, p. 28)[7]

This issue is discussed further below in relation to recent changes in British drink-related attitudes and behaviors.

GENDER AND TEMPERANCE

Just as attitudes to intoxication throughout Britian were increasingly divided along class and religious lines from the Middle Ages on, so, too, it has been suggested that there was a growing disapproval of women's public drinking and public drunkenness. During the medieval period and up to the 16th century—at a time when people tended to drink steadily throughout the day, and abstinence was yet to be considered a virtue—women "drank very freely and without serious censure" (Warner, 1997, p. 99). Female and male wages were relatively high for the late medieval postplague population, and both the quality and quantity of food and alcohol for the lower classes improved in the wake of recurring epidemics and consequent population control.

By the 16th century, however, "low literature" began to be critical of women's drinking and drunkenness in public, advocating temperance as a feminine virtue. Warner (1997) has suggested that the emergence of temperance as a virtue specifically for women occurred during the economic crisis of the early modern period, characterized by a growing population, inflation, a sharp decline in real wages, and chronic underemployment. The quality of the average diet deteriorated markedly and household budgets could no longer afford alcohol consumption at the high levels of the late medieval period. In these circumstances, Warner suggests, "we may assume that women's consumption of alcohol declined relative to that of men" (1997, p. 103).

Thus, female temperance effectively sanctioned the redistribution of diminishing household resources in favor of men, resulting in the reduction of women's social access to the alehouse and the development of a drinking culture outside the home—in settings from which women were increasingly excluded. It was also at this time that

tastes were shifting away from the crude and often sour ales concocted by women at home in favour of beers manufactured by men...beer started to eclipse ale at about the same time that it was becoming unacceptable for women to drink in public places; that is, at a time when drinking was becoming a more strictly recreational activity conducted by men outside the home. (Warner, 1997, p. 105)

Furthermore, the entwining of gender and socioeconomic class is discernible in this exclusion of women from the alehouse: "It is clear that the

FIGURE 2.1 William Hogarth, *Gin Lane* (1751). © The Trustees of the British Museum. All
rights reserved.

campaign to enforce temperance on women also belonged to a larger campaign designed to ensure submissive behaviour among women in particular
and among the lower classes in general" (Warner, 1997, p. 106).

Consequently, it was in the alehouses of pre-Puritan and preindustrial
England that we can see the origins of the class-based and gender-based regulation of intoxication in the public domain, as well as of the discourses of temperance, morality, and respectability. Alongside the development of drinking
as a "recreational activity conducted by men outside the home" (Warner, 1997,
p. 105), female temperance came to be associated with virtue, modesty, and
femininity, whereas female drunkenness was equated with moral and sexual
depravity. This sentiment was most graphically illustrated in Hogarth's infa-
mous engraving, entitled *Gin Lane* (1751), in which the central character is

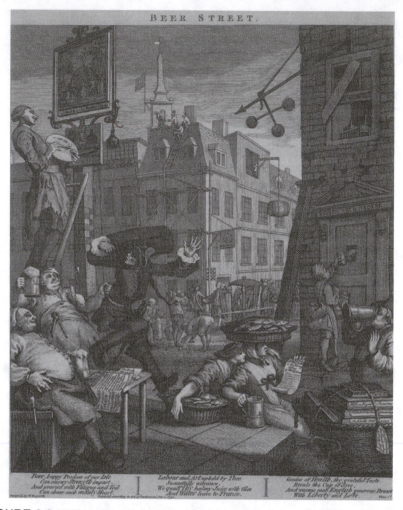

FIGURE 2.2 William Hogarth, *Beer Street* (1751). © The Trustees of the British Museum.
All rights reserved.

a woman representing the antithesis of feminine modesty and decorum, as well
as of maternal love and protection…. Dishevelled, half-naked and oblivious to
all but the snuff that she is taking, she allows her child to fall headlong into the
stairwell of a gin-cellar and to certain death. (Riding, 2006, pp. 190–192; see
also O'Malley & Valverde, 2004)

This portrayal of the consequences of heavy consumption of (Dutch)
gin—forcefully depicted as the source of misery, squalor, and death—and *Gin
Lane's* companion engraving, *Beer Street* (1751), depicting images of security,
order, and wellbeing associated with moderate consumption of (British) beer,
could arguably be considered the first images used in a public health campaign against drunkenness (see Figures 2.1 and 2.2).

Such concerns about the debilitating and debasing effects of intoxication on women and the lower classes are echoed more than 250 years later in relation to the anxieties around the apparent reemergence of women's public drinking and public drunkenness, associated with their growing educational and employment aspirations and opportunities. The focus on the changing drinking patterns of the "modern woman" echoes criminological debate in the 1970s about the "new female criminal" (Adler, 1975) and the idea that, as women's lives increasingly emulate men's in the workplace, we might also expect their behavior to emulate men in terms of a range of deviant or criminal behaviors, such as heavy drinking, drug use, violence, or acquisitive crime. However, as Smart (1979) noted in relation to such criminological speculation, women more likely to be involved in such problem behaviors may be among the demographic groups who are less likely to have benefited from any changes in educational and employment opportunities.

National surveys illustrate the complexities of the interplay between gender, socioeconomic class, and drinking patterns. Working women in Britain report higher alcohol consumption than economically inactive women (the latter are more likely to have caring responsibilities than their working counterparts). Among working women, those in managerial and professional positions are more likely to report consuming above recommended sensible drinking levels than women employed in routine and manual occupations; yet, the latter group is more likely to report "binge" drinking than managerial and professional women workers (Office for National Statistics [ONS], 2005). Thus, while the rise of women's binge drinking has been explained as a part of an emergent *ladette* culture, alongside women's increased disposable income and delayed marriage and motherhood, such concerns relate as much to the anxieties about women's changing position in society as to the realities of equality. Women's pay remains below men's, despite over 30 years of equal pay and sex discrimination legislation in the United Kingdom, and there has been a recent noted downturn in the number of women in higher executive positions in British industry (Equal Opportunities Commission, 2007). Research suggests that there is a complex relationship between drinking patterns and women's changing roles in employment, domestic responsibilities, and wider society (e.g., Gmel, Bloomfield, Ahlström, Choquet, & Lecomte, 2000; Hajema & Knibbe, 1998).

THE REGULATION AND CRIMINALIZATION OF INTOXICATION

The regulation of alcohol consumption in the United Kingdom has taken many forms over the years. Some of the earliest and most sustained public efforts have been directed at the control and criminalization of intoxication per se. The first statute on alcohol related to drunkenness and drunk and disorderly behavior (the Alehouse Act 1552, see London Metropolitan Archives, 1998); meanwhile, controls on the sale of alcohol in licensed premises related to the degree of intoxication as assessed by the landlord (and, more recently, the server) and whether or not the landlord/server will intervene and withhold access to alcohol. Thus, outward and subjective interpretations of socially appropriate levels of intoxication can potentially result in restricted access to alcohol and even arrest for both server and customer. The commercial sale of alcohol in licensed premises is therefore related to the apparent intoxication of customers, their behavior in public drinking places, and the potential harm that may result from excessive consumption for the individual, fellow drinkers, or the wider society (Graham, 2005). However, for those unable to purchase and consume alcohol legitimately in licensed premises—whether because of being intoxicated or under age—street drinking is an alternative, if more risky possibility (Coleman & Cater, 2005; Galloway, Forsyth, & Shewan, 2007). The strict enforcement of legislation controlling the sale of alcohol in licensed premises, combined with the higher price of alcoholic beverages in pubs and nightclubs, can result, therefore, in a polarization of young people's drinking into outdoor, isolated, and excessive drinking or indoor, underage but more moderate consumption due to social and financial restrictions.

As Törrönen and Karlsson (2005) have discussed in relation to moral regulation, and Wacklin (2005) in relation to social control, the regulation of drinking and drunkenness is symbolic of broader attitudes to appropriate public behavior. In an overview of Wacklin's and Törrönen and Karlsson's studies, Rudy (2005) draws attention to how changes in drinking, drinking-related behavior, and drinking establishments suggest that "moral regulation of these real and ideological spaces focuses the attention of various interest groups on the nature of drinking (civilised and controlled versus deviant)" (pp. 128–129). Törrönen and Karlsson's study juxtaposes the "civilized" picnic park drinking of the middle classes with rowdy and offensive youths and street drinkers in Finland. In the recent "binge" drinking debates, the British government advocated extending trading hours through the Licensing Act 2003 as a measure to reclaim city centers for the law-abiding, respectable majority while discouraging the wild lawlessness of "binge" drinkers, who were portrayed by the media as having turned these centers into "no-go" areas for the over-30s population (Measham & Brain, 2005; Roberts, 2006), discussed in more detail below.

REPRESENTATIONS OF INTOXICATION

Changes in attitudes to intoxication are evident in the changing nature of representations of intoxication in media such as the press, television programs, and feature films across the course of the 20th century, which both reflect and reinforce wider sociocultural values.

In the first part of the 20th century, British films portrayed intoxication in a largely positive light. It was represented as convivial drinking, in which alcohol bonded ordinary folk and even epitomized a spirit of defiance against the authorities and the "nanny state"; examples were the Ealing comedies *Whisky Galore!* (Mackendrick, 1949) and *Champagne Charlie* (Cavalcanti,

1944). In the United States, the glamorous high society "good time" image of alcohol in the postprohibition era gave way to a more sober tone during the Second World War (Rorabaugh, 2003); in the postwar era, intoxication was increasingly associated with negative portrayals of alcohol and the dark side of excessive consumption—alcoholism, withdrawal, and mental instability—seen in films such as *The Lost Weekend* (Wilder & Brackett, 1945). The (shorter term) pleasures of intoxication were associated with the (longer term) "slippery slope" to alcoholism and ruin, excessive consumption being used as a pivotal plot device and marker of "badness." The nature of this "ruin" was dependent on the social status and gender of the central protagonists: For example, in the case of *Days of Wine and Roses* (Edwards, 1962), the male character suffered professional ruin, as the female character suffered sexual ruin (Room, 1989).

In the late 20th century there was a period of positive and largely unproblematic portrayal of excessive drinking, shown in a series of 1970s comedy fraternity films such as *Animal House* (Landis, 1978). From that point onward, however, positive representations of intoxication were sidelined in favor of an emphasis on either the negative consequences of long-term consumption—for example, *28 Days* (Thomas, 2000)—or the setting of the bar as a workplace and social space for the film's protagonists—for example, *Cocktail* (Donaldson, 1988).

In terms of representations of intoxication and socioeconomic class, Hersey (2005) has argued that the chief plot developments involving alcohol in films and television programs increasingly focus on addiction and recovery from addiction, while successful recovery from alcohol addiction tends to occur predominantly in White characters from higher socioeconomic and professional groups, in films such as *Clean and Sober* (Gordon Caron, 1988), *When a Man Loves a Woman* (Mandoki, 1994), and *28 Days* (Thomas, 2000). In these instances, intoxication is portrayed as having a major negative impact on family relations: For instance, Meg Ryan's character in *When a Man Loves a Woman* hits her child when intoxicated, and Sandra Bullock's character in *28 Days* spoils her sister's wedding by knocking over the wedding cake and stealing and crashing a limousine while drunk.

Is it possible to disentangle such representations of intoxication from representations of addiction, however? Hersey (2005, p. 477) argues that, though "earlier alcoholism movies focused almost exclusively on the progressive decline of characters, rarely acknowledging their pleasurable periods of using," intoxication (whether from alcohol or illicit drugs) is not portrayed as problematic in itself in the later 20th century films and therefore can be considered as distinct from addiction. In each of the three films under consideration in Hersey's study, not only do the films recognize that intoxication had been fun for the addicts at some earlier point in their lives, but that intoxication could also be pleasurable for the friends, family, and colleagues of the addict: "Instead, the films imply that the nature of addiction is found within the individual character rather than in specific substances" (Hersey, 2005, p. 477).

More recently, within television broadcasting and the press, public and political concerns about "binge" drinking by young Britons have developed in tandem with a growing genre of exposés, docu-dramas, and "fly on the wall" reality television programs. The format of these "police, camera, action"-style reality specials often entails following groups of young people out and about in the city at night in the process of becoming intoxicated. The ambivalence to young people's leisure-time drinking can be seen in television programs such as *Booze Britain*, which holds intoxication by young people up for simultaneous viewer condemnation and voyeuristic entertainment.

This combination of horror and fascination at intoxication and its consequences for specific social groups (youth, the working classes, women) has historical continuities from Hogarth's *Gin Lane* and *Beer Street* onward. Although Hogarth's engravings were considered to be "popular" prints with the general public, Riding (2006) has suggested that, given their price of one shilling each, "a sum well beyond the means of the majority of Londoners…, Hogarth's prints—and their stark message—could only have reached the wide audience he purportedly sought through public display" (p. 181). Thus, Hogarth's prints were more likely to reflect and reinforce middle- and upper-class concerns about drunkenness and its relationship to crime, disorder, and idleness, providing entertainment to the higher classes through representations of the "reigning vices peculiar to the lower class of people" (Hogarth, quoted in Paulson, 1989, p. 145). Hayward and Hobbs' (2007) analysis of this "spectacle" of excessive consumption, notes that,

> [f]rom the comfort and safety of one's own armchair, the transgressive utility of normative space and normative consumption can be observed. Violence, vomit, vandalism and obscene behaviour test the boundaries… [and] stage managed battles between the representatives of the state and violent youth… (p. 449)

This raises the question about the extent to which we are seeing the periodic media demonization of youth and young adults (Cohen, 1972/1973; Pearson, 1983) or whether there is a genuine and significant shift in attitudes toward drinking and drunkenness in the early 21st century.

Alcopops and the Media: Another Moral Panic?

It has been argued that the U.K. has seen a shift away from a traditional model of controlled, cross-generational drinking in working-class community pubs (e.g., Gofton, 1990). This shift has been in part the consequence of broad socioeconomic change—in particular, the decline of the traditional manufacturing basis of British industry—and in part the result of changes in British leisure. Such has been the magnitude of developments in the manufacture and sale of alcohol beverages, the redesign of drinking venues, and the broadening customer base that it has been suggested elsewhere by the author that we have seen a "revolution" in the late modern alcohol order, with a consequent increase in the amount consumed per drinking session by young women and men (Measham, 2006; Measham & Brain, 2005; see also Hadfield, 2006). Six phases in the recommodification of alcohol beverages in the U.K. over the last 15 years can be identified:

1. *Early 1990s:* high-strength bottled beers and lagers, white ciders, and fortified wines.
2. *1995:* the introduction of first-generation alcopops or alcoholic lemonades in the U.K. from Australia.
3. *Late 1990s:* second-generation alcopops or flavored alcoholic beverages (FABs).
4. "Smart," "buzz," or energy drinks containing legal stimulants such as caffeine and guarana, often sold in licensed premises as spirit mixers.
5. *Early 2000s:* shots, shooters, or slammers containing mixtures of liqueurs and spirits in small shot glasses, often sold in licensed premises at discounted price for multiple purchases.
6. *Mid-2000s:* third-generation FABs and ready-to-drink spirit mixers (RTDs) with a growing emphasis on premium, fresh, and high fruit content beverages—for example, premium flavored lagers, ciders, premixed branded cocktails, and milk-based products.

The development of alcopops led to the recasting by the media of alcoholic beverages as a temptation for young people, whereas the reality of beverage choice was somewhat different. Brain and Parker (1997) suggested that youths early in their drinking careers continued to prefer purchasing cheap, strong alcohol such as lager, cider, and fortified wines rather than the emergent and relatively expensive alcopops and spirit mixers in the mid-1990s, illustrating the importance of price as a factor influencing younger drinkers (discussed further in chapter 5). It has been suggested that instead of the youth-oriented imagery of alcopops attempting to tempt children in their early teens into their first alcoholic drink, these beverages were marketed to appeal to an older age group—the young adult clubbing customer base—in an attempt to lure them from the alcohol-free, illicit psychoactive consumption of acid house parties and raves during the "decade of dance" between 1988 and 1998 in the U.K. (e.g., Collin, 1997; Forsyth, 2001). Furthermore, Forsyth (n.d.) describes the ways in which alcohol was remarketed to appeal to the 1990s rave generation not only through the development of a wide range of new products outlined above, but (using a 4 Ps marketing analysis of "products, price, promotion, and place," based on Kotler, Armstrong, Saunders, & Wong, 1999) also through price, promotion, and place, using such methods as alcohol sponsorship of individual bars at music festivals. Forsyth argues that "in this way the alcohol industry can be seen as having employed 'brand-stretching' techniques to equate their drug with currently popular forms of music" (n.d., p. 10; see also Forsyth & Cloonan, 2008).

Concerns about "novel" alcoholic beverages are nothing new. As early as 18th century England, as Warner (2003) has explored in her colorful history of the Gin Acts and gin as "the original urban drug," recurring practical and moral concerns about drunkenness circled around cheap, potent, easily available "new" alcoholic drinks, favored by the working classes at a time of rapid socioeconomic development and urbanization. Warner suggests that then, as now, "concerns over drunkenness bore very little correspondence to actual consumption" (2003, p. 4), and that Parliament only paid attention to alcohol consumption during peaceful times and saw it primarily in terms of revenue-raising potential in times of war. Rudy (2005) noted in relation to studies on Finland and Russia,

> ...through media accounts, political forums, temperance movements, and policing campaigns, upright consciences are brought together to validate the value of civilised drinking and to stigmatize deviant drinking. Middle-class picnic drinking is civilised and youth drinking is deviant; and drinking in private settings is fine but not in beer halls. (p. 129)

Similarly, British politicians and the press distinguished between the allegedly moderate and "civilized" consumption of the theatergoer, who might want a late-night glass of wine, and the rampaging rowdy young women and men drinking to excess, immoderately dressed, and dominating public space, allegedly making British city centers no-go areas for the over-30s (Hadfield, 2006; Measham & Brain, 2005; Measham & Moore, in press).

It has been suggested by the author elsewhere that the development of high-strength alcohol beverages and modern city-center café-bars that appealed to the emergent young adult customer base has facilitated a new "culture of intoxication," resulting in increased sessional consumption and "determined drunkenness" in the U.K. from the early 1990s onward (Measham, 1996, 2006). Just as the 19th century established public drinking and public drunkenness as signs of lower socioeconomic groups and lack of respectability (with the higher classes being *seduced out of* the local pub), the late 20th and early 21st centuries have seen a shift to intoxication becoming less of a taboo for young people, with a growing range of socioeconomic groups and young women *seduced into* the new café-bars (Bauman, 1988, 1998). Given the evidence to suggest that this determined drunkenness or "warp speed intoxication" (Hayward & Hobbs, 2007, p. 447) is a widespread feature of youth and young adult consumption in the U.K. across sociodemographic groups (Engineer, Phillips, Thompson, & Nichols, 2003; Measham & Brain, 2005), individualizing and pathologizing risk factor analysis is as limited in value as seeing the alcohol industry as the key causal factor when attempting to understand changing drink-related attitudes and behavior (see Parker, 2003, for a critique of risk factor analysis). We need to move beyond the micro-level to macro-level developments in order to understand the changing nature of attitudes to drinking, drunkenness, and excess.

"Extended Adolescence" and Sociocultural Change

What is suggested here—and is evident in some of the subsequent chapters—is the need to understand the backdrop to changing attitudes to intoxication: a period of rapid socioeconomic change where a work hard/play hard millennial lifestyle increasingly emphasizes the maximization of pleasure and the minimization of problems within an individualistic and consumption-oriented society (e.g., Rojek, 2000). In this analysis, changing attitudes to drinking, drunkenness, and excess are evidence of socioeconomic and cultural change, which has impacted particularly on young women and men in the late 20th and early 21st centuries.

Such changes in the transition from childhood to adulthood have led to a period known as *extended adolescence* (e.g., Furlong & Cartmel, 1997; see also chapters 4 and 5). The rapid expansion of higher education in the U.K.—student numbers doubled in the 1990s—combined with a substantial reduction in state financial assistance for students, has resulted in increased economic dependence on parents. According to recent data, over half of 25-year-olds are now still living in the parental home (ONS, 2005). This has resulted in the delayed onset of key life stage markers and adult responsibilities, such as marriage, mortgage, and parenthood, along with increased disposable income for some young people, increased debt for many more, the longest working hours in Europe, and an extended period without a private home within which to socialize with friends.

At the same time, there has been a rapid expansion of the night-time economy (Hobbs, Hadfield, Lister, & Winlow, 2003; Hobbs, Lister, Hadfield, Winlow, & Hall, 2000), indicated, for example, by the doubling of overall capacity of licensed premises in the late 1990s, together with a doubling of sessional consumption, leading to greater numbers of increasingly visible 18- to 24-year-olds inebriated on the streets of British towns and cities (Roberts, 2006). Unlike in many countries (as Thornton [1995] has discussed in relation to the inclement weather and the traditional appeal of pubs and clubs to British youth), the lack of alternative leisure space in the U.K., and the expansion and enhanced appeal of modern leisure venues and alcohol beverages have added to a mixture of factors resulting in increased attendance at a rising number of licensed premises and consequent increased drinking by a growing sociodemographic range of young people. This widening array of licensed leisure venues has made drinking the primary purpose rather than the backdrop to the creation of social spaces and "cultural milieux" in the "creative city" (Landry, 2000; Richardson & Budd, 2003; Roberts, 2006). The problem is that this rapid expansion of the British night-time economy has occurred at the same time as an increase in alcohol-related crime and disorder in the very same city streets (Hobbs et al., 2003).

Nevertheless, it would be inaccurate to portray the pursuit of altered states of intoxication as simply an indulgent desire to lose control by young people during a period of extended adolescence. There is evidence that "determined drunkenness" may be bounded in terms of minimizing individual harms, such as negative health or safety consequences (Measham & Brain, 2005), supporting the work of Featherstone (1991) on the "controlled decontrolling" of emotions and calculated hedonism in postmodern society and Measham's (2002) identification of a "controlled loss of control" specifically in relation to the motivations and expectations surrounding the consumption of alcohol and drugs. However, alongside the concept of "extended adolescence," commentators have suggested that the globalization of goods and services has been accompanied by a globalization of emotional insecurities (Elliott & Lemert, 2005), and criminologists such as Young (2003) have noted the irony of the post-9/11 world resulting in a growing "culture of control" (Garland, 2001), of increased surveillance, and state control being combined with increased individual ontological insecurity. With a perceived growing lack of control over one's individual life, intoxication itself may be repositioned as an attempt to regain such control. In this context,

> the seductiveness of binge drinking…is not only linked to the inherent excitement of the alcoholic rush, but also to the more general feelings of self-actualisation and self-expression to which it also gives rise. It is a means of seizing control, a way of reacting against the "unidentifiable forces that rob one of individual choice." (Hayward & Hobbs, 2007, p. 447; see also Lyng, 1990, p. 870)

Moreover, this is not simply a rational response to contemporary ontological insecurities, but is combined with the emotionality and pleasures of intoxication and the search for the "liminal experience," evident in an increased willingness to experiment with a widening repertoire of easily available and affordable legal and illegal psychoactive substances to achieve altered states of intoxication (Measham & Moore, in press; Moore & Measham, in press; Parker & Measham, 1994). It is this potential pleasure that is a characteristic of—and, indeed, a motivation for—extreme drinking.

Who are we talking about when we discuss this purposeful pursuit of intoxication? Contemporary academic and political debate surrounds the extent to which extreme drinking and determined drunkenness might be a characteristic of a distinct minority of youth and young adults, or are changing to become a majority pursuit. A Home Office study of "binge" drinking found that "young people often go out with the definite intention of getting drunk, and … many deliberately accelerate or intensify their drunkenness by mixing drinks, drinking before they go out, or drinking beverages that they know have a strong effect on them" (Engineer et al., 2003, p. 16). At a national level, this new determined drunkenness has informed U.K. government policy, with the Prime Minister's Strategy Unit (2004) noting that "drinking is often viewed as an end in itself, and public drunkenness is socially accepted, if not expected.… Particularly evident…is a culture of going out to get drunk. This culture is particularly associated with…16–24 year old drinkers" (p. 23).

In a culturally and ethnically diverse country such as the U.K. caution is needed, however, in generalizing about the uniformity of the changes identified above and understanding the multi-faceted nature of attitudes to intoxication. Longitudinal studies of young people show how the complexities of the interaction between ethnicity, religion, and cultural background, as well as age and generational characteristics, influence young people's drinking-related attitudes and behaviors and suggest why simplistic risk factor analysis cannot fully predict protective factors for probable high-risk groups. For certain minority ethnic groups, cultural and religious factors will combine with socioeconomic position, education, employment, and housing conditions. Although, for example, British Asian Muslims in their earlier teens appear to engage in very little drinking and drunkenness compared with their peers, there is evidence that, by the late teens, some second- and third-generation Asian Muslims who move away from their families and communities then become more involved in a social life that includes alcohol (Parker, Aldridge, & Measham, 1998). Among British adults, apart from Irish respondents, both men and women in minority ethnic groups were less likely than the general population to have had a drink in the week prior to interview or to have drunk above the daily recommendations. For example, only 1% of Bangladeshi men had consumed more than four units on their heaviest drinking day in the previous week, compared with 56% of Irishmen and 45% of the general male population (ONS, 2005).

CONCLUSION

A consideration of changing attitudes to intoxication shows the historical continuities in official concerns about drunkenness, public disorder, the sociodemographic mix of drinkers, and broader issues of social control. Discourses about drunkenness, both official and popular, have shaped the state regulation of alcohol, focusing such measures on the perceived "problem" drinkers from lower socioeconomic groups, women, and youth and on popular leisure locations as sites of intervention—from the "gin madness" of the 18th century; to the beer houses, music halls, and gin palaces of Victorian England; to the 1990s policing of raves and dance clubs (Redhead, 1995; Shapiro, 1999); and the alcopops "panic" and our contemporary debate surrounding millennial city centers and "binge" drinking. The regulation and criminalization of intoxication are both symbolic of these anxieties and instrumental in their perpetuation. We can see continuities in the social regulation of leisure and pleasure linked to licensing legislation and the regulation of public drinking and drunkenness, the problem of leisure being recycled in the form of middle class "respectable fears" of the crowd (working class, the young, and women) out and about on the streets. In fact, however, research suggests a controlled loss of control, a bounding of consumption. Drunkenness is as much a facilitation of, as a rebellion against, the pressures of the working week, because drunkenness is itself subsumed by and facilitated by the working week.

However, the role of intoxication has shifted, as have attitudes to the role of alcohol within the changing landscape of work, leisure, and pleasure. From carnivalesque excess, to pressure valve to sustain the capitalist working week, to an integral part of late modern capitalist society and marker of individual consumer identities, intoxication reflects far broader socioeconomic and cultural change. As this chapter has attempted to illustrate, the reasons for changing attitudes to intoxication relate not simply to changes in the British alcohol and leisure industries, the expansion of the night-time economy, and the development of new products, places, and promotional strategies, but also to the transition from childhood to adulthood, extended adolescence, and the construction of identity. A government policy of economic liberalization through licensing legislation and increased criminalization of "flawed" drinkers (with excessive or illegal consumption) link the persistent problems of leisure with a new culture of intoxication that targets young women and young men in public space. As this book is testament, such motivations for intoxication are increasingly complex and contradictory for young people growing up in contemporary late modern capitalist society, seeking to balance a broader sense of lack of control with the re-exertion of control through the "controlled loss of control" in leisure, driven by both a rationality and emotionality in drinking and drunkenness.

REFERENCES

Adler, F. (1975). *Sisters in crime: The rise of the new female criminal*. New York: McGraw-Hill.

Alcohol the "New British disease." (2004, May 20). *BBC Online*. Retrieved June 12, 2007, from http://news.bbc.co.uk/1/hi/uk_politics/3731025.stm.

Bancroft, A. (2008). *Drugs, intoxication and society*. Oxford, U.K.: Polity.

Bauman, Z. (1988). *Freedom*. Philadelphia: Open University Press.

Bauman, Z. (1998). *Work, compensation and the new poor*. Philadelphia: Open University Press.

Bell, D. (1976). *The cultural contradictions of capitalism*. London: Heinemann.

Bennett, J. M. (1991). Misogyny, popular culture, and women's work. *History Workshop Journal*, *31*, 166–188.

Brain, K., & Parker, H. (1997). *Drinking with design: Alcopops, designer drinks and youth culture*. London: Portman.

Campbell, C. (1987). *The romantic ethic and the spirit of modern consumerism*. Oxford, U.K.: Basil Blackwell.

Cavalcanti, A. (Director). (1944). *Champagne Charlie* [Motion Picture]. United Kingdom: Ealing Studios.

Cohen, S. (1973). *Folk devils and moral panics: The creation of the mods and rockers* (Rev. ed.). St Albans, U.K.: Paladin. (Original work published 1972)

Coleman, L., & Cater, S. (2005). *Underage "risky" drinking: Motivations and outcomes*. York, U.K.: Joseph Rowntree Foundation.

Collin, M. (1997). *Altered state: The story of ecstasy culture and acid house*. London: Serpent's Tail.

Dean, A. (1997). *Chaos and intoxication: Complexity and adaptation in the structure of human nature.* London: Routledge.

Donaldson, R. (Director). (1988). *Cocktail* [Motion Picture]. United States: Interscope Communications.

Edwards, B. (Director). (1962). *Days of wine and roses* [Motion Picture]. United States: Jalem Productions.

Edwards, G. (2000). *Alcohol: The world's favorite drug.* New York: St Martin's.

Elliott, A., & Lemert, C. (2005). *The new individualism: The emotional cost of globalization.* London: Routledge.

Elliott, L. (2007, February 26). Live now, pay later culture here to stay. *The Guardian.* Retrieved June 12, 2007, from http://business.guardian.co.uk/economy/story/0,,2088361,00.html.

Engineer, R., Phillips, A., Thompson, J., & Nicholls, J. (2003). *Drunk and disorderly: A qualitative study of binge drinking among 18- to 24-year-olds.* Home Office Research Study No. 262. London: Home Office.

Equal Opportunities Commission (EOC). (2007). *The gender agenda: The unfinished revolution.* Manchester, U.K.: Author.

Featherstone, M. (1991). The body in consumer culture. In M. Featherstone, M. Hepworth, & B. S. Turner (Eds.), *The body: Social process and cultural theory* (pp. 170–196). London: Sage.

Forsyth, A. (2001). A design for strife: Alcopops, licit drug—familiar scare story. *International Journal of Drug Policy, 12,* 59–80.

Forsyth, A. (n.d.). *From illegal leisure to licenced disorder: Rave culture as marketing opportunity for the licensed trade (drinks) industry.* Unpublished manuscript.

Forsyth, A, & Cloonan, M. (2008). Alco-pop? The use of popular music in Glasgow pubs. *Pop Music and Society, 31,* 1.

Furlong, A., & Cartmel, F. (1997). *Young people and social change.* Buckingham, U.K.: Open University.

Galloway, J., Forsyth, A., & Shewan, D. (2007). *Young people's street drinking behaviour: Investigating the influence of marketing and subculture.* Unpublished final report by Glasgow Centre for the Study of Violence, Glasgow Caledonian University.

Garland, D. (2001). *The culture of control: Crime and social order in contemporary society.* Chicago: University of Chicago Press.

Gmel, G., Bloomfield, K., Ahlström, S., Choquet, M., & Lecomte, T. (2000). Women's roles and women's drinking: A comparative study in four European countries. *Substance Abuse, 21,* 249–264.

Gofton, L. (1990). On the town: Drink and the "New Lawlessness." *Youth and Society, 29,* 33–39.

Gordon Caron, G. (Director). (1988). *Clean and sober* [Motion Picture]. United States: Imagine Entertainment.

Graham, K. (2005). Public drinking then and now. *Contemporary Drug Problems, 32,* 45–56.

Gusfield, J. (1991). Benevolent repression: Popular culture, social structure, and the control of drinking. In S. Barrows & R. Room (Eds.), *Drinking: Behavior and belief in modern history* (pp. 399–424). Berkeley, CA: University of California Press.

Hadfield, P. M. (2006). *Bar wars: Contesting the night in contemporary British cities.* Oxford, U.K.: Oxford University Press.

Hajema, K., & Knibbe, R. (1998). Changes in social roles as predictors of changes in drinking behaviour. *Addiction, 93,* 1717–1727.

Harrison, B. (1971). *Drink and the Victorians: The temperance question in England 1815-1872.* London: Faber & Faber.

Hayward, K., & Hobbs, D. (2007). Beyond the binge in "Booze Britain": Market-led lim-
    inalization and the spectacle of binge drinking. *British Journal of Sociology, 58*,
    437–456.
Heath, D. (Ed.). (1995). *International handbook on alcohol and culture*. Westport, CT:
    Greenwood.
Heath, D. (2000). *Drinking occasions: Comparative perspectives on alcohol and culture*.
    Philadelphia: Brunner/Mazel.
Hersey, C. (2005). Script(ing) treatment: Representations of recovery from addiction in
    Hollywood film. *Contemporary Drug Problems, 32*, 467–493.
Hey, V. (1986). *Patriarchy and pub culture*. London: Tavistock.
Hobbs, D., Hadfield, P., Lister, S., & Winlow, S. (2003) *Bouncers: Violence and gover-
    nance in the night-time economy*. Oxford, U.K.: Oxford University Press.
Hobbs, D., Lister, S., Hadfield, P., Winlow, S., & Hall, S. (2000). Receiving shadows:
    Governance and liminality in the night-time economy. *British Journal of Sociology,
    51*, 701–718.
Kotler, P., Armstrong, G., Saunders, J., & Wong, V. (1999). *Principles of marketing* (2nd
    ed.). London: Prentice Hall Europe.
Landis, J. (Director). (1978). *Animal house* [Motion Picture]. United States: Universal
    Pictures.
Landry, C. (2000). *The creative city: A toolkit for urban innovators*. London: Earthscan.
London Metropolitan Archives. (1998). *Licensed victuallers records*. Information Leaflet
    No. 3. London: Author.
Lyng, S. (1990). Edgework: A social psychological analysis of voluntary risk taking.
    American Journal of Sociology, 95, 851–886.
Mackendrick, A. (Director). (1949). *Whisky galore!* [Motion Picture]. United Kingdom:
    Ealing Studios.
Mandoki, L. (Director). (1994). *When a man loves a woman* [Motion Picture]. United
    States: Touchstone Pictures.
McInernay, J. (2006, October 21). Toast of the town. *The Guardian*. Retrieved
    August 27, 2007, from http://books.guardian.co.uk/departments/generalfiction/
    story/0,,1927718,00.html.
Measham, F. (1996). The "Big Bang" approach to sessional drinking: Changing patterns
    of alcohol consumption amongst young people in North West England. *Addiction
    Research, 4*, 283–299.
Measham, F. (2002). "Doing gender"—"doing drugs": Conceptualising the gendering of
    drugs cultures. *Contemporary Drug Problems, 29*, 335–373.
Measham, F. (2006). The new policy mix: Alcohol, harm minimisation and determined
    drunkenness in contemporary society. *International Journal of Drug Policy, 17*,
    258–268.
Measham, F., & Brain, K. (2005). "Binge" drinking, British alcohol policy and the new cul-
    ture of intoxication. *Crime, Media, Culture: An International Journal, 1*, 263–284.
Measham, F., & Moore, K. (in press). The criminalization of intoxication. In P. Squire
    (Ed.), *ASBO nation. Anti-social behaviour: Critical questions and key debates*.
    Bristol, U.K.: Policy.
Moore, K., & Measham, F. (in press). "It's the most fun you can have for twenty quid":
    Motivations, consequences and meanings of British ketamine use. *Addiction
    Research and Theory*.
Office for National Statistics (ONS). (2005). *General Household Survey 2004*. Retrieved
    June 12, 2007, from http://www.statistics.gov.uk/ghs/.
O'Malley, P., & Valverde, M. (2004). Pleasure, freedom and drugs: The uses of "pleasure"
    in liberal governance of drug and alcohol consumption. *Sociology, 38*, 25–42.

Parker, H. (2003). Pathology or modernity? Rethinking risk factor analyses of young drug users. *Addiction Research and Theory, 11*, 141–144.

Parker, H., Aldridge, J., & Measham, F. (1998). *Illegal leisure: The normalization of adolescent recreational drug use*. London: Routledge.

Parker, H., & Measham, F. (1994). Pick 'n' mix: Changing patterns of illicit drug use amongst 1990s adolescents. *Drugs: Education, Prevention & Policy, 1*, 5–13.

Paulson, R. (1989). *Hogarth's graphic works*. (3rd ed.). London: The Print Room.

Pearson, G. (1983). *Hooligan: A history of respectable fears*. Basingstoke, U.K.: Macmillan.

Presdee, M. (2000). *Cultural criminology and the carnival of crime*. London: Routledge.

Prime Minister's Strategy Unit. (2004). *Alcohol harm reduction strategy for England*. London: Author.

Redhead, S. (1995). *Unpopular cultures: The birth of law and popular culture*. Manchester, U.K.: Manchester University Press.

Richardson, A., & Budd, T. (2003). *Alcohol, crime and disorder: A study of young adults*. Home Office Research Study No. 263. London: Home Office Research, Development and Statistics Directorate.

Riding, C. (2006). Crime and punishment. In M. Hallett & C. Riding (Eds.), *Hogarth*. London: Tate Publishing.

Roberts, M. (2006). From "creative city" to "no-go areas": The expansion of the night-time economy in British town and city centres. *Cities, 23*, 331–338.

Rojek, C. (2000). *Leisure and culture*. Basingstoke, U.K.: Macmillan.

Room, R. (1989). Alcoholism and Alcoholics Anonymous in U.S. films, 1945–1962: The party ends for the "wet generations." *Journal of Studies on Alcohol, 50*, 368–383.

Rorabaugh, W. (2003). Drinking in the "Thin Man" films, 1934-47. *The Social History of Alcohol and Drugs, 18*, 51–68.

Rudgley, R. (1993). *The alchemy of culture: Intoxicants in society*. London: British Museum Press.

Rudy, D. (2005). Societal response and the moral regulation of public-space drinking. *Contemporary Drug Problems, 32*, 127–130.

Schechner, R. (1993). *The future of ritual*. London: Routledge.

Shapiro, H. (1999). Dances with drugs: Pop music, drugs and youth culture. In N. South (Ed.), *Drugs: Cultures, controls and everyday life* (pp. 17–35). London: Sage.

Smart, C. (1979). The new female criminal: Reality or myth? *British Journal of Criminology, 19*, 50–59.

Stedman Jones, G. (1971). *Outcast London: A study in the relationship between classes in Victorian society*. Oxford, U.K.: Oxford University Press.

Stedman Jones, G. (1983). *Languages of class: Studies in English working class history, 1832–1982*. Cambridge, U.K.: Cambridge University.

Thomas, B. (2000). *28 days* [Motion Picture]. United States: Columbia Pictures Corporation.

Thompson, E. P. (1988). *The making of the English working class*. London: Penguin. (Original work published 1963)

Thornton, S. (1995). *Club cultures: Music, media and subcultural capital*. Hanover, NH: Wesleyan University Press.

Törrönen, J., & Karlsson, T. (2005). Moral regulation of public space and drinking in the media and legislation in Finland. *Contemporary Drug Problems, 32*, 93–129.

Wacklin, J. (2005). Drinking and public space in Leningrad/St. Petersburg and Helsinki in the interwar period. *Contemporary Drug Problems, 32*, 57–92.

Walton, S. (2001). *Out of it: A cultural history of intoxication*. London: Hamish Hamilton.

Walvin, J. (1978). *Leisure and society 1830-1950*. London: Longman.

Warner, J. (1997). The sanctuary of sobriety: The emergence of temperance as a feminine virtue in Tudor and Stuart England. *Addiction*, *92*(1), 97–111.

Warner, J. (2003). *Craze: Gin and debauchery in an Age of Reason*. London: Profile.

Weiss, S. (2001). Religious influences on drinking: Illustrations from select groups. In E. Houghton & A. Roche (Eds.), *Learning about drinking* (pp. 109–127). Philadelphia: Brunner-Routledge.

Wilder, B. (Director/Screenplay), & Brackett, C. (Screenplay/Producer). (1945). *The lost weekend* [Motion Picture]. United States: Paramount/C. Brackett.

Young, J. (2003). Merton with energy, Katz with structure: The sociology of vindictiveness and the criminology of transgression. *Theoretical Criminology*, *7*, 389–414.

Chapter 3

Beyond Boundaries
Youth and the Dream of the Extreme

Véronique Nahoum-Grappe

A group of youths jumping to the lively rhythm of the music during the traditional May Day parade in Paris displayed a large banner: *"I WANT NOTHING. RIGHT NOW!"* Such extreme and nihilistic impatience may be the latest version of the famous May 1968[1] slogan, "We want everything. Right now!" an echo of that slogan 40 years later. Reflected in it is a desire to *live for the present* that is so typical of youth. There is a close link between being young and dancing with abandon, listening to blaring music, being agitated, shouting, fighting, laughing wildly, not wanting to go home, spending sleepless nights of extreme drinking, and accelerating to top speed (whether on motor bikes or through experiences). There is also a connection between impatience and acceleration, acceleration and excess, and a "thirst for drunkenness" from a generation yearning to live its youth to the fullest, *beginning tonight*. The adjective *extreme* is characteristic: It denotes the impatience, the feeling of urgency for things to happen "right now." And thus, the expression *extreme drinking* precisely encapsulates this yearning for "everything, now." The quantity of alcohol consumed is closely tied to the acceleration of consumption: The faster one drinks, the faster and more extreme the drunkenness.

The question here is this: Why is it that young people in contemporary Western society, those poised between the end of childhood and the beginning

---

[1] The May 1968 Paris uprising began as a series of student protests and eventually led to the collapse of the De Gaulle government.

of adulthood, an interval that varies from one individual to another, engage in particular drinking patterns (more excessive, more extreme than those of adults) when they celebrate? This chapter addresses the question from an anthropological rather than a psychological perspective. Whatever the motivation of those who drink—a combination of pleasure-seeking, anxiety, depression, mounting excitement, and being mindlessly driven on, glass by glass, and by collective euphoria (Nahoum-Grappe, 2005)—the important parameter for the ethnologist is its relationship with the short-term, the present, this evening, tonight.

We therefore propose here a comprehensive and descriptive approach to asking certain questions and putting them into context (Augé, 1994; see also issue 185 of *L'Homme: Revue Français d'Anthropologie*, 2008). Here, the concept of *culture* is neither "ethnicized," nor defined by geographically delineated cultural areas. In modern societies, one can observe a growing extension of Western lifestyles elsewhere: Patterns of consumption, clothing styles, and means of transportation are becoming more and more homogenous worldwide. In this context, just as the "culture of poverty" concept was developed by the ethnologist Oscar Lewis (Lewis, 1961, 1998), it seems equally relevant to hypothesize about a "culture of youth," a notion that became increasingly consistent and distinctive over the course of the 20th century. Originating in the Northern Hemisphere, the signs and esthetics of this culture have spread across borders: its music, its style, but also its "myths" (see Barthes, 1957),[2] a system of collective images, narratives, beliefs, and patterns of consumption and expression. The term *extreme* is one of the most typical symbols of today's youth culture; and extreme drinking is one of its manifestations.

What does the adjective *extreme* mean in defining drinking patterns? Is there such a thing as a "culture of youth," one that is wilder, more intense, more excessive than the mainstream? And, finally, is there a link between youth culture and certain patterns of consumption that the word *extreme* might help us identify? The answers to these questions are linked to the "esthetics of vertigo" and their significance for contemporary youth, as well as to the definitions of thresholds, borders, and limits: One may suppose that, in some contexts, "too much" and "extreme" not only constitute the overstepping of limits, but become an injunction, a temporary norm that takes over for the evening.

First, the issue of "extreme drinking" by young people in contemporary societies requires a brief explanation of the concept of "extremes" in today's youth culture (this chapter draws primarily on French sources; for an overview of drinking patterns among young people in France, see Case Study, "Young People's Drinking in France," below). Second, we need to describe from an anthropological perspective what it is like to "be young" in modern society and define the particular place of drunkenness during this crucial period of transition from childhood to adulthood. And, finally, we should put extreme

---

[2] The word *myth* is used here as defined by Roland Barthes (1957): "a system of communication," a "message," a "mode of signification" (p. 109).

drinking in its context, to understand the setting—the party, the soirée, the celebration—that makes it a special event. It is usually at night that the party reaches full swing, and drunkenness becomes extreme. The question is, then, what does "partying" mean to today's youth?

Case Study: Young People's Drinking in France

Marie Choquet

France is an alcohol producer and a "wet" country, when compared to the United Kingdom and most Nordic European countries—meaning that alcohol consumption is relatively frequent and integrated into everyday life. However, two important international surveys, the WHO/Health Behaviour in School-aged Children (HBSC) study (Currie et al., 2004) and the European School Survey Project on Alcohol and Other Drugs (ESPAD, Hibell et al., 2004), agree that young people in France drink less than in most other countries in Europe. Figures 3.1 and 3.2, based on the ESPAD data, clearly illustrate this finding. France is also among the European countries with the lowest prevalence of repeated "binge drinking" (defined as the consumption of five or more drinks in a row): 9% of 16-year-olds in France reported it during the last 30 days versus 32% of their peers in Ireland, 28% in the Netherlands, 27% in the United Kingdom, and 25% in Sweden (Hibell et al., 2004).

Informal influences appear to be particularly important in moderating drinking among young people in France. Thus, when compared to their Dutch peers, French adolescents perceived alcohol as less easily available; it has been suggested that this perception was more related to parental attitudes and

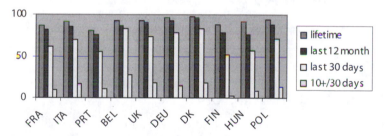

FIGURE 3.1 Alcohol consumption (%) among 16-year-old males in Europe. Adapted from: Hibell et al. (2004)

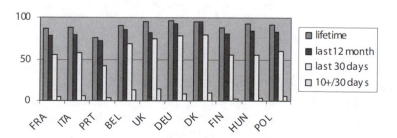
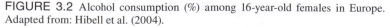

FIGURE 3.2 Alcohol consumption (%) among 16-year-old females in Europe. Adapted from: Hibell et al. (2004).

informal controls than to availability in stores or bars (Knibbe, Joosten, Derickx et al., 2005). Because the informal controls aimed at prevention of intoxication are high, French adolescents also reported more problems with parents and peers because of alcohol when compared to respondents in other countries (Knibbe, Joosten, Choquet et al., 2007). A survey by the Institut de Recherches Scientifiques sur les Boissons (IREB) provided more information about adolescents' (13- to 19-year-olds) drinking attitudes, contexts, and lifestyles (Choquet, Com-Ruelle, & Leymarie, 2003). According to its findings:

- **Drinking to intoxication is not a common behavior in France.** While most young people have drunk alcohol at least once during their life (97%), only 37% have reported being intoxicated, and 5% have been intoxicated at least 40 times during their lifetime.
- **Drinking to intoxication appears in France, as in most countries, outside parental control.** So, while alcohol is mostly experienced for the first time in a family context, intoxication is normally experienced with friends (86%), during a party (61%), or dinner (25%).
- **Whatever their age, French adolescents do not systematically become intoxicated when they go out with friends.** At ages 13 to 14 years, 34% go to a party at least once a month (6% at least once a week), while 2% have been drunk during the last 30 days. At ages 15 to 16 years, 50% go to a party at least once a month (9% at least once a week), while 9% have been drunk during the last 30 days. At ages 17 to 18 years, 61% go to a party at least once a month (13% at least once a week), and 18% have been drunk during the last 30 days.

In conclusion, most data coming from France, in comparison with other countries, indicate that, for adolescents in France: (1) parental and informal controls seem to be more important than official alcohol availability and regulations; (2) drunkenness is not systematically related to overall per capita consumption.

"EXTREME" IN YOUTH CULTURE

The way *extreme* was commonly used at the end of the extreme 20th century moved this adjective away from its classic definition, when it traditionally served to enhance the inherent meaning of a noun (as in the expressions *extreme hunger*, *extreme poverty*, or *extreme passion*), toward something else: a style, an esthetic, a stream of dizzying activity beyond the usual slow, dull life. Though a bout of drunkenness ends with its very opposite, a heavy sleep that erases the evening's memories, opting for the "extreme" often also leads to risk-taking. The extreme is an exploit, a performance, a limit pushed to the point of no return (e.g., Cloarec, 1996). An extreme act will disrupt the peace of mind. Indeed, in our current usage, the term emphasizes intensity of sensation, like the experience of vertigo or a rapid ingestion of a strong alcoholic beverage; this "strong sensation" is an inner upheaval, but one that has no substance.

Consider the following title of an article that appeared in a major French daily, *Libération*: "The Extreme Merry-Go-Round" ("Le manège de l'extrême," 1995). The article refers to Space Mountain, a ride inaugurated in spring 1995 in the Disneyland amusement park near Paris, and warns that "it elicits strong sensations that may upset delicate people." Riding in the car of this rollercoaster as it loops and twists through a darkness sprinkled with stars and meteors, one is exposed to accelerations and sensations of vertigo that are more audacious and more violent than in other rides of its kind.

In this example, state-of-the-art technology has created the necessary speed to suspend weightless bodies in paradoxical immobility, where the enveloping darkness and emptiness change the very nature of vertigo, no longer pulling the individual toward the ground, but in all directions. This extreme sensation endangers the body's very verticality and the functioning of consciousness, resembling the experience of drunkenness. We hardly need statistics to predict that the main customers for the Space Mountain are young people looking for a thrill.

Like all psychoactive experiences, the Space Mountain targets kinesthesia, the physical consciousness of self. "Extreme" refers here to the cumulative effects of physical dizziness, due not only to acceleration of the rollercoaster cars, but also to the void created by darkness and the absence of a background, a feeling of weightlessness, and lack of spatial points of reference. With its thirst for violence through acceleration and tailspins, the Space Mountain offers an emblematic representation of the meaning of hurling through time toward the edge of the abyss, all reference to the harmoniousness of nature, a landscape that makes its quiet circles around the thinking man, erased and annihilated. A solid base, a pillar, a steadying horizon, even daylight—all these disappear when the ride is "extreme." The image of a void or vacuum is also therefore implied in the concept of "the extreme."

As one young practitioner of extreme sports described it:

> In fact, I am looking for a sensation of fear because, you know, in your daily life, are you fearful of anything? You're never afraid. Now, you cross a road, a car comes close to you, you are so used to it, you don't even pay attention anymore, it is no longer even fear. You have to look outside your daily life— parachute jumps, diving; I mean the extreme stuff, bungee jumping, anything out of the ordinary. You jump, you jump. When you first jump, you leap, you don't see anything for three seconds, everything is dark. You see yourself from the plane, you jump out, and—boom!—nothing for three seconds and then, all of sudden, hop, you wake up as if you had been asleep for three seconds. You wake up and you see your parachute open. It is exactly the same thing. A leap into the unknown. (Marcel, 25 years) (Groupe de Recherche et d'Etudes sur les Conduites Ordalique, 1994, p. 156)

The speaker's description of his experience has much to tell about the social representation of the "extreme": The use of the word *asleep* implies a loss of consciousness as the suspense reaches its peak and darkness sets in, permeating everything—even breathing ceases. This sought-after sensation is thus not only fear; the leap into the unknown is accompanied in the conscious mind by a peculiar sequence of destruction, that intense moment of emptiness and discontinuity when the "extreme" is at last experienced, linking together drunkenness and the thrills of fear. The experience also evokes a particular setting, a mood, and an esthetic—a desert, a high mountain, an immense deserted space, and the void of the vast nocturnal sky (wishing for "nothing, right now")—which, like the night, allow a temporary and purely theatrical liberation from "daytime" society and Western "civilized" lifestyles, with their shades of concrete gray and tedious November mornings, through which we come and go in the daylight, active and sober.

The dream of the "extreme" encapsulates specifically the moment of leaping into a void, heeding the momentary impulse, the moment of unconsciousness, the pursuit of which is at the very core of the narrative of the extreme: It is the spasm, the loss of consciousness, the loss of perception that invades all awareness with darkness. The "extreme," thus, is the opposite of everything "ordinary." The night, violent and short, is an awakening from the routine and the "happy medium," where the price for longevity is the absence of "extremes." It signifies the rejection of the shackles of *"métro-boulot-dodo"* (literally, "metro, work, sleep"); sleeping at night and working during the day is a sequence that the culture of "extreme" rejects with rage and disgust.

This sentiment is nothing new and has been captured in song, poetry, and film. "But what does an eternity of damnation matter to one who has found for one second the infinity of pleasure?" Charles Baudelaire wrote in 1862 (Baudelaire, 1869/1993). Another, more recent "poet of the extreme" is the young French filmmaker Cyril Collard, who died of AIDS in 1993, director of the film *Les Nuits Fauves*, translated into English as "Savage Nights" (Collard, 1992). In the film, Collard depicts the imagery of the "extreme" behaviors of his generation: torrid nights, heavy drinking, drugs, and frenetic and risky sexual practices. Shortly before his death, the director was asked what he would do if he were cured of AIDS, to which he responded, "We would have a great party. All together, once more... I would find a freighter, a jungle, a guerilla, an automatic weapon, a lost cause, a girl, a boy, another disease" (cited in Fessard, 1995, p. 12). Such wish for renewed perdition can only be understood within the context of a particular esthetic choice of those who prefer to lead a life of "savage nights," risky sexual practices, and dangerous places created by both nature (jungle) and humans (war) and acts of violence to the idea of a sanitized life, diurnal, organized, "grandfatherly." Heroes of the "extreme" prefer to die young after a life (or a night) of intense experiences.

Fauve can also be translated as "tawny," the color of a feline's fur; it is warm, torrid, and tinted with sensual cruelty—in short, presenting a multiplicity of risks. It is particularly at night that the extreme unfolds, where many different forms of intoxication are drowned in that first among them, the drunkenness that follows extreme drinking. Alcohol intoxication is at once the peak and the low point of excess, binding the two together, marking both beginning and end—without it, nights would be less wild (*fauves*).

The "extreme" has a particular relationship with time, reducing it to a *dense ball of immediacy*: the unusual and the vertiginous, in unstable suspension over a void, those "three seconds of darkness" between the springboard and the abyss. Consequently, all action on the brink of the vacuum, all dizzying experiences (for example, extreme acceleration), every violent and sudden act is likely to be called "extreme": leaping into the void, climbing a high wall, embarking on an unexplored and dangerous journey. This adjective signifies a mindset on the observer's part: It implies a model of excellence for the actor, pushing intensity to one's absolute limits, demonstrating the "real life" and proving the quality of self when put to the test. The notion of risk is therefore central to the imagery of the "extreme," but it does not sum it up. Risk-taking can always be viewed from the "extreme" angle by the actor-observer, yet its roots show an internal expansion, a growing self-definition, like the voice of a singer swelling to new heights.

In the imagery of "extreme," excellence does not represent the perfection of a finished work. Rather, it refers to a specific form of perfection, captured entirely in the gesture and manner of its expression. What is moral is not "extreme"; what is well done is not "extreme." But what is sudden and unstable, violent and vertiginous is likely to be seen as extreme. The frequent use of this adjective in today's rhetoric indicates a form of voluntary sympathy among young people for the style, nuance, or type of action the adjective conveys. The rhythm of the "extreme" is the same as the pace of sexual pleasure, with its progression of intensity and tension to the point of annihilating climax.

"Extreme action" designates an area of human excellence, the highest point of instability in the performance: Its best image is that of dizziness, atop a tightrope spanning an emptiness, immediately preceding the downward dive. High speeds, the use of legal and illegal psychoactive drugs, anything that dizzies the senses can be invested with this positivism of identity implied by the "extreme." It becomes a proof of density, a test of one's own value and choices.

Speed itself has undergone a technological acceleration in recent history (Studeny, 1995), and is in and of itself an emblematic manifestation of the metaphor of the "extreme." Generally speaking, every rise to the extreme, every pushing of limits carries a positive value. Competitions to drink faster and more are naturally extreme behaviors; but drunkenness is the most basic, the easiest to achieve (one only has to drink to intoxication), the most predictive of other extreme behaviors. It is the most ordinary but also the most important in the absence of any others; those preparing for an illegal nocturnal skydive do not need to get drunk.

"WILD YOUTH"

Our contemporary representation positions adolescence as characterized by a lifestyle of "partying" longer into the night, more frantically, and more frequently than adults. One might even say that this is precisely what being young is all about: "going out" and "having fun." A young person getting drunk on a Friday night and then being killed in a motorcycle crash not only frequently makes it into the news, it is also a cliché, a stereotype of "wild youth."

The concept of the extreme is inevitably coupled with that of risk when it comes to young people. The "heroes" of the extreme "thirst for drunkenness" are typically young men, and, once the period of "wild youth" is over, most of them will either slow down their extreme drinking or cease it altogether. Few adults can say they have never engaged in at least some form of this behavior, and it is this inverse relationship between risky consumption patterns and age that makes "extreme drinking" transcend the realm of medicine and enter the domain of the social sciences.

A narrative—a "myth," as Barthes (1957) would say—of the "extreme" is continually evolving in youth culture, itself full of variations and contradictions. The *"extreme"* is the face of excess pushed further still, the symbol and proof of "wild youth" attained. The adjective *extreme* implies an urgency and an abyss, a rise in intensity that seems linked to excessive behavior, mostly nocturnal and more typically characteristic of youth than advanced age. The "extreme" becomes almost a style, that of youth freed from its shackles and defining itself through its favorite activity: to "go out!" at night. The night is the background to its exploits, the chronological niche of these excesses so typical of youth. The popular French expression, "Il faut bien que jeunesse se passe" ("Youth must have its fling"), excuses the disorderly evenings of youngsters who have drunk too much and defines the predictable range of youthful exploits—the risk of going too far beyond the boundaries to the point where there are no more limits.

The first level of excess appears to be a constant one, involving the quest for drunkenness, with its accelerated, rapid, and repetitive drinking aimed at attaining a marked psychoactive effect. Parties involving young people but not featuring alcohol are rare. The expression "extreme drinking" is a double superlative in French because the verb *to drink* (*boire*) is already a synonym for drinking to excess. The expression *he drinks* (*il boit*), for instance, refers to an alcohol-dependent drinker. Therefore, "extreme" surpasses the concept of "too much." It encompasses all excessive celebration and even the context for celebrating, where intoxicated drinkers search for a more violent state of drunkenness through an even more intense ingestion of ethanol, while they are "having a blast" and think they are "living intensely," pressing the gas pedal of their motorbikes, jumping barriers, or speeding toward the edge of a precipice.

Partying for a group of youths is a way of overcoming constraints that stand in the way of creating an *esthetic of communication* that opens the way for all other kinds of excess. This excess might take a number of forms: noise, various transgressions, public disorder, theft, brawls. In a beautiful text, Donald W. Winnicott described adolescents by quoting Shakespeare from memory: "I would like there to be no age between 16 and 23, or that youth should spend its time sleeping: between these two, what else do they do than get girls pregnant, disrespect the elderly, steal, and fight?" (Winnicott, 1984/1994, p. 186).[3] Winnicott stressed that, unlike adults, "young people do not want to sleep" and that "during these sleepless nights, they multiply risky behaviors: incivility, robbery, and at times sexual violence." At the end of the 20th century, a public health perspective added both licit and illicit psychoactive substances to the list of risks for young partygoers. Yet, in older literary sources, drunken nights are largely commonplace, not considered "noble" enough (or even significant enough) to deserve more than passing mention.

One might analyze the stereotype of youth's excessive behaviors from a historical perspective, putting the role of drunkenness in the celebratory behavior of youth into its proper context (Nahoum-Grappe, 1991). But our study is about contemporary behaviors. However deep-rooted the historical stereotypes about "youth" and its "thirst for drunkenness," it is the current forms of young people's "extreme drinking" that are of interest to us here. It is almost impossible to introduce a "generational" variable into research in the humanities, even though historians, sociologists, and anthropologists have often felt the importance of generational differences in their work. As Claude Lévi-Strauss wrote (1986):

> We do not have sufficient hindsight to identify the way the family unit evolves because of technical, economic, and psychological changes that are happening before our eyes in Western societies: married women working, increasing numbers of domestic partnerships, growing importance of the media that favors horizontal communication between members of each generation to the detriment of the communication that was previously essentially vertical, from one generation to the next. (p. 12)

For technological and sociological reasons, communication is more "horizontal"—among peers—in some societies than in others. Without doubt, the formation of a relative "cultural autonomy" of a particular age group also creates a similar common horizon where information circulates actively between siblings, cousins, friends, and confederates: Models and positions, values and preferences, behavioral patterns can be shared out of sight of adult eyes. This gap between parents and children—more sociological than geographic—plays an important role in establishing the eventual and relative autonomy of "youth" as a culture.

The consistency of young people's behavioral patterns is at issue, with their esthetic, their quirks, their particular ways of consuming and dressing, and their relationship with alcohol and extreme drinking. In fact, the tension between generations, which has been widely depicted on stage and screen and

---

[3] Shakespeare's original text from *Winter's Tale* (Act 3, Scene 3) is as follows: "I would there were no age between sixteen and three-and-twenty, or that youth would sleep out the rest; for there is nothing in the between but getting wenches with child, wronging the ancientry, stealing, fighting—Hark you now! Would any but these boiled brains of nineteen and two-and-twenty hunt this weather?"

through our most canonical literature since Molière at least, has helped define the peculiarities of youth: their thirst for "freedom(s)," both singular and plural, sexual and romantic, freedom from submission to parental restraints, freedom in choosing identity and lifestyle, and freedom to choose how to spend the night. The ties between youth and the expression of moral liberties and freedom of choice are nothing new. The thirst for the "extreme" is a short-term consequence of its expressions: "going out!" "living for the moment!"; "everything, right now!"; or better still, "nothing, right now!"

The ability to think in terms of childhood and youth depends on historical and social conditions that are not universal. A number of elements play a role in the creation of this specific *identity category*: the age for entering the workforce, the age of marriage, the presence or absence of an educational system accessible to all, the duration of schooling, the formation of an economic market centered on the "young" age group, and the growing individualization of political citizenship—these are the various factors (among many) that support the creation of a specific, autonomous, and consistent category of identity, *youth* morphed into *adolescence*. At stake in this transitional period from childhood to adulthood is the ability to achieve a successful break, a gradual process of disconnection that occurs over the course of several years during adolescence. To recognize oneself in the mirror, to go out at night, to encounter alcohol, tobacco, and sexuality are more problematic for young people than for adults, who have come to terms with their faces and bodies and who can turn down another drink if they feel they have already had enough.

While young children may accept (after a struggle) what to eat, when to sleep, what to wear, and what to do, moody adolescents take a more critical view. They may balk at their reflection in the mirror for they do not want to look like their parents' dream child. As they grow older, they begin to resist adult authority by controlling their own appearance, despite parental disapproval, choosing their haircuts and insisting on what to wear. They decide what to eat and drink, typically marking the end of childhood with coffee, tobacco, and alcohol (all forbidden for children, whose main "addiction" is sugar). They change and claim ownership over their schedule, refusing to get up in the morning and go to bed at night, eager to explore the night's party scene. Drinking and eating patterns are in fact markers of social identity (Fischler, 2001). It would seem that tobacco, alcohol beverages, and excessive behaviors are visible and predictable choices for some age groups more than others, and for one gender more than the other, and our social imagination is full of expectation and anticipation over these differences of style and choices.

Young people want to leave the nest that has been woven around them by the dreams and expectations of their parents, and this difficult and at times confrontational attempt to break with parental control is reflected in consumer choices, self-presentation, and a violent desire to "go out!" at night. In some cultures, societal safeguards exist within the community itself to deal with this transition: At the end of childhood, severe regulations and a collective monitoring system are put into place, often in a highly ritualized way. It is an effort to control the dangerous gap that exists between purely biological reproduction and the social transmission of goods and identity. In many Western societies, young people enjoy a relative degree of freedom in their amorous adventures and many other behavioral choices (clothing, food, pastimes). In this context, a number of parameters should be noted, including the history of mores, laws, and differences between the genders in terms of sexuality. The progressive and relative disappearance of the taboo of virginity among Western girls is a key illustration of this history.

But one should also keep in mind that periods of "freedom of choice" throughout history have not been reflected in an increase in marriage among different social classes and ethnic groups; in reality, the freedom of choice in marriage only rarely clashes with family conventions, the world of romantic fiction notwithstanding. The celebratory context—the night—is a rare moment during which this anthropological need to disconnect can find a stage. Oblivion, particularly from the parental world, is played out with an intensity heightened by noise, laughter, and intoxication. Parents demand of their children, "Tell me where you are going and what time you are coming home," as they try to keep a connection. But extreme drinking will intrude even on this relationship and the young person's consciousness. It can break this connection: "How would my parents know where I am when I am drunk and don't know myself?" We cannot understand extreme drinking without putting it within the context of the need to break away from the world of childhood and to become integrated into the broader circle of social life. The more difficult this break, the greater is the importance of youthful "nights out" and the more potent is the seduction of the extreme and the notion of the "wild youth," with its short but intense bouts of "drunkenness" (achieved through alcohol or by other means).

EXTREME DRINKING IN CONTEXT: WHAT IS "PARTYING"?

A rapid typology of celebrations in Western societies enables us to distinguish at least two main stages, rooted in history and tradition:

1. *The ceremonial celebration*: Normally, the first phase of a social gathering, religious or secular, but always permeated by a particular liturgy, in which gestures, postures, and behaviors are specified, as during parades, ribbon-cutting ceremonies, awards of medals or trophies, christenings, or weddings. Mona Ozouf's book *La Fête Révolutionnaire* (1976) offers a good illustration of this stage, as it traces the invention of ceremonial celebrations at the end of the 18th century. Such occasions are normally held in honor of a person or an event, with most participants acting as spectators of the action occurring before them, usually at the altar, throne, stage, or podium. Although drinking vessels may be present in

the beginning of the event, its official, ceremonial part is typically a
time for sobriety.

2. *Merry-making*: The period of merry-making often follows the ceremonial celebration. "The people need to have fun," is an expression from
   the ancien régime. The "people" (Bakhtine, 1982; Barrows, 1981), the
   working masses, like the youth of today, were perceived as groups in
   need of fun from time to time, because this is part of their very identity. During such festivities, song, dance, and laughter are associated
   with unlimited drinking, where empty bottles are no longer counted
   (Braudel, 1949, 1958; Dion, 1959).

The more "popular" the festivities and the more diverse the crowd, the
more drunkenness (combined with song and dance) is likely to be "extreme,"
while the norms of keeping one's distance, composure, and codes of good
conduct no longer hold sway as they do during times of nonfestive sobriety.
The celebration is a space of temporary and tolerated impunity, not so much
in legal terms but with regard to mores, according to Montesquieu's distinction: Certain sins and transgressions will be overlooked, albeit within limits,
for there is an implicit second threshold of what is acceptable during times of
popular celebration. Chaos and danger are put in perspective within the context of the "extreme" celebration (but this is a topic for another day).

At the center of the celebration and the festive space, it is the young who
are the most joyful and the wildest; they will be the last to leave and have
come the farthest to be able to join in. For them, a party and a chance to
rejoice are a true adventure and an eagerly anticipated event, as though specifically created for them. The connection between the idea of "youth" and
that of celebration as an occasion for collective rejoicing is nothing new. Who
is the central player in the celebration? Who is first in line to have fun? It is
the young person, possibly male, the inventor of various competitions, ready
for any stunt. Drinking and eating competitions, which have been described
extensively under the ancien régime, show that excessive behavior enjoys a
privileged place in the culture of celebrations, as do the exploits of young boys
and indeed grown men. While *moderation*, the refusal of excess (of food and
of alcoholic beverages), was the central norm promoted by the religious, medical, educational, moral, and civil authorities throughout the ancien régime,
immoderate, excessive behavior was also the rule of conduct during periods
of celebration and belongs to our Western mode of celebratory communication. Excessive drinking and eating here are a humorous test, staged amidst
fun and laughter, but, in the case of drinking, they are also a test of the "true"
man, an assessment of strength and ability to fight his own body. Before our
contemporary culture of the "extreme," there existed in Europe a traditional
popular culture of festive excess, where immoderate drinking and eating were
the rule (Bakhtine, 1982), a behavior that continues in the carnivals of the 21st
century (see chapter 2).

A night of celebration is never consistent or homogeneous, it gains
momentum, it "bursts" (as do laughs and stomachs), and reaches its peak well

after midnight. As the night advances, collective drunkenness leads to adventurous ideas, proposed by the most festive element, the young people. The performances and stunts that follow are often linked to the feeling of vertigo/lightheadedness: climbing a steeple, a tree, a cliff, a tower—or out-drinking one's friends. It is important to stress here the existence of a historic and social tradition of collective enjoyment that leads young people to test themselves though sampling excess. But this analysis digresses into the realm of work initiated by "folklorists," the forerunners of ethnographers at the turn of the 20th century, who observed rural and urban celebrations in traditional French society, recording their rituals and peculiarities (van Gennep, 1937).

Opportunities for celebration are many and often relate to moments of transition during the year (solstice, New Year's Eve), across one's life stages (births, baptisms, weddings), and throughout the events of collective life (athletic or military victory, a remarkable exploit). Drunkenness is often present during these moments, especially among young participants. Here, the old culture of celebration in Europe, where drunkenness accompanies and sets the pace for other acts of immoderation and excess, meets the contemporary culture of youth that values an esthetic of extreme in the sense defined above. Today, the extreme has become the highest embodiment of liberation of mores and norms, an almost physical search for a radical, intense, and deep sensation, stronger than simply pleasure—a real, albeit temporary, modification of the consciousness of self.

To what degree are our celebratory habits the legacy of traditional ways and in what way have they been reinvented? The usage of the celebration in traditional societies (Corbin, 1992; Le Roy Ladurie, 1979) has been reinvented today by groups of young drinkers on the prowl for extreme transgression. On contemporary festive occasions, one can still distinguish the two stages of a traditional celebration, described above—but the expressions of excess, the stunts performed under its spell, have changed with time: Today's speeding in vehicles, be it on two or four wheels, offers a form of horizontal headlong plunge, reminiscent of the vertical giddiness of climbing a church steeple. Variations on this theme—of how best to induce the feeling of vertigo (Baudry, 1991; Le Breton, 1991)—are being constantly reinvented by young people in full party mode.

"GOING OUT!"

What is it that makes youth different—with its rosy cheeks and bursts of laughter, often represented in unkind movies as sulky and disturbed, addicted and truant, "burning the candle at both ends" and burning their bodies with tobacco and alcohol—if not the way they "go out" and have fun? How do they celebrate? What do they think they have to do to "have fun"? The choice of entertainment is limited to a number of forms of celebratory behaviors that have been passed down through centuries and have recently evolved sociologically. But for young people, "having fun" always begins with "going out" and going out to "have fun," an effort that can either fail or succeed. There are "good" ways to have fun, and drinking to extreme and engaging in other risky behaviors (speeding, performing dangerous stunts) are often included in this "trip."

Going out involves an imagined sequence with a temporary (just for the night ahead) physical and psychological closeness to the narrative of the "extreme" that is characteristic of contemporary youth. "Going out" is also an important step in the difficult but necessary process of disconnecting from one's family that marks the end of childhood. It is these two quite disparate parameters that enables extreme drunkenness—that goal of attaining not refreshment but a dizzying psychoactive effect and an altered state of consciousness, "forgetting everything" (above all the vigilant parental eye), being outside oneself, and wanting "everything/nothing, right now!"—to serve, through the effects of ethanol on the nervous system, as a convenient, mechanical means of switching gears and entering another stage of life. Escaping, the flight of youth, "quitting everything" are illusory dreams for adults but make perfect sense to young people. The terrible sentence, "I don't care about anything," that expresses adolescent malaise implies this vertigo of "nothingness" and is also embedded in the slogan quoted at the beginning of this chapter: That phrase encapsulates the desire for a radical break, which sometimes only extreme drinking can temporarily make real, even if it is just for one night.

"Going out" in our modern, urban Westernized society is not nearly as constraining and codified as it is in other more traditional, more religious, and more isolated cultures. "Going out" becomes anonymous and undefined, where "real life" must invent and prove itself with its many extreme and intense experiences, of which the most reliable (because it is both biological and mechanical) is drinking in "sufficient" quantities (excessive from a public health perspective, but "sufficient" as far as achieving drunkenness is concerned). It is in this festive space, mostly at night, that chance may bring an amorous or at least a sexual encounter. This encounter is the anticipated highlight of the night and truly the culmination of that ascent to the extreme. Couples who are already together leave the party before others do, they drink less, and "want to go home." Extreme drinking is far more interesting for the singleton, for the young person possessed by the dream of an encounter.

Whatever the sociological consistency of the idea of "youth," and its reality or "unreality" (Huerre, Pagan-Reymond, & Reymond, 1990), there is a need for the child to become an adult; it is a prerequisite for the continuation and transmission of all societies. Young people must traverse the circle of their own childhoods, surrounded by family, to become a part of their time, their age, their city; "going out" is a natural step in this rupture, both physical and spatial. Drunkenness can also be understood as the inner fulfillment, within the consciousness of self "outside the self," of this essential severing process. Encounters with the other sex and peers outside the family circle are part of the profile of this process.

REFERENCES

Augé, M. (1994). *Pour une anthropologie des mondes contemporains* [*An anthropology of contemporaneous worlds*]. Paris: Aubier.

Bakhtine, M. (1982). *L'œuvre de François Rabelais et la culture populaire au Moyen Age et sous la Renaissance* [*Rabelais and the folk culture of the Middle Ages and the Renaissance*]. Paris: Gallimard.

Barrows, S. (1981). *Distorting mirrors: Visions of the crowd in late nineteenth-century France.* New Haven, CT: Yale University Press.

Barthes, R. (1957). *Mythologies.* Paris: Editions du Seuil.

Baudelaire, C. (1993). The evil glazier. In *Baudelaire, Rimbaud, Verlaine: Selected Verse and Prose Poems* (pp. 102–104). New York: Carol Publishing Group. (Original work published 1869)

Baudry, P. (1991). *Le corps extrême: Approche sociologique des conduites à risque* [*The body extreme: Sociological approach to risky conduct*]. Paris: Gallimard.

Braudel, F. (1949). *La Méditerranée et le monde Méditerranéen à l'époque de Philippe II* [*The Mediterranean and the Mediterranean world in the age of Philip II*]. Paris: Armand Colin.

Braudel, F. (1958). La longue durée. *Annales, 725–753.*

Choquet, M., Com-Ruelle, L., & Leymarie, N. (2003). *Les 12–20 ans et l'alcool en 2001* [*The 12–20-year-olds and alcohol in 2001*]. Paris: Institut de Recherches Scientifiques sur les Boissons.

Cloarec, J. (1996). Le corps acteur et le corps agi [The body actor and the body acted]. *Communications, 61,* 5–10.

Collard, C. (Director). (1992). *Les Nuits Fauves* [*Savage Nights*]. [Motion picture]. France: Banfilm.

Corbin, A. (1992). *Le village des cannibales* [*The village of the cannibals*]. Paris: Aubier Montaigne.

Currie, C., Roberts, C., Morgan, A., Smith, R., Settertobulte, W., Samdal, O., et al. (Eds.). (2004). *Young people's health in context. Health Behaviour in School-aged Children (HBSC) study: International report from the 2001/2002 survey.* Health Policy for Children and Adolescents No. 4. Copenhagen, Denmark: WHO Regional Office for Europe.

Dion, R. (1959). *Histoire de la vigne et du vin en France: Des origines au XIXe siècle* [*History of vine and wine in France: Origins in the 19th century*]. Paris: Clavreuil.

Fessard, S. (1995). L'incurable retard des mots [The incurable delay of words]. *Cités: Journal d'Information et de Prévention de la Toxicomanie et du Sida, 2,* 12.

Fischler, C. (2001). *L'Homnivore.* Paris: Odile Jacob.

Groupe de Recherche et d'Etudes sur les Conduites Ordaliques (GRECO). (1994). *Toxicomanie et mort : Addictions et conduites de risque* [*Drug-addiction and death: Addictions and risky conduct*]. Paris: Hôpital Marmottan.

Hibell, B., Andersson, B., Bjarnason, T., Ahlström, S., Balakireva, O., Kokkevi, A., et al. (2004). *The ESPAD Report 2003: Alcohol and other drug use among students in 35 European countries.* Stockholm: Swedish Council for Information on Alcohol and Other Drugs (CAN).

Huerre, P., Pagan-Reymond, M., & Reymond, J.-M. (1990). *L'adolescence n'existe pas* [*Adolescence does not exist*]. Paris: Universitaire Paris.

Knibbe, R., Joosten, J., Choquet, M., Derickx, M., Morin, D., & Monshouwer K. (2007). Culture as an explanation for substance-related problems: A cross-national study among French and Dutch adolescents. *Social Science and Medicine, 64,* 604–616.

Knibbe, R., Joosten, J., Derickx, M., Choquet, M., Morin, D., Monshouwer, K., et al. (2005). Perceived availability of substances, substance use and substance-related problems: A cross national study among French and Dutch adolescents. *Journal of Substance Use, 10,* 151–163.

Le Breton, D. (1991). *Passions du risque* [*Passion of risk*]. Paris: Métaillé.

Le manège de l'extrême [The extreme merry-go-round]. (1995, June 1). *Libération*, 11.

Le Roy Ladurie, E. (1979). *Le Carnaval de Romans: de la Chandeleur au mercredi des Cendres 1579-1580* [*Carnival in Romans: Mayhem and massacre in a French city*]. Paris: Gallimard.

Lévi-Strauss, C. (1986). Preface. In A. Burguière, C. Klapisch-Zuber, M. Segalen, & F. Zonabend (Eds.), *L'histoire de la famille* [*The history of the family*] (Vol. 1, pp. 9–13). Paris: Armand Colin.

Lewis, O. (1961). *The children of Sanchez: Autobiography of a Mexican family.* New York: Random House.

Lewis, O. (1998). The culture of poverty. *Society, 35,* 7–9.

L'Homme: Revue Français d'Anthropologie. (2008). Special issue. No. 185. Availabe: http://lhomme.revues.org.

Nahoum-Grappe, V. (1991). *La culture de l'ivresse : Essai de phénoménologie historique* [*The culture of intoxication: A historical test of phenomenology*]. Paris: Quai Voltaire.

Nahoum-Grappe, V. (2005). *Soif d'ivresse* [*Thirst for drunkenness*]. Paris: STOCK.

Ozouf, M. (1976). *La fête révolutionnaire, 1789–1799* [*The revolutionary festival, 1789–1799*]. Paris: Gallimard.

Studeny, C. (1995). *L'invention de la vitesse: France, XVIIIe–XXe siècle* [*The invention of speed: France, 18th to 20th century*]. Paris: Gallimard.

van Gennep, A. (1937). *Manuel de folklore français contemporain* [*The handbook of contemporary French folklore*]. Paris: Picard.

Winnicott, D. W. (1994). *Déprivation et délinquance* [*Deprivation and delinquency*]. Paris: Science de l'Homme Payot. (Original work published 1984)

Chapter 4

What Motivates Extreme Drinking?

Barbara Leigh and Christine Lee

Recent public concern in many countries has drawn much attention to young people, among whom extreme drinking peaks in late adolescence to early adulthood (e.g., Hibell, Andersson, Ahlström et al., 1999; Hibell, Andersson, Bjarnason et al., 2004; Kuntsche, Rehm, & Gmel, 2004). This drinking pattern is prevalent among young adults and is often seen by them as a culturally appropriate behavior (Engineer, Phillips, Thompson, & Nicholls, 2003). It is also primarily a social phenomenon, typically occurring in public places, such as pubs, bars and nightclubs, and in groups.

Alcohol consumption in general can be viewed as a developmental rite of passage for young adults. This practice transcends culture and social class, with drinking being perceived by many youths as more normative than not drinking. However, young people who engage in *extreme* drinking are at risk for many immediate physical effects—for instance, hangovers, blackouts, impaired cognitive and motor coordination, and injury—as well as the more delayed social consequences, such as having problems at home, school, and work. Moreover, alcohol consumption in or around nightclubs, pubs, bars, or taverns increases the risk of violence as compared to drinking in other contexts (Pernanen, 1991; Richardson & Budd, 2003).

In light of these potentially negative consequences, why do young people engage in extreme drinking? We examine this consumption pattern in a young adult population and review research that can help put this behavior into context. Throughout the chapter, examples from focus groups of young people in a number of countries are highlighted. The subsequent chapter in this volume will present findings of recent focus groups that explored the issue of extreme drinking among young people in Brazil, China, Italy, Nigeria, Russia, South Africa, and Scotland (see chapter 5).

DRINKING AS CENTRAL LEISURE ACTIVITY

When young people are asked how they spend their free time, alcohol consumption takes pride of place. In focus groups of adolescents and young adults in the United Kingdom (U.K.), drinking was nearly always mentioned spontaneously as a prominent leisure activity, and, indeed, many young people felt that they had few other options available (MacAskill, Cooke, Eadie, & Hastings, 2001). Moreover, drinking alcohol among this population usually involves going out, and visiting drinking venues is a central element in the young adult lifestyle. In another U.K. study of 18- to 24-year-olds, going to a pub, a party, or a nightclub was second only to watching television as the common pastime; three-quarters of respondents reported visiting such venues in the last month (Richardson & Budd, 2003). Among college students in the United States (U.S.), parties, dates, and socializing were found to be the most common events where extreme drinking occurred (Clapp & Shillington, 2001). Drinking with friends, drinking beer and liquor, and having many other intoxicated people at an event were found to be predictive of extreme drinking in this U.S. population (Clapp & Shillington, 2001; Clapp, Shillington, & Segars, 2000).

Extreme drinking occasions among young people in many countries are normally planned in advance rather than being accidental or unintended (Brain, Parker, & Carnwath, 2000; Coleman & Cater, 2005; Engineer et al., 2003; MacAskill et al., 2001; Sheehan & Ridge, 2001). "Getting drunk" is often the goal of a big night out, with many young people engineering their intoxication by drinking quickly, choosing beverages with high alcohol content, or drinking at home before going out (Engineer et al., 2003; Gofton, 1990; Measham & Brain, 2005; see chapter 5). Although the most-emphasized aim of drinking among this population involves its social aspects—including spending time with friends and meeting new people—the second most likely object is to "feel drunk" (Richardson & Budd, 2003). For many young people around the world, the goal of extreme drinking is to "have a good time," which includes drunkenness as a principal objective and an inevitable feature of the excursion (Engineer et al., 2003; MacAskill et al., 2001; chapter 5).

Although most young adults, when asked, provide reasons for their drinking—including social facilitation and enjoyment—for some it is so routine that they have difficulty explaining why they do it:

> You don't have to know the reason for it. You just do it anyway. Everybody does it, it is the way the world is. (Male, 18–20, nonmanual worker) (Engineer et al., 2003, p. 24)

> I dunno why, it's just what we normally do. (Male, 14) (Coleman & Cater, 2005, p. 21)

> Tonight I found myself drinking more out of habit than anything else. It seems that drinking on Friday night is the thing to do. It is the end of the week, and it is so acceptable. (Rabow & Duncan-Schill, 1995, p. 57)

DEVELOPMENTAL CONTEXT DURING EMERGING ADULTHOOD

To understand extreme drinking among young people, we must address the context in which it occurs: Developmental, cultural, and social factors all play a part. The ages between 18 and 25 years, often referred to as *young adulthood* or *emerging adulthood*, are a distinct period in the lifespan, characterized by experimentation and exploration (Arnett, 2000). In many countries, the transition to early adulthood is marked by prolonged schooling, delays in acquiring full adult roles and responsibilities (such as marriage and parenting), increased autonomy, and residential changes (Arnett, 2000).

The developmental transition from adolescence to adulthood brings a number of new normative demands and expectations in multiple domains (Arnett, 2000; Schulenberg, Maggs, & O'Malley, 2003), and young people are provided with many new environments and opportunities to meet these demands (Schulenberg & Maggs, 2002). The setting of personal goals allows individuals to become active participants in their achievement of age-graded developmental steps (Nurmi, 1993; Salmela-Aro & Nurmi, 1997), such as establishing new relationships, exploring different identities, and gaining autonomy from parents (Schulenberg et al., 2003).

Experimentation with alcohol and other substances increases in emerging adulthood, and often reaches peak lifetime levels during this period (e.g., Johnston, O'Malley, Bachman, & Schulenberg, 2004). Despite the negative consequences individuals may face from excessive consumption, drinking alcohol may serve many constructive functions (Schulenberg, Maggs, & Hurrelmann, 1997). Experimenting with alcohol may be developmentally appropriate and interpreted as a way for individuals to obtain and work toward certain goals and tasks listed above—for instance, by helping them make new friends, explore "adult" behaviors, and achieve identity (Baumrind, 1985; Dworkin, 2005; Jessor & Jessor, 1977; Maggs, 1997; Silbereisen, Noack, & Reitzle, 1987). Thus, alcohol may be used for a variety of reasons by emerging adults: to ease peer relations, to cope with the instability of the context or identity confusion, to exercise newfound freedoms and autonomy, and to try new things before accepting full-time adult roles (Arnett, 2005). In qualitative studies, young people in different countries report drinking for these very reasons (e.g., Engineer et al., 2003; chapter 5).

Drinking to Facilitate Peer Relations

Peers play an important role in young adult lives, providing a reference group or identity and social support (Brown, Dolcini, & Leventhal, 1997). Cultural norms often promote heavy drinking as a rite of passage during these years, excessive drinking being viewed as normative, fun, and a bonding experience with friends. Many young people enrolled in colleges or universities have been found to overestimate the frequency and quantity of peer drinking, adding to the perception that extreme consumption is normative for this age group (e.g., Borsari & Carey, 2003; Perkins & Berkowitz, 1986).

Much of youthful drinking occurs in social milieus, and young adults are more likely to drink with friends and in groups than with a spouse or a partner (Richardson & Budd, 2003). Getting drunk is acknowledged by some youths as a way to meet new people, make new friends, and increase bonds with existing friends (Coleman & Cater, 2005). The relationship between alcohol use and friendships is complex. A study of U.S. college students found that frequency of extreme consumption was associated with more intimate relationships with same-sex peers (Nezlek, Pilkington, & Bilbro, 1994). In addition to the actual drinking event being a time of socializing, drinking alcohol may increase the bond between friends both during the event and afterwards, when negative consequences may enhance intimacy. For example, female participants in U.K. focus groups often described holding back each other's hair as they were vomiting as part of the group support dynamic (MacAskill et al., 2001).

Forming romantic or sexual relationships is an important developmental task of emerging adulthood. Many young people go to bars, nightclubs, and parties for the opportunities to meet potential romantic or sexual partners; alcohol in these settings may help facilitate the courtship process. Among U.S. college women, Nezlek and colleagues (1994) found that participants who engaged in extreme drinking reported more intimate relations than those who did not. In Swedish young adult focus groups, both men and women said that alcohol facilitated flirtation, creating the opportunity for interaction and giving the drinker confidence to pursue the interaction:

> That it's easier to flirt with someone after you've been drinking, that is definitely true, but mostly this thing about contact, going to a club and flirting in a sober state, people will react, um, then they might think: *my, she's desperate!* (Abrahamson, 2004, p. 12)

In the Swedish study, women also indicated that drinking alcohol helped them take sexual initiative, but up to a limit, whereas men reported that alcohol helped them be more daring and open with women (Abrahamson, 2004). According to many young adults, the main benefit of drinking is alcohol's ability to facilitate the interaction by lowering inhibitions and raising confidence, but it may also lead to unplanned sexual behavior:

> From my experiences, hookups always happen at parties, thus with alcohol and drugs. Many situations involve alcohol and drugs because people lose inhibition and wear beer goggles, increasing the likelihood of hooking up. (Female, 20) (Paul & Hayes, 2002, p. 646)

Drinking to Cope with Problems

Developmental transitions are marked by discontinuity, as well as continuity (Schulenberg & Maggs, 2002; Schulenberg et al., 2003), involving major qualitative reorganizations in one's perception of self and others' perception of self (Cowan, 1991). Individuals need to adopt new behaviors and beliefs in order to address the new tasks and demands placed on them by society. Thus, youths may drink to cope with the new demands of young adulthood—for instance, finding one's identity in work and romance and overcoming fights or breakups with friends or partners:

> If, I mean I've had a couple of times when I've been with one of my girlfriends, if we've split up. I go out with my mates and get bladdered. Stress. Exams, especially. If I've muffed up an exam I go out that very same night and I will get bladdered. (Male 17) (Coleman & Cater, 2005, p. 18)[1]

Drinking to cope is not new in the alcohol literature. This behavior is aimed at managing, minimizing, or eliminating problems or negative emotions (Cooper, Frone, Russell, & Mudar, 1995). Among adolescents and young adults, alcohol consumption and problem drinking have been positively related with depression, subjective stress (Camatta & Nagoshi, 1995; Hussong & Chassin, 1994), and negative affect (Kushner & Sher, 1993; Kushner, Sher, Wood, & Wood, 1994; Wills, Sandy, Shinar, & Yaeger, 1999; Wood, Nagoshi, & Dennis, 1992). Drinking to cope is positively related to alcohol consumption and prevalence of alcohol problems (Bonin, McCreary, & Sadava, 2000; Carey & Correia, 1997; Cooper, 1994; Kassel, Jackson, & Unrod, 2000; Lecci, MacLean, & Croteau, 2002; Park & Levenson, 2002).

Although much of the literature on the issue conceptualizes this motivation to drink as the polar opposite of "drinking for sociability" (e.g., Cooper et al., 1995; Farber, Khavari, & Douglass, 1980), there is often a large social component among young adults in drinking to cope. Thus, a young person who is troubled by problems may be taken out drinking by peers, creating a context in which alcohol consumption can both relax the drinker and help him or her forget problems in the company of supportive friends (Coleman & Cater, 2005).

Drinking to Explore Increased Freedoms

Young adulthood is characterized by more freedoms than adolescence. Many emerging adults have more autonomy from their parents as they move out of the parental home and take on new and different responsibilities. Even those who continue to live with parents are likely to have less confining rules and more disposable income than when they were younger. Many emerging adults are furthering their education, and so delaying full-time work, marriage, and parenting. This period of growing independence, before accepting full-time

---

[1] From *Underage "Risky" Drinking: Motivations and Outcomes* by Lester Coleman and Suzanne Cater, published in 2005 by the Joseph Rowntree Foundation. Reproduced by permission of the Joseph Rowntree Foundation.

adult roles, is often used by young people for experimentation with alcohol and other substances, including extreme drinking.

Because of shifting societal demands, age-related changes in drinking patterns occur among young people in their late teens to mid-20s: The 17- to 19-year-olds with few demands on their leisure time become 20-somethings for whom responsibilities require limited alcohol consumption. The "good night out" at some point becomes less attractive than a quiet night at home, especially for those with children and financial constraints. In addition, as drinkers get older, they are less able to cope physically with the consequences of heavy alcohol consumption—for instance, longer hangovers (MacAskill et al., 2001).

Young people themselves are aware of this drinking trajectory, and can look back at previous experiences and forward to future changes. Although they may not consciously see drinking as a rite of passage, they think that everyone in their age group goes through this natural progression, and they see themselves as able to cut down in the future as they develop other responsibilities:

> I'm a student just now and I think I drink more because I've not got work in the morning. I think as you get older and you've got kids and things, you won't be able to go out and get plastered and feel how you do, because you'll have to get up. I think it'll change. I hope it does. (MacAskill et al., 2001, p. 10)

> There's a carefree attitude experiencing college…my friends and I refer to it as the safety bubble of school, you can do whatever you want. You can get up at 8 in the morning and drink for a football game, you're not an alcoholic, you're a party animal. But if you do that in the real world, then you'll go to treatment. (Dworkin, 2005, p. 232)[2]

Drinking as Goal-Directed Behavior: "Drinking for Fun"

Among young drinkers, the central motivation for alcohol consumption is to "have fun" (Coleman & Cater, 2005; Engineer et al., 2003; MacAskill et al., 2001; Parker, Aldridge, & Measham, 1998; Richardson & Budd, 2003; Sheehan & Ridge, 2001). Aspects of this motivation include promoting confidence, being sociable, meeting people, feeling good, and "enjoying" drunkenness. The sociability aspect of drinking is paramount, accompanied by a sense of personal pleasure in getting intoxicated. The pleasures of drinking among this age group—whether the drinking occasion is motivated by personal pleasure, stress reduction, or alleviation of boredom—always include other people as part of the drinking situation (Engineer et al., 2003). The increasing confidence in one's ability to engage in social interaction (whether friendly or sexual) is key, and young people often report feeling that alcohol

---

[2] Dworkin, J. *Journal of Adolescent Research*, *20*, 219–241, copyright ©2005 by Sage Publications. Reprinted by permission of Sage Publications, Inc.

helps in social processes by way of its disinhibiting qualities (Richardson & Budd, 2003).

Multiple studies of young drinkers demonstrate that young people from various countries drink (whether moderately or extremely) largely for personal pleasure (e.g., Brain et al., 2000; MacAskill et al., 2001; Measham & Brain, 2005; Park, 2004). Such behavior has been labeled *hedonistic*, although one might argue that the use of such a term, with its connotations of self-indulgence and carelessness, is disparaging; and it raises the question why this term is applied to young people and not to older adults, who also drink for pleasure. For example, a *Binge Drinking Fact Sheet* from the London-based Institute of Alcohol Studies, an organization with roots in the temperance movement, describes with veiled disapproval the consumption of "psycho-active substances to achieve an altered state of consciousness" (Institute of Alcohol Studies [IAS], 2005)—although it is unlikely that people would use these substances (including alcohol) if no alteration of consciousness was involved.

Brain, Parker, and Carnwath (2000) have described such drinking among young people with few social responsibilities and considerable free time as "unbounded" hedonism. For some drinkers, hedonism is "bounded" by external limitations as well as demands on time and income, including work, sports, school, and—most importantly—children. Measham and Brain's (2005) study of young adult drinkers in a British city center found that their drinking was rarely unbounded: Consumption was usually limited by an awareness of safety, security, and financial considerations for drinkers, in particular getting home safely. MacAskill and colleagues' (2001) study of young people in Scotland reported that even drinkers with few external constraints acknowledged the need to be capable for activities that were important to them and planned their excessive drinking around these activities. For example, they acknowledged the need to drink less on the night before an early call at work or an important sports event. Thus, these drinkers struck a balance between the pursuit of a good time by getting drunk and the recognition of other demands on their time and income. Another example is the finding that traditionally aged U.S. college students (18- to 22-year-olds) engage in heavy drinking primarily during weekends, often beginning on Thursday nights as the academic demand lessens for the week (Baer & Carney, 1993; Rabow & Duncan-Schill, 1995).

The balance between the desire to get drunk and the need to meet external responsibilities leads to "strategic" drinking, which balances the aspects of the drinking event (for instance, cost, duration, and level of intoxication) with these other demands (such as work, family, and financial responsibilities) (MacAskill et al., 2001). Drinking strategically might include the following: interspersing short periods of intoxication with periods of abstinence; confining heavy drinking to certain days of the week, planned around other priorities; and aiming for a "buzz" rather than intense drunkenness on a "good night out."

A key factor in bounded, controlled, or strategic drinking is "getting your money's worth" or most "bangs per buck" (Coffield & Gofton, 1994;

MacAskill et al., 2001; Measham, 1996). Alcohol is drunk for its psychoactive properties and, therefore, part of its utility lies in that "alcohol…is judged according to how long it takes to produce a hit and at what financial cost" (Coffield & Gofton, 1994, p. 20); that is, the intensity of the effects experienced from drinking needs to be "worth" the money expended (see also chapter 5). Parker and Measham (1994) have interpreted this tendency as part of a more general psychoactive culture in which an array of substances is available to young people, leading to a "pick 'n' mix" approach to experimentation with both legal and illegal drugs, as a result of a normalization of adolescent recreational drug use (Parker et al., 1998). Additionally, many young adults engage in drinking games as a way to socialize and to intentionally become intoxicated more quickly (Borsari, Bergen-Cico, & Carey, 2003; see chapter 5).

"GOOD" AND "BAD" CONSEQUENCES OF DRINKING

Alcohol can have paradoxical effects for the individual, causing both pleasure and pain in the same drinking episode. Young people are not unique in expecting good things to happen when they drink: Surveys and interviews of individuals of different ages show that people expect largely positive effects from drinking—most people drink because they enjoy it. When asked to list the effects of alcohol, many respondents tend to list the positive rather than negative effects and to list the positive effects first (e.g., Gustafson, 1988, 1989; Leigh & Stacy, 1994; Parker et al., 1998). Moreover, people view the positive outcomes as more likely to occur than the negative ones. For instance, in Roizen's (1983) analysis of a U.S. national survey, the most commonly reported consequences of alcohol consumption (mentioned by 70% to 80% of respondents) were generally positive (such as being friendly, talkative, or romantic). Unpleasant outcomes, such as feeling sick, aggressive, argumentative, sad, or mean, were reported less frequently. Interestingly, it was not the case that some people reported positive effects and others reported negative effects. Instead, people who reported *any* effects mentioned positive ones, and, as the number of the effects being listed became larger, negative effects were included. Thus, people reported either no effects, positive effects, or both positive and negative effects, but no one reported negative effects without positive effects. The results from several similar surveys clearly demonstrate that drinkers (including heavy drinkers) experience more positive outcomes than negative outcomes from drinking—at least subjectively (Maggs, 1993; Mäkelä & Mustonen, 1988, 1996, 2000; Mäkelä & Simpura, 1985; Miller, Plant, & Plant, 2005; Mustonen & Mäkelä, 1999; Nyström, 1992; Park, 2004; Parker et al., 1998).

Although positive consequences of alcohol consumption are paramount among young people who drink to intoxication, negative consequences are readily acknowledged (Coleman & Cater, 2005; Engineer et al., 2003; MacAskill et al., 2001; Parker et al, 1998; Perkins, 2002; Richardson & Budd, 2003). Such consequences include physical effects of intoxication (vomiting and hangovers), social effects (making a fool of oneself, fighting, or having unplanned sexual experience), and negative impacts on work or studies. However, these negative outcomes are often perceived as inevitable and not reason enough for concern. Thus, interviews of young extreme drinkers in the U.K. showed that many negative consequences—including vomiting, hangovers, injuries, and embarrassing behavior—were seen by them as "routine" consequences of alcohol consumption and did not serve as deterrents to drinking heavily in the future (Coleman & Cater, 2005; Engineer et al., 2003; MacAskill et al., 2001). As one respondent noted:

> You can't control that sort of thing, it just happens. You've got to know that sort of thing happens occasionally and you've got to accept it. (Male, 18–20, student) (Engineer et al., 2003, p. 45)

Whereas negative outcomes were accepted as part of the process of drinking, those who experienced them were seen as deserving of sympathy rather than condemnation. More serious concerns were expressed about spiked drinks, fighting, and vulnerability to potentially dangerous situations (for instance, walking home alone or being unable to escape aggression). Serious consequences, such as police involvement and long-term health implications, were commonly viewed as remote and irrelevant to drinking decisions; indeed, police involvement was often described in humorous terms (MacAskill et al., 2001).

Although one might expect that negative consequences would dissuade young people from drinking to extreme, their acceptance of the inevitability of such consequences suggests some reasons why drinking continues in the face of such outcomes: Positive consequences appear to youths to be more important and frequent; negative outcomes are delayed and infrequently experienced; and bad effects are often minimized by the drinkers as "not so bad."

Positive Consequences Are Much More Important and Frequent

People who know about potential negative consequences of alcohol consumption also expect positive consequences (and more of them). Most research into positive and negative outcomes of drinking has demonstrated that positive consequences are experienced much more often than negative ones (Mäkelä & Mustonen, 1988, 1996, 2000; Mäkelä & Simpura, 1985; Miller et al., 2005; Mustonen & Mäkelä, 1999; Nyström, 1992; Park, 2004). Because negative effects of drinking occur less frequently than positive effects, the expectations of their occurrence may be "swamped" by the much more probable likelihood of pleasurable consequences. Thus, although young people generally know that negative effects may occur, they may be more motivated by the likelier positive effects when they drink.

For example, in a study of U.S. college students (Park, 2004), drinking episodes with positive outcomes were described as being more extreme and more frequent than episodes with negative outcomes. Heavier drinkers reported more positive and negative consequences, but it was the positive consequences that were perceived as more influential in future decisions.

MacAskill and colleagues (2001) noted that

> [y]oung people could compile a formidable list of things that might go wrong when drinking alcohol, although they tended not to acknowledge these alcohol-related risks on a personal basis. What might objectively be seen as risks tended to be seen as transitory difficulties and even part of the fun and targets to aim for. In other words, any potential negative factors were far outweighed by the benefits of drinking. More serious consequences such as addiction or liver damage, while acknowledged, were rationalised away as future risks for *other people, not me*" or accepted fatalistically. (p. 19)

The positive consequences of drinking are especially likely to predominate among young people. Surveys in Finland, the United Kingdom, and the United States suggest that younger people report more positive effects from drinking than older people, even when drinking habits are controlled. For example, in a Finnish survey on drinking outcomes (Mäkelä & Mustonen, 2000), respondents aged under 30 years reported *both* positive and negative consequences (other than long-term health problems) more often than their older counterparts. Age differences in positive consequences were concentrated in social aspects (getting to know someone better, becoming closer to the opposite sex), and age differences in negative consequences were also concentrated in aspects of social interactions that require the presence of other people (becoming loud/boisterous, regretting something said or done, getting into quarrels or fights). Thus, these age distinctions in effects reflect the importance of social interaction in drinking occasions in young people.

In the U.K., a survey assessed drinking level and patterns, negative consequences from drinking (including problems with work, relationships, studies, or finances; accidents; fights; health problems; and immediate physical consequences, such as nausea and unsteadiness), and positive drinking consequences (relaxing, enhancing social situations, enjoying oneself, and being less sexually inhibited) (Miller et al., 2005). Heavier drinkers reported more positive experiences than lighter drinkers, but this was only the case among people who drank once or twice a week, compared with drinkers who spread out their consumption over the week. Moreover, this effect was present only in drinkers aged between 18 and 24 years. In this age group, respondents who drank once or twice a week but less than 14 total drink units a week listed a mean of 3.9 positive experiences from drinking, while once-or-twice-weekly drinkers who consumed 15 or more units a week reported an average 5.5 positive consequences. In short, positive effects of drinking in this sample were highest among young extreme drinkers.

A U.S. national survey of drinking habits may shed some light on whether younger drinkers enjoy drunkenness more than older drinkers (Leigh, 1990). When asked about the likelihood of a list of positive outcomes of drinking, younger respondents were more likely to report that they would "enjoy the buzz" than their older counterparts: A "likely" or "very likely" response was given by 61% of 12- to 17-year-olds, 66% of 18- to 25-year-olds, 64% of 26- to 35-year-olds, 55% of 36- to 45-year-olds, 38% of 46- to 60-year-olds, and 29% of those 61 and older.

Negative Outcomes Are Delayed and Infrequently Experienced

Many positive effects of alcohol are immediate, "feel good" consequences, whereas many negative effects are delayed by minutes (loss of coordination), days (loss of job), or years (loss of liver function). The relative importance of desirable and undesirable consequences in drinking motivation might then be a function of the immediacy of the consequence. Thus, the pleasurable, more immediate reinforcing "ups" may have a greater impact on learning about drinking and its effects than the more delayed "downs." A drinking episode might end badly, but its pleasurable beginnings are more powerful motivators (Marlatt, 1987; Stacy & Widaman, 1987).

In addition, some severe negative consequences of drinking, including accidents and long-term physical damage, are never experienced by most drinkers and are thus not learned by direct experience. Drinkers who have not experienced these consequences will perceive them as unlikely to occur in the future, and they may not figure strongly in drinking decisions. Young people in the U.K. who drank to excess reported rarely engaging in criminal or disorderly activity themselves, and others stated that only extremely serious consequences would motivate them to cut down their alcohol consumption, but that those consequences "hardly ever happen" (Richardson & Budd, 2003).

Bad Effects "Aren't So Bad"

Labeling alcohol effects as *positive* or *negative* is problematic, since effects that are desirable to some people may be undesirable for others. A striking example of this subjectivity comes from a study by Leigh and Stacy (1994) in which U.S. college students were asked to list the positive and negative effects of alcohol. Whereas 14% of men and 5% of women listed increased sexuality as a positive consequence of drinking, 6% of men and 13% of women mentioned it as a negative consequence. Clearly, some alcohol effects are perceived as positive by some and negative by others.

In general, heavier drinkers tend to perceive negative drinking outcomes less negatively than do lighter drinkers and nondrinkers (Cahalan & Room, 1974; Critchlow, 1987; Gustafson, 1991, 1993; Leigh, 1987, 1989; McCarty, Morrison, & Mills, 1983; Roizen, 1983). These perceptions may result from the norms of drinking situations: If heavy drinkers consume alcohol mostly with other heavy drinkers who are also experiencing negative consequences, they may accept these consequences as normal (McMahon, Jones, & O'Donnell,

1994). If negative outcomes are seen as "not so bad," they may not effectively limit drinking.

Although young people can easily name undesirable consequences from problem alcohol consumption, many do not see them as particularly serious and do not care whether they occur or not. Most negative consequences tend to be perceived by young drinkers as routine and transitory, and some consequences (e.g., daring behavior and pranks) may be seen as "part of the fun" (Engineer et al., 2003). As mentioned above, many negative consequences are judged by young people as an inevitable part of the whole experience, and the prospect of their occurrence is not seen as serious enough to deter future drinking (Coleman & Cater, 2005). In a California survey (Leigh, 1984), participants under 25 years of age rated certain "negative" consequences of drinking—including "doing things I would otherwise not do" and "becoming silly"—less negatively than their counterparts aged over 25 years.

Moreover, even though harm (as judged by a parent or health professional) does occur from drinking, the prevailing memory of the drinking episode in young people is not necessarily a bad one:

> [T]he two categories of experience were interconnected with the good and not so good times occurring as part of that one experience. The risks and occasional negative outcomes from drinking were all considered as part of the total experience and bigger story. There appears to be no clear distinction between positive and negative times, as all alcohol experiences subsequently contribute to the whole, becoming the "good" anecdote. The horrible hangover the next morning or the uncomfortable situation with a boy do not exist on their own. They are accepted elements of the socializing that afforded a good time, a pleasurable interaction, and a shared experience that can be savored and recounted with embellishment if necessary. (Sheehan & Ridge, 2001, p. 355)[3]

In focus groups of young drinkers, negative consequences are sometimes acknowledged only when brought up by the researchers, rather than being spontaneously mentioned as a feature of personal experience. In a study of young Australian women, 75% of the participants reported at least one harmful consequence of drinking, and the mean number of harmful consequences was 4.6. (These harmful consequences, defined by the researcher, included lying to parents, having conflicts with friends, vomiting, making a fool of oneself, having trouble getting home, and experiencing or inflicting damage to property.) However, only 19% of the sample reported that they could recall actual negative experiences from their own perspective (Sheehan & Ridge, 2001). The harmful consequences suggested by the researchers simply did not play a part in respondents' drinking stories and were not seen by study participants as worthy of consideration. As one young woman explained, "I wouldn't really say that having an argument with your friend was a real harm.

---

[3] *Substance Use and Misuse* by Sheehan, M., & Ridge, D. Copyright 2001 by Informa Healthcare-Journals. Reproduced with permission of Informa Healthcare-Journals via Copyright Clearance Center.

It's not like getting killed in a car, bashed up, raped, or something…I mean they're real problems" (p. 355).

> Drinking which is fun thus tends to carry some risks—risks not only for the drinker, but also for those around the drinker. In the real world of drinkers, rather few of whom stick precisely to the [government dietary guidelines] all the time, the pleasures of drinking are not so separable from the problems. The drinker, along with those around him or her, has to put up with the thorns to enjoy the rose. (Room, 2000, p. 250)[4]

Or, as another young woman put it succinctly, "And, you know, having a hangover in the morning is, like, minor compared to the fact you've had loads of fun the night before" (Female 17) (Coleman & Cater, 2005, p. 51).

FACTORS THAT INCREASE THE RISK OF EXTREME DRINKING AND ITS CONSEQUENCES

Cultural Acceptance of Drunkenness

It is clear from studies of young people in a number of countries that drunkenness and frequent intoxication are often perceived as acceptable behaviors by those who engage in them (Coleman & Cater, 2005; Engineer et al., 2003; MacAskill et al., 2001; Measham & Brain, 2005; Rabow & Duncan-Schill, 1995; Wechsler, Dowdall, Maenner, Gledhill-Hoyt, & Lee, 1998; Windle, 2003). In many countries, drunkenness is such a common pastime among youths that it may be viewed by them as a normal part of the transition to adulthood (Coleman & Cater, 2005). According to a young woman in her early twenties in the U.K., "We are a culture that goes out and gets drunk, and we don't go out to drink, we go out to get drunk" (Engineer et al., 2003, p. 24; see also Case Study, "Drinking among Young People in the United Kingdom," below).

Although some young people recognize that society at large disapproves of drunkenness, such considerations are often dismissed. Participants under age 25 in a California survey (Leigh, 1984) were more likely than older drinkers to agree that it was "all right" to get drunk whenever one felt like it, that drunkenness was not irresponsible, and that getting drunk "was nothing to be ashamed of." Moreover, drunkenness is frequently seen by young people as a common adult behavior and is assumed to be an integral part of celebration (MacAskill et al., 2001). Thus, emerging adults may think that drunken behavior is tolerated by society, and view only the most extreme outcomes (for instance, a police record or addiction) with anything other than sympathy or amusement. As one young Australian woman put it, "It's not even seen by us

---

[4] Reprinted from *Drug and Alcohol Dependence*, Vol. 60, R. Room, "The more drinking, the more fun; but is there a calculus of fun, and should it drive policy?" pp. 249–250. Copyright 2000, with permission from Elsevier.

as anything major—I mean everyone drinks, some people get really pissed, others stay in control…there are plenty of worse things…we could be doing drugs and stuff" (Sheehan & Ridge, 2001, p. 357). This is not to suggest that attitudes toward intoxication are not mediated by gender (see chapter 2).

The acceptance of drunkenness among young people and its perceived acceptance by the rest of society stand in sharp contrast to the official disapproval of such behavior. As Room (2000) noted,

> Officially and publicly, in American culture and in others like it, intoxication is disapproved.… Genevieve Knupfer wrote of "covert norms of approval" for drunkenness, since it is so hard to get American respondents to acknowledge that they ever enjoy getting drunk. We used to joke about our survey research findings that it was as if all drunkenness in America happened only by accident, as a miscalculation. (p. 249)[5]

Socializing in Groups

When young people talk about leisure time, they mostly talk about a good night *out*—not a good night *in*. In both developed and developing countries, young adults are more likely to consume alcohol outside the home than older people, and this is even truer for heavier drinkers (Single et al., 1997). In the United States, 42% of current drinkers aged between 21 and 25 years reported that they drank in a bar or a nightclub the last time they had five or more drinks in a row, compared to less than 30% of drinkers in their 30s and 20% of drinkers in their 40s or 50s (Centers for Disease Control and Prevention, 2004). Surveys in the U.K. show that younger respondents are less likely to drink at home and more likely to drink in pubs, bars, and nightclubs than their older counterparts (Lader & Meltzer, 2002; Parker et al., 1998; Richardson & Budd, 2003). Younger people, as well as heavier drinkers, are also more likely to drink in groups and with friends rather than with a spouse or a partner.

Extreme drinking is linked to larger groups and *circuit drinking*—that is, alcohol consumption in a succession of venues, some public, some private, over the course of an evening (e.g., Richardson & Budd, 2003). Several aspects of group drinking in some cultures precipitate heavier consumption, including buying in rounds, which encourages participants to drink at the speed of the fastest drinker, and the norm of reciprocity, where participants stick around until it's their turn to buy (see Case Study, "Drinking among Young People in the United Kingdom," below).

The tendency to drink in groups in public places has several implications for drinking outcomes. If young people are consuming alcohol in public, their drunken behavior is more visible to others. Although the young drinkers themselves may see this kind of behavior as innocuous (see above), those

---

[5] Reprinted from *Drug And Alcohol Dependence*, Vol. 60, R. Room, "The more drinking, the more fun; but is there a calculus of fun, and should it drive policy?" pp. 249–250. Copyright 2000, with permission from Elsevier.

around them probably do not. Such behavior in private locations (for instance, in one's own home) is not likely to be as alarming to the public; thus, the tendency of young people to drink heavily in public places leads to visible behavior that is socially disapproved. Moreover, spending time in public places means increased exposure to other people. This is exactly the reason why young adults go to public drinking venues (to socialize and meet new people), but the presence of others can lead to problems of aggression, whether major or minor. For example, much drinking-related disorder in the U.K. happens at pub closing time when a surge of predominantly young patrons competes for taxis home and when groups from very different venues converge on the streets (Engineer et al., 2003).

Case Study: Drinking among Young People in the United Kingdom

Fiona Measham

Of all the countries discussed in this book, it is perhaps the United Kingdom which is most frequently associated with problematic alcohol consumption by young people, however that might be defined. British young people both at home and when on holiday overseas are characterized as heavy sessional or "binge" drinkers, with the attendant alcohol-related health, crime, and social problems linked to this pattern of consumption.

Both national and international studies confirm this impression that British youth and young adults drink large amounts of alcohol concentrated into a short space of time with adverse consequences (e.g., Foreign and Commonwealth Office, 2007; Marsh & Kibby 1992; Plant & Plant, 2006; Richardson & Budd, 2003; Tuck, 1989). While, in terms of overall consumption of pure alcohol per person, the U.K. is about average in international "league tables" at just over 11 liters per capita per annum (Department of Health, Home Office, Department for Education and Skills, & Department for Culture, Media and Sport, 2007, p. 14), if we look specifically at young people's sessional consumption, it is clear that youthful extreme drinking of the sort discussed in this book is more frequent in the U.K. than in most other countries (e.g., Hibell et al., 2004). Drinking follows a northern European pattern, which emphasizes weekend beer and spirit consumption in pubs with friends, rather than the southern European style of wine drinking with the family at mealtimes within the home (see chapter 5). Young people start to drink in their early teens, most usually at home and then with friends at private parties in friends' houses and in public places, progressing to bars, pubs, and nightclubs by their late teens (e.g., Fuller, 2007). By young adulthood, approximately a quarter of British young people report drinking above the recommended sensible drinking levels: 27% of 16- to 24-year-old men reported drinking more than 21 units a week in 2005, and 24% of young women drank more than 14 units a week, particularly on a Friday and Saturday night in licensed premises (Goddard, 2006).

As much a cause for public and political concern as "binge" drinking has been the broader question of British drinking culture and the extent to which British young people have an increasingly favorable attitude to drunkenness. There has been an apparent growing acceptance of public drunkenness by both young women and young men, with evidence that the state of intoxication is seen as a positive effect to be purposefully pursued (Engineer et al., 2003; Hayward & Hobbs, 2007; Measham & Brain, 2005; see also chapter 2). Such concerns about public drunkenness have resulted in a new National Alcohol Strategy, which aims to "challenge the attitudes and practices that underlie cultural attitudes towards alcohol" in the U.K., specifically "a willingness to tolerate drunkenness and antisocial behaviour as a 'normal' part of life" (Department of Health, Home Office, Department for Education and Skills, & Department for Culture, Media and Sport, 2007, pp. 57–58).

It is important to recognize, however, that alcohol consumption by young people appeared to have peaked at the turn of the century and is now leveling off or even decreasing in the U.K. and other countries in northern Europe with some of the highest levels of "binge" drinking in the world, whereas other developed countries may be "catching up" (e.g., Hibell et al., 2004). Furthermore, it should not be presumed that extreme drinking is a general characteristic of all young British drinkers. Indeed, a growing polarization is evident between extreme drinkers and abstainers, with increasing numbers of young people delaying the onset of teenage drinking and classifying themselves as abstainers in self-report surveys (Fuller, 2007). The reasons for this apparent downturn in young people's drinking in the last two or three years, the increase in abstainers, and the sustainability of these emergent trends are not yet clear (see Measham, in press).

The government and the alcohol industry have responded to concerns about public drinking and drunkenness by young people with stricter controls on the purchase and consumption of alcohol in licensed and off-license premises, as well as the growing regulation of street drinking in public places. Alongside the relaxation of trading hours through the Licensing Act 2003 (Plant & Plant, 2005), both the Licensing Act and Violent Crime Reduction Act 2006 include new enforcement powers to combat alcohol-related crime and disorder. Initiatives have been developed to toughen the restrictions on underage sales of alcohol, currently illegal to young people under the age of 18 in the U.K., as well as the development of proof of age schemes, strengthened restrictions on street drinking, and increased restrictions on parentally supervised drinking.

One possible concern surrounding this more vigilant enforcement of 18+ alcohol purchase laws and the greater regulation and criminalization of drinking by young people under 18 in the U.K. is the potential displacement effect. With a hostile climate for many months of the year and few alternative indoor leisure venues for under-18-year-olds, the appeal of licensed bars, pubs, and nightclubs is self-evident, particularly with the rapid expansion of the night-time economy (NTE) in British towns and cities, leading to a leisure/pleasure landscape designed and marketed to appeal primarily to the under-25s (Chatterton & Hollands, 2003; Hobbs, Hadfield, Lister, & Winlow, 2003). From the mid-1990s, "the NTE was regarded as the driver of this civic revival, streets being brought to life by large numbers of visitors, or—more accurately—consumers" (Hadfield, 2006, p. 45). The policing of underage drinking in both licensed leisure venues and open spaces reduces the opportunities for British teenagers to drink alcohol, however it might have been obtained. Research suggests that a significant minority of teenagers under 18—excluded from the nocturnal delights of the emergent "24-hour cities"—increasingly engage in risky alcohol-related behaviors such as drinking alcohol in isolated, potentially more dangerous parks, open spaces, and wasteland. While underage drinkers might successfully evade the prying eyes of the authorities, they are also less likely to be drinking alongside older and more experienced drinkers with a degree of formal security (however variable in practice) in licensed premises and are conversely more exposed to potentially harmful and violent situations in unsupervised open spaces at night (Coleman & Cater, 2005; Galloway, Forsyth, & Shewan, 2007).

Drink Promotions and Drinking Context

It is no secret that many public drinking venues have promotions that may lead to heavy alcohol consumption (for instance, "2-for-1 deals," happy hours, and speed-drinking bars). In MacAskill and colleagues' (2001) study of young Scottish drinkers, the participants reported that such promotions were widely known. Although the drinkers recognized that these promotions were being driven by profit, they saw them as mutually beneficial to sellers and buyers of alcohol and agreed that these deals would encourage drinking. Participants in the interviews were all aware of marketing campaigns and discussed them enthusiastically, expressing interest in new products.

In the case of the U.K., it has been suggested that commercial promotion targeted at young adults is an outgrowth of changes in drinking patterns in the last 30 years, along with the appearance of the acid house and rave scene. As alcohol consumption in Britain switched from the pub to the home in the 1970s and 1980s, beer and spirits sales fell. The subsequent arrival of the rave scene and development of the dance club culture encouraged younger drinkers to think of alcohol as just one in an array of substances to use for intoxication. From the mid-1990s onward, drinks promotions built on this trend in youth culture to choose from a psychoactive repertoire through catchy design and naming of products (Coffield & Gofton, 1994; Collin & Godfrey, 1997; Gofton, 1990; McKeganey, Forsyth, Barnard, & Hay, 1996; Measham, 1996; Measham & Brain, 2005; Measham, Aldridge, & Parker, 2001; Parker et al., 1998; see also chapter 2).

POLICY ISSUES

The focus on public disorder as an outcome of extreme drinking poses a question: If young people were getting drunk in private, would it be "okay"? Given that most young people "mature out" of problematic consumption patterns before experiencing serious consequences and that many young drinkers never experience such consequences, is the biggest problem with extreme drinking in this population the fact that they really annoy the rest of us? Note that there are other contexts in which public drunkenness is seen as acceptable for adults—fiestas, tailgate parties, and Midsummer, to name a few. Note also that fairly recently public intoxication was not seen as such a bad thing. In a 1997 World Health Organization (WHO) study of public drinking in 12 countries,[6] public intoxication, although generally disapproved, was not viewed as a major social problem (Single et al., 1997).

The public discourse on extreme drinking often focuses on behavior and social controls rather than on health effects of excessive consumption. This is illustrated by the comments of one British judge: "What is the pleasure, night after night, in getting drunk, turning out on to the streets, fighting, vomiting,

---

[6] Australia, Canada, Chile, the Congo, Fiji, Finland, France, India, Israel, Japan, Poland, and Trinidad and Tobago.

being carted off to hospitals? It's highly disagreeable, highly anti-social, and we don't want to see it get any worse" (Muir & Wintour, 2005, para. 18). Statements like these suggest that it is the *disorder* that is bothersome. They also demonstrate that policy-makers may not understand that these kinds of consequences are simply not important to young people and that getting drunk on purpose is "fun" for them. As one U.K. commentator noted, "[Professor Dick Hobbs of Durham University] believes that binge drinkers have become the 'folk devils' of our day. They are noisy, prone to violence and antisocial behavior such as urinating and vomiting publicly, and nobody wants them at the end of their street" (Gunnell, 2005, para. 7).

As Brendan O'Neill (2005) wrote:

> [T]he handwringing in political and media circles about strange town centres where young people do weird things like *get drunk on purpose*—and the tortured debate about how we might change this behaviour—expresses the establishment's own sense of dislocation from the masses. They are bamboozled by us, seeing us as peculiar creatures who do peculiar things; we're even more foreign to them, it seems, than actual foreigners, who at least drink in sedate cafés rather than in rowdy Superpubs. Britain's apparent binge-drinking crisis is really the fevered imagining of an elite that feels it has little connection with certain sections of the public, especially the youth (the judges yesterday described young people's behaviour as "inexplicable").... That is why they obsess over the boozing issue in particular: we are even more foreign to them when we're drunk, when we consciously seek to go a bit wild and when potentially anything might happen. (para. 9)

For further discussion of both the continuities and change in British alcohol consumption with reference to the binge drinking debate, see Measham and Brain (2005).

Potential Interventions: As Proposed by Young Drinkers

MacAskill and colleagues' (2001) study of young Scottish drinkers included discussion of the participants' views on potential interventions to reduce risky alcohol consumption. The authors concluded that the main limitations on drinking were from external circumstances, like having children, jobs, and financial obligations (the bounded, controlled, or strategic drinking discussed earlier); in contrast, potential direct moderating influences, such as parents, schools, media, and law enforcement, had only a weak effect. Legal restrictions and interventions—such as proof of age and curfews—were seen by respondents as ineffective, and police intervention provoked frustration because of a perception that it was selective and inconsistent.

MacAskill et al. (2001) found that the participants' detailed knowledge of alcohol advertising stood in sharp contrast to their lack of knowledge of mass media health messages. There was considerable confusion about whether the "official" drinking recommendation was for moderate drinking or abstinence.

Although many were aware of the potential health benefits of moderate alcohol consumption, they did not realize that these benefits only accrue for people much older than themselves. Study participants did not actively seek out information on drinking; they felt confident about their own behavior patterns and their knowledge of their own limits. Importantly, they had little awareness of the recommended number of maximum drink units (except for when driving). Other surveys, however, show greater knowledge of units. For example, in the U.K., 61% of the adult population had heard of the government guidelines on recommended daily consumption in 2004, with this figure rising each year (Lader & Goddard, 2004).

Another U.K. study (Engineer et al., 2003) reported that, when young people were asked to suggest interventions to reduce problems, most of them focused on environmental interventions, including:

- extended drinking hours to enable patrons to leave the pubs in their own time, encourage a slower pace of drinking, and avoid triggers for violence in a closing-time crowd flow;
- a greater range of venues where young people can either drink or hang out "after hours";
- increased police presence outside drinking venues;
- use of plastic bottles and glasses to reduce risk of injury in fights;
- improved public transport after drinking-venues' closing time.

This group of drinkers felt that advertising messages were unlikely to affect their behavior. They liked to go out drinking and would continue doing so until something bad happened to them; until then, they would not worry about the risks involved (Engineer et al., 2003). This lack of enthusiasm for advertising was echoed in a *Guardian* (U.K.) article:

> At the moment, sources at the Department of Culture, Media and Sport are staying sagely unisex about their plans: "We have all seen people lying in gutters, stumbling around and falling over. We want to change public attitudes so they know it is not acceptable to go out and binge drink like that."
>
> It would be an astonishing triumph of advertising if someone cooked up a message so compelling that it "changed public attitudes" to that degree. Give or take the odd couple that likes a sober perambulation down a high street on a Saturday night, binge drinkers operate in a self-selecting environment. That's to say, if you find yourself surrounded by the revolting spectacle of people falling over, then the chances are that it's just gone closing time, and the very fact that you're not at home suggests you yourself are stumbling a little, or else there's something seriously wrong with your satellite navigation. (Williams, 2005, para. 5–6)

Young people's focus on environmental interventions might reflect a perception that environmental factors are easier to change than individual motivations—or might indicate that many emerging adults view the responsibility for the problems of extreme drinking as lying with external agencies rather than themselves (Engineer et al., 2003). Alternatively, it may simply reflect realism among the young drinkers who know that they like to get drunk and that they may well change when they are older.

CONCLUSIONS

Drinking is the most common leisure-time pursuit in young people in many countries. It is largely normative during the period of emerging adulthood and is integrated into certain developmental tasks. Many young people drink for fun and for personal pleasure and many enjoy getting drunk. Alcohol consumption in this age group can be strategic, balancing hedonistic motivation against external constraints. Although potential negative consequences of extreme drinking and drunkenness are readily acknowledged, they are largely accepted with little concern. Expectation of positive effects from alcohol consumption predominates, particularly among frequent extreme drinkers. Risk factors for young extreme drinkers include the view of drunkenness as an acceptable behavior, the tendency of young adults to drink in public and in groups, and the targeting of young public drinkers by irresponsible promotions that may encourage excessive alcohol consumption (for example, happy hour specials). Interventions that attempt to change cultural norms through advertising are often viewed by young people as unlikely to succeed, when compared with interventions targeting the drinking environment. The discussion of policies and interventions that may be implemented to target young extreme drinkers is continued in chapters 7 and 8, respectively.

REFERENCES

Abrahamson, M. (2004). Alcohol in courtship contexts: Focus-group interviews with young Swedish women and men. *Contemporary Drug Problems, 31*, 3–29.

Arnett, J. J. (2000). Emerging adulthood: A theory of development from the late teens through the twenties. *American Psychologist, 55*, 469–480.

Arnett, J. J. (2005). The developmental context of substance use in emerging adulthood. *Journal of Drug Issues, 35*, 235–254.

Baer, J. S., & Carney, M. M. (1993). Biases in the perceptions of the consequences of alcohol use among college students. *Journal of Studies on Alcohol, 54*, 54–60.

Baumrind, D. (1985). Familial antecedents of adolescent drug use: A developmental perspective. In C. L. Jones & R. J. Battjes (Eds.), *Etiology of drug abuse: Implications for prevention* (pp. 13–44). NIDA Monograph 56. Rockville, MD: National Institute on Drug Abuse.

Bonin, M. F., McCreary, D. R., & Sadava, S. W. (2000). Problem drinking behavior in two community-based samples of adults: Influence of gender, coping, loneliness, and depression. *Psychology of Addictive Behaviors, 14*, 141–161.

Borsari, B., Bergen-Cico, D., & Carey, K. B. (2003). Self-reported drinking-game participation of incoming college students. *Journal of American College Health, 51*, 149–154.

Borsari, B., & Carey, K. B. (2003). Descriptive and injunctive norms in college drinking: A meta-analytic integration. *Journal of Studies on Alcohol*, *64*, 331–341.

Brain, K., Parker, H., & Carnwath, T. (2000). Drinking with design: Young drinkers as psychoactive consumers. *Drugs: Education, prevention and policy*, *7*, 5–20.

Brown, B. B., Dolcini, M. M., & Leventhal, A. (1997). Transformations in peer relationships at adolescence: Implications for health-related behavior. In J. Schulenberg, J. L. Maggs, & K. Hurrelmann (Eds.), *Health risks and developmental transitions during adolescence* (pp. 161–189). New York: Cambridge University Press.

Cahalan, D., & Room, R. (1974). *Problem drinking among American men*. New Brunswick, NJ: Rutgers Center of Alcohol Studies.

Camatta, C. D., & Nagoshi, C. T. (1995). Stress, depression, irrational beliefs, and alcohol use and problems in a college student sample. *Alcoholism: Clinical and Experimental Research*, *19*, 142–146.

Carey, K. B., & Correia, C. J. (1997). Drinking motives predict alcohol-related problems in college students. *Journal of Studies on Alcohol*, *58*, 100–105.

Centers for Disease Control and Prevention (CDC). (2004). *Behavioral Risk Factor Surveillance System*. Retrieved December 14, 2006, from http://www.cdc.gov/brfss/.

Chatterton, P., & Hollands, R. (2002) Theorising urban playscapes: Producing, regulating and consuming youthful nightlife city spaces. *Urban Studies*, *39*, 95–116.

Clapp, J. D., & Shillington, A. M. (2001). Environmental predictors of heavy episodic drinking. *American Journal of Drug and Alcohol Abuse*, *27*, 301–313.

Clapp, J. D., Shillington, A. M., & Segars, L. B. (2000). Deconstructing contexts of binge drinking among college students. *American Journal of Drug and Alcohol Abuse*, *26*, 139–154.

Coffield, F., & Gofton, L. (1994). *Drugs and young people*. London: Institute for Public Policy Research.

Coleman, L., & Cater, S. (2005). *Underage "risky" drinking: Motivations and outcomes*. York, U.K.: Joseph Rowntree Foundation.

Collin, M., & Godfrey, J. (1997). *Altered state: The story of ecstasy culture and Acid House*. London: Serpent's Tail.

Cooper, M. L. (1994). Motivations for alcohol use among adolescents: Development and validation of a four-factor model. *Psychological Assessment*, *6*, 117–128.

Cooper, M. L., Frone, M. R., Russell, M., & Mudar, P. (1995). Drinking to regulate positive and negative emotions: A motivational model of alcohol use. *Journal of Personality and Social Psychology*, *69*, 990–1005.

Cowan, P. A. (1991). Individual and family life transitions: A proposal for a new definition. In P. A. Cowan & E. M. Hetherington (Eds.), *Family transitions* (pp. 3–30). Hillsdale, NJ: Erlbaum.

Critchlow, B. (1987). A utility analysis of drinking. *Addictive Behaviors*, *12*, 269–273.

Department of Health, Home Office, Department for Education and Skills, & Department for Culture, Media and Sport. (2007). *Safe. Sensible. Social. The next steps in the National Alcohol Strategy*. London: Department of Health & Home Office.

Dworkin, J. (2005). Risk taking as developmentally appropriate experimentation for college students. *Journal of Adolescent Research*, *20*, 219–241.

Engineer, R., Phillips, A., Thompson, J., & Nicholls, J. (2003). *Drunk and disorderly: A qualitative study of binge drinking among 18- to 24-year-olds*. London: Home Office Research, Development and Statistics Directorate.

Farber, P. D., Khavari, K. A., & Douglass, F. M. (1980). A factor analytic study of reasons for drinking: Empirical validation of positive and negative reinforcement dimensions. *Journal of Consulting & Clinical Psychology*, *48*, 780–781.

Foreign and Commonwealth Office (FCO). (2007, August). *British behaviour abroad report*. London: Author.

Fuller, E. (Ed.). (2007). S*moking, drinking and drug use among young people in England in 2006*. A survey carried out for The Information Centre for Health and Social Care by the National Centre for Social Research and the National Foundation for Education Research. London: National Centre for Social Research/The Information Centre.

Galloway, J., Forsyth, A., & Shewan, D. (2007). *Young people's street drinking behaviour: Investigating the influence of marketing and subculture*. Unpublished final report by Glasgow Centre for the Study of Violence, Glasgow Caledonian University.

Goddard, E. (2006). *General household survey 2005: Smoking and drinking among adults, 2005*. London: Office for National Statistics.

Gofton, L. (1990). On the town: Drink and the new lawlessness. *Youth and Policy, 29*, 33–39.

Gunnell, B. (2005, August 29). What we don't know about drinking. *New Statesman*. Retrieved March 1, 2007, from http://www.newstatesman.com/200508290014.

Gustafson, R. (1988). Self-reported expected effects of a moderate dose of alcohol by college women. *Alcohol and Alcoholism, 23*, 409–414.

Gustafson, R. (1989). Self-reported expected emotional changes as a function of alcohol intoxication by alcoholic men and women. *Psychological Reports, 65*, 67–74.

Gustafson, R. (1991). Is the strength and the desirability of alcohol-related expectancies positively related? A test with an adult Swedish sample. *Drug and Alcohol Dependence, 28*, 145–150.

Gustafson, R. (1993). Alcohol-related expected effects and the desirability of these effects for Swedish college students measured with the Alcohol Expectancy Questionnaire (AEQ). *Alcohol and Alcoholism, 28*, 469–475.

Hadfield, P. M. (2006). *Bar wars: Contesting the night in contemporary British cities*. Oxford, U.K.: Oxford University Press.

Hayward, K., & Hobbs, D. (2007). Beyond the binge in "Booze Britain": Market-led liminalization and the spectacle of binge drinking. *British Journal of Sociology, 58*, 437–456.

Hibell, B., Andersson, B., Ahlström, S., Balakireva, O., Bjarnason, T., Kokkevi, A., et al. (1999). *The 1999 ESPAD report: Alcohol and other drug use among students in 30 European countries*. Stockholm: Swedish Council for Information on Alcohol and Other Drugs (CAN) and the Pompidou Group at the Council of Europe.

Hibell, B., Andersson, B., Bjarnason, T., Ahlström, S., Balakireva, O., Kokkevi, A., et al. (2004). *The ESPAD Report 2003: Alcohol and other drug use among students in 35 European countries*. Stockholm: Swedish Council for Information on Alcohol and Other Drugs (CAN)/Pompidou Group at the Council of Europe.

Hobbs, D., Hadfield, P., Lister, S., & Winlow, S. (2003) *Bouncers: Violence and governance in the night-time economy*. Oxford, U.K.: Oxford University Press.

Hussong, A. M., & Chassin, L. (1994). The stress-negative affect model of adolescent alcohol use: Disaggregating negative affect. *Journal of Studies on Alcohol, 55*, 707–718.

Institute of Alcohol Studies (IAS). (2005). *Binge drinking: Nature, prevalence and causes*. St. Ives, U.K.: Author.

Jessor, R., & Jessor, S. L. (1977). *Problem behavior and psychosocial development: A longitudinal study of youth*. New York: Academic Press.

Johnston, L. D., O'Malley, P., Bachman, J., & Schulenberg, J. (2004). *Monitoring the Future national survey results on drug use, 1975–2003. Vol.1: Secondary school students*. Bethesda, MD: National Institute on Drug Abuse.

Kassel, J. D., Jackson, S. I., & Unrod, M. (2000). Generalized expectancies for negative mood regulation and problem drinking among college students. *Journal of Studies on Alcohol, 61,* 332–340.

Kuntsche, E., Rehm, J., & Gmel, G. (2004). Characteristics of binge drinkers in Europe. *Social Science and Medicine, 59,* 113–127.

Kushner, M. G., & Sher, K. J. (1993). Comorbidity of alcohol and anxiety disorders among college students: Effects of gender and family history of alcoholism. *Addictive Behaviors, 18,* 543–552.

Kushner, M. G., Sher, K. J., Wood, M. D., & Wood, P. K. (1994). Anxiety and drinking behavior: Moderating effects of tension-reduction alcohol outcome expectancies. *Alcoholism: Clinical & Experimental Research, 18,* 852–860.

Lader, D., & Goddard, E. (2004). *Drinking: Adults' behaviour and knowledge in 2004.* London: Office for National Statistics.

Lader, D., & Meltzer, H. (2002). *Drinking: Adults' behaviour and knowledge in 2002.* London: Office for National Statistics.

Lecci, L., MacLean, M. G., & Croteau, N. (2002). Personal goals as predictors of college student drinking motives, alcohol use and related problems. *Journal of Studies on Alcohol, 63,* 620–630.

Leigh, B. C. (1984). Unpublished data, 1984 Drinking Attitudes Study, conducted by the Alcohol Research Group, Berkeley, CA, USA.

Leigh, B. C. (1987). Beliefs about the effects of alcohol on self and others. *Journal of Studies on Alcohol, 48,* 467–475.

Leigh, B. C. (1989). Attitudes and expectancies as predictors of drinking habits: A comparison of three scales. *Journal of Studies on Alcohol, 50,* 432–440.

Leigh, B. C. (1990). Unpublished data, 1990 National Alcohol Survey, conducted by the Alcohol Research Group, Berkeley, CA, USA.

Leigh, B. C., & Stacy, A. W. (1994). Self-generated alcohol expectancies in four samples of drinkers. *Addiction Research, 1,* 335–348.

MacAskill, S., Cooke, E., Eadie, D., & Hastings, G. (2001). *Perceptions of factors that promote and protect against the misuse of alcohol amongst young people and young adults.* Glasgow, U.K.: Centre for Social Marketing, University of Strathclyde.

Maggs, J. L. (1993). *Adolescent alcohol use as a goal-directed behaviour.* (Doctoral dissertation, University of Victoria, Victoria, British Columbia, Canada).

Maggs, J. L. (1997). Alcohol use and binge drinking as goal-directed action during the transition to postsecondary education. In J. Schulenberg, J. L. Maggs, & K. Hurrelmann (Eds.), *Health risks and developmental transitions during adolescence* (pp. 345–371). New York: Cambridge University Press.

Mäkelä, K., & Mustonen, H. (1988). Positive and negative experiences related to drinking as a function of annual alcohol intake. *British Journal of Addiction, 83,* 403–408.

Mäkelä, K., & Mustonen, H. (1996). The reward structure of drinking among younger and older male drinkers. *Contemporary Drug Problems, 23,* 479–492.

Mäkelä, K., & Mustonen, H. (2000). Relationships of drinking behaviour, gender and age with reported negative and positive experiences related to drinking. *Addiction, 95,* 727–736.

Mäkelä, K., & Simpura, J. (1985). Experiences related to drinking as a function of annual alcohol intake and by sex and age. *Drug and Alcohol Dependence, 15,* 389–404.

Marlatt, G. A. (1987). Alcohol, the magic elixir: Stress, expectancy, and the transformation of emotional states. In E. Gottheil, K. A. Druley, S. Pashko, & S. P. Weinstein (Eds.), *Stress and addiction* (pp. 302–322). New York: Brunner/Mazel.

Marsh, P., & Kibby, K. F. (1992). *Drinking and public disorder: A report of research conducted for The Portman Group by MCM Research.* London: The Portman Group.

McCarty, D., Morrison, S., & Mills, K. C. (1983). Attitudes, beliefs and alcohol use: An analysis of relationships. *Journal of Studies on Alcohol, 44*, 328–341.

McKeganey, N., Forsyth, A., Barnard, M., & Hay, G. (1996). Designer drinks and drunkenness amongst a sample of Scottish schoolchildren. *British Medical Journal, 313*, 401.

McMahon, J., Jones, B. T., & O'Donnell, P. (1994). Comparing positive and negative alcohol expectancies in male and female social drinkers. *Addiction Research, 1*, 349–365.

Measham, F. (1996). The "Big Bang" approach to sessional drinking: Changing patterns of alcohol consumption amongst young people in North West England. *Addiction Research, 4*, 283–299.

Measham, F. (in press). The turning tides of intoxication: Young people's drinking in the 2000s. *Health Education*.

Measham, F., Aldridge, J., & Parker, H. (2001). *Dancing on drugs: Risk, health and hedonism in the British club scene*. London: Free Association Books.

Measham, F., & Brain, K. (2005). "Binge" drinking, British alcohol policy and the new culture of intoxication. *Crime, Media, Culture: An International Journal, 1*, 263–284.

Miller, P., Plant, M., & Plant, M. (2005). Spreading out or concentrating weekly consumption: Alcohol problems and other consequences within a U.K. population sample. *Alcohol and Alcoholism, 40*, 461–468.

Muir, H., & Wintour, P. (2005, August 11). Blunkett offers concessions on drinking hours. *The Guardian*. Retrieved March 1, 2007, from http://politics.guardian.co.uk/homeaffairs/story/0,11026,1546777,00.html.

Mustonen, H., & Mäkelä, K. (1999). Relationships between characteristics of drinking occasions and negative and positive experiences related to drinking. *Drug and Alcohol Dependence, 56*, 79–84.

Nezlek, J. B., Pilkington, C. J., & Bilbro, K. G. (1994). Moderation in excess: Binge drinking and social interaction among college students. *Journal of Studies on Alcohol, 55*, 342–351.

Nurmi, J. E. (1993). Adolescent development in an age-graded context: The role of personal beliefs, goals, and strategies in the tackling of developmental tasks and standards. *International Journal of Behavioral Development, 16*, 169–190.

Nyström, M. (1992). Positive and negative consequences of alcohol drinking among young university students in Finland. *British Journal of Addiction, 87*, 715–722.

O'Neill, B. (2005, August 1). A licence to bash the masses. *Spiked Online*. Retrieved March 1, 2007, from http://www.spiked-online.com/Articles/0000000CACEB.htm.

Park, C. L. (2004). Positive and negative consequences of alcohol consumption in college students. *Addictive Behaviors, 29*, 311–321.

Park, C. L., & Levenson, M. R. (2002). Drinking to cope among college students: Prevalence, problems, and coping processes. *Journal of Studies on Alcohol, 63*, 486–497.

Parker, H., Aldridge, J., & Measham, F. (1998). *Illegal leisure: The normalization of adolescent recreational drug use*. London: Routledge.

Parker, H., & Measham, F. (1994). Pick 'n' mix: Changing patterns of illicit drug use amongst 1990s adolescents. *Drugs: Education, Prevention & Policy, 1*, 5–13.

Paul, E. L., & Hayes, K. A. (2002). The casualties of "casual" sex: A qualitative exploration of the phenomenology of college students' hookups. *Journal of Social and Personal Relationships, 19*, 639–661.

Perkins, H. W. (2002). Surveying the damage: A review of research on consequences of alcohol misuse in college populations. *Journal of Studies on Alcohol Supplement, 14*, 91–100.

Perkins, H. W., & Berkowitz, A. D. (1986). Perceiving the community norms of alcohol use among students: Some research implications for campus alcohol education programming. *International Journal of the Addictions*, *21*, 961–976.

Pernanen, K. (1991). *Alcohol in human violence*. New York: Guilford.

Plant, E., & Plant, M. (2005). A "leap in the dark?" Lessons for the United Kingdom from past extensions of bar opening hours. *International Journal of Drug Policy*, *16*, 363–368.

Plant, M., & Plant, M. (2006). *Binge Britain: Alcohol and the national response*. Oxford, U.K.: Oxford University Press.

Rabow, J., & Duncan-Schill, M. (1995). Drinking among college students. *Journal of Alcohol and Drug Education*, *40*, 52–64.

Richardson, A., & Budd, T. (2003). *Alcohol, crime and disorder: A study of young adults*. London: Home Office Research, Development and Statistics Directorate.

Roizen, R. (1983). Loosening up: General population views of the effects of alcohol. In R. Room & G. Collins (Eds.), *Alcohol and disinhibition: Nature and meaning of the link* (pp. 236–257). NIAAA Research Monograph No. 12. Rockville, MD: National Institute on Alcohol Abuse and Alcoholism.

Room, R. (2000). The more drinking, the more fun; but is there a calculus of fun, and should it drive policy? *Drug and Alcohol Dependence*, *60*, 249–250.

Salmela-Aro, K., & Nurmi, J.-E. (1997). Goal contents, well-being and life context during transition to university: A longitudinal study. *International Journal of Behavioral Development*, *20*, 471–491.

Schulenberg, J. E., & Maggs, J. L. (2002). A developmental perspective on alcohol use and heavy drinking during adolescence and the transition to young adulthood. *Journal of Studies on Alcohol Supplement, 14*, 54–70.

Schulenberg, J. E., Maggs, J. L., & Hurrelmann, K. (1997). Negotiating developmental transitions during adolescence and young adulthood: Health risks and developmental transitions. In J. Schulenberg, J. L. Maggs, & K. Hurrelmann (Eds.), *Health risks and developmental transitions during adolescence* (pp. 1–19). New York: Cambridge University Press.

Schulenberg, J. E., Maggs, J. L., & O'Malley, P. M. (2003). How and why the understanding of developmental continuity and discontinuity is important: The sample case of long-term consequences of adolescent substance use. In J. Mortimer & M. Shanahan (Eds.), *Handbook of the life course* (pp. 413–436). New York: Kluwer Academic/ Plenum.

Sheehan, M., & Ridge, D. (2001). "You become really close…you talk about the silly things you did, and we laugh": The role of binge drinking in female secondary students' lives. *Substance Use and Misuse*, *36*, 347–372.

Silbereisen, R. K., Noack, P., & Reitzle, M. (1987). Developmental perspectives on problem behavior and prevention in adolescence. In K. Hurrelmann & F. Kaufmann (Eds.), *Social intervention: Potential and constraints. Prevention and intervention in childhood and adolescence* (pp. 205–218). Oxford, U.K.: Walter De Gruyter.

Single, E., Beaubrun, M., Mauffret, M., Minoletti, A., Moskalewicz, J., Moukolo, A., et al. (1997). Public drinking, problems and prevention measures in twelve countries: Results of the WHO project on public drinking. *Contemporary Drug Problems*, *24*, 425–448.

Stacy, A. W., & Widaman, K. F. (1987, August–September). *A "positivity" bias in attitude models of alcohol use*. Paper presented at the 95th Annual Convention of the American Psychological Association, New York.

Tuck, M. (1989). *Drinking and disorder: A study of non-metropolitan violence*. Home Office Research Study No. 108. London: Her Majesty's Stationery Office.

Wechsler, H., Dowdall, G. W., Maenner, G., Gledhill-Hoyt, J., & Lee, H. (1998). Changes in binge drinking and related problems among American college students between 1993 and 1997: Results of the Harvard School of Public Health College Alcohol Study. *Journal of American College Health*, *47*, 57–68.

Williams, Z. (2005, August 15). Sobering and sexist. *The Guardian*. Retrieved March 1, 2007, from   http://society.guardian.co.uk/drugsandalcohol/comment/0,8146,1549894,00. html.

Wills, T. A., Sandy, I. M., Shinar, O., & Yaeger, A. (1999). Contributions of positive and negative affect to adolescent substance use: Test of a bidimensional model in a longitudinal study. *Psychology of Addictive Behaviors*, *13*, 327–338.

Windle, M. (2003). Alcohol use among adolescents and young adults. *Alcohol Research and Health*, *27*, 79–85.

Wood, M. D., Nagoshi, C. T., & Dennis, D. A. (1992). Alcohol norms and expectations as predictors of alcohol use and problems in a college student sample. *American Journal of Drug and Alcohol Abuse*, *18*, 461–476.

Chapter 5

Focus Group Results
Brazil, China, Italy, Nigeria, Russia, South Africa, and Scotland, United Kingdom

The tendency among some young people to drink to intoxication has been a growing concern internationally. This pattern of alcohol consumption is associated with a wide range of negative health and social outcomes. Termed *extreme drinking*, the behavior is driven largely by thrill-seeking and risk-taking and goes beyond "binge" drinking, which is constrained by its quantitative definition. Extreme drinking requires a qualitative analysis, emphasizing the *process* and *outcomes* of getting drunk (see chapter 1).

The focus groups presented in this chapter aim to compare reports of intoxication among young people in the research literature with how young people themselves view getting drunk. Extensive research on the influence of alcohol expectancies on drinking behaviors was discussed in chapter 4. This work has helped to develop some approaches (such as social norms marketing) that have shown promise in changing drinking culture (see chapter 8). Deeper understanding of how behaviors related to intoxication are perceived by young people is likely to contribute further to the development of other promising initiatives aimed at this population.

This chapter's analysis of extreme drinking is based on information provided by young people themselves in describing their views on drinking and drunkenness. The information was gathered in a series of focus groups made up of youths and young adults of legal drinking age from seven countries: Brazil, China, Italy, Nigeria, Russia, South Africa, and Scotland. These countries were chosen in part for their diverse drinking patterns. For consistency, guiding questions developed by ICAP were used in all the countries (Annex 2), and focus group moderators were provided with standardized guidelines for procedures and participant selection (Annex 1). It should be noted that some leeway was given in how focus groups were conducted to allow for cultural considerations and idiosyncrasies within each group. For example, moderators in Nigeria chose to include a quantitative component in their definitions of an "extreme drinker"; and the discussions in China, although guided by the sample questions in Annex 2, primarily reflected local logic and priorities. Whereas focus group participants were offered compensation for attending the sessions in some instances, in others they were not. Finally, because of the small sample sizes in each of the focus groups, the opinions expressed do not represent the views of all youths in these countries. Nevertheless, they may be used to gain a general sense of young drinkers' attitudes, relaying some of the voices behind the statistics on alcohol consumption. Although the overall approach of focus groups was consistent, the differences noted above may account for some of the variations in views among the participants in different countries.

OVERVIEW OF FOCUS GROUP RESULTS

The results from the different countries show striking similarities in the way young people understand alcohol consumption, its role, and the factors that influence it. At the same time, each set of results reflects a particular drinking culture, which manifests itself in a range of disparate consumption patterns and views on the issue of extreme drinking. Each focus group was encouraged to discuss the following topics: (1) drinking in general; (2) extreme drinking; (3) contexts for extreme drinking; and (4) reasons for extreme drinking. All sessions were recorded by the moderators and later reviewed and collated to produce the seven country reports in this chapter.

General Views on Drinking

To frame the discussions, the participants were asked to share their opinions on drinking in general. All groups broadly agreed that alcohol consumption was primarily associated with enjoyment and socializing, normally taking place at communal gatherings (such as parties, festivals, family celebrations, and sporting events) and in public venues (for instance, bars, pubs, and, in China, restaurants), in the presence of friends, peers, or family. Across focus groups, a description of a "successful drinking experience" included going out with friends, socializing, drinking, and "having fun," but also avoiding problems and negative experiences that would detract from the pleasure.

A large part of the discussions centered on the satisfaction and enjoyment young people associated with drinking in general. According to a Chinese participant, "Drinking is a way to communicate, to establish and maintain relationships…. It's a bridge between people." In Brazil, a male participant described it as a positive contribution to his wellbeing, stating that "wellbeing is feeling self-confident." Another young man in this group said he "can also talk to all the women" when he drinks, exemplifying the perceived increased confidence associated with alcohol (this was a recurring theme in all groups, among both men and women). Meanwhile, in Russia, a participant enjoyed drinking because it helped him "get back to normal" after a long day at work. Likewise, the majority in the Scottish sample identified alcohol intake as an important part of feeling "happy/enjoying myself." From all these remarks, it can be deduced that expectations of increased self-confidence, enjoyment, and relaxation are three significant contributors to young people's drinking generally. At the same time, however, participants of all the focus groups also mentioned heavy alcohol use as a means of self-medication during high-stress situations and under negative circumstances.

What constitutes a "typical" drinking occasion varied widely among the respondents and was in all cases influenced by age, sex, relationship status, and living arrangements. For example, for most participants living with long-term partners, a typical drinking experience generally consisted of a drink or two at home with their spouse or partner. Young people still living with parents, on the other hand, were more likely to drink outside the home—in pubs, bars, and nightclubs—and to engage in extreme drinking. And those living on their own were more likely to drink at home, accompanied by friends. In general (and with the exception of large house parties), drinking at home was associated with moderate alcohol intake, whereas drinking at bars, pubs, or nightclubs was associated with higher consumption levels.

One of the key factors cited as influencing the drinking experience was financial solvency. In general, drinking was most likely to occur (and tended to be heavier) on paydays and when free or discounted alcohol was available. As summed up by a Nigerian respondent, "Drinking is fun; I will drink every day if I have the money." Although the notion of drinking regularly on weekends was typical in the Scottish sample, extreme drinking was more likely to occur when "other people are providing the alcohol," or on "Tuesdays, Thursdays, and paydays" when financial resources were available.

The focus group participants were also asked about their first drink and the initiation of regular consumption. In many cases, regardless of culture, young people had been introduced to alcohol by their parents, often at an early age and in the context of family celebrations and other social occasions. In fact, drinking with family was the predominant consumption pattern among Chinese youths. At the same time, regular and, in particular, extreme drinking in the presence of adults was mostly considered inappropriate. Thus, overwhelmingly, friends and peers played an important role in young people's drinking patterns beyond the alcohol debut. Other cultural influences, such as social stigma surrounding women's drinking in some countries, appeared to affect the age of the first drink and any subsequent consumption patterns.

Excessive Drinking and Drunkenness

For many respondents, regardless of the country they were from, extreme drinking was part of the "typical" drinking situation with peers. However, there were clear differences in extreme drinking as *purposeful* behavior: While getting drunk was an unintended outcome of a night out for some, it was the main goal for others. "I do not go out to get drunk, but neither do I go out *not* to drink," one of the male participants from Brazil said during his session. "The party environment encourages drinking a lot more than you planned for," said a female respondent from the Nigerian group. Nonetheless, the Nigerian, Russian, Scottish, and South African groups all had respondents who felt that people at times consumed alcohol with the expressed intention of becoming intoxicated.

Interesting contrasts were provided by the Italian, Brazilian, and Chinese samples. In Italy, drunkenness was perceived to be an undesirable outcome of a drinking occasion; and in both Italy and Brazil, the main reason for going out and drinking was to meet friends, which was not merely an *excuse* for drinking. Meanwhile, in China, complex rules governed when it was appropriate for a young person to exhibit intoxication (normally a shameful behavior), including within a business setting.

Because of the variation in the responses on main motivations for getting drunk, it was important to assess the type of occasions that typically led to extreme drinking. In Brazil, the *balada* (a slang term used to denote any kind of party; for instance, a rave, a bar outing, or any other collective amusement) seemed to be a common occasion for extreme drinking, the presence of alcohol being seen as a prerequisite for a successful event. Excessive alcohol consumption was most commonly a goal of drinking among the participants in the Scottish focus group. In all groups, extreme drinking behavior typically occurred in the presence of peers and friends: Many respondents noted that heavy drinking often took place when "catching up with friends."

Young people's drinking was generally inhibited when they were with their family. In all groups, lower levels of alcohol were typically consumed when family members were present. The participants also cited several responsibilities as deterrents to extreme alcohol intake. Specifically, being a designated driver or having an early commitment the next day were two of the reasons for drinking "a little." The participants also listed wanting to stay "in control," feeling ill, and running out of money as reasons for limiting their consumption.

The need to remain in control was an important element evoked by several focus groups. In large part, retaining control and, conversely, extreme drinking are about "alcohol maturity." The ability to control one's level of consumption and the outcomes of drinking are determined by age and experience, and, in turn, define what it means to "get drunk." Similarly, the type of alcohol consumed and the location where drinking takes place helped determine the ultimate level and pattern of drinking. For example, consuming cheap alcohol beverages while playing drinking games, as one Brazilian participant described, normally led to excessive alcohol intake. These views illustrate some other issues that determine drinking patterns and behavior.

The majority of the participants believed they were responsible consumers of alcohol, even if they participated in extreme drinking. So, when the focus groups were asked *why* do young people drink to get drunk, the responses often included some mention of age, inexperience, and the desire to experiment—along with expectancies of enjoyment and entertainment. Some participants also mentioned drinking to excess as a way to deal with insecurities and problems. Such problems included loneliness, having a bad day, relationship difficulties, and employment issues. The use of alcohol in these situations coincided with participants' comments about alcohol's role in increasing one's self-confidence.

Some respondents believed that alcohol consumption was common among people who used illicit drugs. A number of young people mentioned having used a drug, such as cannabis, during a night of heavy drinking. On the other hand, others believed that tobacco use, and not the use of illegal drugs, was more common among youths who get drunk. Culture likely also plays an important role in this regard. For example, in the Italian sample, in a country, where alcohol consumption is an integral part of everyday life and "no special occasion is needed for drinking," none of the respondents saw a relationship between alcohol and illicit drugs. Nevertheless, there was a general consensus in the groups that heavy alcohol consumption contributed to people breaking the law. These crimes included alcohol-impaired driving, vandalism, and assault.

Finally, although looking for self-confidence, enjoyment, sociability, and relaxation were the primary reasons for drinking, the participants also were aware that a range of "bad things" may occur when one drinks to intoxication. The focus groups mentioned unplanned sex, violent behavior, traffic crashes, trouble with the police, hangovers, embarrassing situations, losing possessions, alcohol poisoning, and other reckless conduct (for instance, going "swimming with crocodiles" in South Africa) as some of the negative outcomes of extreme drinking. Focus groups cited serious health conditions, pregnancy, and experiencing a severe trauma (particularly, sexual assault among women) as potential reasons to reconsider their current drinking patterns. They mentioned learning from their mistakes; however, it appears that the events actually leading to changed drinking behaviors were often tragic. Respondents brought up numerous morning-after speeches, where they would vow during a hangover never to drink alcohol again. Unfortunately, the participants generally agreed that this "never-again" vow was quickly forgotten the next time they were in a heavy drinking environment.

The full results of the focus groups are presented in the subsequent sections. It was decided not to standardize the presentation of the studies (for instance, not all country studies attributed their participants' quotes by gender and age), but to allow them to retain their unique flavor and character. Although none of the groups represent the experiences of all young people in a given country, we hope they will provide an interesting cultural snapshot of young people's experience with alcohol.

BRAZIL

Mônica Gorgulho and Vera Da Ros

Brazil is the fifth largest country in the world, with an estimated population of over 189 million inhabitants, 81% of whom live in cities and towns (for more information on Brazil, see the Web site of the Brazilian Institute of Geography and Statistics: http://www.ibge.gov.br). The official language is Portuguese.

In 2004, the Brazilian Information Center on Psychotropic Drugs (Centro Brasileiro de Informações sobre Drogas Psicotrópicas—CEBRID) conducted the latest in its series of comprehensive surveys on alcohol and drug use among the country's youth aged between 10 and 20 years (Galduróz, Noto, Fonseca, & Carlini, 2004; regarding results of the 1987, 1989, 1993, and 1997 CEBRID surveys of this population, see Galduróz & Caetano, 2004). According to the 2004 data, beer was the most popular beverage among this group, reportedly consumed by 70% of the participating students, followed by wine (27%) and distilled beverages (nearly 3%).

A comprehensive household study in 107 Brazilian cities revealed that the prevalence of lifetime alcohol use was 68.7%; among the respondents aged between 12 and 17 years—that is, young people under Brazil's official drinking age of 18 years—48.3% had already tried beverage alcohol (Carlini, Galduróz, Noto, & Nappo, 2002). Moreover, 5.2% of adolescents aged 12 to 17 years were alcohol-dependent (Carlini et al., 2002; see also Galduróz & Caetano, 2004). In a study of alcohol consumption among students in two medical schools in the state of São Paulo, 11.8% of male and 1.3% of female students exhibited "harmful alcohol use"; 4.2% of males and 0.8% of females were alcohol-dependent (Borini, Oliveira, Martins, & Guimarães, 1994).[1] Despite these relatively high levels of problem drinking, alcohol is not perceived as a problematic substance by Brazil's general population.

The Focus Group

Our focus group comprised 10 members. Fifteen young people initially confirmed their participation, but three failed to show up for the group discussion and two arrived too late. In the final group, the average age of participants was 21.1 years, with four women and six men. According to their own or family/household income, they belonged to B (upper-middle) and C (middle)

---

[1] Borini and colleagues defined "harmful use" and "alcohol dependence" in the study according to the International Classification of Diseases, 10th Revision (ICD-10; see World Health Organization [WHO], 1992).

TABLE 5.1 Brazil Focus Group: Participants' Demographic Profile

Participant	Occupation	Economic class	Lineage
Female, 18	Student (Std.)	C	African
Male, 20	Student	B	Caucasian
Female 1, 21	Student	B	Caucasian
Female 2, 21	Std./part-time job	B	Hispanic
Male 1, 21	Student	B	Hispanic
Male 2, 21	Std./part-time job	B	Caucasian
Female, 22	Std./part-time job	B	Caucasian
Male 1, 22	Student	C	African
Male 2, 22	Std./part-time job	B	Caucasian
Male, 23	Student	B	Hispanic

economic classes, based on a scale that varies from A (upper class) to E (very poor) (Instituto Brasileiro de Opinião Pública e Estatística [IBOPE], 2000).[2] All group participants were students; four were also employed part-time. Table 5.1 provides the demographic profile of the group.

After a brief introduction, the purpose of the focus group was explained (see Annexes 1 and 2), and the respondents were assured that all answers would remain confidential. It was stressed that the minimum drinking age in Brazil is set at 18 years and that organizing this group did not denote approval of extreme or underage drinking. At the same time, it was noted that the prevalence of such behaviors has been growing globally, leading to the creation of the present study.

Results

Drinking in General

Few participants recognized that drinking may be a way of relieving tension or coping with problems. Instead, it was primarily perceived as an attribute of leisure, relaxation, lack of obligations, and a reason to meet friends. According to the respondents, drinking was such a natural behavior in their peer group that those who did not drink were seen as outsiders:

> [The person] who doesn't drink feels uncomfortable... feels shy among drinkers. (Female, 18)

---

[2] IBOPE (Brazilian Institute of Public Opinion and Statistics; www.ibope.com.br) divides the country's population into five broad categories: class A (A1 = average annual household income of 7,793 Brazilian real [BRL]; A2 = 4,648 BRL); class B (B1 = 2,804 BRL; B2 = 1,669 BRL); class C (927 BRL); class D (424 BRL), and class E (207 BRL) (see IBOPE, 2000). In July 2007, 1 BRL = 0.543154 U.S. dollars. For most recent exchange rates, see Banco Central do Brasil: http://www.bcb.gov.br.

The majority in this focus group did not see drinking alone as a typical or enjoyable drinking occasion:

It [drinking alone] is possible but ungraceful. (Female 1, 21)

Alcohol consumption was perceived as a collective experience, with the main goal of:

Reaching "level one," feeling a bit happy. (Male 2, 21)

However, the ultimate goal the respondents pursued as they consumed alcohol was not expressly to reach intoxication:

Nobody drinks alcohol just to get drunk! (Female, 22)

Many participants reported that they enjoyed the taste of alcohol—"even of warm beer," which may be willingly consumed under some circumstances (in the winter, for example). It was said that, after a certain point of intoxication, or when the "optimal level"—the so-called "level one"—starts to wear off,

...you can drink anything at 5 in the morning! (All respondents speak at once, followed by laughter)

The theme of consuming warm beer was evoked again in the debate about controlling alcohol intake during typical social gatherings, such as weekend barbecues. On these occasions, a "guardian of the drinks," a person responsible for keeping the beer at the best temperature for drinking, naturally arises. In this context, the battles between "let's drink it right now" and "let's wait until [the beer] is cooler" are inevitable:

There is always the "guardian of the drinks" who may want to drink it all immediately or wait a bit more...I've been on both sides. (Male 2, 21)

However, what ultimately defined a typical experience of drinking for group participants was the positive group feeling:

The temperature of the beer doesn't matter that much [in the end]. Drinking becomes an act of companionship: We are drinking together—let's do it! (Male 2, 21)

Whereas drinking warm beer could be considered a positive experience under special circumstances, mixing many types of spirits was not deemed acceptable—at least in theory. Many participants agreed that, "once the beer runs out, the party is over!"

Influences on Drinking

According to this focus group, the presence of friends, free drinks, a decline in the level of intoxication ("level one"), and—in particular—a limited budget influence alcohol consumption. All respondents agreed: "While there is money, there is drinking." Alcohol beverages were considered expensive, and using credit cards was described as a known nightmare, generally to be avoided:

> You don't want to wake up the next day, realizing there is now a hole in the bank account; [you] drank some beer and…bye-bye money…. We want to live! (Female, 22)

Planning and setting limits on one's own consumption were closely linked to the money young people had to spend and not to the effects and the volume of alcohol already consumed or to be consumed. However, on the prospect of free drinks the group responded:

> Sometimes, it's more expensive to go to [an open bar] party because of the costs that losing the wallet, getting hurt, or crashing the car…can mean. (Contribution of the entire group)

Presence of family seemed to inhibit young people's alcohol consumption. Although some respondents saw their parents, grandparents, and uncles as frequent or even heavy drinkers, all said that they themselves would avoid any extreme behaviors at family gatherings:

> People [at family events] get drunk without feeling shy, but no one wants to see the granddaughter drunk. (Female, 22)

Relatives, especially parents, seemed to know about their children's drinking habits. However, they did not appear to have an exact idea about how much young people drink. The majority of respondents said that mothers in particular were likely to worry about their offspring's behaviors, including drinking too much; but the expression of this worry did not lead young people to consider a behavior change:

> My mother stays up, waiting for me to come home from the parties. When she realizes that I am drunk, she threatens me, like, to forbid me to take the car again. (Male, 20)

> My mother even offers to pay for my taxi home and shouts at me if I insist on doing things my own way. I still do. (Male 1, 21)

> I know my mother gets disappointed, even when she doesn't know exactly what happened. (Male, 20)

When asked about their "first experience with alcohol," the respondents recounted their first experiences of getting drunk. The simple question about "the first experience" caused a commotion in the group:

> I got completely wasted…. It was the first time in my life. (Male, 23)

> It started badly! (Said by several people, eliciting laughs from the group)

I got … baaaaaah! I almost got into a coma! (All participants speak at once in a very chaotic way and with much bravado, especially among the men)

The moderators clarified that the question was about the first experience of *trying* alcohol and not the first time drinking too much. That revealed that the initial experiences with alcohol among the participants occurred at a young age and always at home, often with the parents' permission.

The family thinks it's cute. (Female, 18)

I've lived in an environment of barbecues and lots of drinking. I used to compare beer with *guaraná* [Brazilian soft drink] from when I was very young.… I used to take a sip of beer without planning to get drunk. Tried [beer] and went back to *guaraná*. (Male, 23)

In general, nobody enjoys the first beer.…. It is like cigarettes! The first ones are not good. Then, you learn how to appreciate it. (Male 2, 21)

It was the old story of trying the foam of [a parent's] beer. (Male 2, 22)

According to the sample, however, this situation is changing, as adults become more informed about the risks of problem drinking in young people and act less permissively with our group's younger siblings.

All participants reported having their first *intentional* experience with alcohol around the age of 10:

For my 4th grade graduation, the teachers got completely drunk on champagne. Then, four of my classmates and I stole a bottle and drank it in the corner, while the party was still going on. (Male 2, 21)

The first time was at my grandfather's place. He liked to offer me a martini, and I tried but hated it… (Female, 2, 21)

For my first time, I drank wine with my father. (Male, 2, 22)

When I was younger, I didn't like beer, but, when I was around 10, I tried vodka with coke. (Female, 1, 21)

I was around 10, and it was Christmas. There was lots of champagne to toast. I saw everybody drinking and tried some beer. But I didn't like the taste. (Female, 18)

Frequently present at family celebrations, beverage alcohol was clearly linked by the respondents to moments of socializing. Several young people reported drinking alone and when they felt sad or unwell, but this was usually a single experience that they have not since repeated:

It is not frequent, but possible. I drank alcohol when I was sad once, but that just made the situation worse. (Female, 18)

Drinking alcohol alone looks like you are unaware [of what you are doing]....
(Male 2, 21)

Once, at a [soccer] match, I drank alone...but I was among many people on the stands, and it was all right. (Male, 23)

Yes, I drank alone, but because I had to wait for someone...sometimes, when I travel alone (I do that a lot!), I also can drink by myself. (Female, 22)

"Typical" Drinking Occasions and a "Successful Night Out"

It was impossible to obtain a single definition for a typical drinking experience. The participants' descriptions varied from drinking one drink to reaching the "level one." However, all respondents agreed that drinking was "a collective behavior":

There is the issue of staying safe...if you are alone in a bar, start drinking, and get drunk. If you are with a friend, with some friends, then you know that, if you fall down, there is always somebody to help you. (Male, 20)

In general, a successful evening was described as drinking to "level one" without exceeding one's limits. Not losing control, not having a headache, and not experiencing memory loss on the morning after were also mentioned as markers of a positive night out. The presence of friends was associated with pleasant situations or a celebration:

I go out to celebrate anything with my friends. (Male 2, 21)

For example, I met some friends last night and had a beer in a nice bar by my university. (Male, 1, 22)

According to some participants, a successful evening was possible without alcohol:

Once I went to a soccer match, watched the game, and didn't drink anything....
(Male 2, 22)

It depends on where and with whom [you are].... (Male 2, 21)

If it's a dancing party, with friends, there is no need to have alcohol. (Female 2, 21)

I went to a rock concert in a stadium...I just ate a very big sandwich...and that was okay. (Male, 23)

For the majority of male respondents, however, the lack of alcohol was rarely justified in a successful evening:

Aah…but I cannot dance without alcohol! (Male 2, 22; many other male voices chimed in to agree)

A *balada* has to have alcohol. A nice *balada* without alcohol is still to happen [is impossible]! (Male, 20)

Everyone agreed on one chief concern after a night out when alcohol was involved:

The only thing that worries me…bumping my mother's car! (Male, 20)

I ask myself how I got home, and I don't believe I was able to…it's great to be home without any problem with [mom's] car! (Female 1, 21)

The next day, the very first thing I do is check: Is it possible that my car is not there? (Male, 2, 21; with a reaction from the whole group and lots of anxious laughs)

Although not stressed by young people themselves, these comments illustrate a worrying trend among young Brazilians to drink and drive.

The idea of setting limits on one's own drinking was questioned by the participants. For most, the evening can be very pleasant even when going beyond "level one," although they admitted to worry about ruining their friends' evening or experiencing some physical harm as a result:

You may feel ill [afterward], but you are also [suddenly] able to speak English very well! Fluently! (Male 1, 22)

We can also talk to all the women! (Male, 23)

And I am even able to sing opera! (Male 2, 21)

It gives you a feeling of wellbeing…. Wellbeing is feeling self-confident! (Male 2, 22)

I feel a giant! (Male 1, 21)

"Feeling a giant" was considered a normal, positive, and pleasant consequence of drinking. It seemed to be the borderline between pleasurable drinking and extreme drinking.

Extreme Drinking

"Extreme drinking" was understood by the group as a dramatic experience—for instance, drinking until falling down. However, in practice, pleasurable drinking ("feeling a giant") and extreme drinking often got confused:

The purpose [when you want to drink moderately] is not to go over the limit, in other words, not to fall down. (Female 1, 21)

> Those who do not appreciate [alcohol] don't drink; but those who drink don't have a limit. (Female, 18)

For the majority, what was in essence extreme drinking did not mean "getting drunk." None agreed with the suggestion that they might go out specifically to get drunk:

> It depends on the occasion. [You] wouldn't drink a lot at a barbecue with the family, but at a *balada*, yes! (Female 1, 21)

> I do not go out to get drunk, but neither do I go out *not* to drink. (Male 1, 21)

Getting drunk at a *balada* was seen as a normative behavior, so the respondents did not see their experiences during such occasions in a negative light.

The focus group members reported that feeling unwell did not stop them from drinking more; they simply moved on to another type of beverage alcohol. They complained about the high price of water, citing it as the reason for not choosing water as their next beverage. Given their limited budgets, the participants said they chose those drinks from which they expected to "gain the most":

> I choose what will make me higher. So, I won't drink simple water! (Male, 20)

> At a *balada*, water and beer have the same price. It [water] is too expensive! Water shouldn't cost anything. (Male 2, 21)

The group did not reach a consensus on the definition of "extreme drinking," mentioning a variety of variables, including age and physical disposition. The group did come up with an important ingredient of excessive intake, however. Extreme drinking, according to these young people, depended on alcohol maturity, defined as a gradual learning process about personal limits and preferences. Thus, getting drunk was a different thing depending on the age and the experience of the drinker:

> One learns to recognize the limits. (Female, 22)

> ...and to have total self-control. (Female 1, 21)

> After a certain age, you don't want to feel sick anymore. Between [the ages of] 13 and 16, people are completely out of their minds!! They drink till they drop! Teens don't have anywhere to go or money to spend, so, they drink any alcohol they can find. (Male 2, 22)

> When I was 15, I would never go out, it was too rare. But, when my parents allowed me to go, I thought, "I will take all the possible advantage of this!" (Female, 18)

The notion of alcohol maturity also included having more disposable income with age, which leads to a better choice of what to drink. Otherwise, respondents reported drinking a liquor of the worst quality mixed with equally suspicious nonalcohol beverages:

> When I didn't have money, I used to buy a bottle of *51* [a popular and cheap *cachaça*, Brazil's traditional spirit made from sugar cane] and mixed it with Tang [orange juice powder].... It's cheap. (Male 1, 21)

Although the idea of alcohol maturity was strongly approved by the respondents, it was not perceived by the majority as a guarantee of total self-control. According to some, until the second bottle of beer,

> ...it's possible to know what you are doing [and to control yourself]. After that, though, everything...it's all gone! (Male, 20)

Still trying to define the concept of extreme drinking, the participants did not agree on what constitutes "self-control." Respondents admitted to feeling, at times, more in control than they really were. Looking back, they remembered testing their self-control and personal limits in the context of drinking games:

> We started drinking when I was very young. In high school, we used to play the game called "Little Coin." Everybody knows it! If you manage to throw the coin into the glass, you have the right to order someone to drink anything. And it goes on until nobody stands.... (Male 2, 21)

> My brother is 18 and that [engaging in drinking games] also happens. I don't like to go out with him because he always gets too drunk. (Male 2, 22)

Everyone recognized that alcohol consumption changes with age:

> Our outings change and, with them, our relationship with alcohol becomes different. (Female, 22)

What the population over 20 defined as a "normal" pattern of drinking—given their acquired experience, knowledge of their own limits, and access to better-quality drinks—was pointed out by them as an extreme pattern for 16- and 17-year-olds.

Recognizing drunkenness in themselves was reported as difficult by the respondents. They said that it was much easier to notice in friends, and this state was not readily approved:

> Ah...it is a shame! It [means] making a fool of yourself! (Male, 20)

> Happy drunks are great fun! But, when they feel sick, it becomes so boring. (Female, 22)

> Drunk people don't listen to others. (Female, 2, 21)

...and don't care when someone tells them that they passed their limit. (Male 1, 21)

[As good friends,] we help by offering water, but there are friends and "friends".... (Female, 18)

When asked about being drunk themselves, the respondents indicated that they considered it a problem only if they felt ill afterwards—otherwise, the experience was considered "fun":

If you feel ill, it's boring, but if you are just feeling happy, that's ok. (Male 2, 22; this phrase was repeated by other respondents)

Yet, again, the definition of "drinking too much" was unclear. There was a tendency among respondents to think positively of occasions when they did not remember what had happened. They thought it was "fun" when their friends told them what they did when drunk—unless told that they "made a fool" of themselves, like vomiting, whispering "I love you" inappropriately, and so on.

This high tolerance toward one's own drunkenness could be a behavior learned from parents, often referred to as "professional drinkers" by the respondents (many participants said that their parents "drink a lot" and "act as if they know everything about it," like professionals know about their area of expertise). When asked who drinks more, older or younger generations, the group reacted with excitement and what seemed to be a lack of consensus. Asked individually, they replied that:

Young people drink a lot, but older people who are used to drinking, [do so] more than us. (Female, 18, and Male 1, 22)

Older people are more resistant if they start getting boozed. They have a better self-control, a stronger resistance. (Male 1, 21)

Older people drink more, but they know how to control themselves, and they don't get drunk easily. They know how to keep to the limit. (Male, 23)

Young people drink more nowadays; we can go to a bar every day. Our generation drinks more, more frequently.... Older people worry about going to work [the next day]. (Female 2, 21)

All young people drink alcohol, and just *some* old ones do. (Male, 20)

Older people drink much more alcohol! But young people are drinking more than [they did] in the past. (Female, 22)

What happens is that we drink quicker. I think there is this anxiety at present: Time flies quicker! (Male 2, 21)

Although this sample characterized older people as "good drinkers" (drinking a lot), there was strong agreement that, when at their age, their parents drank less than the participants in the group do today. Looking into the future, some youths thought they would continue to drink "a lot," consuming as much as their parents or even more as they grow older; the majority, however, were inclined to believe that they would reduce their drinking in the coming years.

When I get old, I think I will drink a lot! (Male, 20)

No, I think, we will show more responsibility. I will have a wife and kids. (Male 1, 22)

I think I will drink more, but with more responsibility. (Male 2, 22)

Because the respondents had not mentioned anything about their sex life and related consequences of extreme drinking, the researchers asked them about condom use. The participants thought that unsafe sexual behavior was "the same as other risks" related to drinking excessively—such as traffic crashes and experiencing car theft—they did not know enough to worry about this risk in particular.

Conclusions

The participants of this focus group considered themselves, in their own words, "intensive drinkers," but none admitted to being problematic drinkers. They had difficulty in acknowledging their involvement in the negative aspects of extreme consumption.

The expression "reaching level one" was a spontaneous construction from the group, not a term currently used in the scientific literature. According to the sample, this drinking level has a desired effect on self-perception, especially among men, who reported feeling more adult and self-assured ("I feel a giant!").

The notions of limits and transgression were constant themes in young people's responses. Group participants hoped to reach "alcohol maturity," a point when they would be able to differentiate between "getting wasted" and appreciating a drink—and without counting on family or social support to do so.

Drinking excessively, however, was not seen purely as a matter of individual choice. Family and society play an important role in how young people model their drinking. Families were characterized as tolerant toward alcohol use in general, with the adults often providing an illustration of drunken behavior and adult family members introducing adolescents to their first drink. On the other hand, relatives—especially mothers—appeared to be central in helping youths to build a positive self-image, an important factor in young people's decision not to engage in extreme drinking. The presence of relatives was also deemed to be a moderating factor in young people's alcohol consumption. This dichotomy needs to be addressed in future research.

On the whole, Brazilian culture is full of symbols related to alcohol consumption, especially in the arts and some social rituals, which often equate drinking with elegance, sophistication, and national pride (for instance, Brazilians are fond of *cachaça*, the country's national drink, and alcohol consumption is an important ingredient of festivities during the Carnival). This background seems to weaken societal limitations on drinking and related behavior. In addition, television—a social aspect of great influence in Brazil—is generally not recognized as an educational tool by prevention specialists. There is an evident lack of moderate drinking campaigns in television programming, whereas images of excess are broadly displayed. Importantly, young people in this focus group indicated general openness to comprehensive and objective awareness-building messages about alcohol and appropriate patterns of its consumption.

CHINA

Ian Newman[3]

In the West, alcohol is frequently discussed in terms of health or social *problems*. As a result, most Westerners are well informed about (or are at least aware of) the significance of alcohol-related social issues. This is not the situation for most Chinese people.

In China, alcohol consumption has been an integral part of daily life for centuries, perceived in the light of the pleasures it provides rather than the problems it may cause. Some concern is expressed when *problem* drinking results in traffic crashes and alcoholism. However, questions about drinking per se are often met with surprise. Few people have considered alcohol use as a potentially risky behavior, and many have no formulated perspectives from which to answer Western-style problem-oriented questions.

At the same time, alcohol is treated differently from other beverages. As one future teacher stated in our focus groups, "China has her alcohol culture. When people speak while holding a cup, it seems their words are more

[3] Acknowledgements: Many people assisted in organizing the discussion groups upon which the report on China is based. Not all of them can be acknowledged here, but special thanks go to those who participated in the discussions and shared their personal experiences. The project would not have been possible without the significant assistance of Qu Ming, Nebraska Department of Health and Human Services; Qian Ling, National Institute for Health Education, Chinese Center for Disease Control and Prevention; Li Huipu, Institute for Mental Health, Peking University; Chunmen Yan, Baotou Institute for Health Education; Pu Jia, Shanghai; Zhao Jie and Michelle Maas, Nebraska Prevention Center for Alcohol and Drug Abuse; and Cheng De, Baotou City.

convincing and important." A psychology student added, "Alcohol culture lasts thousands of years in China. Why has it lasted so long? Because alcohol has positive significance in itself...it brings benefits to us." The role of alcohol in traditional medicine illustrates this point: "Chinese people put herbs...in their alcohol to cure many diseases and reactivate their blood. They drink a small amount [of alcohol] each day."

Many Chinese proverbs suggest that alcohol plays a special role in society and has done so for centuries: "A thousand cups of liquor is still not enough if you drink with a bosom friend," "There is no feast without alcohol," "The cup you are holding contains alcohol but also friendship and sincerity," "Drink top down [empty the cup] for strong friendships; sip lightly for weak friendships." This elevated (yet integral) role of alcohol contrasts with its place in many Western cultures. As a participant in our focus groups noted, "In the West, you see somebody take a bottle of beer from the refrigerator and just drink it, as if it were Coke. Alcohol here [in China] has a special social meaning." In China, alcohol is distinguished from other beverages by the subtle meanings associated with patterns of its consumption, the frames of reference that dictate meaning, the spoken and unspoken rules that direct drinking practices, the special ways status and power dictate drinking obligations, and the manner in which drunkenness is defined by circumstance and environment as much as by the amount of alcohol consumed. When the Chinese wonder, "Why do you ask so many questions about alcohol?" they illustrate the degree to which alcohol is an integral and unquestioned part of their life.

Alcohol Consumption in China

The evidence of alcohol production in China dates back more than 7000 years. Drinking is common and apparently has been so throughout history. *Jiu*, "alcohol" in Mandarin, holds significant cultural, social, and historical meanings. It is frequently mentioned in well-known classical literature as a representation of happiness and the embodiment of auspiciousness; but it is also one of the "four vices" or disasters: womanizing, gambling, drinking, and smoking (Singer, 1972).

The Chinese use *jiu* in cooking, and it is considered an important ingredient in traditional medicine. Alcohol is regarded as food, and convention suggests that alcohol beverages should be consumed slowly to enhance the pleasure—"not to quench the thirst, but to appreciate every drop," as a common Chinese saying goes. Drunkenness, especially in public, is condemned. However, there are certain situations and occasions when intoxication is permissible, for example, at weddings, banquets, birthday celebrations, and other family gatherings (Sue, Kitano, Hatanaka, & Yeung, 1985). Men who consume large amounts of alcohol and maintain their sobriety are greatly admired (Shen, 1987).

Chinese history suggests that, as early as 2010 B.C., emperors recognized both the merits and the potential problems associated with alcohol. Emperor

Yu (2205–2198 B.C.) imposed a *jiu* tax to reduce consumption. Around 200 B.C., a fine of four ounces of silver was levied if four or more people were found drinking together, illustrating a perception of alcohol's potential role in trouble-making. However, a second-century decree ordered the provision of a ration of *jiu*, meat, and corn for old men, implying that alcohol may have been seen as part of everyday diet. In 147 B.C., alcohol production and sale were prohibited; this ban was lifted in 98 B.C., but only for government officials.

Punishments for violating alcohol laws were often severe. According to reports from the year 2000 B.C., offenders were sentenced to death. Around the fifth century, alcohol consumption was so great that the emperor ordered all manufacturers, sellers, and consumers of alcohol to be beheaded. Similar penalties were evident in the eleventh and twelfth centuries, when the Yuen emperors, the Mongols, banished alcohol makers. Historical record suggests that different Chinese governments over the centuries have tried virtually all the strategies used today to reduce the consumption of alcohol—without great success.

At present, China is the world's largest producer of beer and spirits. How this production translates into consumption patterns is difficult to determine. Estimates vary. According to the World Health Organization (WHO), China's increase in annual per capita consumption of pure alcohol among adults over age 15 was the second highest in the world, climbing from 1.03 liters in 1970–1972 to 5.17 liters in 1994–1996, a 501.94 % rise (WHO, 1999). In 2003, using total midyear population and production data, the World Advertising Research Center (2005) estimated annual per capita consumption of spirits alone to be 3 liters of pure alcohol; spirits, beer, and wine combined amounted to 4.0 liters. In 1994, surveys of consumption in six areas of China placed yearly adult per capita consumption of pure alcohol at 3.6 liters. Men were reported to drink 18.6 times more than women (Hao, Young, Xiao, Li, & Zhang, 1999).

According to the latest Nutrition and Health Situation Survey of Chinese Residents (Behaviors and Lifestyles), 20.9% of urban and 21.1% of rural dwellers—and 39.6% of male and 4.5% of female respondents (see Figure 5.1)—had at least one drink a week (Ma & Kong, 2006). The trajectory of urban and rural drinking rates was similar (see Figure 5.2). The survey defined "current drinkers" as individuals who had at least one drink per month.

Fermented drinks such as beer are the oldest form of *jiu* produced in China, but distilled products (liquor) are the most consumed alcohol beverages in the country. The introduction and popularization of commercially produced beer are relatively recent phenomena. As a result, beer has become the *jiu* of choice for young people: Rates of beer consumption are highest among drinkers aged under 39 years, especially in the urban areas (see Figure 5.3). None of these estimates account for noncommercial alcohol production and consumption.

Socially, China is a country of contrasts. Known for large cities and free-trade coastal regions, it is, in fact, predominantly rural—60% of the population consists of farmers and villagers. Rural China is dotted with small

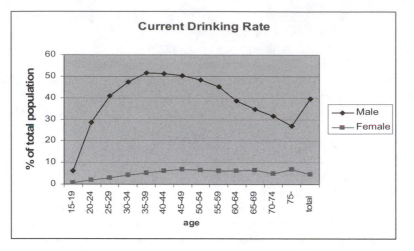

FIGURE 5.1 Trends in current drinking rate by age and gender. Adapted from: Ma and Kong (2006).

villages that are as close together as individual farmhouses in some other parts of the world. "Rural," thus, does not necessarily mean "isolated," but refers to groups of people living in small communities surrounded by agricultural land, employed in agriculture-related work. In addition to the Han, the largest ethnic group in China, 55 other minority ethnic groups are recognized. An attempt was made to seek a reasonable degree of diversity in the focus groups on which this section is based.

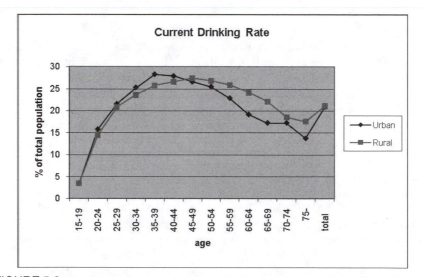

FIGURE 5.2 Trends in current urban and rural drinking rates by age. Adapted from: Ma and Kong (2006).

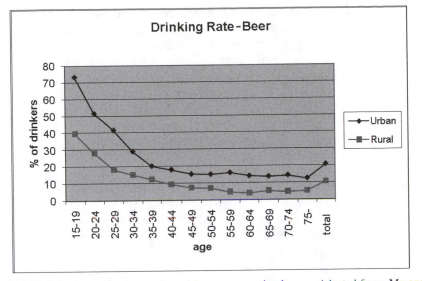

FIGURE 5.3 Trends in urban and rural beer consumption by age. Adapted from: Ma and Kong (2006).

Young People in China

Today's urban Chinese young people have more freedom, more money, more opportunities, more products to buy, more media to consume, more education, and more to dream about than any previous generation. This is not the case for rural youths. However, on the whole, Chinese young people of today are the product of a society vastly different from that of their parents and grandparents. Thus, a 30-year-old in 2007 was born a year after Mao Zedong's death, when Deng Xiaoping started the push for the "Four Modernizations": agriculture, industry, defense, and science. Import of Western technology was allowed, and, in the countryside, farmers were being reintroduced to a free-market economy; Coca-Cola was introduced into the Chinese market. A young person aged 25 was born two years after the establishment of the special economic zones in Shenzhen that led to the showcase cities known to most Westerners. A 20-year-old in 2007 was 2 years old when the events of Tiananmen Square were unfolding. And a 15-year-old was born the year the first stock market opened in Guangzhou. With a few exceptions, urban young people aged under 28 years are the product of the one-child policy, having been raised without brothers and sisters and with two parents and four grandparents to dote on them.

The Focus Group

This case study is based on four focus groups made up of young people aged 18 to 28 years; a total of 49 young people were involved (23 men and 26 women).

Two focus groups were conducted in Beijing, one in Baotou (Inner Mongolia), and one in Shanghai. The young people involved represented university students, recent university graduates working in a variety of occupations, and service workers and salespeople who had not graduated from college and had migrated to Beijing from the provinces, seeking work and a brighter future. The focus groups were held in the private dining rooms of restaurants or meeting rooms. Three of the four focus groups were conducted by Chinese health workers who had experience conducting group discussions but not necessarily focus groups. One group was conducted by the author of this section, with the assistance of a Chinese translator.

The conversations in the three groups convened by Chinese organizers were translated into English by the moderators. The transcript of the group conducted by the author was translated by a third party; two additional observers recorded notes and comments for this group. All discussions were based on ICAP's Guiding Questions for Focus Groups (Annex 2) and followed the procedures specified in Annex 1.

Results

Benefits of Alcohol Consumption: "An Elixir of Friendship"

In our discussions, it was the benefits of alcohol that our Chinese respondents brought up first. The topic of extreme drinking needs to be seen in the context of these views. In addition to conferring health benefits, alcohol was viewed as conducive to communication, understanding, and friendship. These latter effects were described as indispensable in creating and maintaining social connections, achieving success in business, and seeking happiness.

"Voyaging needs a steersman, enhancing friendship needs *jiu*," declares an Inner Mongolian saying. Alcohol was seen as a great facilitator of human contact, which in turn strengthened friendship. According to a recent university graduate, "Drinking is a way to communicate, to establish and maintain relationships. If you have a toast you feel closer to each other and can establish good relationships. It's a bridge between people." A university student put it this way: "We drank to let everyone speak out, no matter if it was a good experience or a bad experience. Drinking facilitates our communication and enhances our friendship."

Toasting with alcohol is a long-standing tradition in China. It can be formal, as when the toaster makes a short speech to the assembled group, followed by the raising of glasses and the drinking of their contents—or it can be brief and simple, such as a nod to someone across the table, followed by emptying of the glasses together. A few words may accompany an informal toast, but this is not necessary. In either case, verbal or nonverbal, the message of toasting is one of goodwill and friendship. In the words of focus group participants:

People can communicate without putting their ideas into words. They exchange ideas through the language of the table while drinking alcohol. This allows them to speak from the bottoms of their hearts and ultimately enhance their friendships.

I drank because it was the last big gathering with my classmates. I treasured our friendships so much. I wanted to say what I wished to say to them, but it's hard to express everything through words. So I chose to drink.

Alcohol can make you bold. Many people can speak out after drinking. Alcohol helps communication and allows people to talk in a more relaxed way.

Friendships carry with them deep emotions. As the above comments suggest, alcohol helps translate emotions into words. It also provides an opportunity for emotional expression that would be seen as unacceptable for a sober person:

I drank at a big party with about 120 people last Saturday. Quite a few of my [male] friends cried after drinking. They cried because they have very strong feelings towards each other, and it's not normally a custom [for men] to cry. However, after drinking, it's okay.

Communication is a reciprocal process between a sender and a receiver. Along with its benefits comes the risk of misunderstanding. In some cases, alcohol-assisted communication can go wrong:

When you get drunk, you can share your private thoughts with others. My cousin said a lot of things that she should have never said. She talked about her emotions, and her relationships, and complaints, and hatred for some family members. She made it known to everybody. The person whom she said she hated must've felt bad because [that person] got up and left. Other people went to comfort [this person], saying that my cousin was drunk and not to take her words too seriously.

In this case, *jiu* facilitated the communication of strong and long-suppressed emotions. Whereas the sender may have been relieved to speak out, the receiver was hurt. This situation was interesting because the observer attributed to alcohol the power to open communication *and* the potential for it to be blamed if the communication goes wrong.

The presence of alcohol can change significantly what is acceptable and what is not. For sober individuals, showing emotions—even the positive emotions engendered by friendship—is typically unacceptable. Alcohol's role in facilitating friendship through communication was encapsulated in two comments by young service workers in Beijing:

The best thing about drinking is that it allows you to see each other's hearts and make your relationship closer.

Saying words deep in your heart is a good thing.

Drinking within Acceptable Limits

When alcohol is seen as the elixir of friendship and good communication, it raises the question, "Is more always better?" At what point and under what circumstances is alcohol consumption, because it affects the central nervous system, counterproductive? In Chinese society, the rules are subtle, complicated, and critical to personal success.

The notion of defining excessive consumption by a set number of standard drinks, as does the term *binge drinking* in North America, is incomprehensible to most Chinese. The concept of a "standard drink" is impractical in the Chinese context. The alcohol content of drinks can go from 4% to more than 60% alcohol by volume (ABV). The size of bottles varies from 100 ml to a liter or more. Drinking cups also range from small (holding 1.2 ml) to rice bowls. Waiters, waitresses, and good hosts keep guests' cups "topped up" [full]; for drinkers, emptying the cup in one swallow is often an obligation, not a choice. All these factors make it difficult to keep track of the quantity of alcohol consumed. Besides, it was the *act* of drinking, not its quantitative components, that was important to our Chinese respondents.

The discussion that follows highlights the differences between acceptable and unacceptable levels of alcohol consumption. Group participants noted that what may constitute "extreme drinking" in the eyes of sober observers is often perceived as normal, traditional, expected, dutiful, or respectful in the eyes of the drinker. In fact, "extreme drinking," as a notion, was not necessarily seen in a negative light, but had many positive attributes that most often, but not always, outweighed any "bad" effects.

Drinking with Family: A Common Practice   The most common drinking patterns often carry special meanings, such as showing respect, sharing, and feeling included in a group:

> On social occasions, you drink a little to show respect for everybody. If they all drink except you, you feel very isolated, outside the sphere, not accepted. If you drink a little, people will think you are sociable.

One of the most typical drinking patterns in China is drinking with the family. Despite the events of the last 50 years that seemed to be designed to break up traditional family structures, the Confucian principles of order and respect still prevail. It is within the family that young people learn to drink and gain their first understanding of what to expect from *jiu*:

> I usually drink at home during Spring Festival, when family members come together. My mother will serve me several glasses of alcohol. I appreciate the different good tastes.

> When we drink at home the atmosphere is more casual…. We drink at home without social pressure from others…sometimes our parents will stop us from getting drunk.

FIGURE 5.4 Shui women offering rice alcohol at the New Year Festival, China. © Christophe Boisvieux/Corbis.

I drink a lot on some occasions like Spring Festival and other festivals. I drink a little with my family, usually red wine, because my mother is a nurse and says that drinking a little is good for health, especially red wine.

For the first time in my life [speaking of the alcohol debut], I drank at home. My parents encouraged me to drink, especially before I went to college. They think I am an adult now. It's inevitable that you drink with classmates at parties and on business occasions. So, if we have not drunk at home in the past, it might cause problems when you drink outside [the home]. You may feel dizzy and even vomit. So my parents helped me when I drank at home. That was very helpful. Neither my father nor my mother has a big drinking capacity. They drink a little with each meal and never experience any [negative outcomes]. So I drink under the direction of my parents. I haven't drunk [spirits] yet. They allow me to drink some wine and beer. I don't actually like wine.

Not all drinking at home is without problems, as one future teacher explained:

If the father comes home after drinking, his violent behavior may hurt the feelings of the family. It can affect the relationship between parents and children. They will be hurt. He may be a bad influence on the children. If the son drinks too much, he may quarrel with his parents or even beat his parents.

Another participant said,

I drink with my family, especially at festivals, and particularly the Spring Festival. I do not drink very much. Just as a courtesy, I drink. Drinking provides us with the feeling and the atmosphere for getting together.

This comment introduces the subject of the "drinking atmosphere," which arose frequently in the discussions. It was important in young people's decision to drink and was reflected in the outcomes they were likely to experience.

Drinking Atmosphere   Drinking atmosphere, the environment in all its dimensions, plays a large part in any drinking occasion. The mere presence of alcohol changes the atmosphere:

> When friends get together without any special reason, we drink just a little. We drink just for fun, just for the atmosphere. The atmosphere is different if there's alcohol with the meal as compared to when there's no alcohol at all.

The atmosphere dictates the ease of intoxication and the acceptability of alcohol-impaired behavior. As a young government employee said, "When I am happy, I often get drunk, even with just one bottle of beer." Another respondent added, "Sometimes I can get drunk after just one glass, but, on other occasions I can drink a whole bottle of liquor without getting drunk. It depends upon my mood and on the atmosphere."

The "atmosphere" starts with the physical location and extends to the mood. There is a difference between drinking in restaurants and drinking in bars:

> When drinking in a restaurant, you enjoy the dishes and appreciate little by little the taste of the alcohol. When drinking in a bar, you enjoy the music, the dances, and the relaxation.

It was said that it is easier to get drunk in a bar than in a restaurant. A young waiter suggested that the real reason for the difference is that one drinks faster at a bar than at a restaurant. In China, restaurants are everywhere, but Western-style bars are rare, except in large cities, where they first clustered to accommodate foreigners and tourists, and where they have now spread to areas with younger populations, such as near university campuses.

Bars and restaurants have different atmospheres. The atmosphere may even dictate a person's choice of drink: "I drink liquor at a restaurant. At a bar, with the music playing, drinking liquor does not match the atmosphere, so I drink beer."

Searching for the Limits   Strong social pressures suggest to young people that drinking "a little" is good: It is good for social relationships, enhancing friendship and camaraderie, showing respect, digesting food, and as a medicine. Where this goodness declines is the beginning of "extreme." The very concept of "goodness" in relationship to alcohol consumption is complicated because, as the quantity consumed increases, the ability to make decisions weakens.

According to our focus groups, obvious benchmarks exist in China for *over*drinking, even for an inebriated person, but these are sometimes confounded by other considerations. The most obvious indicator of exceeding the limit was vomiting. A young restaurant worker put it this way, "The best [thing about drinking] is to speak words from the bottom of your heart. The worst is to be nauseated and vomit." Vomiting was not seen as socially acceptable. Among other concrete indicators that the limit has been exceeded, young people mentioned passing out, falling down, or starting to "talk nonsense."

The signs of approaching the limit were "muddle-headedness," "feeling like mud," "feeling like stepping on cotton," "being about to fly," "being about to fall," and having a clear mind but no control of limbs (for instance, "Not even able to pick up a glass!").

On the other hand, in certain situations, *under*drinking was seen to be just as unacceptable. A person must be careful not to move so far away from overdrinking as to inadvertently ruin the atmosphere or the communication, or threaten friendship or business relations:

> There is a custom related to drinking that you should drink as much as the others when you drink together.

> Self-control is emphasized. One's self-control can be shown by drinking.

> "Drinking a little" is a strange concept. In my opinion, you either don't drink at all or you drink to your heart's content.... How much is your heart's content depends on the atmosphere.

The attitudes, values, and behaviors described by focus group members closely parallel those identified in studies using the Chinese Adolescent Alcohol Expectancy Questionnaire (CAEQ). We developed this instrument between 1997 and 2003 to measure what high school students expected would result from drinking alcohol (Newman, Qian, Shell, Qu, & Zhang, 2006a, 2006b; Newman, Shell, Qu, Xue, & Maas, 2006; Newman, Xue, & Fang, 2004). Data collected from high school students in several parts of Inner Mongolia, Shanghai, and Beijing identified eight factors reflecting expectancies of benefits and harms from drinking. The expectancy factors were: Traditional Drinking Expectations ("If I drink medicinal alcohol, it is good for my health"), Global Negative Consequences ("If I drink alcohol, my judgment would be impaired"), Negative Personal Effects ("If I drink alcohol, my reputation would be ruined"), Positive Physical and Mental Effects ("If I drink alcohol, I will feel relaxed"), Positive Social Perceptions ("If I drink alcohol, it would help me make friends"), Social Courtesy Consequences ("If I refuse someone's toasting, I am afraid of hurting his/her feelings"), and Family Reactions to Drinking ("If I drink alcohol, my family will be angry"). These factor labels and sample belief statements suggest the complicated role alcohol plays in Chinese society.

The eighth expectancy factor identified by Newman and colleagues was Sexual Expectancies ("If I drink alcohol, I will be more attractive to opposite-sex classmates or friends"). The focus group discussions described here did not venture into questions about alcohol-related sexual expectancies. Sex-related discussions are not yet especially comfortable for many young Chinese, and it is important to remember that most drinking is done in groups for many reasons unrelated to sex.

When It Is "Okay" to Exceed the Limits

In most societies, there are times when sanctions on excessive alcohol use are suspended. In China, this occurs during festivals or rites of passage, like weddings and birthdays. However, specific circumstances may also call for the suspension of responsible alcohol use. The following example illustrates how vomiting was a small price to pay for the pleasures of an evening with a friend not seen for a long time:

> In the winter of 2002, around New Year's Day, I was in my hometown in northeast China. It was snowing that day. One of my former classmates who had been in the military and I had not seen him for three years was home. We were classmates in high school and I missed him very much. We went out drinking, staying out until midnight. I was living on the 17th floor. The elevator had already stopped operating for the night. I climbed the stairs to my apartment. I don't remember how I got there. As soon as I opened the door, I went straight to the toilet and vomited.... It was a very special day for two reasons: I had not seen my classmate for a long time and I was really, really very happy to meet him again, and it was snowing and I am very fond of snow. So I drank several glasses more than usual.

Drinking as an Excuse   Complicating the search for limits, somewhere on the edge of the unacceptable is the excusable: When drunk, "you can give the wrong answers to others' questions without being blamed." The Chinese have a saying, *sa jiu feng,* meaning "alcohol madness"—behavior brought on by drinking that is out of the ordinary but somewhat socially acceptable: "I know of some girls who are usually reserved, but when they drink, they just hug the boys next to them." Alcohol as a man's excuse for crying publicly (described above) seems to fall under this heading.

"Pushing"   When friends get together and the atmosphere is good, people "push" (put pressure on) each other to drink more:

> Most pushing occurs among close friends. If people are not very close, they will control themselves even if someone pushes [drinks on them]. Otherwise one will feel embarrassed and leave a bad impression of getting drunk in front of unfamiliar people.

> When several girls and boys drink together, girls will push boys and boys will accept. In turn, girls will not drink more than one cup, even if they are pushed by several boys. It is much easier for girls to push boys, than for boys to push girls.

Drinking as Punishment   Further complicating the determination of the limits of acceptable drinking is the role alcohol can play as a means of punishing another or punishing oneself. As one male participant recounted:

My friend invited others to a banquet but ignored me. He later invited me to drink with him to make up. I did not accept his invitation since he had invited all the others without me. "Why don't you forget me altogether?" I asked.... So he promised he would drink as much as I drank to apologize to me, if I agreed to accept his invitation. There were four of us, including two girls. My friend and I drank on and on. I can't remember exactly how much we drank, but there were empty beer bottles all over the room. We didn't have many dishes to eat. The two girls sent us back home. I didn't wake up until the next day. The atmosphere that day was really unhappy. I was drinking for the release of my anger. [My friend] followed my example. I wanted to get him drunk at that moment, but later, when I woke up the next day, I regretted it. I was unhappy because he had ignored me. But getting drunk didn't solve anything.

A female respondent remembered:

Another girl and I arrived late at the banquet. We drank three glasses as soon as we arrived to punish ourselves for the late arrival.

Obligatory Drinking   Friendship drinking, even with its games—"pushing" or punishment drinking—is usually a drinking situation where it would be possible to opt out. There are other drinking occasions today in China, particularly in business-related settings, where opting out is not possible. It has become common practice that business deals are negotiated and finalized with drinks:

Good friends compel one another to get drunk for fun. With business clients, it's a different situation. You must drink with the client all through the banquet, even if you get drunk. I drink with clients, and, in many cases, clients are quite capable of drinking, but you have to stay up and continue to drink with them. It's drudgery.

It's not possible to sign a contract while drinking tea. You have to drink [alcohol] at that crucial point. It's easier to sign the contract if you drink liquor with the others. Liquor is the bridge between you.

"Without alcohol, there is no banquet," goes the Chinese saying. When you have a banquet with a superior, then the saying is, "If the glass is not full, there is no sincerity." You have to drink a full glass of alcohol to show your sincerity, even if you may get drunk.

The boss of my company was at the table dealing with people from another company over a contract. He said he couldn't drink. But the others insisted that he did, no matter how little. They drank him "under the table" and then sent him back to his hotel. The next day, when he awoke, he was told that the contract had been signed. On some occasions, you have to get drunk for your own good.

Sometimes in social situations younger colleagues are called upon to "protect the boss," by fulfilling their superior's drinking obligations. In this way, young employees may show their loyalty to the boss:

If you drink to protect the boss, even if you vomit, you are regarded as loyal,
capable, and having face and dignity in front of others. So, sometimes, even if
you don't like to drink at all, you have to.

The rules of business drinking are complicated. Drinking is strongly
related to social hierarchy. One of the moderators described the complicated
business drinking system. Young people who have just begun to work are considered to belong to the lowest class and have to drink a lot in business situations. When you drink with your boss, you drink to the bottom of your glass,
while the boss can just sip—an obvious show of the status difference between
the two of you. A boss can ask subordinates to drink his or her share of alcohol "according to the courtesy of the table," as a way to express a favor toward
the subordinates, while the reverse is not allowed and would be offensive.

In addition to hierarchy, gender is also factored into the formula of what
is courteous and what is not in a business drinking situation:

> If a man and a woman have a toast, the man drinks to the bottom of his glass,
> while the woman just sips—not because a woman is superior to the man, but to
> show that the man is superior to the woman. Alcohol is a symbol of power and
> prestige.

> Say, my boss is a woman and can drink a lot. Since she is the boss with a big
> appetite, I must drink as much as she.

> If a young woman applies for a sales position, she will often write on her resume
> how much she can drink.... If your staff can win in the competition of drink-
> ing—that is, get the rivals drunk while your team stays sober—it is a sign of
> having face. The response will be, "If you can drink all of this alcohol today, I
> will sign the contract."

Tricks of the Table   There are many "tricks of the table," deceptions designed
to protect the drinker from getting sick or embarrassed, while at the same
time maintaining relationships and observing social courtesies. For example,
one may drink a glass of alcohol and then pretend to drink some tea, spitting
some alcohol into the tea cup. Or, one could wipe his or her mouth with a
towel, transferring some alcohol onto the towel:

> Many people cheat like this. Sometimes, we will fill bottles with water, some-
> times we dilute the liquor to preserve the smell of alcohol on the bottles.
> Sometimes we recognize cheating and allow it. Sometimes we don't: We take
> our partner's glass and fill it from our bottle, requiring them to drink it all in a
> toast. That is also cheating in a way.

Flushing Reaction   Differential rates of alcohol metabolism, dictated by
the enzymes alcohol dehydrogenase (ADH) and aldehyde dehydrogenase
(ALDH), can reduce the body's ability to break down alcohol. The result is a
flushing reaction, thought by many to be a protective factor against problem

drinking and dependence, especially among Asian populations. However, as the following comments suggest, the social meaning of flushing in China is far from clear:

> It's very normal when someone's face turns red. The person who flushes is not easily drunk. It is related to blood circulation. Some people's face turns white when drinking. It depends on individual differences.

> I belong to those who will get drunk after one glass. I remember once turning red, including my eyes, after the first glass, and my heart was beating fast. What's more, when I finished the second glass, I vomited. So I don't think flushing means bigger drinking capacity.

> Some people flush even after one sip of alcohol. It does not mean that person has drunk too much.... I hear that, for people who flush, alcohol follows the stomach path, and, for people who turn white, alcohol follows the kidney path.[4]

> I don't think turning red or turning white is a big issue. I won't turn red when I drink, but my heart pounds and I become sweaty.

> If I am with strangers, I usually say I do not drink. I flush when drinking. I think it's not a good image of myself, so I don't drink with strangers. I only drink with acquaintances and friends. I don't drink much usually, but, when my mood is good, I will drink more.

This last comment suggests that the social meaning of flushing may be as important as the physiological reaction. The respondent said she can drink more when "in the mood" (essentially overcoming the physical discomforts of flushing), suggesting that appearance and comportment were very important in front of strangers, especially for women. The significance of social roles is also illustrated in the following comment, "If the girl turns red, others will not push [her to drink more], but, if the boy turns red, others will push."

In a different questionnaire study of 442 university students in central China (Zhang, Merrick, Newman, & Qian, 2007), the respondents could not reach a consensus on the social meaning of flushing. However, the data did show that perceptions of other people's reactions to flushing differed by gender. If the "flush reaction" happened to a man, 41.9% of the male and 49.2% of the female respondents thought the other *men* would encourage the flushed person to drink more. If a "flush reaction" happened to a woman, 7.8% of the male and 10.5% of the female respondents thought the *men* would encourage the woman to drink more. No one thought women would encourage either their male or female peers to drink more if they were flushing. This illustrated that social pressure to drink (especially among men) could trump one's negative physical responses to alcohol.

---

[4] The idea of a liquid's "separate paths" through the body is a core concept of traditional Chinese medicine.

Conclusions

Since the mid-1980s, economic changes have made China the world's leading producer of beer and liquor, resulting in lower prices and greater alcohol availability. The average urban Chinese has more income and more freedom than ever before. Personal luxuries, such as automobile ownership, have introduced new consequences of problem drinking: traffic crashes caused by alcohol-impaired driving. In spite of diversity and recent economic change, China has a fairly unified alcohol culture—a set of traditions, esthetics, and rules surrounding drinking.

In our focus groups, both drinking "too much" and not drinking at all were viewed as "unhealthy." In general, there was widespread confidence in the health benefits of drinking *some* alcohol. Confucian and Taoist philosophies encourage moderation, a standard widely applied to alcohol consumption (at least in theory, if not always in practice). Furthermore, the alcohol culture is set within the Chinese social traditions that minimize the role of individuals and maximize the role of social groups. Within social groups, the Confucian values of loyalty to the leader, obedience, and social order are evident. An individual's actions, including drinking, are shaped by these important considerations. The high value that an individual places on group membership means that much individual time and energy are devoted to communication, relationships, and friendships. Eating and drinking together are activities central to forming relationships and maintaining the solidarity of a group. In our focus groups, the most common drinking pattern was drinking with a meal that is shared with others; drinking alone was rare, as was drinking alcohol by itself, without food. As the discussions reported here suggest, alcohol consumption is admired for the way it promotes harmony and closeness among people, and for the ways it facilitates the expression of private feelings that cannot acceptably be expressed when a person is sober.

In general, a drinker is expected to control his or her behavior, even when intoxicated. People who can drink large amounts of alcohol and maintain the appearance of sobriety are greatly admired. Bad behavior by a drunken person is not only shameful for that individual, but also reflects badly on his or her social group.

In a society changing as fast as China, a key question facing policy-makers is how young people will accommodate to the change. Today, more than ever before in China, young people are exposed to foreign ideas and practices, encouraging them to question and sometimes reject traditional values. Our previous research suggests that young Chinese who are more open to Western culture are also more likely to drink and to drink more than those young people who maintain strong traditional beliefs (Xue, Newman, Shell, & Fang, 2005). How educators and policy-makers react to young people's drinking in the future will determine whether alcohol will continue to play an important, positive role in society or become a public health problem.

ITALY

Enrico Tempesta

In its history, social traditions, and economy, Italy has a long-standing and close relationship with beverage alcohol. Italy is often held up as an example of the Mediterranean drinking pattern, a culture where drinking is well integrated into everyday life, serves as an accompaniment to meals, and is part of the social fabric. Wine, traditionally the dominant beverage, is generally considered to be nourishing (Cottino, 1995), but its use also marks special events and occasions.

The cultural context surrounding drinking in Italy is thought to provide a safeguard against the problematic drinking patterns that seem to characterize countries of northern Europe (Cottino, 1995). Three distinct cultural control mechanisms have been identified. The first of these may be referred to as "regulated abuse," specific social occasions when drunkenness is not only condoned, but also expected, usually associated with rare, important events. The second is the strong association between drinking and food in Italian culture. Drinking outside mealtimes has traditionally been frowned upon and viewed as a challenge to work and sociability. The final safeguard is that Italian culture discourages loss of control over alcohol; individuals unable to control their drinking are not viewed favorably by society. However, there is evidence to suggest that some of these patterns may be shifting. In particular, there appears to be an increase in reported drinking outside mealtimes, often in bars and nightclubs (Pala, 2004).

Most Italians drink: 67.2% identify themselves as regular drinkers (defined as consuming alcohol at least once a week), an additional 13.2% drink occasionally (less than once a week), and 19.6% report abstaining from alcohol (Osservatorio Permanente sui Giovani e l'Alcool [Osservatorio Permanente], 2006). As in other cultures, men are more likely to drink than women, and drinking cuts across all social and economic groups. While a drop in overall alcohol consumption has been reported for Italy in recent years, the number of consumers has increased, particularly among women and young people (Pala, 2004). In addition, recent data suggest that the traditional preference for wine has gradually given way to the consumption of beer, especially among younger age groups (Hibell et al., 2004; Osservatorio Permanente, 2006).

Young Italians and Drinking

For young people in Italy, an introduction to alcohol takes place relatively early in life, within the context of the family, mealtimes, and special events. This introduction commonly involves wine, and, as survey data indicate, many young people in Italy are unable to recall the exact age at which this may have occurred (Osservatorio Permanente, 2006). For most individuals, drinking wine is associated with meals and family, whereas beer and other beverages are linked to drinking with peers. Early introduction to alcohol is also reflected in Italy's legally mandated minimum purchase age of 16 years (WHO, 2004a).

According to a survey conducted by the Rome-based Osservatorio Permanente sui Giovani e l'Alcool (2006), 80% of all Italians aged 12 years and older and 72% of young people aged between 13 and 24 years report ever consuming alcohol. In the latter group, 47.5% describe themselves as "regular drinkers" (drinking at least once a week). These figures vary by region, with drinking more prevalent in the north of the country than in the south. As in other countries, young people's drinking is influenced by a range of external factors, including relationships with parents (Zambon, Lemma, Borraccino, Dalmasso, & Cavallo, 2006) and the drinking patterns of peers (Donato et al., 1994).

The cultural attitudes toward drinking in Italian society that safeguard against heavy consumption and are also reflected in the drinking patterns of the country's young people. Although a considerable number of youths report having consumed alcohol, only 5% of Italians aged 13 and older report being drunk at least once during the past three months. Among young people in the 13 to 24 age group, this number increases to 9%, males being more likely to report being drunk than females (Osservatorio Permanente, 2006). These relatively low figures for intoxication among young Italians are further supported by evidence from the 2003 European School Survey Project on Alcohol and Other Drugs (ESPAD), which examined the use of various substances among secondary school students aged 15 to 16 years in 35 countries (Hibell et al., 2004). According to this survey, 4% of the Italian participants were drunk 10 or more times during the preceding 12 months. This stands in stark contrast to 34% of their counterparts in Denmark and 24% in the United Kingdom.

In an analysis of "binge drinking" (defined as having at least five drinks in two hours and not in conjunction with any meals), such behavior was reported by 10% of all young people between the ages of 13 and 24 years, with 15% for boys and 6% for girls (Osservatorio Permanente, 2006). Youths aged over 15 years were more likely to have "binged" than those in the lower age group. According to the ESPAD data, 13% of Italy's 15- to 16-year-olds had reported having five or more drinks in a row three or more times in the preceding 30 days. Other studies have estimated rates of binge drinking among Italian university students to be as high as 33% (D'Alessio, Baiocco, & Laghi, 2006).

The Focus Group

The present study addresses the results of a focus group conducted in Rome in September 2005. This group consisted of 27 men and women, aged 16 to 25 years, from different socioeconomic backgrounds and walks of life, including high school, technical school and university students, young people already in the workforce, and the unemployed. The group was led by two moderators;

three assistants kept a record of the entire discussion and a hostess welcomed the participants.

The focus group followed this schedule: The moderators began the discussion by explaining the study's main purposes; the assistants then distributed a short questionnaire about drinking (based on the guiding questions in Annex 2), which the participants had 15 minutes to fill out. These questionnaires were used to facilitate discussion focused on four main topics: drinking in general, extreme drinking, contexts in which people tend to drink to excess, and why people drink to excess. The inquiry was carried out in accordance with the ICC/ESOMAR International Code of Marketing and Social Research Practice (International Chamber of Commerce [ICC] & European Society for Opinion and Marketing Research [ESOMAR], 1994) and the Italian law on privacy (L. 196/03). At the end of the focus group meeting, all respondents were compensated for their participation with gift cards valued at around €30 (for instance, cinema tickets and prepaid mobile phone cards).

Results

A "Typical" Drinking Experience

In this focus group, drinking alcohol was a common behavior, though participants aged between 16 and 21 years reported lower levels of consumption than those aged between 21 and 25 years. On average, young people tended to drink not less than twice but not more than three times a week, usually during weekends, evenings, and holidays. For all group members, drinking generally

FIGURE 5.5 Young couple at outdoor café, Rome, Italy. © Simon Watson/Corbis.

occurred when they were in the company of others—mostly with friends, for instance, going to a bar after dinner. According to the respondents, being with friends, rather than alcohol consumption by itself, was central during such outings: "Nobody would go out *just* to drink."

According to their drinking habits, members of this sample could be further divided into three main subgroups:

1. *Group 0:* Composed of male and female respondents aged 16 to 21 years. These youths viewed drinking as an important (but not an indispensable) part of socializing. For this group, there were few situations in which they could consume alcohol during the week, so drinking mostly occurred during weekends or in the evenings. Group members reported drinking "moderate amounts" of alcohol—mostly beer—and none felt ashamed or awkward if they were the only ones choosing *not* to drink among peers at a given occasion.
2. *Group A:* Composed of young people (especially women) aged over 21 years. This group also saw drinking as an important ingredient of social interaction, but was more selective and set about the beverage types (generally preferring wine). As with the previous subgroup, no one in Group A reported feeling ashamed or awkward if he or she declined a drink among alcohol-consuming peers.
3. *Group B:* Composed of young people (especially men) aged over 21 years. Although the concept of drinking to socialize remained, many youths in this group agreed with the following when they thought of their typical drinking experience: "We went out for the company [to be with friends], but we were also together because we all like drinking when we go out." In addition, respondents in this group reported drinking alone, especially if they were already in the workforce (drinking as "a pick-me-up" at the end of the workday). Only one member of this group reported feeling ashamed or awkward if (s)he decided not to drink in the company of alcohol-consuming peers.

Probing the topic of typical drinking occasions further, the moderators asked about drinking in nightclubs—public venues where, according to some research (e.g., Pala, 2004), youths tend to drink more than in other settings. This hypothesis (nightclubs as emerging new locations for increased alcohol consumption) did not ring true to our group's respondents. Drinking in nightclubs was more expensive than in pubs, they explained: "[At nightclubs,] the first drink is included in the admission ticket, but, if you want to drink more, you must spend a lot of money." Overall, the price of alcohol seemed to have a considerable influence on young people's drinking choices.

According to the sample, drinking did increase during vacations, because "people could sleep in and did not have to study," or go to work the next morning:

[You tend to drink more when you are on vacation], because your mood changes and you can let yourself go, as if you were in another world....

Motivations for Drinking

Two motivations that, according to international research (see chapter 4), normally feature in young people's decisions to drink alcohol were investigated: drinking to "let go" of inhibitions and drinking to "do something forbidden."

On the former—using alcohol to feel less inhibited and, therefore, more at ease in social contexts—participants expressed several divergent views. Group 0 respondents did not see alcohol as a means to aid their interaction with friends. When they drank with peers, many stressed that they did so "using good judgment, not drinking too much." These youths preferred having beer during meals and on special occasions and generally disliked spirits. Overall, Group 0 reported not letting themselves be pressured by friends to drink (or to drink excessively) when they did not want to do so.

The results were somewhat different among older respondents. Group A participants strongly agreed that "alcohol makes you feel at ease," and that "being a little tipsy helps you feel better [about yourself]...you speak more and easier, so others appreciate you more." These youths reported that sometimes the desire to "feel at ease" led them to "drink more than I should have." Conversely, young people in Group B said that, when they drank—and sometimes drank "a bit too much"—they were not motivated by alcohol's disinhibiting qualities. Rather, they drank because they liked it:

I like having a good glass of wine or some beer. Basically, I drink because I like it; when I am with a friend, we have a nice chat while drinking a beer or a cocktail.

According to Group B, drinking did not so much influence their behaviors or self-perception as it enhanced the atmosphere of the occasion: "...the taste of a good glass of wine is a pleasure."

No one in our sample saw the connection between drinking and "doing something forbidden." The youngest respondents (Group 0) said that, when they do drink, they do so freely in front of parents, relatives, and friends "without feeling guilty." Among these youths, drinking normally took place at communal events, such as parties, banquets, and anniversaries, and was thus an essential part of their human, familial, and social experiences. A similar attitude was exhibited by young people in Group A. The lack of perceived connection between drinking and doing something forbidden, however, was also illustrated in this group by an emerging tendency to drink alone, without giving it much thought. Thus, a 25-year-old Group A respondent said, "Sometimes, I drink at home, because I'm alone and I don't have anyone [else] to drink with." Another young woman said, "I don't drink much, even if I recently started drinking more than I used to...beer and wine...in pubs, pizzerias, restaurants, at home if I am alone...."

Group B respondents contributed to this discussion by bringing up their early drinking experiences. They reported "feeling older" when they drank as adolescents, but this did not entail a sensation of doing something "forbidden." These youths generally had easier access to alcohol from relatively younger ages than the participants in Groups 0 and A:

> In my family, you can always find a bottle of wine during dinner. Mine is not a family that prevents children from drinking; for instance, if my parents were making a toast, I was allowed to drink champagne.

Drinking in the context of the family appeared to shape a perception among these respondents of alcohol as food, rather than a substance of abuse, allowed only under certain circumstances. According to a Group B member:

> No special occasion is needed for drinking. We just go to drink when and if we want to. Some weeks we don't get anything to drink, in others we drink every evening.

This rather relaxed view of alcohol in our focus group translated into a relative lack of awareness about its effects—for instance, about the impact of drinking on driving a vehicle:

> I really like drinking beer, wine, it depends on the situation. During the last six months...at university, I let myself go [drank a lot]...then I would go to sleep for several hours and go to classes in the morning. Sometimes, I try to drink moderate amounts, though, especially when I have to drive.... Unfortunately, this last law about drinking and driving probably [will not let me do that any more].... different people suffer from different effects....

Alcohol and Drugs

The majority of the participants did not think that people who drank alcohol were more likely to use drugs and to break the law. All respondents wanted to make it clear that, although they considered themselves "regular drinkers," none used illegal substances. Whereas they linked drinking alcohol to terms such as *fun*, *good company*, and *friendship*, they always connected drugs to unpleasant situations; using drugs was defined as an "extreme" and "unusual" behavior. A minority of respondents, however, thought that people who used drugs were more likely to drink to intoxication: "People who abuse drugs go overboard with alcohol too."

Extreme Drinking and Drunkenness

Very few participants (particularly among the younger people in Group 0) reported ever getting drunk. Among those who did, some thought that the experience helped them limit their drinking in the future; others said it had no bearing on their habits.

No episodes of drunkenness were reported by women in Group A, although the norms and stories they provided gave evidence of remarkable consumption. These respondents were very critical of drinking to intoxication:

> I got drunk once in my life and I think that was enough...so I try not to drink to excess. I control myself, because drinking to excess spoils my evening.... People should be aware of their limits, because drinking can spoil their and everyone else's evening.

Group B youths were similarly critical of extreme drinking and drunkenness ("In my opinion, people should never drink so much that they get drunk"). Interestingly, some in this group felt that, if someone had gotten drunk once, he or she was more likely to get drunk in the future ("If you cannot keep away from it once, you will never be able to do it").

When asked whether or not they drank more when feeling sad, young people in Group 0 were mystified: They had no experience of such drinking and were surprised at the concept. Older individuals were more open to the possibility of drinking to cope. Broadly, their responses can be illustrated by four quotes. The most common opinion, especially among women, was that:

> ...when you have problems (with your partner, for instance), alcohol can make the situation worse. So you do not drink at all, and you have no wish to go out with friends.

Some individuals, however, particularly young men and those already in the workforce, agreed that:

> People tend to associate alcohol with fun. When somebody drinks to feel better, [he or she] must be in real trouble.

Several young nonstudents (mostly men) took this perception further:

> Drinking can help you feel better, work better, be happier, and face problems with your boss and with others in general.

For a minority of respondents, drinking to excess was associated with extraordinary, negative circumstances:

> I do not get drunk when I'm with my friends. I get drunk when I'm alone, if I'm in trouble.

When asked what it means to "get drunk," how much someone would have to drink to be considered "drunk" or intoxicated, and how they would act, the discussants felt that: (1) the definition of "being drunk" depends on the individual and on "how much alcohol [he or she] can [normally] handle"; (2) to "get drunk" signifies losing control of oneself and the situation; (3) people never plan to get drunk, and this result is generally avoided. Older respondents were more outspoken about their views on the matter, also sharing their own experiences of excessive consumption and drinking outcomes. For instance, the following responses exemplify the opinions of Group A participants:

...to get drunk means to talk childishly, to have slurred speech...it can be fun to drink without being aware of it. I have gotten drunk that way, but, [whether or not I have fun], does not depend on drinking, otherwise I wouldn't be very healthy.

The feeling of "getting drunk" goes from starting to lose some reflexes to losing consciousness.

I associate drunkenness with being sick, feeling dizzy...when the next day you have a headache and decide never to get drunk again.

To get drunk means to feel sick. [When I felt drunk in the past,] I always remembered what I had done [during the night out], because, though my reflexes slowed down, I remained conscious. I remember getting home was annoying: It was like a never-ending trip.

Group B members added:

To get drunk means to lose consciousness, to forget [what has happened]. I have gotten drunk [before], but without planning to.... For instance, I don't feel like I have to get drunk on [a certain date]. It depends on the situation, on the people you are with, on how much [alcohol] you can handle. I can take a lot of alcohol. In my opinion, though, getting drunk is not good; maybe being a little tipsy is fine, it makes me feel good.

In my opinion, [the definition of "getting drunk"] strictly depends on the individual. In general, it means to lose consciousness, to lack quick reflexes, not remembering what has happened. I never plan to get drunk. I got drunk at most twice in my life, under some really special circumstances.

In the past, I sometimes drank too much, and I had a headache afterwards.... [When I felt that way,] I felt like only drinking water from then on.... I never forgot what I had done while drinking, though....

I do not particularly like getting drunk. When I got drunk in the past, I remembered all the things I had done. I was on vacation in Greece at the time.

For my part, I've never got drunk. At most, I drank a little bit more than usual, enough to feel sick the next morning.... I didn't want to have breakfast even.... But I never planned it... [it just happened during] an evening with friends.... but I don't like being sick. I try to control myself.

Changing Current Drinking Behaviors

The participants were asked if they could think of any experiences that would make them consider abstaining from alcohol in the future. The idea of giving up drinking altogether surprised young people in our sample, but temporarily changing one's consumption patterns was mentioned under certain extreme circumstances:

> A friend of mine was involved in a car [crash] after drinking, and that struck me deeply. [He stopped drinking for a while.] Now he is better and has started drinking again, but I'm more aware of the consequences of drinking…you must pay attention….

Although very few participants indicated that they knew of peers with problematic drinking patterns, they agreed that, "It [would be] really sad to see a friend who cannot keep away from drinking." In general, the discussion revealed that young people were not well informed about the potential negative outcomes of drinking.

Conclusions

In this focus group, young people normally drank during weekends, in the evenings, or when on vacation. They thought of drinking in the context of socializing with friends or family, seldom drinking alone, and never "just to drink." Their consumption was generally moderate, but the volume tended to increase with age. Drinking at home in the context of the family (and with meals) was common; most youths had their first experience with alcohol between the ages of 10 and 11 years for boys and 13 or 14 for girls (during lunch or dinner, with parents). Young people did not think that their current drinking patterns would change dramatically over the years; all participants thought that their drinking behavior was similar to that of their parents in the past.

Unlike some recent studies that detected growing rates of extreme drinking among young Italians and pointed to nightclubs as venues where such drinking might occur, this pattern of consumption was viewed by the young people in our focus group as unusual (although many said they enjoyed "feeling a little tipsy" on occasion). High prices for drinks at nightclubs prevented them from listing such venues as their primary drinking settings or places where their consumption was likely to be higher than normal. In our group, bars and parties were regular drinking locations—young people went to bars with friends after dinner, and some drank to excess as a result; meanwhile, a noticeable increase in consumption was reported during vacation from school or work.

At the same time, drunkenness was strongly criticized by all respondents. In our group, "getting drunk" was primarily equated with losing control and feeling sick (none of the participants had themselves experienced serious negative consequences beyond hangovers). Reaching intoxication was unintentional; of youths who had ever experienced being drunk (primarily, men over 21), many said the experience made them more cautious in the future. Importantly, an overwhelming majority did not feel awkward or ashamed to drink nonalcoholic beverages "when they felt like it," even if everyone else around was drinking alcohol.

Although the results of this focus group support recent findings of relatively low prevalence of intoxication among Italian youths, a worrying theme did emerge. Namely, a rather relaxed approach to alcohol seemed to contribute to young people's lack of awareness about the effects of drinking. They reported that they limited their alcohol consumption if they had to drive, but most participants had only a vague idea of its precise impact on blood alcohol levels and the ability to drive, pointing to a possible gap in current prevention initiatives that should be filled in the future.

NIGERIA

Olabisi Odejide, Olayinka Omigbodun, Ademola Ajuwon,
Victor Makanjuola, Afolabi Bamgboye, and Frederick Oshiname

Despite existing alcohol policies, research indicates a major increase in alcohol availability and consumption in Nigeria over the past three decades, particularly among the country's young people (Adelekan et al., 2001; Odejide, 1989; Odejide, Ohaeri, Adelekan, & Ikuesan, 1987). This section offers an overview of two separate focus groups containing young men and women, held in 2005 in the city of Ibadan. The focus groups discussed the participants' current alcohol consumption and views on extreme drinking behaviors.

Present Legal Climate: Alcohol Policy in Nigeria

At the outset, an important distinction must be made between alcohol policies in southern states of Nigeria (where our study took place and which are the focus of this discussion) and the predominantly Muslim states in the north, governed by Sharia, the Islamic legal code (WHO, 2004a). Prior to the year 2000, Sharia applied only to civil law in northern Nigerian states, but, in the past seven years, individual state houses of assembly began to promulgate legislation that gradually extended Sharia to cover penal law. As a result, consumption, sale, and advertisement of alcohol in all parts of Sharia-governed states are banned, regardless of individual religious beliefs.

Non-Sharia Nigerian states impose state control over alcohol production and sale, including restrictions on hours and place of sale for off-premise consumption. Alcohol advertising over the electronic media (television and radio) is partially restricted but the regulations are unevenly enforced. There are no limits on advertising in print media and on billboards, and no provisions exist for health warning labels on alcohol products. Sponsorship of sports and youth events by beverage alcohol companies is permitted, but all alcohol consumption is banned from sporting events and workplaces. Partial restrictions are placed on drinking alcohol in healthcare establishments, educational buildings, and government offices, but it is allowed in public transport and parks, on streets, and during community leisure activities, such as concerts.

The maximum blood alcohol concentration (BAC) level for driving is 0.0 mg/ml, but the use of random breath testing is yet to be adopted as a policy (WHO, 2004a). Finally, the minimum purchase and drinking age for alcohol in non-Sharia Nigerian states is 18 years; however, this limit is rarely enforced.

Country Background

In the precolonial era, alcohol obtained from palm wine, palm wine distillate, and fermented cereals was commonly used at social gatherings and at the end of the daily labor (usually farming). At that time, the use of alcohol was the preserve of male adults, forbidden to women and adolescents (Netting, 1964; Odejide, 1989; Odejide & Odejide, 1999). However, with colonization, the influx of European culture changed indigenous patterns of alcohol use, introducing commercially produced Western beverages. Alcohol drinks became readily available to adults and youths of both sexes (Odejide et al., 1987). In the past three decades, several studies from Africa have noted the growing consumption of alcohol particularly by young people (e.g., Adelekan, Abiodun, Imouokhome-Obayan, Oni, & Ogunremi, 1993; Adelekan, Makanjuola et al., 2001; Odejide et al., 1987). Some researchers have also observed that, within the last three decades, young people, who constitute the largest proportion of the population in African countries, have become the target audience for alcohol marketing (e.g., Jernigan, 2001). In the present study, we were interested in whether the focus group participants would list marketing of alcohol beverages as a factor influencing their drinking (see discussion below).

The consumption of beverage alcohol across Africa now includes both local and commercially produced drinks (Haworth & Simpson, 2004; Riley & Marshall, 1999). Just like adults, young people of both sexes consume alcohol essentially for pleasure and to overcome psychological and physical problems (Odejide & Odejide, 1999). However, as remarked by researchers in South Africa, alcohol use, along with its pleasures and benefits, may contribute to many problems in developing societies, such as an elevated incidence of trauma, violence, organ system damage, various cancers, unsafe sexual practices, injuries to the developing fetus, and broader negative economic and social consequences (Parry, Plüddemann et al., 2005).

The pattern of alcohol drinking behavior among young people in Nigeria has not been extensively studied. In previous research, Odejide and colleagues (1987) found that children and young adults were more involved in alcohol use than their parents at the same age, first alcohol experiences occurring between the ages of 11 and 13 years. Further observations from the study revealed that traditional alcohol beverages were not regarded as psychoactive substances, and alcohol in general was culturally perceived as a recreational liquid, traditionally consumed by males at the end of the day's activities. Moreover, it was pointed out that commercially produced drinks were widely available to young persons despite cultural constraints, and that adolescents and young adults had been noted as occasional drinkers who at times drank to intoxication. Young women were found to be on a par with their male counterparts in terms of alcohol consumption and problem drinking (Odejide et al., 1987). In Nigeria's non-Sharia states, alcohol beverages are usually sold in supermarkets and are easily accessible to young consumers.

The present study was designed to serve as a window into some of the reasons behind youthful drinking and extreme drinking behaviors in Nigeria today.

The Focus Group

To prevent cultural bias in attitudes to drinking by men and women from restricting the responses of female participants, two focus groups were constituted, separated according to gender. In the male group, the age range of the 16 respondents was from 18 to 25 years, with a mean age of 22.8 years. The female group consisted of 13 participants, aged between 19 and 24, with an average age of 21.2 years. The three largest ethnic groups in Nigeria—Hausa, Ibo, and Yoruba—were represented in the study, as well as three smaller groups, Ijaw, Edo, and Itsekiri. Yoruba, Hausa, and Ibo inhabit the southwest, north, and south-east of Nigeria, respectively, while the latter three live in the riverine areas (Delta Region) of the country. The two focus groups were comprised of students from secondary and tertiary institutions (13), civil servants (2), traders (7), a fashion designer, an unskilled laborer, and the unemployed (5). Tables 5.2 and 5.3 provide the demographic profile of the group participants.

TABLE 5.2 Nigeria Focus Groups: Female Participants

S/N	Age	Occupation	Ethnic origin
1	23	Unemployed	Yoruba
2	24	Unemployed	Yoruba
3	21	Higher National Diploma student	Ibo
4	22	Higher National Diploma student	Itsekiri
5	20	Fashion designer	Yoruba
6	24	Civil servant	Yoruba
7	19	University student	Yoruba
8	20	Higher National Diploma student	Yoruba
9	21	University student	Yoruba
10	22	Higher National Diploma student	Ibo
11	24	Businesswoman	Yoruba
12	21	Nursing student	Yoruba
13	20	University student	Ibo

TABLE 5.3 Nigeria Focus Groups: Male Participants

S/N	Age	Occupation	Ethnic origin
1	22	Computer shop assistant	Yoruba
2	23	Shop assistant	Yoruba
3	25	Civil servant	Yoruba
4	21	Unemployed polytechnic graduate	Yoruba
5	24	Unemployed university graduate	Yoruba
6	23	Higher National Diploma Polytechnic student	Yoruba
7	20	Unemployed university graduate	Ibo
8	24	Unskilled laborer	Ijaw
9	21	Higher National Diploma Polytechnic student	Yoruba
10	24	Businessman	Ibo
11	25	Telephone card dealer	Edo
12	22	Higher National Diploma Polytechnic student	Edo
13	18	Secondary school student	Yoruba
14	25	Marketer	Hausa
15	22	Marketer	Hausa
16	20	University student	Hausa

The focus groups' discussions were tape-recorded and transcribed for content analysis. The study sample does not represent the entire youth of Nigeria, but the mix of members in both focus groups covered the various categories of young adults from different ethnic backgrounds.

At the beginning of the discussion in both groups, the concept of extreme drinking was explained. Thus, in the Nigerian focus groups, an "extreme drinker" was defined as a male who consumed five or more drinks in a row or a female who consumed four or more drinks in a row at least once in a two-week period (this and the following definitions were not specified by the ICAP guidelines for focus groups—see Annexes 1 and 2—but were applied independently by the authors of this section). An "occasional extreme drinker" was defined as an individual who consumed 5+/4+ drinks one or two times in a two-week period, whereas a "frequent extreme drinker" engaged in this behavior three or more times in a two-week period. A "drink" was defined as 12 ounces of beer, 4 ounces of wine, or a 1.25 ounce shot of distilled spirits. For the sake of simplicity, extreme drinking was equated to drunkenness.

Results

Legal Drinking Age and the Actual Onset of Drinking

Participants in both groups claimed to be unaware of any legal age restrictions for purchasing or drinking alcohol, despite the Federal Government's law setting the official limit at 18 years. Female respondents indicated that they began drinking between the ages of 12 and 18 years. Similarly, the age of onset among male respondents varied from 10 to 18 years. The average age of drinking onset for men and women can be put at 15 years, the median and modal age suggested by the two groups.

Types of Alcohol Consumed

Beer was the most prevalent alcohol beverage used by young men, followed by palm wine and spirits. Among young women, alcohol drinks mixed with a variety of fruit juices ("teezers") were more frequently used than beer. The consumption of local beverages appeared to be diminishing among youths in both groups. This may be attributed to the current high availability of commercially produced alcohol products.

Influences on Drinking Behavior

The consensus among members of the two groups was that most young people drink under the influence of their peers—and, to a lesser extent, their parents—or in an attempt to solve emotional problems.

Fathers seemed to play a particularly important role in young people's first taste of alcohol. For instance, according to a female participant,

> I was influenced by my dad—anytime he is drinking, he offers me a small quantity. I was about 6 years old when I had the first experience.

Parental influence was also discussed in the male group, with one young man noting,

> I used to taste beer at my father's meetings which he hosted. I have always felt there is something good or special in alcohol.

For others, the first experience came with friends: "I started drinking with a couple of friends," said one young woman, as a male respondent recounted, "For me, I started drinking because of my friends." Experimentation and self-discovery were common themes during these early drinking episodes. For example:

> I have watched my father drinking as a child. When I was 14 years old, I decided to experiment with my father's "stuff" when he was away. I wanted to know what effects alcohol would have on me. I got hooked to this self-experimentation whenever I was alone at home. (Male)

In terms of peer pressure, men in particular reported that they drink not to be left out, to appear important to their peers, and because it is seen as one of the attributes of being with friends. According to one male discussant,

When you go to a party and alcohol (beer) is served and everybody takes theirs, you now look somehow odd if they have to go and look for soft drinks for you. Next time they go to a party, you will be left out as you will be described as "not being the type," "not being a big boy," or "not being up to their level."

Another young man noted,

When I come home during holidays, my friends and I have a lot to do together and drinking together is just one of them.

The choice of alcohol beverage was also primarily dependent on the preferences of peers, and drinking could be opportunistic. As one male participant explained:

Actually, some people drink because of their friends—like me, when I see most of my friends taking [local beer brand], I better join them though I prefer [another beer brand]. I simply join them because there will be more of the [local beer brand] available and I drink a lot.

In addition, the participants in both groups talked about the influence of alcohol advertising on their positive attitude toward alcohol use. For example, one young female respondent said:

Whenever I watch the advert on [a beer brand], it gives me the impression that it is a tonic, that is good for the body... [The advertisement says,] "It is good for you. It is black, it is good, it gives strength, it is beautiful. It is good for you."

The glamorization of alcohol in videos, films, and television seemed to attract young adults to alcohol.

Although social drinking was prevalent in both groups, drinking alone was also mentioned. This behavioral pattern was attributed to attempts to solve emotional problems, as captured in the following response in the male group:

The most common scenario is when one has a problem, you know, depression. There was a girl I was crazy about, really crazy. Suddenly, she just took off and I just couldn't believe it. That day, I continued drinking alone in my room until I passed out and I slept it off. So most times it depends on your mood, especially when you are depressed.

Overall, both groups indicated that drinking typically took place at weekends, so occasional consumption was the predominant pattern. Drinking occasions were described in mostly positive terms. For instance, one male discussant declared, "Drinking is fun. I will drink every day if I have the money," whereas, according to a female participant, "A good night out is to drink, go to a club, to eat, and catch my fun.... I like to drink."

Drinking and Sexual Behavior

Most members of the two groups mentioned increased libido and lowering of inhibitions in sexual behavior after drinking. They were also of the opinion that taking alcohol enhanced sexual performance. Twelve out of 16 male participants (75%) said that they felt more confident talking to women when drunk:

> When I am drunk is when I have the guts to "toast" [chat up] any woman I like. If I am not drunk, I cannot do such.

> Drinking disinhibits and you feel free to do other things. And, if she would not mind, I can take it to any level, even at the same spot. When you take alcohol to a level, you have better sex because the erection is prolonged.

One of the major consequences of drinking, as expressed directly by 10 out of 16 male respondents (62.5%), was their ability to have better sexual experiences.

Female respondents also indicated that drinking enhanced their sexual ability:

> When I take alcohol, I feel high... [I] discovered that, if I drink, I have good sex, and if I don't, the sex is not good.

> I drink before I have sex because I am fat and I don't move easily to have good sex [otherwise].

> If my boyfriend says I'm not good in bed, I will take alcohol to impress [him] because it enhances my sexual performance.

Use of Other Substances

In both focus groups, differing views were expressed on the relationship between alcohol and the use of illegal drugs. Some of the participants thought that youths who smoke cigarettes were more likely to progress to illegal drugs than those who drink ("...people who smoke are more likely to try Indian hemp than people who drink").

In general, respondents perceived a stronger link between cigarette smoking and cannabis use than between drinking and cannabis use. As one female participant told us,

> When I got to 100 level [the first year of college], I started smoking cigarettes and later tried weed [cannabis]. Later, I stopped smoking [cigarettes] when I started having chest pains, but I didn't really stop smoking weed.

However, among men, out of the nine respondents who gave their opinions on the use of cannabis when drinking, four felt that alcohol plays the same role as cannabis and that the two together give a faster feeling of "being high":

Cannabis actually reduces the number of bottles you take. So, if you normally take 10 bottles of beer, with cannabis you may take only 3 bottles [because] cannabis disturbs your brain.

The essence of drinking beer is to get high...cannabis and cigarettes are [also] involved in getting you high, so they work together. Actually, when you want to drink and don't have enough money, after taking one or two bottles, you might use cannabis to achieve the high.

Both male and female participants referred to the tendency to smoke cigarettes during drinking, especially if alcohol consumption was heavy. As one young woman put it,

I think drinking is incomplete without smoking. Smoking plus drinking is equation balanced!

Apart from cigarettes and cannabis, no other substances were associated with alcohol consumption.

Reasons for Drinking to Get Drunk

The general impression in both groups was that getting drunk helped people feel "on top of the world," relax, increase fluency of speech, and cope with problems. One male participant said, "Getting drunk makes a person feel confident and bold to do what you can't do when you are sober." A female discussant noted that getting drunk helped her forget misfortunes or get over problems. Yet, respondents from both groups accepted that it is fun to drink without getting drunk:

When you are drunk, you can destroy things and behave badly, so it is better to drink without getting drunk.

Extreme Drinking

About 60% of the participants in both groups claimed that extreme drinking happened when alcohol was free:

Most young people only get drunk when the drinks are cheap or free.

I think when young people go out to drink, they really don't want to get drunk, only to get tipsy, but when the drinks are free, they overdo it.

A third of male discussants said they drank excessively to "increase their boldness or courage to meet the challenges of life":

It depends on your mood and the environment. For example, if someone owes you money, you may purposely get drunk so that you can be bold enough to talk anyhow, or if you are going to ask a girl out, you may also get drunk to build up your courage.

Drinking to excess usually happened with friends, as described by one participant:

As for me, I only get drunk whenever I am happy or if something good happens to me. I just call some of my friends so that we will refresh together.

The respondents in both groups also indicated that one could drink more than planned, particularly if friends declare that the drinks are free:

You go out to have a few bottles, say two bottles of beer, but you run into a friend who has just "hit pay" [received his paycheck] and he invites everybody to drink on him, "serve them round," so you generally will drink more than you intended to. Anyway, you know people like that will not give you money, so you had better drink the free beer offered by him. (Male)

According to both focus groups, the situation influenced drinking behavior:

The party environment encourages drinking a lot more than you planned for. (Female)

Getting drunk might come out of competition, we might decide to test who can drink more than the others among us. (Male)

Reasons to Drink Moderately

Participants in both groups tended to limit their drinking in the presence of parents:

I take a little alcohol when I am at home so that my parents, especially my dad, will not think I drink too much, but, at school, I can take as much as I want. (Female)

Among men, the following statement was a good example of the common sentiment:

At times, I drink little, so that my parents would not suspect that I take alcohol. (Male)

All women also indicated that they tried to control the amount of alcohol consumed in the presence of men, "so that boys will not take advantage of them, such as raping them or messing them up [sexually assaulting them]." It was the consensus among male participants that they "drank a little" when they did not have enough money or when they were sick. In both groups, few had attempted to stop drinking either on doctor's advice or because of other complications.

Risky Behavior Associated with Extreme Drinking

Some of the risky behaviors that both groups associated with extreme drinking were: risky sexual conduct (for instance, engaging in unplanned or unsafe sexual activity); violent behaviors (such as committing vandalism); alcohol-impaired driving; unintended injuries at home (for instance, from falls); embarrassing behavior (e.g., exposing oneself in public); alcohol poisoning; inability to keep up with daily duties (for instance, dropping out of school); and going swimming while alcohol-impaired (with high potential for drowning or incurring injuries).

Reasons to Reconsider Own Extreme Patterns

When asked about the experiences that could cause attitudinal change toward their own extreme drinking, the participants mentioned rape, accidents, anesthesia not working, broken relationships (being jilted) because of drinking, a major embarrassment, and knowledge of parents or religious leaders about the drinking habit. For instance:

> When I was still in the University of Ibadan, I stayed at a boys' quarters at Abadina. We went drinking one night, mixing gin and beer. By the time we came back, we were very drunk and tired. So we took off our shirts, trousers, and boxers, ready to sleep. Then one of us started looking for cigarettes and the rest of us felt the same way. Mama Calabar [a cigarette seller] was just across the road from us but nobody wanted to go over to get it. When I woke up the following morning, I learnt that I went over to purchase cigarettes without my clothes on (naked), that I was actually smoking on my way back to the room. The girls who saw me that night started asking me, "Which kind of beer did you drink last night?" (Male)

After this incident, the respondent felt embarrassed and stopped drinking "for a while."

Looking into the Future

When asked to anticipate future trends related to drinking in Nigeria, nearly all respondents believed that extreme drinking would increase. They gave various reasons for this opinion, for instance:

> It will increase because of the social gatherings we have now. People want to say, "My party was a hit," they want their party to be remembered for something.

> Alcohol use will increase, and, I believe, [the onset of drinking] will be earlier in these younger ones coming after us because of the foundation we, their elder brothers, are laying for them.

Societal or marital problems may also be contributing factors:

> If one has a nagging wife, like in the case of my father now who knows he is coming home to face queries, then he will "take care of himself very well" so that when he gets home, he will just sleep.

The respondents indicated that their drinking patterns do not resemble those of their parents because of changing economic conditions and growing disposable incomes:

> No, I think their own time is quite different from our time. The difference is that during their own time, a boy of 15 was not likely to have N100 [one hundred naira; 1USD = approx.126 naira] on him, but these days 15-year-old boys may have up to several thousands of naira on them. Times have changed.

Discussion

While this study does not represent all the youth of Nigeria, it provides an interesting insight into some of the reasons behind youthful drinking in this country. In this sample, frequent drinking was a common practice, largely influenced by peers and, to a smaller degree, the parents. Curiosity was a common theme, with young people wanting to find out the effects of alcohol on themselves, thereby experimenting and exploring their limits.

According to the participants, drinking by individuals of any age or sex revolves round social occasions, such as weddings, house warming parties, naming ceremonies, and festivals. This supports an earlier finding (Odejide & Odejide, 1999) that a strong link exists in Nigeria between alcohol and pleasure, and draws a picture similar to Netting's 1964 observation of a predominantly convivial drinking pattern.

However, this drinking environment also means that young people may be exposed to alcohol at an early age, and, since drinks at such social events are often free, many youths (whether accidentally or intentionally) drink to excess—indeed, some discussants claimed to go to such events deliberately to get drunk because the alcohol was complimentary or paid for by friends. Moreover, previously abstinent individuals may get initiated into alcohol consumption in the spirit of taking part in the social gathering. These findings are in tune with past studies of drinking patterns in Nigeria, particularly of students in secondary and tertiary institutions, which reported an early onset of drinking among younger generations and noted a pattern of occasional consumption and problem drinking during weekends and when the drink is free (Abiodun, Adelekan, Ogunremi, Oni, & Obayan, 1994; Adelekan, Abiodun et al., 1993; Odejide, 1989; Odejide et al., 1987; Oladimeji & Fabiyi, 1993).

Importantly, in surveys of Nigerian undergraduates in the 1980s, many students reported that they drank because they "enjoy drinking" (Oladimeji & Fabiyi, 1993). This is in accord with our present findings. Moreover, we found no gender differences in the reasons given for alcohol use. Both male and female groups mentioned drinking to enhance their sexual ability, promote boldness in confronting certain social situations (for instance, asking an acquaintance to return the money he or she borrowed), and boost their confidence. Whereas the majority indicated that they drank to socialize, some also drink to cope with problems.

The two groups were in agreement on associating smoking cigarettes with alcohol consumption (and especially heavy drinking), but their opinions on the use of cannabis varied. While some of the discussants felt that cannabis reduced the amount of alcohol use, others indicated that it was an intoxicant that could damage the brain. The claim that alcohol consumption may act as a gateway for the use of psychoactive drugs was not supported by the outcome of the study, but this issue needs further exploration in future research. Uncontrolled sexual behavior, traffic crashes and other unintentional injuries, social misbehavior, drinking oneself into a stupor, and family disruptions were common consequences of excessive drinking mentioned by the participants. Previous research has similarly identified these complications (e.g., Odejide & Odejide, 1999).

When the respondents' future drinking pattern was discussed, the consensus was that episodes of extreme drinking would continue as long as social events continue. It is therefore essential to promote prevention methods that take into account local cultural perspectives (Whitehead, 1996). As noted above, a strong link between alcohol and pleasure is evident in Nigeria. However, although there is tacit approval for drinking, drunkenness is forbidden. Odejide and Odejide (1999) underscored this: "The general attitude towards drinking was summed up in the words, 'A person with good upbringing can drink but he must not drink to excess'" (p.343). Ohaeri and colleagues' fascinating study (1996) of alcohol consumption among a nationwide university student club, "The Kegites," is germane to the discussion of pleasurable uses of a traditional alcohol brew, palm wine, within a regulated drinking setting. The authors recommended that elements of the ideals of the Kegites Club, especially its emphasis on discouraging extreme drinking and enforcing rules related to drinking norms, can provide a model for preventive alcohol education. This would strengthen attempts to enforce existing national policies.

References by our focus groups to the effects of advertising on their drinking underscore the need to review existing regulations on responsible alcohol advertisement, which are either partially enforced or nonexistent in Nigeria (WHO, 2004a). Advertising practices that glamorize alcohol consumption may induce young people to experiment prematurely with this substance.

It is equally necessary to create awareness that occasional bouts of extreme drinking among both young people and adults can be hazardous to self and society and to dispel common myths regarding alcohol and sexuality. Finally, a longitudinal study is desirable to identify possible risk factors and outcomes for young persons with early drinking problems.

In short, in order to moderate young people's relationship with alcohol in Nigeria, there must be a change in the social environment that surrounds youth drinking. This can be done by mounting early prevention programs that are ongoing, consistent, and involve all aspects of a child's life—home (fathers and other male relatives in particular), school, and community.

Conclusions

The present two focus groups of young men and women confirmed previous findings and provided further insight into youthful drinking in Nigeria. Although the predominant pattern of consumption is periodic, alcohol is widely used and abused by young people in this country. The age of alcohol onset was found to be low among both genders, possibly because of the influence of the sociocultural environment and lack of enforcement of existing alcohol regulations. To moderate youth drinking culture, it is necessary to devise prevention strategies that combine traditional norms of drinking behavior with modern national policies and enforcement.

RUSSIA

Eugenia A. Koshkina

Despite the current public emphasis on drug use, extreme drinking, particularly among the young, remains a fundamental health and social concern in Russia. Learning about the traditions surrounding alcohol consumption (or abstinence from it) is part of the all-important socialization process experienced by young people. The consequences of problem drinking for this group include immediate medical, psychological, economic, and social problems. Early patterns of extreme consumption may also pose long-term risks, as youths may develop various health problems later in life or have children with birth defects and developmental disabilities. Although extensive information is available on drinking among the general population, further research is needed on young people (Altshuler, 2000; Dmitriyeva, Igonin, Klimenko, Kulagina, & Pishchikova, 2003; Gofman & Ponizovsky, 2005; Ivanets, 2005; Koshkina & Kirzhanova, 2005; Nemtsov, 2003; Pelipas & Miroshnichenko, 2002; Sheregi & Arefiev, 2003). For the purposes of this section, modern qualitative and quantitative methods were used to explore the prevailing aspects of young people's drinking culture and related high-risk behavior. All data discussed here pertain to the capital city, Moscow, and further studies are necessary to determine how these results compare with young people's drinking in other parts of Russia.

Russia's Young People: Quantitative Research

The general atmosphere of permissiveness toward problem drinking has been reflected in largely lax public controls over the issue of drunkenness, encouraging young people's experience with alcohol. Epidemiological studies conducted in Russia in the recent past confirm these trends.

The Russian component of the European School Survey Project on Alcohol and Other Drugs (Hibell et al., 2004) examined the prevalence and patterns of alcohol consumption among 16-year-olds in Moscow's public schools: 2,937 students took part in the study in 1999, and 1,925 were involved in 2003 (Hibell et al., 2004). In 1999, 48.1% of the study's participants were male and 51.9 % female; in 2003, these numbers were 45.7 % and 54.3%, respectively.

The results of the 2003 ESPAD survey for Russia were as follows (Hibell et al., 2004):

- 93% of participants had tried alcohol at least once. The average age of first drink (wine or beer) was 11 years or younger—a significant shift from the 1999 average (14 years of age).
- 39% consumed alcohol "regularly" (defined as lifetime use of 40 times or more).
- Rates of regular alcohol consumption were higher among male than female participants (44% and 34%, respectively).
- In terms of beverage preferences, beer was in the lead, followed by wine and spirits. The prevalence of wine consumption underwent significant changes, however: The percentage of respondents who reported drinking wine increased from 38% in 1999 to 47% in 2003. This was particularly evident among boys, whose consumption grew by 16% since 1999 (up from 30.7% to 46.6%). Increased wine consumption was also noted among girls (up from 45.3% to 53.8%).
- In 2003, about a quarter of respondents reported getting drunk at least once in the last 30 days, and one in 10 was drunk three or more times within that period. According to the same data, 37.8% of respondents reported consuming five or more drinks in a row at least once in the last 30 days, and 16.5% did so three or more times. These patterns of consumption were more prevalent among male participants.

In another 2003 study, Koshkina and colleagues (2004) examined the varying patterns of alcohol consumption among two groups of young Muscovites aged 14 to 21 (Group 1) and 22 to 30 (Group 2). Almost all study participants reported lifetime alcohol consumption of 40 times or more (Group 1: 73.8%; Group 2: 91.1%); and 14.1% in Group 1 and 34% in Group 2 had consumed alcohol 6 to 9 times in the last 30 days. Meanwhile, 11.9% in Group 1 and 22.7% in Group 2 had drunk more than 10 times in the past month.

In Group 1, the majority (74%) consumed a variety of alcohol beverages: 74% said they drank beer, 74% wine, and 53% spirits. Moreover, almost all respondents had experienced alcohol intoxication at least once in their lifetime, and nearly half (48%) had been drunk in the last 30 days. Among Group 2 participants, 91% consumed a variety of alcohol beverages (84% wine, 82% beer, and 70% spirits). Risky patterns of drinking were more prevalent in this older group: Nearly all respondents had drunk to intoxication in their lifetime, and 57% reported being drunk in the last 30 days.

TABLE 5.4 Russia Focus Group: Participants

Gender	Age	Occupation
Female	18	University student, majoring in Russian literature
Male	19	Systems administrator
Male 1	20	Military service
Male 2	20	IT specialist
Female 1	21	Opera singer
Female 2	21	Kindergarten teacher
Female 3	21	Social worker
Female 4	21	English instructor at a university
Female 5	21	Psychologist, Center of Psychological Assistance to Families and Children
Male	22	Jeweler
Female	24	Computer sales manager
Male	25	Interpreter
Male	26	Worker, Moscow power plant
Male	30	Engineer

The Focus Group

In 2005, the Moscow-based National Research Center on Addictions conducted a focus group on young people's health decisions and behaviors with regard to drinking, including the patterns of so-called "extreme drinking." The aims of the research were: to describe drinking behaviors and determine typical consumption models; and to discuss the topic of extreme alcohol intake, its causes, consequences, and related high-risk behaviors. The focus group followed a previously developed scenario (see Annexes 1 and 2), the entire session was tape-recorded, and all participants were guaranteed anonymity.

The group met in Moscow and consisted of 14 participants (7 men and 7 women). The invitation to the study was extended to young adults of legal drinking age (18 years in the Russian Federation), including both alcohol consumers and abstainers. The age of respondents ranged between 18 and 30 years, with an average age of 22.1. Table 5.4 provides a snapshot of the focus group participants.

Results

At the outset, the respondents were asked about their beverage preferences and the age of their first drink. Men mostly consumed spirits, whereas women preferred beverages with lower alcohol content (wine and beer). It was noted that, for men, the first alcohol experience generally occurred around the age of

10 years—on average, four years earlier than that for women (14 years). Beer was the beverage figuring most prominently in these early experiences. As a rule, respondents first tried alcohol either at home (with parents' permission) or among a group of peers (during some celebration):

> My parents let me try a sip of beer at 7. Intentionally, though, I tried wine at 13. (Male, 22)

> I was 13... I tried champagne, during a New Year's celebration. (Female 2, 21)

> [At] 15, I had wine, celebrating [with friends]. Well, it was at my [secondary technical school], we were celebrating the end of the first semester. (Female 1, 21)

Further discussion revealed five broad consumption models, typical for most of the participants.

1. Drinking *during holidays and special events*: The type and quantities of alcohol consumed on such occasions depend on family and/or group traditions; usually, the beverages of choice are wine, champagne, or cognac.

> I drink rarely.... Normally, my friends and I celebrate a successful end of the school term, as it is usually done. I drink about two glasses of wine, not more.... Very often, no celebration goes on without alcohol, in particular, celebrating birthdays and various important dates. Well, for example, when my brother got into one of Moscow's universities, of course, we drank a glass of wine each, but not more than that. (Female 2, 21)

2. *Drinking with colleagues*: This model is also driven by group dynamics and culture, and occasions for drinking vary. As a rule, however, it involves drinking spirits, mostly vodka, often in large quantities:

> I work with a tight-knit group, with [factory] workers, so it's not hard to find a reason to drink. Mostly, of course, we drink vodka.... Some drink until they drop, others—until they run out of vodka.... At a minimum, six bottles [of vodka] are bought for five to ten people. (Male, 30)

3. *Drinking with friends to socialize*: Usually, this involves "weaker beverages" (wine and beer) for regular get-togethers and spirits, especially vodka, on special occasions. The amount consumed is guided by the group dynamic. For instance:

> Usually, I drink with friends. [We drink] during weekends and sometimes after work, also weaker beverages [beer and wine]. It happens about once a week, maybe once in two weeks. With friends, I mostly drink beer, although lately we've started to drink wine more often. (Male, 19)

> Everything depends on the group, on where and with whom you're drinking. If it's fun, then, of course, the party will go on. With another run to the store, if need be.... Then you no longer think of the consequences. (Male, 22)

4. *Drinking in nightclubs*: This involves drinking "to relax," as part of the club culture. Usually, the consumption is confined to beer and cocktails; less frequently, it may include spirits. It must be noted that drinks in such establishments are relatively expensive, which limits the volume consumed in a given venue. However, several participants mentioned drinking at home before going out.

> I now often go to clubs [about twice a week]. And in clubs it's impossible to feel comfortable—you know, feel happy and have a good time—without drinking one or two shots of something strong…like liquor or some cocktail. (Male, 22)

> In clubs, since everything is kind of expensive, I can have one tequila…I guess 40 or 50 grams [of tequila]. I can't [afford to] buy more than one drink. But in general, I drink cocktails or beer. [On an average night at a club], I drink about two bottles of beer [0.3 to 0.5 liter bottles], for example, and one cocktail. (Female, 24)

5. *Drinking beer*: A distinct and prevalent consumption model, particularly among men, is based around drinking beer (one or two bottles at a time), especially after work to relieve fatigue or to relax. Cold beer may also be consumed daily during summer months to help overcome the heat:

> Mostly, I drink beer after work…maybe twice a week. (Male, 25)

> After work, I also sometimes take a bottle of beer. Work can be stressful at times. And, in addition, I have a very long commute home…. So, before I get home, [a bottle of] beer, for example, stimulates the appetite…in order to get back to normal. (Male, 26)

> I drink beer to wind down and be able to sleep after work. If I had to work late, there is all this exhaustion piling up, so, in order to fall asleep more easily, I drink a bottle of beer. And this summer, it was hot, so, you could say, not one day passed without beer. (Male 2, 20)

> I don't really like beer, although sometimes during a hot day, [I may get] some cold beer, but not much, because it is bitter and so on. (Female, 18)

On recounting their perceptions of a "successful drinking occasion," all respondents alluded to drinking in good company and pleasant surroundings, while consuming quality alcohol and without negative consequences:

> For example, I just remembered one particular time: We were drinking Glühwein [mulled wine] in this cozy café with great, close people—and that was really wonderful. (Female 2, 21)

> [A "successful drinking experience"] is when you drink a small amount of alcohol, depending on the situation. I think that there is nothing better than real Stavropol cognac or another good cognac, while having a pleasant conversation and in moderate amounts. (Male 2, 20)

FIGURE 5.6 Three Russian paratroopers drink vodka celebrating National Paratrooper Day in Gorky Park (1993, Moscow, Russia). © Vassily Korneyev/AFP/Getty Images.

> I think, it means drinking without negative consequences. (Female 3, 21)

Interestingly, the absence of negative consequences was mentioned primarily by female participants, who also noted the need for nondrinkers in the group to watch over those who drink: "They are watching out for me and can help if needed" (Female 4, 21). During a drinking session, the behavior of nondrinkers in the group may be followed by those choosing to drink as an example of controlling their own behavior. The quality of the beverage was also considered key to a positive drinking experience, since "there are so many counterfeit products out there" (noted by several participants).

Respondents related the incidence of excessive consumption primarily to the drinker's age: The younger the person, the more likely he or she is to experiment, including with alcohol ("he surrenders to his hormones, and gets 'a high' from any alcohol"). Such experimentation, according to the group participants, normally takes place among the 15 to 25 age group. During this period, reaching intoxication is largely intentional—to show off, "see what it feels like," and "have fun"—but may also be accidental, due to inexperience; this often depends on the surroundings and circumstances:

> I drank alcohol to experiment. But I wasn't drinking excessively, just experimentally. I was curious about how alcohol would affect my state of consciousness, my body. In general, I could always control these sensations, with the exception of those times when I would cross the line intentionally.... (Male 1, 20)

> I just see more young people getting drunk [than older people], and, usually, [such] drinking occurs in groups of 15- to 17-year-olds.... I don't know what the reasons for drinking may be. Maybe, one of the reasons is experimentation, wanting to see what it'd be like, how it feels if you get drunk. Of course, then

you can just transfer responsibility for your actions on to somebody else. And [another reason may be] to show off…. (Female 2, 21)

[University students] drink without, really, any particular goals. Sometimes they drink because they are happy or because they are sad, and sometimes just to get drunk. It's simple to get drunk…just get a couple of boxes of vodka. (Female, 18)

Nearly all participants agreed that purposeful excessive drinking ceases after the age of 25, because of family responsibilities and a realization that negative consequences (for instance, hangovers) are inevitable after such behavior. By that age, people tend to develop a sense of their own limits and self-control. One knows how much to drink and when it is time to stop:

As you become older—I am now over 25—you know how to control yourself and there is no more of this…bravado—you know, out drinking your friend [drinking more than your friend]—this is no longer there, it just goes away, [and] you begin to understand that the consequences [of getting drunk] are inevitable…. (Male, 30)

Getting drunk then becomes largely accidental, due to special circumstances (for instance, "if there are several parties in one evening, it might begin at a nightclub and move to a local park or to someone's apartment" or because of the low quality of the beverage). The leading reasons for excessive consumption among individuals over 25, in the respondents' view, are "drinking to forget" problems, loneliness, drinking to celebrate an important occasion (for instance, getting a new car), and the desire to keep up an acquaintance:

With age…24, 25, 26, so my peers…people drink less, they control themselves more, because they are no longer alone, they have responsibilities with regard to their boyfriend or girlfriend, or family…. I have some [female] friends, though, who get offered alcohol, somebody buys it for them, since they are by themselves, so they can't say no…you know, to keep up the conversation. They drink too much sometimes. But they hope to find someone special—so, I guess, it's from loneliness…. When you are in a couple, when you know that somebody is waiting for you at home… then there is just no reason. But [my friends] are not looking for adventures either, they are kind of worried about each other, actually, when they drink like that…. (Female, 24)

When asked about potential negative consequences of extreme drinking, the group mentioned unmotivated aggression (which may result in fights, brawls, and hooliganism), other reckless behaviors that may endanger the drinker's health and wellbeing, memory loss, "feeling unwell," and engaging in uncharacteristic behaviors. Risky behaviors related to excessive drinking, according to the respondents, are very diverse. Among the leading examples were family violence ("he can get drunk, come home, and beat up his wife and kids"), traffic incidents, and hooliganism, as well as the fact that an intoxicated individual is more likely to get into a number of dangerous situations:

I have an acquaintance, who, for example, cannot stop after just one bottle of beer—he doesn't know what it means to stop…. He has got into some bad situations [after drinking]. Like, when he moved to Moscow from another city and he just got his first paycheck, and he also had his passport and [city residency registration card] with him…. Well, he got drunk and was beaten up and robbed. So, he came to Moscow to earn money but, after that incident, could not stay here and had to leave a month later. (Female 1, 21)

The respondents thought that younger people were more prone to "reckless behavior" after extreme drinking but that the consequences of such consumption might become more serious as individuals grew older.

I think, in this case everything depends on age. After all, people stop doing such extreme things as they get older. It's only when you are young, you get drunk and go crazy—like, going to some supermarket and smashing something, breaking a window, or beating up a passer-by on the street…well, different crazy things. With age, when people drink and get drunk, they focus on their own problems, on themselves. There isn't this wish to go and do something, to show off; people think about all of their problems and there is no longer a desire to "play hero." (Female 4, 21)

…and the older a person gets, the more serious are the consequences… Like, for a young guy…maybe there will be a fight, but it would get resolved somehow, and that's it. With an older guy, he gets drunk, climbs into his car, and hits somebody on the road. (Male, 30)

When asked, "How would you rate—negatively or positively—the consequences of extreme drinking?" all respondents rated them as "negative."

The group participants did not agree on whether or not individuals who drink excessively are also more likely to use drugs. Some thought that those engaging in problem drinking were more likely to try drugs (especially among young people who frequently experiment with altering their state of consciousness); others did not see the connection as inevitable.

All respondents thought that negative personal experiences from drinking, as well as those of others, can influence an individual's motivation to change his or her consumption pattern; eventually, an intention develops to lower the dose of alcohol intake and to control one's own drinking to preserve health. Factors that were seen as being particularly capable of contributing to a decrease in drinking were related to health problems; problems at work; negative reaction from close friends/family; an unpleasant experience involving alcohol, the respondent, or his or her social circle; the fear of developing alcohol dependence ("I don't like to feel dependent, particularly on harmful habits"); and pregnancy and breast-feeding in women.

In describing the situations when they would drink "a little" or "a lot," the respondents agreed on the following behavior patterns. They would drink "a little" on regular or everyday occasions (such as meeting with friends, family celebrations, holidays, or drinking after work, before going to a nightclub) that broadly corresponded to the notion of a "pleasant drinking experience."

On the other hand, they would drink "a lot" on either a very happy or a tragic occasion ("if something really serious happens"). In either case, consumption of significant amounts of alcohol was linked with extraordinary occasions, be they positive or negative in nature. Overall, the definitions of "drinking a little" and "drinking a lot" varied among the group participants, largely influenced by their personal experience and attitudes toward drinking:

> I drink moderately when I meet up with friends, so on a completely ordinary occasion...a bottle of beer, for example. As for drinking a lot...well, that's if something serious happens. Like, if there is some tense situation or if something very important is going on...or just when there is something difficult to deal with...then, yes, I'd drink more...I think, from half a bottle of wine to a full bottle per person. (Female 4, 21)

> You drink a little—say, a bottle of beer or two—when you are with people you don't know well, for self-control, so that you won't mess things up.... And drinking a lot, that's when you are among your circle of friends. Even then, how much "a lot" means depends on the mood. I guess, we'd be drinking vodka. And, again, the amount would depend on the mood...maybe half a bottle per person. (Male, 26)

> "A little" is, for example, a couple of bottles of beer before going to a club, "a lot" is, for example, during a quiet night, when I have the apartment to myself, then I can drink. Eat a little after that and go to sleep. "A lot"—when vodka is concerned—is one bottle, probably, in the course of the night. (Male, 22)

> "A little" for me is one bottle of beer, with friends.... "A lot" is for special occasions, like celebrations, probably three bottles of beer. I don't drink more than that. (Female 5, 21)

Conclusions

On the whole, it may be inferred that the patterns of alcohol consumption among young people are diverse and include: drinking during holidays and special events; drinking with colleagues, depending on traditions within a given group; drinking with friends as the necessary attribute of socializing; drinking in nightclubs, as an attribute of club culture and a means to "relax"; and drinking beer for a variety of different reasons. The age of the first drink is relatively low, the initial drinking experiences taking place within the family or while celebrating with friends. The notion of alcohol as a "reason to get together" or as a routine backdrop for "hanging out" is prevalent among young people, whereas the pattern of drinking primarily during holidays remains widespread among the general public. Beer is still the most popular alcohol beverage type, followed to a lesser degree by various cocktails, which have become prominent attributes of youth and club subcultures; vodka plays an important role on special occasions, particularly in the context of extreme drinking.

The results of our focus group complement recent quantitative data and underscore the need for devoting more attention to young people's drinking through policy and outreach. Such initiatives should be based on realistic assessment, monitoring, and epidemiological data from quantitative and qualitative studies and should include preventive and rehabilitative measures targeted particularly at this group's sometimes excessive consumption patterns and related negative social consequences.

SOUTH AFRICA

Chan Makan

This section aims to add to the understanding of young people's drinking in South Africa, focusing specifically on risky patterns of alcohol consumption. The results of the focus group presented below offer a cultural snapshot that should be viewed within the context of available national data and South Africa's historical and social settings.

Alcohol Consumption in South Africa

The history of alcohol consumption in South Africa is linked to the country's history of apartheid, which legally separated the racial groups in this multiracial society and afforded differential socioeconomic development opportunities based on race classification. Society was divided into four race groups: Whites were placed at the top of the racial hierarchy, followed by "Coloureds" (individuals of mixed ancestry) and Asians, with Blacks at the bottom as fourth-class citizens. The different race groups were confined to their own designated residential and trading areas. Hence, many activities that took place in public spaces, including drinking alcohol, were also mainly conducted in racially segregated settings (Parry & Bennetts, 1999). For instance, selective prohibition was applied to Blacks for many years by the apartheid government in order to force them to purchase all their alcohol beverages from municipally owned beer halls. A consequence of this measure was the mushrooming of illicit drinking venues, *shebeens*, which still exist today and present a tremendous challenge for any attempt to regulate the retail end of the alcohol industry in South Africa (Parry & Bennetts, 1998). According to recent WHO estimates, 46% of all adult alcohol consumption in the country is unrecorded (WHO, 2004b).

The advent of a democratically elected government in 1994 marked the end of apartheid. However, race remains a significant differentiator with respect to drinking patterns, and levels of abstention vary significantly by population groups and gender. Thus, according to the 1998 South Africa Demographic and Health Survey (SADHS), 44.7% of male and 16.9% of female South Africans aged 15 years and older were current drinkers (Department of

Health, 1999; Parry, Plüddemann et al., 2005). When differentiated by race, White men (71%), White women (51%), and Coloured men (45%) reported the highest rates of current alcohol consumption, while African and Asian women reported the lowest rates (12% and 9%, respectively). For both genders, current drinking was more likely among older adults, with the lowest rates in the 15- to 24-year age group. Race—but not gender—differences were also found with regard to risky alcohol consumption (defined as having five or more drinks a day for men or three or more drinks for women): African and Coloured respondents of both genders reported significantly higher prevalence than their Asian and White counterparts. Moreover, the incidence of risky drinking among all survey participants was dramatically higher during weekends than weekdays (a four- to five-fold increase). One-third of all "current drinkers" reported risky levels of consumption during weekends; adults in the middle categories for age (25–34, 35–44, and 45–54 years) were more likely to report the behavior than both the youngest (17–24 years) and the oldest respondents (55–64 and 65+ years).

Several more recent surveys have focused specifically on young South Africans. As in adults, their experience with alcohol varies according to race and gender, boys being more likely to drink and drink excessively than girls, and White and Coloured students more likely to report these behaviors than their Black and Asian peers (Reddy et al., 2003). In general, according to the 2002 South African Youth Risk Behaviour Survey, 49.1% of respondents in grades 8 to 11 (aged between 13 and 19 years) had tried alcohol, and one in eight had his or her first experience before the age of 13 years (Reddy et al., 2003). Moreover, 29.3% of male and 17.9% of female students reported "binge drinking," defined as having five or more drinks in a row on one or more days in the past month (Reddy et al., 2003). Several studies conducted as part of the South African Community Epidemiology Network on Drug Use (SACENDU) Project focused on risky youthful drinking in certain urban areas. Thus, in Port Elizabeth, 58% of male and 43% of female students in grades 8 to 11 reported consuming five or more drinks on at least one occasion in the two weeks before the study (Parry, Bhana et al., 2002). Among 11th graders in Cape Town and Durban, such consumption was reported by 36.5% of male and 18.7% of female students and 53.3% of male and 28.9% of female students respectively.

Although, in general, young South Africans may exhibit lower levels of risky drinking than their older counterparts, this group's relationship with alcohol has been emphasized by researchers, given the link between youthful problem drinking and academic failure (Flisher, Parry, Evans, Muller, & Lombard, 2003), victimization (Morojele & Brook, 2006), risky sexual behavior (Morojele et al., 2006), and unintended injuries, for instance, related to alcohol-impaired driving (Matzopoulos, 2005; Peden, 2001; Peden et al., 1996).

The Focus Group

To participate in the focus group, individuals had to be over South Africa's legally mandated drinking age of 18 years and be consumers of alcohol. Although 21 potential participants were initially recruited, only 10 could attend the focus group session. The average age of the sample was 22 years. The 10 respondents comprised seven males and three females, with a racial mix of five Black (meaning of indigenous African origin), three White (meaning of Caucasian origin), and two Asian (meaning of south-east Asian origin). It should be noted that this group was not intended to be representative of South Africa's youth. All recruits were students from the same university, in the province of Western Cape, which is just one of nine provinces in the country. However, the responses provided below can add to our understanding of how some young South Africans view alcohol and describe their relationship with it.

Results

"Typical" Drinking Experiences

Nine of the 10 focus group participants had their first drink between the ages of 13 and 16 years, only one respondent reporting a drinking debut at the age of 19. Most participants described a typical drinking experience as "socializing." The most common drinking settings mentioned were "while watching sports" and during "clubbing" (in nightclubs).

When speaking about their typical drinking experiences and the average amount of alcohol consumed during a drinking session, the group members

FIGURE 5.7 Friends drinking at a shebeen in Soweto, South Africa (1991). © Gideon Mendel/Corbis.

appeared to believe that the extent of peer respect was proportional to one's capacity for alcohol consumption. Each respondent claimed to drink more alcohol on average than the amount claimed by the previous respondent. A degree of exaggeration, therefore, needs to be taken into account when considering the participants' responses relating to the amount of drinking. Claims normally indicated having five to six beers (340 ml per "beer") in one sitting, with some interesting examples: a soccer club team was said to consume between three and four cases of beer (each case comprising 24 cans of 340 ml) after Sunday league games; and a female respondent claimed, with obvious bravado, to regularly share 30 quarts (1 quart equaling 750 ml) of beer with five friends. "Happy hour" promotions that offer two drinks for the price of one were mentioned in some cases as a factor influencing consumption.

Extreme Drinking, Drinking to Get Drunk, and Drunkenness

There was consensus in the focus group that "most" young people engage in extreme drinking and often "drink to get drunk." However, defining such behavior, or how much one has to consume to be considered "drunk" proved difficult. Most participants linked "getting drunk"—and extreme drinking in general—to the type of alcohol consumed. One respondent mentioned that a particular brand of beer always makes her "very drunk." Another said that his body "suddenly tells" him, "You are now drunk."

Being "loud," "talking a lot," and being "much more outgoing than usual" were the main behaviors the participants associated with extreme consumption and drunkenness. According to a female respondent, "many people become very affectionate" as they drink to excess, clarifying that this did not necessarily have a sexual connotation. In comparing the behavior of intoxicated men with that of intoxicated women, one (male) respondent noted that men sometimes become aggressive and want to fight, whereas another (also male) added that "women get very rowdy." The women in the group did not express disagreement with these observations.

All group participants reported that they had been drunk at some time in their life. The majority claimed to have been drunk to the point of needing to vomit, and agreed that it made them "feel terrible." Most respondents also reported that they always have regrets after drinking to excess and usually vow never to drink again. However, according to the sample, such vows do not last beyond the next day or the next weekend. Alcohol-free days in this focus group were restricted mainly to university examination days.

The extent to which extreme drinking played a role in the lives of the group participants was illustrated by their definition of a "successful" drinking experience. Descriptions ranged from "when the drinks run out" and "when you don't run out of money" to "when you don't lose control," "when you remember your night (out)," "when you are just happy," and "when you can still drive home." However, the majority of participants believed that most young people plan to get drunk before they begin their drinking session.

Risks Associated with Extreme Drinking

Awareness of potential risks associated with extreme drinking was probed extensively by the focus group moderators. When asked whether, in their opinion, extreme drinkers have a tendency to use drugs or break the law, some agreed that this was so. One participant said, "I have a friend, and when he is drunk, he starts smoking *dagga* (marijuana)...which I never saw him do before...I don't know where he gets it, but he is more accepting when he is drunk." However, not all in the group agreed that this is always the case. Some participants insisted that no matter how drunk they are, they know what they are doing "at all times."

The focus group was then asked to discuss personal negative experiences and consequences related to extreme drinking. According to one male participant, "I told my woman to hit the road, to get the hell out." He regretted his behavior the following day but could not reach her to apologize. Another respondent remembered driving with his friends, "totally drunk," and getting into a confrontation with another car, which had the right of way. The confrontation was observed by the police, and the respondent and his friends were arrested, spending a night in police custody for alcohol-impaired driving. Another example was that of a female respondent who "fooled around" with a gun while she was drunk. Although she did not discharge it and no one was hurt during the episode, she still does not know whether the gun was loaded. A male participant said, "When I get drunk, I want to go swimming... This is a stupid thing to do because there are crocodiles and hippos in the river, but you feel like you are invincible when you are drunk, so you do it. I do it." Finally, another male respondent mentioned that he was involved in a serious car crash while intoxicated. Although his friend was driving during the incident, the experience taught him never to drive after drinking and never to allow his friends to drive while drunk.

Regarding some of the negative physical outcomes, such as suffering from a hangover, generally feeling sick, and vomiting, most respondents felt that they "didn't mind dealing with it." The consensus in the group was that "little things" can be done to ameliorate or avoid these effects. For instance, some participants claimed that they know which drinks give a bad hangover, and so they simply avoid those drinks.

More specific questions were posed on risk awareness and the negative experiences that could motivate young people to give up or minimize alcohol consumption. "Having a near-death experience" and "surviving a bad injury" were listed as potential motivators for drinking less. In our sample, even severe health problems and a history of negative experiences were not seen as reasons enough to become abstinent. The participant who related his involvement in a serious car crash was asked whether that was reason enough to stop drinking or to drink less. His response was, "It is [reason enough not to drink or to drink less] for a short while, but you are going to drink as much anyway…you just know not to get into a car. Unconsciously [subconsciously], you got that at the back of your mind." Other responses were: "such an experience can make you more scared" and "my friend was diagnosed with a condition, tuberculosis, and the doctor had asked him not to drink anymore, but this didn't stop him from drinking."

Influences on Extreme Drinking

Overall, focus group participants described extreme drinking as a relatively common behavior. An exploration of the factors contributing to extreme drinking was attempted to establish the underlying causes for this pattern of alcohol consumption. When asked whether it would be as enjoyable if one were to drink without "getting plastered," some participants confirmed that it would still be enjoyable because of the socializing that would accompany drinking. However, others disagreed, saying that it "would not be as much fun" since people around them would be more intoxicated. When asked how one assessed that others were more intoxicated, the response was: "You just know by looking at them."

Most participants claimed to feel happy during drinking occasions. Further probing elicited responses such as drinking "makes you have more fun," "makes you feel more relaxed," "makes you more confident," and "helps you get your groove on" (insinuating a sexual connotation, judging from the participant's body language). Despite the wide range of responses, everyone agreed that peer influences played the central role in the participants' decision to drink and how much to drink.

When asked whether the group members or their friends drank when they were sad, bored, or had a problem, the response was in the affirmative among all group members.

On the question of the taste of alcohol, as one of many influences on young people's decision to drink, most participants—and especially the female respondents—claimed not to like the taste of alcohol unless it was sweet.

When asked whether they thought that people drank alcohol because it made them seem older and more sophisticated, one participant explained that, where he came from (Guglethu, a township in Cape Town), "drinking in public with a group of people is seen as a cool thing and there is prestige… young boys will try and emulate that behavior, which is very stupid." Another group member mentioned that she began drinking when she was "in standard 8" (approximately 15 years of age) and that it was "mainly just a rebellion thing," although her parents do not object to her drinking now. She mentioned that she used to drink with friends in a field close to home, which was "very exciting," and explained that, where she lived (in George, a town some 600 km from Cape Town), there was no recreational facility to which she could otherwise go.

Probing family history relating to alcohol consumption elicited a wide range of responses. No pattern in family drinking history explained why the focus group participants consumed alcohol. Responses from participants whose parents did consume alcohol ranged from youths who did not drink in their parents' presence out of respect (a feature of African culture, as pointed out by the Black members of the group) to those who frequently drank with their parents. Among participants whose parents were abstainers, responses ranged from parents not objecting to their children's drinking to parents expressing strong disapproval. In the latter case, it appeared that the parents were not necessarily aware of their children's actual drinking patterns, and young people had a tendency to drink because it was forbidden.

When asked whether extreme drinking was socially acceptable for young people of their age, the group members could not provide a clear answer at first. One of the participants suggested that it was "fine," as long as one did not embarrass oneself, to which there was agreement from the others. This seeming consensus was challenged by one participant, however, who questioned whether extreme drinking was not, in fact, drinking to the point where one embarrasses oneself. Many in the focus group appeared to agree with this definition as well. Clearly, therefore, there was confusion about exactly what was meant by "extreme drinking." It was also clear that the majority did not see themselves as doing anything wrong by drinking (irrespective of how much) as long as they were "in control." It was equally clear that the majority of the focus group did not think of their friends negatively when they saw them drunk. One male participant added that he gets "envious" of friends when he sees them drunk, and went on to say that "you cannot look down on them because you know you have been there before."

Concepts of Extreme Drinking and Moderate Drinking

In an attempt to gain a better insight into the participants' understanding of the concept "extreme drinking," the question was asked whether it was acceptable for older people to drink as much as younger people do (or claim to do) today. Most in the group found that to be unacceptable. The main reason presented was that older people have more responsibilities. One participant elaborated by adding that it would not be acceptable, especially if one had a family.

Many in the group believed that in the days when their parents were young, they did not have access to alcohol as easily as today. Hence, they did not necessarily consume alcohol in excess, if at all. This response was particularly illustrative of Black group members, whose parents' access to alcohol was legally limited under apartheid.

The concept of drinking in "moderate quantities" (or "drinking a little") was not completely alien to the participants in the focus group. When asked about the types of settings in which young people chose to drink in moderate quantities as opposed to those where young people chose to drink in excess, participants consistently answered that it was dependent on "where you are" and "with whom you are." Two drinking contexts that were perceived to encourage moderate consumption were: when eating food or having a *braai* (a South African word for barbecue) and, as reported by male participants, when going out for dinner with one's girlfriend and her mother.

When probed further on whether there was a feeling of satisfaction or dissatisfaction associated with moderate consumption, one response was: "... when old people are around, and you are drinking...sometimes you can't wait to get out of there." Generally, lack of money limited the amount of drinking. Another interesting response was that sometimes, when the participant felt tired, she "drank a little bit" because she "didn't feel like drinking any more."

Conclusions

As a qualitative study, the results of this focus group are but a cultural snapshot that may illustrate statistics on young people's drinking in South Africa. The tendency of the participants to exaggerate their level of alcohol consumption notwithstanding, it would be safe to conclude that extreme drinking behavior is a norm among young people represented by the focus group. This behavior is peer-driven, and intoxication is seen to provide physical and social rewards. A perceived absence of responsibilities, compared to those carried by older people, is offered as justification for the behavior. Although a limited awareness of the risks associated with extreme drinking was demonstrated by many young people, many potential negative outcomes—in keeping with adolescent behavior—are generally dismissed as "insignificant." These attitudes and the general lack of awareness of alcohol's effects on the body are causes for concern and should be addressed by preventive measures.

SCOTLAND, UNITED KINGDOM

Stephen March

This section builds upon the results of a focus group on young people's drinking, conducted in Glasgow in August 2005 by Alcohol Focus Scotland (AFS). It applies secondary research and empirical data to test the extent to which the focus group's responses align with recent United Kingdom and Scottish data.

A total of 17 people (9 women and 8 men), aged between 18 and 25 years, participated in the study. The focus group was comprised of two full-time bar workers, five students, one casual worker, three manual workers, three office workers, and three professionals. Our findings cannot be further refined because of the guarantee of anonymity requested by the participants. The agreement was that no group member would refuse to answer any of the written questions (based on Annex 2) or would underreport their consumption levels, provided that the responses were nonattributable. The participants were willing to talk as a group about the questions, and that enabled the summary of responses to be analyzed by gender.

The sections that follow describe the context within which this study took place and compare its results with other surveys of young people in Scotland and the United Kingdom. In particular, the findings of the AFS group are discussed against those of the 2006 Scottish Executive survey in Aberdeen, Glasgow, Edinburgh, and Falkirk (Citigate Smarts & McArthur Research, 2006).

Legal and Social Context: Scottish Health Initiatives

The timing of the AFS focus group coincided with a period of high national concern in Scotland at both political and public levels about the extent of excessive drinking in the society, particularly among young people.

Legislative Response: The Licensing (Scotland) Act 2005

Scotland's extreme alcohol consumption manifests itself in antisocial behavior, public safety challenges, and serious health consequences. The Licensing (Scotland) Act 2005, which addresses excessive or illegal alcohol consumption and retailing across all age groups, summarizes Scotland's concerns about problem drinking in its five key principles: preventing crime and disorder; securing public safety; preventing public nuisance; protecting and improving public health; and protecting children from harm (Her Majesty's Stationery Office, 2005). Thus, only the fifth principle deals specifically with young people, providing for new penalties and enforcement regimes for sales to—or purchases made on behalf of—underage drinkers.[5]

The Act, which requires bar staff to undergo training every five years to obtain and retain a personal license (effectively that person's license to work in the bar trade), expressly prohibits:

- a person who is already drunk from entering licensed premises (although "drunkenness" is not defined in the legislation, a longstanding case law definition is "having taken intoxicating liquor to the extent that it affects one's steady self-control"—in other words, when one's sensory impairment becomes apparent to the surrounding individuals);
- serving a person who is drunk;
- irresponsible promotions, such as "Happy Hours" and "2 for the price of 1" offers that fuel immoderate drinking;

---

[5] The minimum age for purchase and consumption of beverage alcohol in bars and off-license premises is 18 years in the United Kingdom. The minimum purchase age for certain drinks, however, is 16 when bought for consumption with meals in restaurants or pubs with separate eating areas. These drinks are beer, perry, cider and, in Scotland, wine (for a table showing minimum legal age limits internationally, see the ICAP Web site: http://icap.org/PolicyIssues/YoungPeoplesDrinking/AgeLawsTable/tabid/219/Default.aspx).

- the sale of alcohol with takeout orders and food deliveries (for instance, with pizza ordered by phone for home delivery), unless the vendor can prove that the purchaser is aged over 18 years.

Political Initiatives: Engaging Society in Tackling Problem Drinking

Many keynote speeches were made in 2005 and 2006 on the topic of "binge" drinking. These speeches supported the legislation (Licensing [Scotland] Act 2005) and the practical measures that gave local communities, including parents and schools, a credible voice in tackling this issue. Scotland's Deputy Health Minister, Lewis Macdonald, summed up the sentiment:

> We are attempting to change a centuries-old booze culture—clearly such a change cannot be achieved overnight. Government does have a role to play in tackling alcohol-related problems, but each and every one of us has a responsibility to recognise the effects of alcohol and to drink sensibly. Scottish ministers are committed to working with a range of bodies such as the NHS [National Health Service], the licensed trade, schools, parents, and the police to achieve a major cultural shift in attitudes towards drinking. ("Drink Culture Death Rate Warning," 2006, para. 7–9)

Health Advertising

Traditional Scottish hospitality is legendary, and the "rounds culture" (where people feel pressure to buy drinks for the group and drink the rounds bought by others) is well established. Being drunk (but gregarious) is acceptable conduct; likewise, to be described as "a wee alkie" is to be accepted. This rather affectionate term explains and excuses behavior that would not be tolerated from sober individuals.

The Scottish Executive recognized the "rounds culture" in Scotland's excessive alcohol consumption and in the consequent combination of antisocial behavior and unintended injuries. As a result, an advertising campaign was launched in August 2006, entitled "Alcohol: Don't Push It," which highlighted the fact that buying your round was at least as likely to do your friend harm as it was to be a beneficial, social gesture. Several months after the launch of the campaign, Andy Kerr, Scottish Health Minister, spoke of his determination to eliminate the "rounds culture" in Scotland and to work with the drinks industry to reduce promotions of products such as alcopops that may appeal to the youngest population of drinkers (Kerr, 2006).

Drinking among Young Scots

"Going Out to Get Drunk"

Since the early 1990s, the predominant drinking pattern among many young people in Scotland, and the United Kingdom in general, has been to go out on specified days or occasions with the express intention of getting drunk. This pattern of purposeful drunkenness results in a range of negative outcomes. In 14 focus groups of 9- to 19-year-olds, conducted on behalf of the Scottish Executive in 2001, many respondents reported having fears about or experiencing actual incidences of unsafe sexual encounters, minor crime and vandalism, and a general lack of awareness in connection with drinking occasions when people drink to get drunk (Potter, 2002).

The AFS focus group (discussed below) linked this drinking behavior to the college/university culture of spending a large proportion of available funds on cheap and widely available alcohol in student bars. This also held true for young people who had not undertaken tertiary study: Extreme drinking among friends who had attended college/university convinced them to do likewise. In addition, there is evidence that the team-building ethos in industries and professions where young employees predominate has encouraged a group extreme drinking culture (see chapter 8).

Drinking among Students

A World Health Organization (WHO) study showed that more Scottish girls regularly drink strong alcohol than young women in any other country (Currie et al., 2004). Almost 40% of 15-year-old Scottish girls admitted to consuming spirits each week, compared with 1% in Russia and 7% in the United States. The study reported that Scottish girls have their first drink at the average age of 12 years and that, by the age of 13 they will have experienced their first drunken episode (21.3%). Forty percent of 13-year-old Scots had been drunk on more than one occasion (21.3% female; 19.0% male), as had 6.3% of 11-year-old boys.

By age 15, both England and Scotland reported drunkenness occurring for the first time for 26.9% of young people, but with marginally differing gender percentages (Scotland: 13.4% female, 13.5% male; England: 13.5% female, 13.4% male) (Currie et al., 2004). The percentage of those 15-year-olds who had started drinking at an earlier age and who reported having been drunk twice or more was alarming (51.8% of Scottish females and 51.9% of Scottish males; 54.9% English females and 55.1% English males). The overall figures for 15-year-olds for northern Europe (England, Wales, Scotland, Finland, Denmark, Greenland, Lithuania, and Estonia) were very similar at a combined percentage total for males and females (e.g., 55% males + 60% females = 115) of 104–132.5. These totals were much higher than those for any of the southern and eastern European countries (France: 37; Italy: 39; Russia: 63; Poland: 63; Czech Republic: 66.5). This suggests that it is the traditional attitude and approach to alcohol that causes the problems—"going out to get drunk" in northern Europe rather than "going out to socialize" among south Europeans.

AFS Focus Group Findings and Young People's Drinking Patterns in Scotland

Is the AFS focus group representative of: (1) the average Glasgow young drinker; and (2) the national Scottish young drinker—in other words, is problem drinking in Glasgow different from the rest of Scotland? The results of the AFS focus group are discussed here against the findings of the recent Scottish Executive work with young people (Citigate Smarts & McArthur Research, 2006).

In the Scottish Executive's 2006 Scottish Social Attitudes (SSA) Survey of 300 young adults aged 18 to 35 in Aberdeen, Glasgow, Edinburgh, and Falkirk, 75% of respondents reported that they had "less fun" during an alcohol-free night out; 84% said that drinking was part of their lifestyle; and every Aberdonian interviewed reported a loss of memory during bouts of drunkenness. Finally, 96% of the survey group—288 people— suffered memory loss when drunk.

The AFS focus group reported that drinking was an essential part of socializing because, as one participant put it, "everyone else is drinking and you need to be [drunk] to understand them!" The AFS focus group's feedback on memory loss was limited, but one respondent cited "wanting to remember what happened and how to get home" as a reason for *not* drinking heavily on certain occasions.

In the SSA survey, 56% of all participants were influenced by the amount that others in their group were drinking. Interestingly, the women (68%) in this 56% cohort were more likely to be influenced than the men (43%). Geographical groupings showed that 71% of Glaswegians (but only 41% of Edinburgh interviewees) were likely to be influenced by the consumption of the group of which they were part. This virtually mirrors the responses from the AFS focus group, where two thirds of respondents linked their own drinking to that of peers.

The Scottish culture is to buy drinks in rounds or contribute toward a "drinks kitty." This encourages the practice of keeping pace with the rest of the group for the twin purposes of not losing out on one's contribution to the kitty and also not wishing to appear as a "lightweight." The SSA survey indicated that 28% of men drank because they did not want to appear as a lightweight; this was an issue for 21% of women. It is possible to conclude that, especially for young males, alcohol consumption is linked to their manhood (virility) rather than concerns about liver (cirrhosis) or brain (alcohol-related brain damage, ARBD).

Six (35%) of the AFS focus group participants (4 men and 2 women) reported that their drinking was "*moderate* to *a lot.*" The younger respondents from the AFS focus group said that they regularly socialized together in pubs and clubs, and they did so with the express intention of getting drunk. This involved the rounds culture, contribution to the kitty, and keeping pace with fellow drinkers. Overall, 47% of the AFS focus group members were male, and a 50/50 split occurred between those men who purposefully participated

FIGURE 5.8 Soccer fan. © Jeff J. Mitchell/Getty Images (2006).

in the "rounds/kitty" practice and those who did not set out to keep pace with other drinkers, but did so subconsciously because "someone had got a round in and I lost track because I was chatting/singing/dancing."

Among SSA survey participants, 59% had incurred serious debt during the preceding 12 months because of alcohol consumption. There was no further inquiry on whether the debt also related to loss of earnings from alcohol-induced absence. However, when thinking of the preceding year, 73% reported taking time off work or study because of hangovers.

Two-thirds of the AFS focus group drank in a group "until the money ran out or the lights went out" (lost consciousness), the general consensus being that they would have continued drinking if they had not either been physically sick or had not run out of money. There was no hint of peer pressure, rather a willingness to conform to group behavior norms—and this again surfaced in buying drinks in rounds.

In the SSA survey, 33% of Glaswegians (the highest percentage) reported that they did not feel in control of how much they were drinking; 65% of respondents agreed with the definitive quote: "If I'm drinking in rounds, I find it more difficult to control how much I drink." Seventy-five percent of all women surveyed agreed with this statement, as did 74% of Glaswegians of both sexes.

Nine (53%) of the AFS focus group participants—seven men and two women—reported that peer *behavior* (but not peer pressure) led to a group decision on what was seen as "being drunk," rather than the individual making a conscious decision about the limit. This ties in with the "Everyone else is drinking and you need to be [drunk] to understand them" response from the AFS focus group, cited above. The smaller size of the AFS sample distorts gender percentage comparisons. It is possible that the 75% of females from the larger survey may have included one or more "hen parties" (all-female groups of drinkers) where the rounds culture is similar to that of the men, but this observation is intuitive rather than evidence-based.

According to the SSA survey, 88% of the Glaswegian contingent (of both sexes) admitted to drinking more on a night out than they had intended, and 84% of the female respondents reported excessive consumption as a concern. In contrast, only 58% of the male respondents felt that such drinking was a concern. When the SSA survey asked whether Scotland's "drinking culture" bothered the interviewees, 42% of the sample was "bothered," 53% "did not consider it," and 5% was actually "proud of it."

These results were consistent with the AFS focus group respondents, who felt that it was acceptable to drink to excess when young, without fears for long-term health, with an air of immortality, and with the conviction that they would reduce consumption when they became old ("over 30," because it was not considered "cool" to be "old and drunk").

The SSA survey found that 4% of those questioned had been arrested during the preceding year, despite knowing of the risk to the individual's health, gaining a criminal record, the impact upon public safety and public order, and the cost to the public purse of the police time in dealing with the incidents and arrests.

Seven (41%) of the AFS respondents (4 male; 3 female) reported drinking when sad or when they had problems—this was the nearest question to the SSA survey item regarding health risks and criminal/antisocial behavior. The AFS focus group reported, however, that friends and family almost universally regarded drunkenness as preferable to drug use. This partly reflects the AFS focus group's socioeconomic grouping—most were from the more affluent areas of greater Glasgow.

Conclusions

Overall, the SSA survey and AFS focus group responses were similar in tone and intent, although the differing sizes of the groups rendered percentage comparisons meaningless. The results of the SSA survey and a summary of the expert opinions cited in this section indicate that the AFS focus group responses were representative of young people's drinking habits in Scotland. Overall, our findings are as follows:

• Drinking regularly and excessively is viewed by many young Scots as a rite of passage.
• Social drinking in groups as part of the rounds culture is the norm, peak consumption occurring during weekends.

- Behavior deteriorates as drunkenness takes over and minor trouble/ arrests are viewed as an integral part of the process.
- Getting into debt or never having any money because of alcohol consumption is seen by young people as the cost of the rite of passage.
- The majority were of the opinion that, "You'll grow out of [extreme drinking] before it does you any harm, and we're not bothered about the health messages whilst we're young!"

REFERENCES

Abiodun, O. A., Adelekan, M. L., Ogunremi, O. O., Oni, G. A.., & Obayan, A.O. (1994). Pattern of substance use among secondary school students in Ilorin, Northern Nigeria. *West African Journal of Medicine*, *13*, 91–97.

Adelekan, M. L., Abiodun, O. A., Imouokhome-Obayan, A. O., Oni, G. A., & Ogunremi, O. O. (1993). Psychosocial correlates of alcohol, tobacco, and cannabis use: Findings from a Nigerian university. *Drug and Alcohol Dependence*, *33*, 247–256.

Adelekan, M. L., Makanjuola, A. B., Ndom, R. J., Fayeye, J. O., Adegoke, A. A., Amusan, O., et al. (2001). Five-yearly monitoring of trends of substance use among secondary school students in Illorin, Nigeria, 1988–1998. *West African Journal of Medicine*, *20*, 28–36.

Altshuler, V. B. (2000). Alcoholism in women. In N. N. Ivanets (Ed.), *Lectures on addiction* (pp. 116–134). Moscow, Russian Federation: Knowledge. [Альтшулер, В.Б. (2000). Женский алкоголизм. Под ред. Н. Н. Иванца, *Лекции по наркологии* (с. 116–134). Москва, РФ: Нолидж/Knowledge.]

Borini, P., Oliveira, C. M., Martins, M. G., & Guimarães, R. C. (1994). Padrão de uso de bebidas alcoólicas de estudantes de medicina (Marília, São Paulo): Parte I [Average beverage alcohol use among medical students (Marília, São Paulo): Part I]. *Jornal Brasileiro de Psiquiatria*, *43*, 93–103.

Carlini, E. A., Galduróz, J. C. F., Noto, A. R., & Nappo, S. A. (2002). *Levantamento domiciliar sobre o uso de drogas no Brasil 2001 [Household survey on drug use in Brazil 2001]*. São Paulo, Brazil: Centro Brasileiro de Informações sobre Drogas Psicotrópicas, Departamento de Psicobiologia da Escola Paulista de Medicina e SENAD, Secretaria Nacional Antidrogas, Presidência da República, Gabinete de Segurança Nacional.

Citigate Smarts & McArthur Research. (2006). *Survey on drinking habits of 300 young people (aged 18 to 35 years) in Edinburgh, Glasgow, Aberdeen, and Falkirk*. Unpublished report, commissioned by the Scottish Executive.

Cottino, A. (1995). Italy. In D. B. Heath (Ed.), *International handbook on alcohol and culture* (pp. 156–167). Westport, CT: Greenwood Press.

Currie, C., Roberts, C., Morgan, A., Smith, R., Settertobulte, W., Samdal, O., et al. (Eds.). (2004). *Young people's health in context. Health Behaviour in School-aged Children (HBSC) study: International report from the 2001/2002 survey*. Health Policy for Children and Adolescents No. 4. Copenhagen, Denmark: WHO Regional Office for Europe.

D'Alessio, M., Baiocco, R., & Laghi, F. (2006). The problem of binge drinking among Italian university students: A preliminary investigation. *Addictive Behaviors*, *31*, 2328–2333.

Department of Health. (1999). Adult health risk profiles. In *South Africa Demographic and Health Survey 1998* (chapter 13, pp. 229–249). Retrieved May 23, 2007, from http://www.doh.gov.za/facts/index.html.

Dmitriyeva, T. B., Igonin, A. L., Klimenko, T. V., Kulagina, N. E., & Pishchikova L. E. (2003). *Psychoactive substance abuse (clinical and legal aspects)*. Moscow, Russian Federation: MNTs Infokorrektsia. [Дмитриева, Т. Б., Игонин, А. Л., Клименко, Т. В., Кулагина, Н. Е., Пищикова, Л. Е. (2003). *Злоупотребление психоактивными веществами (клинические и правовые аспекты)*. Москва, РФ: МНЦ Инфокоррекция.]

Donato, F., Assanelli, D., Marconi, M., Corsini, C., Rosa, G., & Monarca, S. (1994). Alcohol consumption among high school students and young athletes in north Italy. *Revue Epidémiologique de la Santé Publique, 42,* 198–206.

Drink culture death rate warning. (2006, January 5). *BBC News Online*. Retrieved May 5, 2007, from http://news.bbc.co.uk/2/hi/uk_news/scotland/4585584.stm.

Flisher, A. J., Parry, C. D. H., Evans, J., Muller, M., & Lombard, C. (2003). Substance use by adolescents in Cape Town: Prevalence and correlates. *Journal of Adolescent Health, 32,* 58–65.

Galduróz, J. C., & Caetano, R. (2004). Epidemiologia do uso de álcool no Brasil [Epidemiology of alcohol use in Brazil]. *Revista Brasileira de Psiquiatria, 26,* 3–6.

Galduróz, J. C. F., Noto, A. R., Fonseca, A. M., & Carlini, E. A. (2004). *Levantamento nacional sobre o consumo de drogas psicotrópicas entre estudantes do ensino fundamental e médio da rede pública de ensino nas 27 capitais Brasileiras* [National survey on the consumption of psychotropic drugs among public elementary and high school students in 27 Brazilian capitals]. Retrieved February 1, 2007, from http://www.unifesp.br/dpsicobio/cebrid/levantamento_brasil2/index.htm.

Gofman, A. G., & Ponizovsky, P. A. (2005). Substance abuse services in Russia, 1999–2003. *Addiction Research, 1,* 30–33. [Гофман, А. Г., и Понизовский, П. А. (2005). Состояние наркологической помощи в России в динамике с 1999 по 2003 гг. *Наркология*, №1, с. 30–33.]

Hao, W., Young, D., Xiao, S., Li, L. & Zhang,Y. (1999). Alcohol consumption and alcohol-related problems: Chinese experience from six area samples. *Addiction, 94,* 1467–1476.

Haworth, A., & Simpson. R. (Eds.). (2004). *Moonshine markets: Issues in unrecorded alcohol beverage production and consumption*. New York: Brunner-Routledge.

Her Majesty's Stationery Office (HMSO). (2005). *Licensing (Scotland) Act 2005*. Retrieved May 1, 2007, from http://www.opsi.gov.uk/legislation/scotland/acts2005/20050016.htm.

Hibell, B., Andersson, B., Bjarnason, T., Ahlström, S., Balakireva, O., Kokkevi, A., et al. (2004). *The ESPAD Report 2003: Alcohol and other drug use among students in 35 European countries*. Stockholm: Swedish Council for Information on Alcohol and Other Drugs (CAN) and the Pompidou Group at the Council of Europe.

Instituto Brasileiro de Opinião Pública e Estatística (IBOPE). (2000). *Levantamento sócio econômico 2000—IBOPE* [*Economic Survey 2000–IBOPE*]. Rio de Janeiro, Brazil: Author.

International Chamber of Commerce (ICC) & European Society for Opinion and Marketing Research (ESOMAR). (1994). *ICC/ESOMAR International code of marketing and social research practice*. Retrieved April 20, 2007, from http://www.esomar.org/uploads/pdf/ps_cg_icccode.pdf.

Ivanets, N. N. (2005, November). *Addiction research today*. Paper presented at the International Conference on Current Achievements in Addiction Research, Moscow, Russian Federation. [Иванец Н. Н. (ноябрь 2005). *Наркология сегодня*. Международная конференция, Современные достижения наркологии, Москва, РФ.]

Jernigan, D. H. (2001). *Global status report: Alcohol and young people*. Geneva, Switzerland: World Health Organization.

Kerr, A. (2006, September 5). Speech delivered at the "Interface between Public Order and Health" session, 49th ICAA International Conference on Dependencies, "What Makes Good Practice," Edinburgh, United Kingdom.

Koshkina, E. A., & Kirzhanova, V. V. (2005). Prevalence of substance abuse among children and teenagers, 2003–2004. *Addiction Problems Journal, 4/5,* 5–12. [Кошкина, Е. А., и Киржанова, В. В. (2005). Распространенность наркологических расстройств среди детей и подростков в 2003-2004 годах. *Вопросы наркологии*, № 4–5, с. 5–12.]

Koshkina, E. A., Pavlovskaya, N. I., Gurtovenko, V. M., & Koshkin, A. V. (2004). *Risky behaviors associated with alcohol consumption among young people*. Moscow, Russian Federation: National Research Center on Addictions. [Кошкина, Е. А., Павловская, Н. И., Гуртовенко, В. М., и Кошкин, А. В. (2004). *Поведенческие риски, связанные с употреблением алкоголя в молодежной среде*. Москва, РФ: Национальный Научный Центр Наркологии.]

Ma, G. S., & Kong, L. Z. (2006). *Nutrition and health situation survey of Chinese residents: Research report No. 9, behavior and lifestyle*. Beijing, China: People's Medical Publishing House.

Matzopoulos, R. (Ed.). (2005). *A profile of fatal injuries in South Africa. Sixth annual report of the National Injury Mortality Surveillance System 2004*. Tygerberg, South Africa: Medical Research Council.

Morojele, N. K., & Brook, J. S. (2006). Substance use and multiple victimisation among adolescents in South Africa. *Addictive Behaviors, 31,* 1163–1176.

Morojele, N. K., Kachieng'a, M. A., Mokoko, E., Nkoko, M. A., Parry, C. D. H., Nkowane, A. M., et al. (2006). Alcohol use and sexual behaviour among risky drinkers and bar and shebeen patrons in Gauteng province, South Africa. *Social Science and Medicine, 62,* 217–227.

Nemtsov, A. W. (2003). *Alcohol-related costs in the regions of Russia*. Moscow, Russian Federation: NOLEX. [Немцов, А. В. (2003). *Алкогольный урон регионов России*. Москва, РФ: NOLEX.]

Netting, R. M. (1964). Beer as a locus of value among the West African Kofya. *American Anthropologist, 66,* 375–384.

Newman, I. M., Qian, L., Shell, D. F., Qu, M., & Zhang, Y. (2006a). Development of Chinese adolescent alcohol expectancy questionnaire. *Chinese Journal of Behavioral Medical Science, 15,* 274–276.

Newman, I. M., Qian, L., Shell, D. F., Qu, M., & Zhang, Y. (2006b). Measurement of alcohol expectancy and development of Chinese adolescent alcohol expectancy questionnaire (CAEQ). *Chinese Journal of Health Statistics, 23,* 426–429, 432.

Newman, I. M., Shell, D. F., Qu, M., Xue, J. P., & Maas, M. R. (2006). Adolescent alcohol use: Mixed methods research approach. *Journal of Guangxi University for Nationalities, 28,* 21–28.

Newman, I. M., Xue, J. P., & Fang, X. Y. (2004). Alcohol use and its risk factors among high school students in Beijing. *Chinese Journal of School Health, 25,* 385–386.

Odejide, A. O. (1989, February 9). *A nation at risk: Alcohol and substance abuse among Nigerian youths*. Inaugural Lecture, University of Ibadan, Ibadan, Nigeria.

Odejide, A. O., & Odejide, B. (1999). Harnessing pleasure for population health ends. In S. Peele & M. Grant (Eds.), *Alcohol and pleasure: A health perspective* (pp. 341–355). Philadelphia: Brunner/Mazel.

Odejide, A. O., Ohaeri, J. U., Adelekan, M. L., & Ikuesan, B. A. (1987). Drinking behaviour and social change among youths in Nigeria: A study of two cities. *Drug and Alcohol Dependence, 20,* 227–233.

Odejide, A. O., Ohaeri, J. U., & Ikuesan, B. A. (1988). Alcohol use among Nigerian youths: The need for drug education and alcohol policy. *Drug and Alcohol Dependence, 23,* 231–235.

Ohaeri, J. U, Oduyela, S. O., Odejide, A. O., Dipe, T. M, Ikwuagwu, P. U., & Zamani, A. (1996). The history and drinking behaviour of the Nigerian students' palm wine drinkers club. *Drugs: Education, Prevention and Policy, 3,* 171–183.

Oladimeji, B. Y., & Fabiyi, A. K. (1993). Trends in alcohol consumption among Nigerian undergraduates. In I. S. Obot (Ed.), *Epidemiology and control of substance abuse in Nigeria* (pp. 88–94). Jos, Nigeria: Centre for Research and Information on Substance Abuse.

Osservatorio Permanente sui Giovani e l'Alcool. (2006). *Gli Italiani e l'alcool 2006: Consumi, tendenze ed atteggiamenti in Italia* [*Italians and alcohol 2006: Consumption, trends, and attitudes in Italy.*] Rome, Italy: Author.

Pala, B. (2004). Il consumo alcolico femminile tra ricerca di parità e aumento del rischio: Quale prevenzione? [Female alcohol consumption between search for equality and increase of risk: Which prevention?]. *Annali dell' Istituto Superiore di Sanitá, 40,* 41–46.

Parry, C. D. H., & Bennetts, A. L. (1998). *Alcohol policy and public health in South Africa.* Cape Town, South Africa: Oxford University Press.

Parry, C. D. H., & Bennetts, A. L. (1999). Country profile on alcohol in South Africa. In L. Riley & M. Marshall (Eds.), *Alcohol and public health in 8 developing countries* (pp. 135-156). Geneva, Switzerland: World Health Organization.

Parry, C. D. H., Bhana, A., Myers, B., Plüddemann, A., Flisher, A. J., Peden, M. M., et al. (2002). Alcohol use in South Africa: Findings from the South African Community Epidemiology Network on Drug Use (SACENDU) Project. *Journal of Studies on Alcohol, 63,* 430–435.

Parry, C. D. H., Plüddemann, A., Steyn, K., Bradshaw, D., Norman, R., & Laubscher, R. (2005). Alcohol use in South Africa: Findings from the first demographic and health survey. *Journal of Studies on Alcohol, 66,* 91–97.

Peden, M. M. (Ed.) (2001). *The sentinel surveillance of substance abuse and trauma, 1999–2000.* Final Report. Tygerberg, South Africa: Medical Research Council.

Peden, M. M., Knottenbelt, J. D., van der Spuy, J., Oodit, R., Scholtz, H. J., & Stokol, J. M. (1996). Injured pedestrians in Cape Town: The role of alcohol. *South African Medical Journal, 86,* 1103–1105.

Pelipas, V. E., & Miroshnichenko, L. D. (2002). Alcohol policy in Russia: A historic overview. *Addiction Problems Journal, 6,* 40–47. [Пелипас, В. Е., и Мирошниченко, Л. Д. (2002). Алкогольная политика в России. История вопроса. *Вопросы наркологии, 6,* 40–47.

Potter, K. (2002). *Consultation with children and young people on the Scottish Executive's Plan for Action on Alcohol Misuse.* Edinburgh, U.K.: Scottish Executive Central Research Unit.

Reddy, S. P., Panday, S., Swart, D., Jinabhai, C.C., Amosun, S. L., James, S., et al. (2003). *Umthenthe Uhlaba Usamila—The South African Youth Risk Behaviour Survey 2002.* Cape Town, South Africa: Medical Research Council.

Riley, L., & Marshall, M. (Eds.). (1999). *Alcohol and public health in 8 developing countries.* Geneva, Switzerland: World Health Organization.

Shen, Y. C. (1987). A survey of alcohol dependence and alcoholism in China. *Chinese Mental Health Journal, 1*, 251–256.

Sheregi, F. E., & Arefiev, A. L. (2003). Substance abuse among young people: Structure, trends, and prevention. Moscow, Russian Federation: TsSP. [Шереги, Ф. Э., и Арефьев, А. Л. (2003). Наркотизация в молодежной среде: Структура, тенденции, профилактика. Москва, РФ: ЦСП.]

Singer, K. (1972). Drinking patterns and alcoholism in the Chinese. *British Journal of Addictions, 67*, 3–14.

Sue, S., Kitano, H., Hatanaka, H., & Yeung, W. (1985). Chinese alcohol consumption in the United States. In C. Bennett & G. Ames (Eds.), *The American experience with alcohol: Contrasting cultural perspectives* (pp. 359–371). New York: Plenum.

Whitehead, S. (1996). The impact of alcohol control measures on drinking patterns. In M. Grant & J. Litvak (Eds.), *Drinking patterns and their consequences* (pp. 153–164). Washington, D.C.: Taylor & Francis.

World Advertising Research Center (WARC). (2005). *World drink trends 2005: Containing data to 2003*. Henley-on-Thames, U.K.: Author.

World Health Organization (WHO). (1992). *The ICD-10 classification of mental and behavioural disorders: Clinical descriptions and diagnostic guidelines*. Geneva, Switzerland: Author.

World Health Organization (WHO). (1999). *Global status report on alcohol*. Geneva, Switzerland: Author.

World Health Organization (WHO). (2004a). *Global status report: Alcohol policy*. Geneva, Switzerland: Author.

World Health Organization (WHO). (2004b). *Global status report on alcohol*. Geneva, Switzerland: Author.

Xue, J. P., Newman, I. M., Shell, D. F., & Fang, X. Y. (2005). Cultural orientation and Chinese adolescent drinking. *Chinese Journal of Behavioral Medical Science, 14*, 71–72.

Zambon, A., Lemma, P., Borraccino, A., Dalmasso, P., & Cavallo, F. (2006). Socio-economic position and adolescents' health in Italy: The role of the quality of social relations. *European Journal of Public Health, 16*, 627–632.

Zhang, J. G., Merrick, T. M., Newman, I. M., & Qian, L. (2007). [The social meaning of alcohol-related flushing]. *Chinese Journal of Health Education, 23*, 171–174.

Chapter 6

Stakeholders and Their Roles

Mark Leverton and Keith Evans

This chapter examines innovative approaches to addressing extreme drinking, with an emphasis on multi-sector involvement. Changing the culture of extreme drinking requires looking beyond traditional responses and calls for employing the capacity of all stakeholders in the field.

Contemporary approaches to alcohol policy tend to emphasize unilateral or bilateral initiatives, often overlooking the opportunities for whole-of-society efforts. The reasons behind this omission have been articulated elsewhere (Stimson, Grant, Choquet, & Garrison, 2007). Whatever the reasons for this omission may be, the inevitable consequence is the inability to capture all of the creative forces that might be directed at achieving a sustained reduction in the incidence and outcomes of extreme drinking at individual and population levels.

Some governments now recognize the need to engage all stakeholders in responding to complex social issues. It is within this context that an opportunity exists to move beyond single-sector approaches to addressing extreme drinking toward multi-sector collaboration, cooperation, and partnership.

A fundamental requirement of the new collective approach to alcohol policy and interventions outlined in this chapter is a willingness to recognize the potential contributions that all key stakeholders can make to achieve the common harm reduction goal. The importance of collective action on the part of the public and private sectors has been acknowledged by international agencies, such as the United Nations and the World Health Organization (WHO). Thus, according to WHO's 1998 *Health Promotion Glossary*, "Social responsibility for health is reflected by the actions of decision-makers in both the public and private sector to pursue policies and practices which promote and protect health" (Nutbeam, 1998, p. 20). WHO's former Director-General Gro

Harlem Brundtland noted in a 1998 speech to the World Health Assembly, "We need open and constructive relations with the private sector and industry, knowing where our roles differ and where they may complement each other" (Brundtland, 1998, p. 5).

WHO ARE THE STAKEHOLDERS?

This chapter identifies some of the key stakeholders who, given their capacity to allocate resources (both human and fiscal), are essential to the process of tackling the issue of extreme drinking among young people. This list is not intended to be exhaustive. All stakeholders will clearly have their own remit and appropriate role. However, it is important to bear in mind that, much like multi-component programs, activities that engage a range of stakeholders are powerful in that the whole is likely to be stronger than the sum of its parts (Thom & Bayley, 2007).

Governments

Governments—whether acting at a regional, national, or local level—have a pivotal role to play in the development and implementation of strategies to address the causes and consequences of extreme drinking. As a social and public health issue, extreme drinking not only has a profound impact on individual consumers, but also affects families, communities, and societies as a whole. A core function of governments in the development of alcohol policy in countries where alcohol consumption is lawful is to ensure that sustainable, balanced, and acceptable regulations are put in place with the dual aim of ensuring reasonable access to alcohol while at the same time minimizing the likelihood of harm, particularly from behaviors such as extreme drinking. Policy measures that are the remit of local and national governments, as well as regional bodies, are discussed at length in chapter 7.

At its broadest, a suggested role for government has been described as follows:

> To provide methods by which the energies of the many millions of individuals as well as various private and public organizations could be harnessed to make possible human advancement and development. The government has a duty to defend the nation from external attack, preserve law and order, establish a degree of regulation essential for interaction between people and institutions, and provide welfare for the genuinely poor, the under-privileged, and the disabled. (Cooray, 1988, chapter 16.3, para. 1)

While this definition is not as inclusive as many would wish (and may be more inclusive than some would desire), it does speak to important issues at the heart of the role of effective government. The notion that it is a responsibility of government to harness private and public organizations and individuals to facilitate human advancement and development fits well with government having a key responsibility in ensuring the same benefits for young people in society. Moreover, the idea that one of the roles of government is to establish a degree of regulation essential for interaction between people and institutions is consistent with the requirement for sensible and targeted regulations aimed at reducing potential harms that may result from problem alcohol consumption, including extreme drinking. Finally, in the definition above, reference is made to the role of government in providing welfare to citizens and groups in particular need of assistance. Although extreme drinking is not confined to any single socioeconomic group, young people who are among the marginalized segments of society because of poverty, unemployment, homelessness, or other factors may be particularly in need of attention (see chapters 7 and 8).

Evans and Roche (2001) addressed the role of governments in shaping the drinking behavior among young people:

> the question for governments to answer is a simple one. What are the key messages one wishes to offer to young people in regard to alcohol? It would appear on the basis of much that has been written regarding the development and implementation of alcohol policies that the dominant orientations to date have been:
>
> • strategies aimed at discouraging alcohol consumption among young people below the legal age for purchase and/or consumption of alcohol; and
> • strategies aimed at highlighting the dangers associated with the consumption of alcohol. (p. 247)

> In recent years, there have been a number of challenges to the traditional precepts underpinning alcohol control policies. One argument is that reduced alcohol consumption is not necessarily required to reduce problems associated with alcohol. (p. 259)

As Österberg (1995) observed:

> In many countries, public emphasis regarding responses to the alcohol question has come to be laid more and more on education, information, and treatment, in recent decades. In addition, market forces and economic considerations have increasingly overshadowed preventive policies, and in some countries, a strengthening of liberal attitudes has led to a stress on individual responsibility and a denial of the justification of any control measures. Accordingly, limiting the physical availability of alcoholic beverages or imposing high taxation as a means to control consumption and related harmful effects are nowadays regarded by an increasing number of people as an archaic patchwork of laws and as irrelevant to contemporary life. (p. 145)[1]

This comment notwithstanding, many governments continue to use and discuss high alcohol taxation and restrictions on physical access to alcohol as public health tools. However, considerable opportunities exist for governments to strengthen the emphasis on harm reduction in an effort to reduce the

---

[1] © Reprinted by permission of Oxford University Press.

incidence and impacts of extreme drinking. Tackling extreme drinking provides an excellent example of moving the emphasis away from the act of drinking to the consequences of drinking. Although some stakeholders might question the impartiality of governments, they are ideally placed to provide a leadership role in this change of emphasis.

National, State, or Provincial Governments

Several key areas are clearly the remit of national, state, or provincial government. Broadly speaking, these include introducing the legislation for policy measures and ensuring their implementation—for instance, mandating, communicating, and enforcing legal drinking age; making sure that an effective system of licensing is in place; and setting other appropriate laws, regulations, and penalties to prevent extreme drinking among young people. Where regulatory measures are accompanied by industry self-regulation, national and state governments can encourage the strengthening of self-regulatory systems and provide legal frameworks in which they can flourish (a system of *co-regulation*). For example, the *Code of Practice on the Naming, Packaging, and Promotion of Alcoholic Drinks*, developed and implemented by the Portman Group in the United Kingdom, was assisted by government support to introduce mechanisms for removing rogue products from the market. In a free-market economy, laws of free trade and competition would generally have frowned upon such practice. In this case, however, the need for working toward a common good was recognized by all involved in the Code's development (Portman Group, 2003).

Governments can also play an influential role in bringing together various stakeholders (Anderson & Baumberg, 2007); similar initiatives can be spearheaded by regional governmental and intergovernmental bodies. For example, the European Commission convened a succession of meetings where stakeholders exchanged views on possible elements of an alcohol policy for the European Union (EU). As a result, the recent communication from the Commission, *An EU Strategy to Support Member States in Reducing Alcohol Related Harm*, mandated the creation of the Alcohol and Health Forum (European Commission, 2006). The Forum's goal is to address a range of issues related to drinking in the EU, generally bringing together EU member states, nongovernmental organizations, alcohol producers, trade associations, media groups, the hospitality sector, retailers, scientists, and others. The creation of the Forum was possible because trust was built between stakeholders whilst exchanging views in the same room.

Although extreme drinking has most immediate implications for health and social order, a wide range of government agencies have a role in ensuring that the twin objectives of providing reasonable access to alcohol and minimizing harm are achieved. However, a critical factor that often bedevils alcohol policy debate is the absence of a unified view among many government departments, which would provide an appropriate policy setting or road map. For instance, health departments and law enforcement agencies, focused on the costs associated with problem drinking and dependence, tend to have a strong regulatory bias and a policy goal of reducing all alcohol consumption, whereas departments of trade, industry, or tourism, interested in revenue growth (for instance, from enjoyable leisure activities) and employment, are more open to maximizing opportunities for increased availability of alcohol outlets. As a result, there is often dissonance between central government agencies as to the key policy objectives to be pursued.

Given the disparate objectives of various departments, governments are often pulled in different directions regarding the best approach to take. Few governments appoint a single individual or department with the role of coordinating policy. As a consequence, government policies to address extreme drinking can be ad hoc, narrowly based, and even contradictory. Different directions for the setting of policy may emerge, which, at worst, could be in direct conflict with each other or, at the very least, make it difficult for the competing demands of the various stakeholders to be accommodated easily. It is also important to note that in some instances—for example, in many developing countries—the pressing demands of other social policy or economic realities are so great that the development of sensible and sustainable alcohol policies ranks low on the scale of priorities.

Since national governments tend to rely primarily on regulation in setting and implementing alcohol policy, it is important that best practice guidelines can be established. In 2005, Australia's National Competition Council commissioned a report on identifying a framework for regulation in packaged retail trading to assist in its consideration of the special status of alcohol (Marsden Jacob Associates, 2005). This report identified the following guidelines for best practice regulation:

(a) Regulation should have clearly identifiable objectives and outcomes.
(b) The development and design of regulation should be scientifically rigorous and evidence based.
(c) Regulation should be enforced and effective.
(d) Regulatory burden should be minimised.
(e) Regulation of social behaviours...must recognise [all tiers of government] and the need for appropriate assignment of regulatory responsibilities and instruments between them. Regulation should be preferably focused on output or performance.
(f) Individual regulations should be designed and assessed.
(g) Local externalities require local action.
(h) The burden of proof that regulation is necessary lies with the proponents.
(i) Processes for judgment and discretion in regulation should be impartial.
(j) Unnecessary impacts should be avoided.
(k) Regulations should not discriminate between different suppliers in competition. (Marsden Jacob Associates, 2005, pp. 52–53)

The European Commission's communication on *An EU Strategy to Support Member States in Reducing Alcohol Related Harm* identified a number of priority areas—considered to be relevant to all Member States—that may add value to national policies and national actions. The resulting alcohol agenda includes efforts to:

- protect young people, children, and the unborn child;
- reduce injuries and death from alcohol-related road accidents;
- prevent alcohol-related harm among adults and reduce the negative impact on the workplace;
- inform, educate, and raise awareness on the impact of harmful and hazardous alcohol consumption, and on appropriate consumption patterns;
- develop and maintain a common evidence base at EU level. (European Commission, 2006, p. 7)

Local Government and Communities

The role of local governments at the county, municipal, or community level is often underestimated or ignored, although it might be argued that extreme drinking and its outcomes are most salient for these jurisdictions. Public safety and order are paramount among the concerns of communities, and many of the functions performed by local governments worldwide are designed to address them. Public drunkenness, graffiti, violence, and property damage are all matters within the purview of local government. The impacts of extreme drinking on taxpayers and local businesses often come to the attention of municipal officers and elected officials; equally, some important interventions—such as the provision of security and law enforcement and late-night public transport in drinking areas—are also frequently managed by local jurisdictions.

These responsibilities make local governments better positioned than their national or state counterparts to address extreme drinking in a given community. Harnessing the capacity of local government as a partner in efforts to reduce the incidence and outcomes of extreme drinking makes good sense: In terms of government action, local government agencies are at the front line and, as such, are ideally placed to identify innovative strategies and to monitor improvements in public safety and social amenity.

Over the past few years, considerable attention has been paid in many countries to increasing local capacity for development of alcohol management plans within communities. For instance, in New Zealand, alcohol harm reduction strategies have been pioneered by a number of local governments. In particular, Wellington City Council has been at the forefront of major innovations aimed at reducing public intoxication and disruption associated with extreme drinking (Wellington City Council, 2003). In Australia, the Council of Capital City Lord Mayors, a body representing all capital cities of the Australian States and Territories, formed the Lord Mayors' Task Force on Drugs, which has identified public alcohol intoxication as a critical issue to be addressed by municipalities across the country (Keith Evans, personal communication, 2006).

A report commissioned by the Joseph Rowntree Foundation in the United Kingdom reviewed the role of communities in the prevention efforts related to drinking (Thom & Bayley, 2007). Approaches to community interventions, according to the authors, have traditionally relied on single-component programs or groups of stand-alone projects aimed at various aspects of drinking and related concerns. As a result, there is often a disconnect at the community level (much as within national government approaches) with regard to alcohol prevention. In comparison to such single-component programs, Thom and Bayley considered multi-component initiatives to be more efficient in the use of resources and more capable, through the partnerships they rely on, to address a range of different issues at once through a comprehensive program of work at the community level. To that end, the authors stressed, for example, improving local policies on alcohol, strengthening networks between professionals and stakeholder groups at the local level, and encouraging direct involvement of communities in effecting change.

The report also introduced a novel idea: In the multi-component approach, "whole communities form the target-intervention group rather than individuals within the community" (Thom & Bayley, 2007, p. 2). Thus, not only is the community involved in developing interventions, bringing resources to the table, and solving its own immediate problems, but it can also *implement* multi-stakeholder projects that address multiple problem areas in an integrated fashion. In the case of extreme drinking, such initiatives may include:[2]

- Police enforcement activities targeting alcohol-related crime and anti-social behavior, such as pub-watch schemes, designed to limit intoxication and alcohol-related disorder by relying on information-gathering and intelligence-sharing among licensees and police to monitor the movement of known trouble-makers.
- Environmental design that introduces closed-circuit television (CCTV) cameras or other surveillance measures in identified community hotspots, or the use of alternative containers and packaging in drinking venues (for instance, plastic or toughened glass).
- Expansion of nonlicensed premises that offer alternatives to drinking as part of socializing (these may be designed and marketed for a younger clientele).
- Limited outlet density where the number of outlets has reached "saturation level."
- Transportation infrastructure that allows the efficient movement of individuals away from hot spots, or incentives for designated drivers and safe-ride schemes.
- Media engagement to educate and inform the public and promote safety campaigns focusing on extreme drinking.
- Media advocacy that engages the local community to change perceptions and norms.

---

[2] Adapted from *Multi-component Programmes: An Approach to Pprevent and Reduce Alcohol-related Harm* by Betsy Thom and Mariana Bayley, published in 2007 by the Joseph Rowntree Foundation. By permission of the Joseph Rowntree Foundation.

- Promotion of responsible drinking among young people through alcohol-free events that focus on changing their perceptions about socializing without alcohol and educating them about alcohol-related issues (adapted from Thom & Bayley, 2007, pp. 22–24). This includes providing attractive entertainment options for underage youth. Where appropriate facilities are lacking (e.g., in rural areas), such events could be held at nightclubs and other venues that normally serve alcohol, so long as the premises offer a "safe, alcohol-free and supervised environment" (New South Wales Office of Liquor, Gaming and Racing, 2007, para. 4).

It should be noted that these approaches are "evidence-based." Which of them may be applied depends on the particular local needs, the drinking culture, and the feasibility of implementation. The effectiveness of the approaches, while possibly low as stand-alone measures, has been shown to be high when implemented in synergy.

Law and Order Authorities

At both the community and local levels, the role of law and order authorities in targeting extreme drinking cannot be overestimated. A considerable amount of police resources and time is taken up in managing incidents related to intoxication and problem drinking. In Australia, for example, problem drinking has been identified as a key factor in 62% of police attendances, 73% of assaults, 77% of street offences, 40% of domestic violence incidents, and 90% of late-night calls to emergency services (Doherty & Roche, 2003; see also English et al., 1995; Matthews, Chikritzhs, Catalano, Stockwell, & Donath, 2002). As a result, police forces around the world are exploring innovative options for more effective management of the impacts of extreme drinking on their workloads; for instance, through collaborative efforts with health and youth organizations. The role of police in the prevention of problem drinking is an issue receiving increased attention globally.

A set of policy approaches has been suggested as strategies for police to prevent episodes of extreme and underage drinking. In the first instance, police have a role to play in ensuring that only persons who are legally permitted to purchase and drink alcohol have access to it. Enforcement of laws is one of the main responsibilities of police. The role of police, however, need not be *purely* punitive, with the necessary criminalization of those who violate laws. Instead, police can be trained to implement different prevention strategies aimed at young people in particular, focusing on identifying and punishing not young people who drink, but adults who enable extreme drinking and either sell alcohol to youth below the legal drinking age or buy alcohol for minors (Alcohol Epidemiology Program, University of Minnesota, 2007). In short, the law and order authorities can assist with the following: developing strategies to identify the sources of illegally obtained alcohol; implementing compliance checks at retail outlets; monitoring of problematic drinking establishments; and building police partnerships with civil society, other community stakeholders, and young people themselves to ensure that laws are upheld and that drinking is responsible.

Beverage Alcohol Industry

As a stakeholder in efforts to promote responsible alcohol consumption, encourage beneficial drinking patterns, and reduce the incidence of harm, the beverage alcohol industry is well positioned with resources and experience. Yet, for some, the involvement of the beverage alcohol industry in activities to address alcohol-related harm is controversial, and sometimes the industry is deliberately excluded from such initiatives. Whereas industry representatives view partnerships in this area as essential, some in the public health community see the industry as a barrier to policy-making (Stockwell, 2007). Finding the right approach to working together may hinge, ultimately, on finding appropriate areas where there is common ground and avoiding those where consensus and common objectives are unlikely.

Industry efforts to combat problem drinking can be traced back over decades; numerous industry responsibility programs exist today, targeting differing types of alcohol-related harm (Grant & O'Connor, 2005; see also Stimson et al., 2007, pp. 202–206). Some of these initiatives are stand-alone industry undertakings and some are conducted in partnerships with others in the public health field. Certain limitations to its involvement notwithstanding, the beverage alcohol industry can make an important contribution and shows an increasing appetite for doing so—an attitude to be welcomed and encouraged.

It should be stated at the outset that the term *beverage alcohol industry* embraces a wide range of industry interests (for an overview of the structure of the beverage alcohol industry, see International Center for Alcohol Policies [ICAP], 2006b). It encompasses producers of different products (such as beer, wine, cider, and spirits); wholesalers and importers; and retailers (including bars, cafes, restaurants, nightclubs, supermarkets, liquor stores, wine merchants, and others). It also includes industry trade associations, representing specific sectors of the industry, and social aspects organizations (SAOs), industry-funded bodies dedicated to promoting responsible drinking and reducing problem drinking. Care needs to be taken, therefore, when talking about "the alcohol industry," to be as specific as possible about which part of the industry is being discussed.

With regard to addressing issues such as extreme drinking, our focus here is on the role of producers and retailers of beverage alcohol, whose involvement lies in the reduction of harm and in encouragement of responsible consumer choices and behaviors.

Beverage Alcohol Producers

In the context of harm reduction, the role of a beverage alcohol producer is, arguably, to manufacture products and to market brands in a way that does not encourage irresponsible drinking of *any* kind. Within this sector of the beverage alcohol industry, standards are set out in industry-wide or individual company codes of practice. These codes typically require all marketing communications to portray only moderate and responsible consumption of alcohol and not condone or encourage excessive drinking. Many codes go further by specifying that marketing communications should not refer in any favorable manner to the effects of intoxication and that there should be no depiction of people drinking heavily or rapidly. Other clauses that are common to many codes and that have some relevance to extreme drinking relate to alcohol content and strength, prohibiting undue emphasis on high alcohol content as the principal basis of appeal to the consumer. Most self-regulatory codes already have such provisions; in the rare instances where they do not, codes can and should be strengthened by their inclusion. An overview of individual codes of practice is offered in chapter 7 (see also Grant & O'Connor, 2005, pp. 177–209).

In June 2006, the International Center for Alcohol Policies convened a meeting of an Expert Committee to consider issues related to responsible drinks marketing. Participants represented the perspectives of marketers, regulators, beverage alcohol producers, researchers, and consumers. The committee made a number of recommendations, including the development of global responsibility messages to help reinforce low-risk drinking norms and enhanced dissemination of research results on issues such as the factors that contribute to extreme drinking (ICAP, 2006a). Although responsible marketing cannot by itself find remedies for all the problems associated with problem drinking in general and with extreme drinking in particular, it is an essential part of the way these issues should be addressed.

Other initiatives taken by the beverage alcohol producers can also help reduce the risks associated with extreme drinking. For example, many producers have a decades-long track record of running campaigns to discourage drinking and driving. Consumer awareness of the risks of alcohol-impaired driving has risen steadily in most high-income societies (Stimson et al., 2007, chapter 5). However, in many low-income countries, where vehicle numbers are now steadily rising, awareness may not be so high and more could be done by alcohol producers, working in partnership with governments and road safety organizations. Similarly, many alcohol producers support "safe ride home" schemes that provide free or discounted travel to consumers. These initiatives are intended to reduce the risk of individuals making unwise decisions after drinking, potentially endangering themselves or others. Clearly, such schemes are of benefit to all drinkers, but they are particularly relevant in reaching young extreme drinkers, a population at increased risk for harm. Chapter 8 offers further discussion of various prevention and intervention efforts that have been implemented—by producers, other stakeholders, or in partnership—to reduce the incidence and consequences of extreme drinking among youths.

Nearly all initiatives in some way try to encourage responsible choices about alcohol. The provision of information about alcohol effects, drinking patterns, and potential outcomes is one approach intended to facilitate responsible decision-making. Some information is provided in a purely factual way. Information labels, for example, are often required by law to state the alcoholic strength of a drink. In countries where the governments issue specific guidelines for maximum daily or weekly consumption, drinks producers can help consumers understand those recommendations by putting unit or standard drink information on alcohol labels. This is a common practice in the United Kingdom, for example, where many alcohol producers do so voluntarily; the practice is mandated by government in Australia. Further study is necessary to ascertain the impact that such information has on extreme drinkers, but the provision of information does serve to raise awareness about alcohol in the general consumer population and may contribute to changing attitudes and drinking culture.

Various other efforts by producers use a range of technological means to convey information to consumers. Web sites for particular organizations, companies, and brands have been set up to educate consumers about different products. For example, in the U.K., the Drinkaware Web site (http://www.drinkaware.co.uk)—run by the Drinkaware Trust, an independent body, supported by voluntary contributions from across the beverage alcohol industry, including producers, pub companies, and retailers—offers an interactive unit calculator that helps consumers work out the number of standard alcohol units in their drink of choice (see http://www.drinkaware.co.uk/how-many-units.html). The site also provides details of the caloric content of alcoholic drinks, as well as information and advice about the effects of alcohol on the body. Similar Web sites have been developed in Ireland, Germany, the Netherlands, and Spain. In 2005, Diageo, one of the largest producers of beverage alcohol, launched a consumer Web site (http://www.knowyourdiageodrink.com) that contains detailed nutritional information on the company's brands. Extreme drinkers may or may not be especially interested in this information, but the intention is to help consumers look at alcohol consumption in the broader context of their overall diet.

All alcohol producers are interested in understanding consumer behavior; they use their marketing expertise to encourage adults to choose their brands on occasions when they choose to drink. A growing number of beverage alcohol producers are now exploring ways in which they can use their consumer insights to promote responsible drinking, or to deal with specific problems such as extreme drinking. Branded responsibility advertisements are now common in the United States, where one frequent focus for such advertisements is a reminder of the legal purchase age for alcohol (21 years of age): Both the Beer Institute and the Century Council (funded by leading spirits producers) regularly run initiatives that aim to prevent the purchase of alcohol by underage young people; so do many of the individual beer and spirits producers, either corporately or under their brand names.

In the U.K. and Ireland, some beverage alcohol producers and industry associations have made extreme drinking a major focus of their responsibility initiatives. Companies such as Diageo have produced broadcast advertisements with hard-hitting messages to those who are engaging or may be tempted to engage in extreme drinking. A common theme of such advertisements is to point out to young adult consumers that drunkenness can be embarrassing (for instance, "you can make a fool out of yourself in front of the very people you want to impress").

All such initiatives need to be supported by research and evaluation to ensure that the right message is communicated, and that the impact is the one that was actually intended. Market research during development of a responsible drinking campaign in Ireland (Diageo Ireland, 2005) indicated that it is possible to come up with effective, responsible drinking messages if an understanding of consumer motivations and beliefs is put at the heart of the campaign development process. In audience research, 75% of consumers said the advertisements were "the kind that made you think" and 57% said they would reconsider how much they drank as a result of viewing the campaign. It is clear that more research is needed to evaluate the effectiveness of such initiatives in the longer term, but, as drinks producers continue to explore the area of social marketing in the context of promoting responsible drinking, more lessons will be learned about how to provide incentives for positive behavior choices. Although it may be impossible to attribute change in extreme drinking *entirely* to one particular initiative or campaign, a range of measures are helpful to evaluate such activities—for example, consumer awareness of the message, consumers' stated behavior intentions, and qualitative changes in cultural attitudes toward extreme drinking.

Beverage Alcohol Retailers

While much of alcohol consumption around the world takes place in people's homes, a lot of it also occurs in public venues, such as bars, nightclubs, cafes, and restaurants. Particularly in urban areas, late-night entertainment activity is often associated with extreme drinking behaviors. The retailing segment of the industry has an important role in creating a comfortable and safe drinking environment in such venues through measures to promote responsible hospitality. The objectives of these efforts are to minimize any risk for harm to individual drinkers and, at the same time, safeguard the quality of life in the surrounding community.

Although an individual licensed retailer can choose from a wide range of initiatives to promote responsible behavior and discourage extreme drinking, the benefits are far greater if the retailers in a city or neighborhood work together with others in the community to address these issues. Partners would typically include local police, transportation authorities, and local government. Joint initiatives that are responsive to immediate needs and concerns of community leaders and citizens and can help to reduce potential harm arc promising approaches.

Policies that address the serving of alcohol are particularly important. To that end, drinking establishments can contribute by training both servers and security staff in identifying and handling intoxicated customers or in providing assistance with finding alternative means of transport for those who may not be fit to drive after drinking. Research from the United States suggests that, for every dollar spent on enforcing laws prohibiting the sale of alcohol to already intoxicated patrons, between $90 and $280 could be saved in the cost of traffic accidents (McKnight & Streff, 1994); common sense suggests that this can also make a contribution to reducing the incidence of extreme drinking. Particular attention is also needed to dealing with minors. Here, initiatives may include training staff to ask for identification to provide proof of legal age. Server training is mandatory in some countries and undertaken voluntarily in many others; more can and should be done to ensure that all retailers of alcohol are proactive in this area of harm reduction.

The following are some examples of approaches to server training that have already been tried and tested:

- The Responsible Hospitality Institute (RHI) in the United States has set up the Responsible Retailers Forum to bring all relevant stakeholders together to tackle the issue of alcohol sales to underage consumers (Responsible Retailing Forum, 2003). Although preventing underage drinking is currently its main focus, there is no reason why such a forum cannot begin to address other areas in alcohol retailing, such as preventing sales to intoxicated individuals and other measures to discourage extreme drinking, particularly among young people.
- A broader approach in Denmark that involved crime prevention is the result of a partnership among a Danish SAO (GODA), local police, licensees and other commercial stakeholders, and the local authorities. The project Safe Nightlife includes equipping staff in on-trade premises (for instance, licensed bars and restaurants) to handle potentially violent situations (European Spirits Organisation [CEPS] and European Forum for Responsible Drinking [EFRD], 2006, p. 8).
- In Scotland, *Guidelines for Developing a Responsible Service of Alcohol Training Programme at National Level* target both on- and off-trade business (the latter include retail shops and wholesalers) and draw on the experience of programs from across Europe. Developed in partnership by the European Forum for Responsible Drinking (a European SAO), the European Trade Union for Tourism, Alcohol Focus Scotland (a national voluntary organization on alcohol issues), and the British Institute of Innkeeping, these guidelines are aimed at trainers and those who run qualification and accreditation schemes (CEPS & EFRD, 2006, p. 11).
- An emphasis on law enforcement drives a training program in Germany, Responsible Serving Initiative, which involves the Federal Ministry of

Health, alcohol producers, and various trade and catering bodies (CEPS
& EFRD, 2006, p. 17).

- In Ireland, an integrated training scheme, the Responsible Serving of
  Alcohol Programme, is jointly funded by the national SAO, Mature
  Enjoyment of Alcohol in Society (MEAS), and the Department of Health
  and Children. The initiative is facilitated by Fáilte Ireland, the national
  hospitality training agency (CEPS & EFRD, 2006, p. 23).
- In Malta, the local SAO, The Sense Group, and the Bartenders'
  Association promote a *Code of Practice for Bartenders*, which applies
  to bars, restaurants, and nightclubs (CEPS & EFRD, 2006, p. 26).

Management and design of drinking premises also have a contribution
to make. Effective management can ensure the wellbeing of patrons through
attention to a range of elements—for instance, the availability of seating and
food, crowd control, and limits on promotional activities that may encourage
immoderate consumption (such as "happy hours" and novelty events). Some
retailers may provide free water or free soft drinks for a designated driver or
offer free nonsalty bar snacks to all patrons (see chapter 7).

A key concern surrounding licensed premises is that of personal safety,
especially from aggression and violence. Many of the elements mentioned
above (for instance, crowd control) can significantly reduce these risks.
Research shows that, while certain types of individuals may be drawn to particular bars and other drinking venues, it is the characteristics of these establishments—and not just their clientele—that are most predictive of violence
(Quigley, Leonard, & Collins, 2003; see also Stimson et al., 2007, chapter 6).
Bar personnel have been identified as the most effective means of managing
violence and aggressive behavior among patrons (Graham, Bernards, Osgood,
Homel, & Purcell, 2005). However, several other approaches have also proven
to be effective: for instance, prompt removal of potentially harmful objects,
such as broken glass, from the premises and substituting plastic for glass containers. So-called "toughened glass" that shatters when broken and cannot
be used as a weapon has been found to reduce the rate of injury in violent
acts around bars and taverns (Coomaraswamy & Shepherd, 2003; Cusens &
Shepherd, 2005; Warburton & Shepherd, 2000).

Case Study: Host Responsibility (New Zealand)

Following substantial changes to the law governing the sale of alcohol in New
Zealand in the late 1980s, the availability of alcohol increased dramatically.
The Alcohol Advisory Council of New Zealand (ALAC) decided to implement
a comprehensive set of strategies that aimed to promote safer drinking environments, culminating in the development of the Host Responsibility initiative
(based on the U.S. concept of "server intervention").

International research indicates that well-managed drinking environments assist consumers in making responsible decisions regarding drinking
and subsequent behaviors (for discussion, see Stimson et al., 2007, chapter 6).
New Zealand's Host Responsibility campaign marked a move away from focusing on the drinker as the key problem to emphasizing the role of the drinking

environment in contributing to alcohol-related harm. Furthermore, it placed the onus of responsibility on the servers of alcohol and their role in limiting or preventing intoxication and its associated problems.

Initially, in an attempt to popularize the concept with the general public, the campaign focused on the private host. During the 1990s, however, Host Responsibility moved into the commercial arena, attempting to deal with the issue of intoxication on licensed premises. In 1999, amendments to the 1989 Sale of Liquor Act saw aspects of Host Responsibility incorporated into legislation, making them legal requirements.

Host Responsibility incorporates six key concepts designed to assist in creating safer drinking environments. Thus, a responsible host: prevents intoxication; provides and actively promotes low- and nonalcoholic drinks; serves alcohol responsibly or not at all; does not serve alcohol to minors; provides substantial food and actively promotes eating; and arranges safe transport options.

The Host Responsibility program has been a considerable success story. The increased recognition by retail outlets of their responsibility for ensuring the nonserving of intoxicated patrons and the provision of nonalcoholic beverages and substantial food has significantly changed the drinking environment in New Zealand.

Source: Adapted from Alcohol Advisory Council of New Zealand (2005).

Public Health

Public health has been defined as the "science and art of preventing disease, prolonging life, and promoting health through organized efforts of society" (Acheson, 1988). Threats to the health of the individual and the community, whether due to lifestyle choices or the environment, are central to "the business" of public health. Thus, public health practitioners are major stakeholders in efforts to address extreme drinking at local, national, regional, and international levels. Since the advent of the public health movement, attention has been paid to identifying appropriate strategies for reducing alcohol-related harm for both individuals and groups.

Broadly, one might define the public health community as including those involved in research, prevention, and treatment. When it comes to extreme drinking, all three groups have distinct and important jobs to perform. This diversity in stakeholders and their role is reflected in the following quote:

[h]ealth promotion employs many strategies and theories to empower communities and individuals to take control of their health. This diversity reflects the complexity of dealing with alcohol-related harm in the community and the diversity of people's concerns and may include anything from harm minimisation through to abstinence, and community development through to social marketing....Health promotion seeks to attain sustainable, long-term social change within identified target communities. Social change is not achieved by delivering a single programme into a community in the hope that individuals will adopt the desired behaviour. It is a complex process that may take years to change attitudes and behaviour that will eventually result in long-term societal change. (Collie, 2002, p. 17)

Public health researchers play an important role in providing the evidence base upon which measures aimed at extreme drinking may be developed and in assessing the effectiveness of various measures that are implemented. Research into drinking patterns of young people, the prevalence of extreme drinking among different groups, and the impact of culture and other environmental factors have highlighted the differences that exist and identified trends that can help in the crafting of new approaches. For example, the European School Survey Project on Alcohol and Other Drugs (ESPAD), which studies substance-related behaviors among 15- to 16-year-olds in 35 European countries, has offered a particularly helpful glimpse into young people's drinking across national lines, including extreme drinking (Hibell et al., 2004). National-level surveys (e.g., Johnston, O'Malley, Bachman, & Schulenberg, 2007; Kalafatelis, McMillen, & Palmer, 2003; Reddy et al., 2003) and global data collection by agencies such as the World Health Organization (Currie et al., 2004; WHO, 2004) have added to the picture of how young people drink, what motivates them, and, ultimately, how harmful patterns such as extreme drinking might be addressed.

Public health also includes practitioners and specialists involved in prevention efforts—not just with regard to drinking, but to health in general—as well as those who provide treatment. Within these groups, two areas should be highlighted as of particular importance when it comes to extreme drinking. First, the involvement of primary healthcare providers in addressing extreme drinking and its outcomes: Lifestyle counseling and interventions apply as much to young people as they do to older age groups, and encouragement to change particular drinking patterns can be a useful and highly effective component of interventions. In order for this to work, however, practitioners need to be equipped with the knowledge and tools to provide information about drinking patterns and possible outcomes. The need for a more systematic integration of primary healthcare into policy measures related to alcohol is addressed at some length in chapter 7.

Treatment services are another key area. These may be combined with mental health services or accident and emergency departments in cases where injury has already resulted from extreme drinking. Of particular note here is the ability to identify young extreme drinkers early, reach them through counseling and brief interventions, and, when necessary, offer treatment for problem drinking or dependence (see chapters 7 and 8 for further discussion on health policy and intervention approaches).

Civil Society

Much controversy and debate surrounds the definition of civil society. Michael Edwards, in his comprehensive analysis of the various civil society paradigms, stated:

> The first thing we need to do is to strengthen the pre-conditions for a healthy civil society—by attacking all forms of inequality and discrimination, giving people the means to be active citizens, reforming politics to encourage more participation, guaranteeing the independence of associations and the structures of public communication, and building a strong foundation for institutionalization of partnerships, alliances and coalitions. (Edwards, 2005, para. 17)

For the purposes of this chapter, we define civil society as individuals and groups who are neither part of government nor of the business (for-profit) sector. Those captured within the meaning of this definition include the voluntary sector, community organizations, trade unions, faith groups, and philanthropic foundations. Engaging these important segments of society in addressing aspects of extreme drinking is critical, particularly in terms of their capacity to reach out to the community, bring about a reassessment of cultural norms, and, where appropriate, act as champions of change.

Although not strictly speaking "stakeholders," consumers also have a role to play in the development and implementation of alcohol policies and measures to reduce harm from extreme drinking. Importantly, policies and interventions need wide public acceptance to be effective. They need to address real needs and do so without negatively impacting personal freedoms; otherwise they will be rejected and circumvented by the individuals and groups they have been designed to protect. Perhaps the most important reason for finding ways to involve consumers is to understand the sort of interventions they would find relevant and to identify the most effective ways of influencing their behavior.

OVERCOMING STAKEHOLDER ASYMMETRY

So-called stakeholder asymmetry exists wherever there are multiple parties working together. It is likely to occur whether potential partners are from disparate sectors (for example, public and private) or from the same sector (as in the case of different areas of government attempting to find common ground). The reasons for such asymmetry are many. Tensions at the local versus the national level have been cited as one of the main reasons (Thom & Bayley, 2007). There is at times a perception that national priorities and concerns may not always be relevant at the local level, and, similarly, that local issues may not be salient at the national level. Compounding this dichotomy is the perceived incompatibility between population-level measures related to alcohol and an emphasis on more targeted harm reduction. In fact, the two approaches are perfectly compatible and may be used in a measured way to complement each other (Stimson et al., 2007).

Other sources of potential disconnect between various stakeholders include different expectations and goals with regard to desired outcomes: For instance, disagreements may arise regarding resource allocation, relative priorities, and the speed with which outcomes are expected. This last issue is of particular concern where the private or commercial sector interacts with the public sector and civil society. Traditionally, the former is results-oriented, expecting to see quick returns on investment, whereas the reality of public health efforts and prevention may move at a slower pace (Stimson et al., 2007, chapters 3 and 10).

Finally, efforts to bring stakeholders together may be hampered further by differences in ideology. As noted above, some controversy surrounds the acceptability of the private sector's involvement in prevention and intervention efforts. The debate regarding the ethics of industry involvement and public-private partnerships is an ongoing and long-standing one that is unlikely to be fully resolved.

Clearly, potential obstacles to effective partnership are bound to exist among stakeholders with diverse backgrounds and points of view. While some will be experienced in working in partnership, others may be suspicious or even hostile to those with whom they have had no working relationship and whom they may regard as having ulterior motives for involvement. It may appear that different viewpoints make it impossible to create consensus. However, under those circumstances, it is essential to recognize that, although differences exist among stakeholders, there is likely to be some common ground—and *that* should provide the foundation for action.

Given these obstacles, any multi-stakeholder effort to address extreme drinking or other harmful behaviors should take into account the following principles (e.g., Grant & O'Connor, 2005; Stimson et al., 2007, pp. 217–225):

- Building trust among stakeholders is essential. This can be achieved through open dialogue conducted by an independent third party, acceptable to all interests.
- Transparency of decision-making will help stakeholders feel confident that they are equals in the decision-making process.
- Mutual respect for each others' opinions is key to building working partnerships.

Promoting responsible consumption of alcohol and reducing the harms associated with problem drinking are the cornerstones of any coherent approach to tackling the negative outcomes of extreme drinking. Failure to engage all relevant sectors of society in reaching these goals will inevitably hinder any sustainable culture shift toward making extreme drinking an unacceptable pattern for individuals, families, workplaces, and communities. Finding creative and enduring solutions, therefore, calls for an open mind when determining the list of necessary participants in policy development.

A report to the government by the Drugs and Crime Prevention Committee (2006, p. xii) in the state of Victoria, Australia, contained the following comments, which are germane when considering the most appropriate response to extreme drinking and its consequences:

...a policy mix of strategies targeting levels of alcohol consumption in the general population as well as specific strategies that target "problematic" drinking populations is an essential tool in reducing harmful alcohol consumption.... The ideal approach is that summed up by the British Academy of Medical Sciences in its report on alcohol policy, *Calling Time* (Academy of Medical Science, 2004, p. 11): "Implemented alone neither the targeted nor the overall approach can constitute an entire policy response. What is needed is an integrated alcohol policy with its constituent elements operating in a mutually supportive fashion, and with the policy sum greater than its parts."[3]

REFERENCES

Academy of Medical Science. (2004). *Calling time: The nation's drinking as a health issue.* London: Author.

Acheson, D. (1988). *Public health in England: The report of the Committee of Inquiry into the Future Development of the Public Health Function.* London: Her Majesty's Stationery Office.

Alcohol Advisory Council of New Zealand (ALAC). (2005). *Host responsibility: Guidelines for licensed premises.* Wellington, New Zealand: Author.

Alcohol Epidemiology Program, University of Minnesota. (2007). *What police can do.* Retrieved May 1, 2007, from http://www.epi.umn.edu/alcohol/policy/police.shtm.

Anderson, P., & Baumberg, B. E. N. (2007). Alcohol policy: Who should sit at the table? *Addiction, 102,* 335–336.

Brundtland, G. H. (1998, May 13). Speech at the Fifty-first World Health Assembly, Geneva. Retrieved May 7, 2007, from http://www.who.int.

Collie, C. (2002). *Strengthening community action on alcohol.* Wellington, New Zealand: Alcohol Advisory Council of New Zealand.

Coomaraswamy, K. S., & Shepherd, J. P. (2003). Predictors and severity of injury in assaults with bar glasses and bottles. *Injury Prevention, 9,* 81–84.

Cooray, M. (1988). 16.3: Working out the limits of government. In M. Cooray (Ed.), *The Australian achievement: From bondage to freedom* [Electronic version]. Retrieved from http://www.ourcivilisation.com/cooray/btof/index.htm.

Currie, C., Roberts, C., Morgan, A., Smith, R., Settertobulte, W., Samdal, O., et al. (Eds.). (2004). *Young people's health in context. Health Behaviour in School-aged Children (HBSC) study: International report from the 2001/2002 survey.* Health Policy for Children and Adolescents No. 4. Copenhagen, Denmark: WHO Regional Office for Europe.

Cusens, B., & Shepherd, J. (2005). Prevention of alcohol-related assault and injury. *Hospital Medicine, 66,* 346–348.

Diageo Ireland. (2005). *Helping to tackle alcohol misuse.* Retrieved May 1, 2007, from http://www.diageo.ie/community/AlchoholAwarness.

Doherty, S. J., & Roche, M. (2003). *Alcohol and licensed premises: Best practice in policing.* Payneham, Australia: Australian Centre for Policing Research.

Drugs and Crime Prevention Committee. (2006). *Inquiry into strategies to reduce harmful alcohol consumption.* Final Report (Vol. 1). Melbourne, Australia: Author.

---

[3] Reproduced by permission of the Honourable Speaker of the Legislative Assembly, Victoria, Australia.

Edwards, M. (2005). *"Civil society," the encyclopedia of informal education.* Retrieved August 10, 2007, from http://www.infed.org/association/civil_society.htm.

English, D. R., Holman, C. D. J., Milne, E., Winter, M. J., Hulse, G. K., Codde, G., et al. (1995). *The quantification of drug caused morbidity and mortality in Australia, 1992.* Canberra, Australia: Commonwealth Department of Human Services and Health.

European Commission. (2006). *An EU strategy to support Member States in reducing alcohol related harm.* Brussels, Belgium: Author.

European Spirits Organisation (CEPS) & European Forum for Responsible Drinking (EFRD). (2006). *Drinks industry initiatives 2006: Voluntary initiatives by the EU spirits industry to help reduce alcohol-related harm.* Brussels, Belgium: Authors.

Evans, K., & Roche, A. (2001). The role of government and law. In E. Houghton & A. Roche (Eds.), *Learning about drinking* (pp. 243–265). Philadelphia: Brunner-Routledge.

Graham, K., Bernards, S., Osgood, D. W., Homel, R., & Purcell, J. (2005). Guardians and handlers: The role of bar staff in preventing and managing aggression. *Addiction, 100,* 755–766.

Grant, M., & O'Connor, J. (Eds.). (2005). *Corporate social responsibility and alcohol: The need and potential for partnership.* New York: Routledge.

Hibell, B., Andersson, B., Bjarnason, T., Ahlström, S., Balakireva, O., Kokkevi, A., et al. (2004). *The ESPAD Report 2003: Alcohol and other drug use among students in 35 European countries.* Stockholm: Swedish Council for Information on Alcohol and Other Drugs (CAN) and the Pompidou Group at the Council of Europe.

International Center for Alcohol Policies (ICAP). (2006a). *Responsible drinks marketing: Shared rights and responsibilities. Report of an ICAP Expert Committee.* Washington, D.C.: Author.

International Center for Alcohol Policies (ICAP). (2006b). *The structure of the beverage alcohol industry.* ICAP Report 17. Washington, D.C.: Author.

Johnston, L. D., O'Malley, P. M., Bachman, J. G., & Schulenberg, J. E. (2007). *Monitoring the future national results on adolescent drug use: Overview of key findings, 2006.* NIH Publication No. 07-6202. Bethesda, MD: National Institute on Drug Abuse.

Kalafatelis, E., McMillen, P., & Palmer, S. (2003). *Youth and alcohol: 2003 ALAC youth drinking monitor.* Wellington, New Zealand: Alcohol Advisory Council of New Zealand.

Marsden Jacob Associates. (2005). *Identifying a framework for regulation in packaged liquor retailing.* Report prepared for the National Competition Council as part of the NCC Occasional Series. Melbourne, Australia: National Competition Council.

Matthews, S., Chikritzhs, T., Catalano, P., Stockwell, T., & Donath, S. (2002). *Trends in alcohol-related violence in Australia: 1991/92–1999/00.* National Alcohol Indicators Bulletin No. 5. Perth, Australia: National Drug Research Institute.

McKnight, A. J., & Streff, F. M. (1994). The effect of enforcement upon service of alcohol to intoxicated patrons of bars and restaurants. *Accident Analysis and Prevention, 26,* 79–88.

New South Wales Office of Liquor, Gaming and Racing. (2007). *Alcohol free entertainment.* Retrieved on August 21, 2007, from http://www.olgr.nsw.gov.au/liquor_info_ young_people_alch_free.asp.

Nutbeam, D. (1998). *Health promotion glossary.* Geneva, Switzerland: World Health Organization.

Österberg, E. (1995). Do alcohol prices affect consumption and related problems? In H. Holder & G. Edwards (Eds.), *Alcohol and public policy: Evidence and issues* (pp. 145–163). New York: Oxford University Press.

Portman Group. (2003). *Code of practice on the naming, packaging, and promotion of alcoholic drinks* (3rd ed.). Retrieved May 1, 2007, from http://www.portman-group. org.uk/uploaded_files/documents/35_152_3rdCode.pdf.

Quigley, B. M., Leonard, K. E., & Collins, R. L. (2003). Characteristics of violent bars and bar patrons. *Journal of Studies on Alcohol, 64*, 765–772.

Reddy, S. P., Panday, S., Swart, D., Jinabhai, C. C., Amosun, S. L., James, S., et al. (2003). *Umthenthe Uhlaba Usamila: The South African Youth Risk Behaviour Survey 2002.* Cape Town, South Africa: Medical Research Council.

Responsible Retailing Forum. (2003). *Responsible retailing forum.* Retrieved May 2, 2007, from http://fcpr.fsu.edu/retail/.

Stimson, G. V., Grant, M., Choquet, M., & Garrison, P. (Eds.). (2007). *Drinking in context: Patterns, interventions, and partnerships.* New York: Routledge.

Stockwell, T. (2007). Working with the alcohol industry on alcohol policy: Should we sometimes sit at the same table? *Addiction, 102*, 1–3.

Thom, B., & Bayley, M. (2007). *Multi-component programmes: An approach to prevent and reduce alcohol-related harm.* York, U.K.: Joseph Rowntree Foundation.

Warburton, A. L., & Shepherd, J. P. (2000). Effectiveness of toughened glassware in terms of reducing injury in bars: A randomised controlled trial. *Injury Prevention, 6*, 36–40.

Wellington City Council. (2003). *Part 23: Liquor control.* Retrieved May 1, 2007, from http://www.wellington.govt.nz/plans/bylaws/part23.html.

World Health Organization (WHO). (2004). *Global status report on alcohol 2004.* Geneva, Switzerland: Author.

Chapter 7

Extreme Drinking, Young People, and Feasible Policy

Marjana Martinic and Barton Alexander

In recent years, concerns about young people's drinking and its implications for health and social order have taken center stage from both a public health and a policy perspective in many countries at national, local, and community levels. In particular, there has been increased concern about extreme drinking and the potential for harm. In an effort to address this issue, governments have grappled with measures to contain extreme drinking within the confines of law and order. Public health officials are striving to craft measures best able to reduce its incidence and resulting problems.

It must be noted, however, that, although numerous measures exist to address alcohol consumption generally and to reduce harm, few approaches are aimed specifically at extreme drinking. Most commonly, policy is developed at the national level, casting a wide net on drinking generally and often relying on restrictions and legislation. Control measures are not specifically tailored to address extreme drinking or other particular drinking patterns with social and health implications, but rather offer blanket approaches that affect populations in their entirety. Specific issues such as extreme drinking require more focused policy approaches that address them directly. To be realistic and feasible to implement, these approaches need to be flexible enough to accommodate different cultures and their idiosyncrasies. They must also be able to address local concerns and priorities using the resources that are available.

The design of reasonable and effective policies hinges upon making use of what is available and proven and combining it with new and responsive approaches. This holds as true in the alcohol field as it does in other areas. This chapter examines the policy context of extreme drinking and ways that feasible policies and targeted approaches might be developed, particularly with regard to young people.

A FRAMEWORK FOR POLICY

A starting point for the crafting of any alcohol policy is an effective regulatory framework. In countries around the world, such frameworks include a range of measures, usually in the form of licensing, taxation, and other restrictions on access to or consumption of alcohol. These cover a wide spectrum from full prohibition to a low level of regulation and enforcement. History has shown that more extreme measures such as prohibition and bans are as likely to have a range of negative as possible positive outcomes in the long run. These unintended consequences of control measures are a serious consideration in the development of policy options. The obvious exception to this is presented by countries (or local jurisdictions) where alcohol consumption is prohibited for religious reasons and there is near unanimous acceptance of these religious principles. Similarly, the lack of structure and regulation at the other end of the scale is also of limited use. When it comes to dealing with young people's drinking in general and extreme drinking in particular, some restrictions can be effective but must also be combined with efforts aimed at changing drinking behavior in other ways and over the long term.

A proper regulatory framework within which targeted measures can be applied is a realistic and desirable basis for alcohol policy development. Such a framework outlines reasonable requirements for production and sale, including taxation and pricing, licensing and consumer access. Typically, provisions as to where or when beverage alcohol may be sold or served are included. Other requirements may define who can be served, for example, prohibiting service to individuals who appear intoxicated or may be under the legal drinking age. The setting and implementation of minimum legal age limits for the consumption and purchase of beverage alcohol goes hand in hand with these requirements. An effective regulatory framework also provides means for appropriate enforcement. There is less agreement on the degree to which regulation alone should be relied on and what other measures can be applied and by whom.

Taxation and Pricing

Taxation and pricing are among the classic panoply of control measures applied to alcohol. While excise taxes are a useful source of revenue generation for governments, they have also been used as a public health tool aimed at lowering consumption across a population (International Center for Alcohol Policies [ICAP], 2006). Proponents of taxation as a prevention measure argue that price increases, by reducing all drinking, will also reduce problem drinking (Chaloupka, Grossman, & Saffer, 1998, 2002; Stockwell, 2006). There is, however, considerable debate regarding whether such measures have an effect on the heaviest or most problematic drinkers. Taxation is a blunt instrument that is nonspecific in its impact; it targets those who drink heavily as much as it does moderate drinkers. Some have argued that it is those who drink moderately who are most affected by increases in cost (Manning, Blumberg, & Moulton, 1995); the heaviest drinkers will simply shift their demand to products that are less expensive (Gruenewald, Ponicki, Holder, & Romelsjö, 2006). Indeed, as Table 7.1 suggests, many countries with high rates of excise tax on beverage alcohol are among those where extreme drinking remains high.

When it comes to young people specifically, there is some evidence of a relationship between the price of beverage alcohol and what and how much is consumed. Young people generally have limited disposable income; as a result, cheaper drinks are likely to be preferred, and the evidence suggests that extreme drinking among this group tends to involve lower-cost beverages (e.g., Chen, Paschall, & Grube, 2006). According to data published in the 2007 Eurobarometer Report (European Commission, 2007), 62% of young survey participants in different countries said that a 25% increase in price would not reduce their purchase of beverage alcohol, whereas 33% indicated that it would. It appears that price elasticity is greatest among the younger age groups examined. The general view held by 68% of surveyed Europeans of all ages, however, is that prices are ineffective at discouraging drinking among young people and heavy drinkers. In the light of these findings, increasing the price of beverage alcohol may, indeed, have some effect on reducing drinking by young people (Chaloupka et al., 2002; Coate & Grossman, 1988; Grossman, Chaloupka, Saffer, & Laixuthai, 1995), but its effectiveness may vary across cultures and may also lead to other unintended negative consequences.

Among the unintended consequences of increasing prices is a shift in demand. Consumers have considerable latitude in the prices they pay for the alcohol they consume (Treno, Gruenewald, Wood, & Ponicki, 2006). This shift may be to other, cheaper commercial beverages or to noncommercial sources (Härstedt, 2004; Haworth & Simpson, 2004; Nordlund & Österberg, 2000), and even to surrogate alcohol (McKee et al., 2005). A rise in price may promote growth of the black market in alcohol and encourage trade in smuggled or counterfeit beverages.

When considering price increases, it is also important to bear in mind that many young people, particularly those who do not yet have their own sources of income, often obtain their alcohol from adults. Where parents are the adult source of drinks, price may not significantly influence access to alcohol for young people. Swedish data suggest that, where parents are willing to supply beverage alcohol, the frequency and intensity of drinking and the likelihood of participating in extreme drinking among young people is increased (Lundborg, 2002). An analysis conducted in the United States by the National Research Council and the Institute of Medicine (2004) showed that most underage drinking requires involvement by adults in selling to or serving young people. Tacit support of underage drinking by many parents perpetuates a permissive culture. These findings suggest not only that parental

TABLE 7.1 Control Policy Measures in ESPAD Countries*

Country	% Getting drunk[b]	Policy Measures[a]						Tax (as % of retail price)		
		Purchase age (On-premise/off-premise)[c]	Advertising restrictions	Sponsorship restrictions	Control of retail sale and production	Off-premise sales restrictions	Taxation (% sales tax/VAT)	Beer	Wine	Spirits
Denmark	34	18/16	Bans and voluntary restrictions	Voluntary restrictions	License for sales	Restricted hours; full enforcement	25.0	34.2	17.6	41.5
Ireland	29	18	Mix of bans and voluntary restrictions	No	Licenses for production and sales	Restricted hours, days, places, and outlet density; full enforcement	24.5	20.4	22.5	41.3
United Kingdom	24	18 (16 for some beverages, with meal and when accompanied by an adult)	Voluntary restrictions	Voluntary restrictions	License for sales	Restricted hours; partial enforcement	17.5	–	–	–
Finland	23	18	Ban	Partial bans	Sales monopoly on wine and spirits; license for sale of beer	Restricted hours, days, places, and outlet density; full enforcement	22.0	38.0	36.0	67.0

Estonia	21	18	Partial bans	None	None	Restricted places of sale; partial enforcement	18.0	13.6	13.0	52.0
Austria	20	16 (18 for fortified wine, spirits)	Voluntary	None	None	None	20	-	0.0	-
Czech Republic	16	18	Partial bans	None	None	None	5	-	0.0	-
Lithuania	15	18	Partial bans	None	Licenses for production and sales	Restricted places of sale for spirits	18	-	-	-
Sweden	15	18/20 (18 for beer with ABV 3.5% or less)	Ban	None	Sales monopoly (for beverages over 3.5% alcohol by volume); license for production	Restricted hours, days, places, and outlet density; full enforcement	25	25.9	33.8	67.1
Iceland	14	20	Ban	Voluntary restrictions	Sales monopoly	Restricted hours, days, places, and outlet density; full enforcement	24.5	64.0	58.0	80.0

(continued)

*Countries are ranked in descending order according to the prevalence of drunkenness. See notes on p. 191.

TABLE 7.1 Control Policy Measures in ESPAD Countries (continued)

| Country | % Getting drunk[b] | Purchase age (On-premise/ off-premise)[c] | Policy Measures[a] | | | | Taxation (% sales tax/VAT) | Tax (as % of retail price) | | |
			Advertising restrictions	Sponsorship restrictions	Control of retail sale and production	Off-premise sales restrictions		Beer	Wine	Spirits
Norway	14	18 (20 for spirits)	Ban	Ban	Production monopoly on spirits; sales monopoly on wine and spirits; licenses for production and sales	Restricted hours, days, places, and outlet density; full enforcement	24.0	-	-	-
Slovenia	13	18	Partial bans	Voluntary restrictions	None	Restricted hours; no enforcement	-	-	-	-
Ukraine	13	18	Partial bans	None	Licenses for wine and spirits production and sales	Restricted places of sale for wine and spirits; fully enforced	20.0	20.0	50.0	85.0
Russian Federation	12	18	Partial bans	Ban	Licenses for production and sales	Restricted places of sale; partial enforcement	20.0	4.0	3.0	35.0

Germany	11	16 (18 for spirits)	Voluntary	None	None	None	16.0	6.6	0.0	13.78
Slovakia	11	18	Partial bans	Voluntary restrictions	Monopoly on spirits production; licenses for production of beer and spirits	None	23.0	7.5	25.0	35.0
Bulgaria	10	18	None	None	Licenses for production of wine and spirits; licenses for sales	Restricted places of sale; partial enforcement	20.0	5.8	9.4	27.7
Latvia	10	18	Partial bans	None	Licenses for production and sales	Restricted hours (wine and spirits); license for production and sales	18.0	4.4	16.9	44.2
Hungary	9	18	Mix of bans, partial bans, and voluntary restrictions	Partial bans	Licenses for production and sales	Restricted places of sale; enforcement rare	30.0	20.0	40.0	27.0

(continued)

TABLE 7.1 Control Policy Measures in ESPAD Countries (continued)

Country	Getting drunk[b] %	Purchase age (On-premise/ off-premise)[c]	Policy Measures[a] Advertising restrictions	Sponsorship restrictions	Control of retail sale and production	Off-premise sales restrictions	Taxation (% sales tax/ VAT)	Tax (as % of retail price) Beer	Wine	Spirits
Switzerland	9	16 (18 for spirits). Varies by canton	Partial bans	Ban	Monopoly on spirits production; license for spirits production	Restricted hours and days of sale; full enforcement	7.5	–	0.0	–
Croatia	8	18	Partial bans	Partial bans	License for beer and spirits production	Restricted places of sale; enforcement rare	22.0	25.0	0.0	53.0
Poland	8	18	Partial bans	Partial bans	Licenses for production and sales	Restricted places of sale and outlet density; full enforcement	22.0	–	–	–
Netherlands	6	16 (18 for spirits)	Voluntary restrictions	Voluntary restrictions	License for sale of spirits	Restricted hours, days, and places of sale; full enforcement	19.0	–	–	–
Italy	4	16	Mix of partial bans and voluntary restrictions	Voluntary restrictions	Licenses for production and sales	None	20.0	11.0	0.0	20.0

Malta	4	16	Voluntary restrictions	None	Licenses for production and sales	None	15.0	-	0.0	-
Romania	4	18	None	None	Licenses for production and sales	Restricted places of sale; no enforcement	19.0	-	-	-
France	2	16 (18 for fortified wine, spirits)	Partial bans	Partial bans	Licenses for production and sales	Restricted places of sale	16.9	8.8	3.1	33.2
Greece	2	17/ None	None	None	License for production	None	18.0	-	0.0	-
Portugal	2	16	Partial bans	Partial bans	Licenses for production and sales	None	17.0	-	-	-
Turkey	2	18	Partial bans	Partial bans	Monopoly on spirits production and sales; licenses for production and sales	Restrictions on hours, days, places of sale, outlet density; full enforcement.	18.0	-	-	-

a. Data on policy measures are taken from the *WHO Global Status Report: Alcohol Policy* (WHO, 2004).

b. Proportion of all students who have been drunk 10 times or more during the last 12 months, as reported in the 2003 ESPAD Report (Hibell et al., 2004).

c. Where on- and off-premise purchase ages are different, this has been indicated. Where they are the same, a single value is reported.

influence has an important role in shaping expectancies and norms, but also that economic constraints may not be a significant factor for many young people, as their alcohol is free.

Thus, even though increasing the price of beverage alcohol through taxation is often proposed as a measure for curbing drinking (and especially heavy drinking) among youth, it should be acknowledged that policies are not implemented in a vacuum, and that a range of costs and consequences (including some that are not obvious) need to be considered in evaluating their relative impact.

Licensing and Access at the Retail Level

Another set of broad-based measures is aimed at those who sell and serve beverage alcohol. Licensing requirements include restrictions on who may sell (or produce) beverage alcohol, where, and when. According to WHO data (2004), among the countries reviewed, 16 relied on state-run monopolies, 80 had some form of licensing requirement, and 13 had no restrictions at all (reviewed in Antalova & Martinic, 2005). Licensing may also differ with regard to type of beverage. For example, while the sale of beer or wine may be permitted in grocery stores and supermarkets in some jurisdictions, the sale of liquor (and, in some cases, wine) may be limited to state-run or specially licensed shops. Yet many establishments that sell or serve alcohol, particularly in developing countries, operate outside the legal framework and remain beyond the reach of licensing authorities, making enforcement difficult.

Zoning requirements around venues that sell or serve alcohol exist in some form in most countries and may also be implemented by local governments and municipalities. Provisions may include restrictions as to where licensed establishments may be located. Many cities implement zoning in order to separate establishments (and entertainment areas, generally) from residential areas in order to reduce potential public disorder and address safety concerns. Zoning may also influence the density of retail outlets in the proximity of schools, libraries, hospitals, places of worship, or other locations of particular concern in the community. Other zoning restrictions may cover the sale of beverage alcohol at gasoline stations and highway rest stops. While sales may be permitted, in some cases the type of beverage(s) available may be limited to those with lower alcohol content.

Other regulations are specifically aimed at minimizing the incidence of drunkenness and public disorder. Outlets may be subject to different operating hours for sale and service or may restrict them on particular days of the week and holidays. The issue of appropriate closing times has received particular attention in conjunction with efforts to avoid the congregation of intoxicated patrons outside bars, nightclubs, and other venues (Chikritzhs & Stockwell, 2002; Plant & Plant, 2005; Talbot, 2006). Some jurisdictions have attempted to solve this difficulty by staggering closing times, thereby avoiding public nuisance and traffic problems.

Many jurisdictions—for example, Spain, the United Kingdom, and the United States—also have requirements as to where and when public drinking is permitted on the street and in public spaces. These are primarily intended to avoid the confluence of large gatherings and intoxication (Single, 1993). Responding to community pressure, some jurisdictions have introduced bans on alcohol in public spaces in order to address concerns about safety. The City Council of Auckland, New Zealand, has implemented a ban on beverage alcohol in the city's central business district and some suburban areas that prohibits people from "bringing, carrying or drinking alcohol in public places within a ban area. This includes the possession or drinking of alcohol in vehicles within ban areas" (Auckland City Council, 2007a, para.12). However, such bans do not cover private property, licensed premises, or outdoor pavement seating attached to licensed premises. Off-licenses, such as retail shops, are also not affected, provided that, once purchased, the alcohol is removed quickly from the ban area (see Case Study, "*Botellón* in Spain," below).

Many of the restrictions and regulations described above are addressed in the requirements for obtaining a license to sell or serve beverage alcohol. However, all of these measures depend on proper enforcement, which may occur through a formal process of government oversight and review (or possible revocation) of licenses. It may also occur through self-enforcement by those who operate establishments. In either case, enforcement must be sensitive and responsive to community needs and concerns.

Case Study: *Botellón* in Spain

Andrés Bascones Pérez-Fragero

In Spain, moderate drinking of beverage alcohol by adults is closely tied to the local culture, culinary traditions, and the way of life. Drinking mostly takes place in the company of others and is historically linked to festivities and social events, many of them in the open air. The phenomenon of the *botellón*, therefore, is nothing new in Spanish culture; only some specific aspects of it are new.

Spain's traditional drinking culture has always included some people—usually a minority—who abused alcohol, whether occasionally or chronically. Nevertheless, extreme drinking was generally penalized by the community, whereas moderate drinking has been accepted and even encouraged. In the past 25 years, overall alcohol consumption in Spain has decreased: Per capita consumption has dropped 25%, and the number of problem drinkers has fallen from 11.2% in 1983 to 5.3% in 2003 (Brugal, Rodríguez-Martos, & Villalba, 2006). These decreases have been reflected in the reduction of problems associated with chronic alcohol abuse, for instance, in mortality from cirrhosis of the liver (Brugal et al., 2006).

Drinking levels among young people in Spain have also decreased since the early 1990s, so that more and more youths report alcohol intake only during weekends (Comas, 2004). In some cases, this concentration of drinking on certain days has led to more compulsive and abusive consumption than in the past (Brugal et al., 2006; Elzo, Laespada, & Pallarés, 2003). In the 1970s and 1980s, when youthful drinking levels were higher than at present, the issue of alcohol was not thought to be a problem (Elzo et al., 2003), but, in recent years, society has become more aware of the dangers of alcohol consumption and abuse by underage drinkers, and these behaviors have become subject to tighter legal restrictions and social pressure. Nevertheless, young Spanish adults mostly continue to drink alcohol moderately and responsibly and tend to reject those among them who abuse alcohol and fail to keep their behavior under control.

We should first try to define the phenomenon, variously referred to in different parts of Spain as *botellón*, *botellóna*, *botelleo*, and so on. Many researchers define it chiefly by the presence of drinking (Baigorri & Fernández, 2004), but, on closer inspection of the practice, *botellón* consists of the gathering of young people in the streets, squares, and parks of towns and cities, normally during weekend evenings, as a way of meeting, having fun, chatting, and drinking beverages of all kinds—mainly, but not exclusively, alcohol drinks (normally bought at shops and supermarkets and then mixed and served by the young people themselves). Current definitions tend to not take account of the fact that *botellón* entails a time of enjoyment, interaction, and, in some cases, personal growth. It is a practice laden with a great deal of symbolism and, hence, is more than a mere meeting of young people for the purpose of drinking alcohol.

The latest surveys report that *botellón* is the predominant choice for weekend leisure activity among young people. *Botellón* gatherings take place in most Spanish towns and cities, but each *botellón* is different, shaped by the idiosyncrasies of its host town, culture, and community. Participants come from all social strata, occupations, educational and political backgrounds, as well as ages. Some *botellón* gatherings attract individuals aged around 50 years; many others—like the *botellón* that meets at Plaza de la Merced in Malaga—primarily involves young adults over 18 years (the minimum drinking age in most Spanish regions), and some events involve many underage drinkers. Young adults' *botellón* gatherings normally take place at a later time than those attracting underage youths.

Botellón has been going on for years, but it was not until the mid- and late-1990s that it took on its present significance and—more importantly—generated the social concern that surrounds it today. Depending on locations and dates, the practice now draws crowds that range from a few dozen to thousands of young people, many of whom take part in the event for many years: For example, youths gathering for the *botellón* at the Plaza de la Merced in Malaga have been doing so for an average of six years (Musitu & Bascones, 2006).

Although the *botellones* are diverse, it is possible to delineate the profile of average participants: normally, single young people of both sexes, aged between 18 and 23 years, students (principally, university students), living with parents, generally in the same city where the *botellón* meeting is held—although some young people come from out of town for the occasion. For instance, among the participants of the *botellón* at the Plaza de la Merced in Malaga, 16% come from outside the city (Musitu & Bascones, 2006). Almost half (47%) of young people gathering at these meetings come by car or motorbike, with the added risk of alcohol-impaired driving: 10% of young people taking part in the *botellón* in Malaga say they "always" or "nearly always" drink and drive (Musitu & Bascones, 2006).

What explains the popularity of the *botellón* gatherings? According to recent research (Baigorri & Fernández, 2004; Consejería de Gobernación, 2006; Musitu & Bascones, 2006; Navarrete, 2002), the main reasons given by the participants themselves include the following: The high price of drinks in bars and nightclubs "forces" them to buy their drinks in shops and supermarkets at a lower price, which they then drink outdoors; the practice has become fashionable and is a new form of leisure; a *botellón* is a meeting-place and an

FIGURE. 7.1 *Botellón* in Valencia, Spain (2006). © Jose Jordan/Sygma/Corbis.

opportunity for enjoyment with the added attraction of being in the open air. The reasons for young people's participation in *botellón*, then, are chiefly economic and social.

The available data on *botellón* gatherings (Baigorri & Fernández, 2004; Consejería de Gobernación, 2006; Elzo et al., 2003; Musitu & Bascones, 2006; Navarrete, 2002; Servicio de Atención a la Movida [SAM], 2004) permit a number of general conclusions. *Botellones* usually draw the largest crowds on Saturday nights, followed by Friday and Thursday nights. Gatherings are more modest during university examination periods. These meetings are normally the first stop during a night out with friends; *botellones* are, therefore, usually held near nightlife areas and near the doors of bars and nightclubs. Depending on the *botellón* in question, the gathering begins between 11 p.m. and 1 a.m. and ends between 2 and 4 a.m. The participants usually go to *botellones* directly from home (69%), the gatherings serving as meeting points for groups of friends at the start of the night's fun (Musitu & Bascones, 2006). Between 3 and 3:30 a.m., fewer young people remain at a given *botellón*: These are generally the individuals who have drunk the most among their peers, make the most noise, and cause the most disturbances to the surrounding communities. At the end of a *botellón* meeting, the majority of young people go on to bars and nightclubs (82%) to continue their *marcha* (which may be roughly translated as "partying," a tour of nightlife venues—the "pub crawl" or "bar hopping"). At the same time, for a considerable number of young people, a *botellón* is the only stop on their nightly *marcha*. On average, most *botellón* participants (92%) spend less than €9 on such an occasion (Musitu & Bascones, 2006).

The majority of *botellón* participants consume beverage alcohol during the event; however, some surveys indicate that around 19% of *botellón* attendees have never tried alcohol (Baigorri & Fernández, 2004). In general, during regular *botellón* gatherings where most participants are young adults, 5% (Musitu & Bascones, 2006) to 8% (SAM, 2004) of people report drinking fruit juice, water, or soft drinks rather than alcohol.

Depending on the venue where the *botellón* is held and its participants, the drinks of choice and the patterns of drinking differ. *Botellones* usually involve the consumption of spirits and soft drinks, mixed by the participants themselves. However, beverage preferences vary by age. Thus, a study in the region of Madrid (Navarrete, 2002) reported that 84% of younger participants aged between 14 and 15 years primarily drank cocktails of red wine and cola (*calimocho*), followed by beer (35%) and spirits (34%). As the respondents neared the age of 18 years, spirits became the most consumed (75%) when compared to *calimocho* (63%) and beer (48%).

The average alcohol consumption during a *botellón* session is about four drinks; some young people drink one or two, while others engage in rapid consumption of 10 to 12 drinks. Most participants think of alcohol as one among several elements of their night out and drink without the intention—at least without an expressed intention—of getting drunk. Rather, young people drink to "have fun" or to get over inhibitions. *Botellón* is also an occasion to consume other substances, chiefly tobacco, followed by hashish and marijuana.

In general, *botellón* gatherings are peaceable and free from conflict. Even though there may be thousands of young people drinking alcohol in one place, fights, aggression, and vandalism are relatively rare. So, despite the fact that some violent episodes may arise, possibly facilitated by extreme alcohol consumption, the link between *botellón* and vandalism, as portrayed by certain media, is unsubstantiated (Baigorri & Fernández, 2004). Where, then, is the problem? Why is there a raging debate in Spain about *botellón*? In this author's view, *botellón* creates two distinct kinds of conflict. The first relates to health. At some *botellón* meetings, alcohol is consumed by minors (aged under 18 years); even where participants are over 18 years, some clearly drink abusively or in inappropriate situations (for instance, when they are going to drive). The second type of conflict—which has done the most to create the bad reputation of *botellón*—involves the side-effects of the practice. A significant part of the adult community is adversely affected by these gatherings in terms of the mess, smells, noise, and the "poor image of the city" that *botellón* may produce. There appears to be a conflict of interest between young people's right to enjoy themselves and local residents' right to sleep at night and enjoy clean and tidy streets.

The measures and bylaws introduced in Spain in response to the *botellón* phenomenon have been many and varied. At the risk of oversimplifying, a range of measures enacted by the authorities (mostly, local and regional) on this issue may be divided into four main kinds: (1) banning or restricting alcohol consumption in public thoroughfares, normally in conjunction with restrictions on the sale, consumption, and advertising of alcohol; (2) promoting alternative leisure pursuits to *botellón* and to going out to bars at night, including sporting events, clubs, and communal games; (3) allotting specific places for young people to gather for *botellón* without being a nuisance to the rest of the community; and (4) implementing prevention and education campaigns to promote responsible alcohol consumption and civic behavior.

The most effective approaches to preventing and reducing the problems currently associated with *botellón* gatherings involve a judicious combination of the four strategies above, achieved through a consensus among the main groups involved: young people, local residents, authorities, and staff at establishments that sell alcohol (Musitu & Bascones, 2006). Since each *botellón* has its own distinct features, action should be taken locally. Although many surveys report significant differences in opinion among young people, community residents, and—for instance—bar staff, they also show that most local residents think *botellón* should be allowed if it is not a nuisance (Consejería de Gobernación, 2006; Musitu & Bascones, 2006). Meanwhile, in at least one study, many young people acknowledged the problems associated with *botellones* (e.g., 84% recognized that the *botellón* might disturb local residents) and expressed an interest in reaching mutually acceptable agreements with community residents (Musitu & Bascones, 2006). It is important to note that heavy-drinking participants of the *botellón* (those consuming between 10 and 12 drinks per night) were the most likely among respondents to oppose any regulation of the gatherings, while the individuals who tended to drink less (one or two drinks per night) were more open to compromise (Musitu & Bascones, 2006). In this respect, it might be useful to involve these moderate drinkers in facilitating dialogue and agreements among the various stakeholders.

Legal Age Limits

Developing measures around young people's drinking, be it extreme or otherwise, relies, at its broadest, on defining what is meant by "young people"; currently, no such definition exists. A World Health Organization (WHO) Study Group has defined a young person as someone between the ages of 10 and 24 years (WHO, 1986, pp. 11–12). Yet, when it comes to drinking, where an appropriate threshold lies within this broad range depends strongly on culture and prevailing societal norms. A first step in addressing issues relevant to young people and their drinking behavior in most countries is the establishment of a legal age threshold for the purchase and consumption of alcohol.

Legal age limits for beverage alcohol are mandated in most countries around the world, but vary with regard to where they are set. Purchase age is generally higher than drinking age (ICAP, 2008b). In the United Kingdom, for instance, alcohol may be consumed legally within the home (under parental supervision) beginning at the age of 5 years, while the age for purchase is 18 (with some exceptions, see Table 7.1). In many countries, the legal right to drink precedes or coincides with the age of legal majority for other activities, such as voting or entering the military. Among the countries reviewed in WHO's Global Status Report on Alcohol Policy (2004), the vast majority of countries set the legal purchase age at 18 years. Out of the 112 countries surveyed for the report, 13% had a lower on-premise purchase age. Among those where the on- and off-premise purchase age is set below 18 years, 16 is the mandated age in a number of countries, including Germany, Jamaica, Portugal, and Spain, but this may depend on the alcohol content of the beverage consumed. A number of countries have no mandated purchase age; 14.8% have no on-premise age limit, while 21.4% have no off-premise limit.

However, some countries have higher age requirements (7.8% of all countries surveyed in the WHO Global Status Report have higher age requirements for on-premise and 8.9% for off-premise purchase). Notable in this category are Indonesia, Micronesia, Palau, and the United States, where the purchase age is set at 21; Iceland and Japan, where the age limit is 20; and Nicaragua and most provinces in Canada, where an age of 19 years is required (WHO,

2004). Some countries further refine their age requirements for on- and off-premise purchase. While the on-premise purchase age in Sweden is 18, its off-premise purchase age for most alcohol beverages is set at 20; in Greece, the on-premise purchase age is 17, but there is no mandated off-premise purchase age; and in Denmark, the age limit is 18 for on-premise purchase and 16 for off-premise purchase. A final nuance is introduced in some jurisdictions with regard to beverage type. Where this is the case, purchase ages for spirits are typically higher both on- and off-premise than they are for beer or wine (for example, in Austria, France, the Netherlands, and Norway).

The application of drinking age laws serves specifically to prevent those under the legal age limit from purchasing and consuming alcohol, and others (with the exception of parents in some cases) from affording them access. A secondary aim of legal limits is to prevent extreme drinking and other similar drinking patterns. Given their relative inexperience with drinking and its possible outcomes, the desire to experiment, and the strong influence of outside pressures, younger people are more likely than older individuals to engage in extreme drinking. However, most make the transition out of this and other thrill-seeking behaviors as they get older. Research evidence suggests that the typical "drinking trajectory" across the lifespan includes heavy drinking in youth, which tapers off as age, maturity, family, and professional obligations increase and gain importance (Schulenberg & Maggs, 2002; Schulenberg, O'Malley, Bachman, Wadsworth & Johnston, 1996). The trend seems to hold across cultures (e.g., Goddard, 2006) and is consistent with the findings of the focus groups described in chapter 5.

Most governments recognize that age limits governing the consumption and purchase of beverage alcohol are important policy measures. Although desirable, such measures also need to be realistic, take into account actual drinking patterns among young people, and correspond to the ability to enforce behavior among individuals they are intended to target. There is a debate as to the appropriate drinking or purchase ages relative to those mandated for other activities, including voting, marriage, military service, and legal majority. Some countries argue that a higher drinking or purchase age for alcohol saves lives in road traffic accidents. This was part of the motivation for implementing the 21-year age limit at the federal level in the United States in 1984 (Title 23 United States Code §158; see U.S. Government Printing Office, n.d.) and also more recently spurred the government of New Zealand to review its own drinking age legislation (Hill & Stewart, 1996; Houlahan, 2006). There is, however, a need to reconcile the legal context of drinking with the reality that many young people are part of the workforce, shoulder responsibilities, and enjoy considerable independence in other aspects of their lives.

Survey results indicate that drinking often begins as young as 13 years of age, well below the legally mandated age in most countries (Currie et al., 2004; Hibell et al., 2004; Johnston, O'Malley, Bachman, & Schulenberg, 2006). The exact meaning of "drinking" is vague in this context; included here are those who just sample alcohol, as well as young people who drink often and to extremes. It should be acknowledged that underage drinkers are a reality. Some governments address the issue by adopting a "zero tolerance" approach—no drinking below the legal age permitted. It has been argued, however, that "[z]ero tolerance is a political response, not an educationally sound solution" (Skiba quoted in "Report: Zero Tolerance No Solution for School," 2001, para. 4) and an example of inflexible policy that ignores reality (Skiba, 2000).

How practical and realistic drinking age limits are should be measured not only by the reality of prevailing drinking patterns among youth, but also by their potential for creating unintended outcomes. The 21-year drinking age law in the United States, for example, has resulted in cross-border traffic of persons below the U.S. legal limit into Mexico where the drinking age is 18, effectively creating an extreme drinking destination for many young people. Where neighboring jurisdictions have different laws regarding drinking age and other restrictions, high rates of traffic fatalities and violent incidents have led to the coining of the phrase "blood border" (Baker, Johnson, Voas, & Lange, 2000; Lange, Lauer, & Voas, 1999; Voas, Lange, & Johnson, 2002). However, other, more targeted measures, such as earlier closing times for bars in border towns frequented by young people, have decreased the problematic outcomes, arguing in favor of combined strategies that are adapted to specific needs (Voas, Romano, Kelley-Baker, & Tippetts, 2006).

An important consideration in developing alcohol policies is that extreme drinking is not confined to young people below the drinking age limit, at whatever age that may be set. Young adults make up a substantial proportion of individuals with harmful drinking patterns. Evidence suggests that the heaviest drinkers in the United States, for example, are young males between the ages of 18 and 29 (Greenfield & Rogers, 1999), whereas in the United Kingdom they are persons between the ages of 16 and 24 (Goddard, 2006). Many of these young people are part of the workforce, have some financial independence, and enjoy a range of freedoms. For them, extreme drinking is often part of a general lifestyle that tests the waters of adulthood. And it is precisely these young people who are the cause of some of the main concerns associated with extreme drinking, including disruption of public order and alcohol-related problems (see chapters 4 and 5).

TARGETED POLICY MEASURES

Countries where heavy drinking among young people is most common are also often those with the most rigorous restrictions on alcohol (e.g., Hibell et al., 2004; see also Table 7.1), clearly as a response to problems. Yet despite the presence of stringent measures, extreme drinking patterns persist, as does resulting harm. In light of the apparent disconnect between policy goals and the reality of drinking behavior, it may be timely to revisit how we think of policies, particularly as they relate to extreme drinking. Although government regulation provides a useful framework within which more targeted efforts can be designed, some regulations such as taxation are inherently too broad to be useful by themselves in addressing particular drinking patterns. Other structured approaches are needed that can be implemented not only at the national level, but also at the local level, and involve a variety of stakeholders. These may be policies implemented by regional jurisdictions or municipalities, and can include internal policies developed and put in place by individual institutions.

The advantage of such a bottom-up approach is that it allows cultural considerations and attitudes around extreme drinking to be taken into account. It also factors in the needed sensitivity to specific local concerns and priorities and improves responsiveness to the most immediate issues. Equally important is the ability to make use of those resources that are on hand and easily accessible. This can help increase a sense of ownership, not just of problems but also their solutions, among those most directly involved. The opportunity to create practical and feasible options exists in a number of different areas.

Consumer Information and Education

Extreme drinking is a cultural phenomenon and, as this book attempts to demonstrate, is in many cases considered a normative drinking pattern, not deviant behavior. As both the focus group results reported in chapter 5 and other data show (e.g., Currie et al., 2004; Hibell et al., 2004; chapters 3 and 4), a culture's permissiveness with regard to intoxication is likely to contribute to the prevalence of extreme drinking on a larger scale. A long-term strategy is therefore needed to shift cultural attitudes toward lesser tolerance of extreme drinking. Currently, as the United Kingdom's 2004 alcohol strategy notes, "public drunkenness is socially accepted, if not expected" (U.K. Prime Minister's Strategy Unit, 2004, p. 28). This applies not only to the U.K. context, but also elsewhere.

Shifts in culture occur over the long term. One vehicle for encouraging changes in attitudes is education in its broadest sense, aimed at three different objectives: as a means of providing information; as a vehicle for raising awareness about an issue and ways to address it; and as a means for ultimately changing specific behaviors or their general acceptance (ICAP, 2004). Education is an important component of alcohol policy and can be built into structured approaches. It may be aimed at the general public or at particular groups in a more specialized and targeted way. Educational approaches to extreme drinking can be devised for young people, for parents and other adults, or for professionals who are in contact with extreme drinking. In each case, the approach needs to be tailored and specific goals must be clearly defined. From a policy standpoint, education can be integrated into broader strategies in a culturally appropriate way.

Educating the Public

Policy measures in many countries include the education of the general public through drinking guidelines and recommendations. These are issued by governments or by professional bodies and largely address the relationship between drinking levels and harm (see ICAP, 2003, 2007). Currently, extreme drinking is not a key focus of most drinking guidelines, although Australia's guidelines, developed by the National Health and Medical Research Council (2001), specifically advise against "binge" drinking. The guidelines are currently being updated, and the Australian National Alcohol Strategy 2006–2009 has outlined its priority areas as including intoxication and public safety around areas where alcohol is served (Ministerial Council on Drug Strategy, 2006). A similar focus has also been integrated into approaches taken in the United Kingdom, both in the *Plan for Action on Alcohol Problems* (Scottish Executive, 2002) for Scotland and the *Alcohol Harm Reduction Strategy* (U.K. Prime Minister's Strategy Unit, 2004) for England. This is a clear reflection of the high priority placed on dealing with extreme drinking and effecting a change in drinking culture.

Other forms of consumer information or reminders at the policy level include nutritional labels on packaging of beverage alcohol (ICAP, 2008a). Although some information is required in most countries, it varies with regard to content. Labeling may, for example, include information about the product itself, its origin and alcohol content, or ingredients and allergens that may be present. It may offer information on standard drink sizes, allowing those who drink to calculate their alcohol intake and reconcile it with any existing official drinking guidelines.

Other types of consumer information or reminders, whether included on labels or in advertising, may warn against drinking during pregnancy, while operating heavy machinery, or when intending to drive. Directional labels point to Web sites and other resources where additional information or advice may be obtained. Whether these different types of consumer information are mandated or voluntary (depending on country), they aim to inform those who drink and raise their awareness about the products and drinking patterns.

In some countries, consumer information or reminders also include warnings about excessive drinking and recommendations for responsible consumption of alcohol. For example:

- In France, advertisements must feature a warning that states, "The abuse of alcohol is dangerous for health: Consume in moderation."
- Similarly, Mexican product advertisements must contain the wording, "Abusing consumption of this product is harmful to health."
- The Dutch social aspects organization STIVA broadcasts the following education message on television advertisements, "Enjoy your drink, but be moderate."
- In Brazil, beverage alcohol packaging must include the wording, "Avoid the excessive consumption of alcohol."
- All advertisements of alcohol beverages in Portugal include the caveat, "Be responsible. Drink moderately."
- In Taiwan, advertising and promotion of alcohol beverages must include the message, "Excessive drinking endangers health."

Consumer information and education also play another important function. Particular attention to extreme drinking and its potential outcomes can help raise awareness among both the individuals who engage in this behavior and the community at large. Creating a culture of disapproval with regard to extreme drinking can help shift public attitudes. Furthermore, education about prevailing laws and the penalties for breaking them is an important component of measures addressing extreme drinking in young people. There must be awareness among the general population, not just among its younger segments, of the levels at which legal drinking or purchase age and blood alcohol content (BAC) limits for driving are set. Education of sellers of alcohol about laws, penalties, and other ramifications may help reinforce responsible behavior.

Educating Young People

Education for young people themselves is a major focus of many prevention efforts around the world, often aimed particularly at extreme drinking. Various programs are discussed in chapter 8, but it is up to policy-makers to ensure that a more formal approach to alcohol education is also taken. Alcohol issues may, for example, be integrated into formal curricula in schools. While existing school education programs on alcohol have received less than resounding endorsements with regard to changing behavior (e.g., Babor et al., 2003), there is also evidence that not all education efforts should be discounted as being ineffective (e.g., Foxcroft, Ireland, Lowe, & Breen, 2002). Accordingly, there is a place for them among the many tools that are available. Young people can be made aware of the relationship between patterns of drinking and their outcomes, particularly with regard to extreme drinking and its possible harmful consequences. Parents and families can play an important role in the effort to educate youth about drinking, and some policies may perhaps best reach young people if they are targeted at parents.

A more structured integration of less formal strategies can also be ensured through policy decisions. For example, one promising approach to informal alcohol education is social norms marketing, which has been integrated in several universities and college campuses in the United States (Berkowitz, 2005; DeJong et al., 2006; Yanovitzky, Stewart, & Lederman, 2006). This approach informs students who may be tempted toward extreme drinking that in reality most of their peers do not drink that way. How young people perceive drinking among their peers and their judgments about their own drinking are found to be reliable predictors of harm (Benton et al., 2006). What differentiates this approach from many other interventions is that it relies entirely on changing drinking culture—young people are made aware that extreme drinking is not necessarily normative behavior among their peers, nor need it be. While the approach may not need to feature formally on any college curriculum, it can none the less be integrated into the general operations of an institution (see chapter 8 for further discussion).

Many young people, both over and below the legal drinking age, have a close relationship with technology and are regular users of the Internet and its resources. Special Web sites have been designed to offer brief interventions and counseling on drinking (e.g., Cunningham, Humphreys, Kypri, & van Mierlo, 2006). Some of these have been specifically adapted for use by young people (Chiauzzi, Green, Lord, Thum, & Goldstein, 2005). There is evidence that some young people may be more likely to access Internet resources if problems arise than to speak directly to an adult, whether a parent or other person of influence, because of social stigma or because they are below the legal drinking age and worried about repercussions. This appears to hold true across cultures (e.g., Hester & Miller, 2006; Wang et al., 2005). Formal integration of such Web sites into other available resources should be encouraged, and awareness of their existence needs to be raised among potential users.

A final but highly important approach to reducing risk is to teach young people who are likely to be (or already are) extreme drinkers about various self-protective strategies and techniques to stay safe (see discussion in chapter 8). These may include always drinking in close-knit groups, in safe environments, or using designated drivers (Benton, Benton, & Downey, 2006). There is evidence that the use of such strategies reduces the likelihood of experiencing harm (Benton, Schmidt et al., 2004). Secondary and tertiary educational institutions may be appropriate venues for teaching such skills, but education in public venues, where drinking takes place, may also be useful. While this approach does not aim to reduce extreme drinking itself, it is at least a pragmatic step in ensuring that the potential for harm is minimized and can be implemented alongside other measures that more directly target the behavior.

Educating Professionals

The third area for educational efforts is directed at professionals, who may deal with extreme drinking and its consequences on a number of different levels—for instance, the healthcare professionals and providers of social services for young people. Education to impart skills to enable these key professionals to recognize problems and offer support is much needed, as is the knowledge necessary to provide adequate referrals.

The curricula of many medical education programs do not include alcohol issues, a structural problem that seems relatively simple to remedy. At present, many continuing education courses are specifically designed to offer the knowledge and resources needed by medical professionals. However, these courses are not a requirement and many primary healthcare providers or social workers are not versed in drinking problems, or in how to deal with them and their outcomes.

Despite the importance of primary healthcare in providing advice and immediate response to various lifestyle issues, many interventions around extreme drinking are likely to take place *after* the harm has already been done. As a result, hospital emergency rooms, for example, can be effective venues for dealing with patients who have engaged in extreme drinking and others who have been harmed by them. They not only provide an opportunity to treat any physical injuries, but can also be used for further interventions and for changing behavior. Again, the ability to provide the services required means that personnel need to be trained in how to screen their patients and offer brief interventions and counseling. The Alcohol Use Disorders Identification Test (AUDIT) and similar questionnaires are powerful tools in identifying individuals who, like many extreme drinkers, engage in harmful drinking patterns but are not alcohol-dependent (e.g., Aertgeerts et al., 2000; Babor, De La Fuente, Saunders, & Grant, 1992; Babor, Higgins-Biddle, Saunders, & Monteiro, 2001; Cook, Chung, Kelly, & Clark, 2005; Kelly, Donovan, Chung, Cook, & Delbridge, 2004; Landry, Guyon, Bergeron, & Provost, 2002; Werner, Joffe, & Graham, 1999). Follow-up brief interventions and lifestyle counseling can be used to modify harmful drinking patterns. At the same time, evidence indicates that a broader approach may also be needed so that the full spectrum of drinking behaviors can be addressed (Hungerford & Pollock, 2003). Where permitted by law, this includes the collection of demographic data about patients to help with tailoring future approaches and interventions, as well as increased integration of new technologies that can facilitate such efforts. While these approaches are important with regard to prevention, they need to be integrated into the structural fabric of healthcare and educational institutions.

Counselors in schools or the workplace are also among the professionals who can provide interventions and offer advice and referrals to young people whose drinking patterns are problematic within the context of their everyday lives. Given that many young people who engage in extreme drinking may be students at the secondary or tertiary level, access to resources that can assist them is needed. Schools and universities seem a logical and appropriate place where such resources can be introduced in a formalized way; for example, through health and guidance services. Protective strategies, already discussed, may be useful skills to teach within these contexts (Benton, Benton, & Downey, 2006). Workplace employee assistance programs and other similar interventions can also be useful in addressing negative drinking patterns (see chapter 8).

Other professionals who deal directly with extreme drinking are those in the hospitality sector, whose training can help reduce the incidence of extreme drinking and of its undesirable social outcomes. Training resources exist in many countries for staff operating and working in on- and off-premise establishments that sell alcohol. Intoxication is a particular focus area for good practice, as illustrated by the host responsibility guidelines introduced by the Alcohol Advisory Council of New Zealand (2005). While there may be limited evidence regarding the effectiveness of such guidelines and other educational tools as stand-alone measures, they are needed to bring about a shift in a culture permissive to intoxication: "Host responsibility must be seen as part of a broader strategy to address intoxication and its associated harms" (Alcohol Advisory Council of New Zealand [ALAC], 2005, p. 6).

Healthcare and Social Services

Targeted policies are also needed in the provision of healthcare and social services. Extreme drinking is closely linked to other aspects of health and social interactions, including broader health issues, sexual health, school attendance, drug use, and social problems (Jessor, Costa, Krueger, & Turbin 2006; Turbin et al., 2006). However, an integrated approach to dealing with young people's drinking problems is rarely implemented. Indeed, when young people with medical problems come in contact with healthcare providers, they may not acknowledge any involvement of their drinking patterns, making a comprehensive diagnosis difficult (Measham, Aldridge, & Parker, 2001). Young people, their drinking, and related negative outcomes are usually dealt with by whichever branch has the first contact with them. Often it is law enforcement, without referral to health and social services. Even where medical care is involved, it is rarely connected to wider health issues and generally does not extend to broader lifestyle counseling.

A particular challenge is posed by people living outside the mainstream of society, in both developing and developed countries. In its recent analysis of social inequalities in health, the WHO Regional Office for Europe showed that the heaviest drinking in the region is centered on individuals and groups at the bottom of the socioeconomic and educational scale (Dahlgren & Whitehead, 2006). Extreme drinking has also been shown to be more common in lower than in higher economic groups in Nordic and west European countries, as well as in the former Soviet republics (Mackenbach, 2006). In addition, individuals at the lower end of the socioeconomic scale are more likely to experience adverse health outcomes than their more affluent counterparts. Any potential problems are compounded by the limited access by many marginalized groups to conventional healthcare, social services, and other forms of assistance. Particularly in developing countries, social exclusion may be the result of a lack of general resources or the difficulty of such resources reaching certain groups of individuals.

Policies in most countries include some provision for addressing the needs of the socially excluded. To what degree this is done varies across countries and depends on the resources that may be available. Yet, even where social services are well developed, emphasis on extreme drinking may not be a high priority. To overcome the gaps in national policy with regard to addressing marginalized populations, alternative measures can be implemented that rely on the available resources and include a range of different and often unconventional stakeholders. For example, training of pharmacists to recognize potential drinking problems and offer brief interventions can be a useful measure where access to primary healthcare is limited. Such a program has been implemented successfully in Chile with the assistance of the private sector, allowing pharmacists to take a leading role in dealing with the problems of the socially marginalized (National Institute on Alcohol Abuse and Alcoholism, 1997). Social workers or teachers might equally be trained to deliver such services; soup kitchens and shelters can offer a useful venue for intervention and can help fill the gap in existing infrastructure. Brief interventions and screening, as well as skills training, can be integrated into the available services. An important corollary is also the need to raise awareness among the young people who might wish to seek assistance that such resources are available to them.

Law Enforcement

Law enforcement has a particularly important role to play with regard to extreme drinking, not merely in criminalizing certain drinking patterns, such as driving while intoxicated, but in offering viable approaches to reducing the potential for harm. Police involvement is important in connection with any violence, public disorder, or other disturbances that may accompany extreme drinking. It is also crucial for enforcement of drinking and driving laws. From a policy standpoint, ensuring that law enforcement is adequate and effective is a priority at all levels of government.

Effective enforcement depends not only on adequate personnel, but also on appropriate training to deal with extreme drinking and its possible outcomes. Law enforcement personnel may be able to deal with situations themselves or may need to refer particular problems to social services, healthcare, or other branches in a better position to address them. For example, sobering-up shelters have been set up in Australia where intoxicated individuals can be taken instead of being locked up in police stations and jail cells (Brady, Nicholls, Henderson, & Byrne, 2006). The argument has been put forward that these shelters can not only help to educate people about acceptable behavior and drinking practice, but also provide referral for counseling, treatment, or other services.

To a large extent, proper enforcement of existing laws and minimization of potential for harm hinge on close interaction between officers and members of the community. These two groups can support each other in monitoring possible problem areas, for example, where extreme drinking is common or where resultant negative outcomes are likely to occur. It should be noted that law enforcement personnel should include not only the police force, but also private security staff (e.g., university police or dedicated personnel hired by establishments or neighborhoods). All of these groups can play an important role, especially when dealing with extreme drinking and young people.

Increased policing during particular hours or times of year when incidents are most likely to occur is another important measure. Closing times of alcohol-serving establishments are a likely occasion for social disruption involving intoxicated patrons. As a result, ensuring that police are present, visible, and on hand to intervene if necessary has proven to be an important deterrent. Similarly, many holiday destinations are known for the high incidence of extreme drinking by young people (Lee, Maggs, & Rankin, 2006). Such places can benefit from seasonal increases in law enforcement. Crowd control and maintaining order in highly frequented areas require particular attention.

There are many examples of community involvement. In some cases, the need for cultural sensitivity and local knowledge is the only effective way to ensure that policing can have an impact. In Australia's Northern Territory, for example, patrols staffed by local Aboriginal women are instrumental in encouraging responsible drinking, settling drunken disputes, and preventing violent incidents. These women also ensure that drunken individuals are brought home safely or at least kept out of harm's way, so that they do not get into dangerous settings, such as lying down by roadsides where they might be injured by passing vehicles (Australian Institute of Criminology, 2006).

Another area for law enforcement and active policing within the community relates to the unlawful sale of beverage alcohol to young people below the legal drinking and purchase ages. A study in the United States has found that between 30% and 70% of retail outlets were likely to sell to minors. However, that study also found that adults, including parents, siblings, friends, acquaintances, and other third parties, were the primary sources of alcohol for young people under the age of 21 (National Research Council & Institute of Medicine, 2004). Accordingly, police monitoring of sales practices in different establishments (often covertly) can help reduce these instances and ensure that penalties are imposed for breaking the rules.

Perhaps the most obvious area for law enforcement when it comes to extreme drinking has to do with alcohol-impaired driving. Certainly, for public safety and community concerns, road traffic crashes are a high priority. Legally mandated BAC levels exist in virtually every country in the world where alcohol consumption in permitted (WHO, 2004). Their enforcement may not prevent extreme drinking per se, but can at least reduce its possible harmful outcomes. There is evidence that sustained road block and random breath testing programs reduce the incidence of alcohol-related traffic crashes and deaths. For example, the introduction of random breath tests in Australia has been linked to a drop in both total and alcohol-related traffic fatalities, and these results were sustained over time (Fell, Lacey, & Voas, 2004; Peek-Asa, 1999). Similar results have been reported for Austria, with a reduction of alcohol-related accidents and fatalities ("Positive Impact of Screening Testing in Austria," 2007). These measures, and others like them, have contributed to a changing culture in which not drinking on a night out has become acceptable. The high visibility of these programs, the constant reinforcement of informal sanctions against driving when drunk, and the undermining of peer pressure to drink to excess has helped change attitudes (Grabowsky & James, 1995/1997). Intensive enforcement specifically in areas known for heavy drinking can be a targeted way of effectively allocating limited funds.

Retail Serving and Sales Practices

Serving and sales practices in on- and off-premise establishments are another important area for targeted policy implementation. Certain venues—such as bars and nightclubs—are particularly popular among young people, and extreme drinking there may be a frequent occurrence. Such settings would seem to offer the perfect opportunity for interventions aimed specifically at extreme drinking. Yet any interventions require the existence of a well-structured framework for responsible hospitality to ensure the safety of patrons and staff alike, as well as of third parties who may not be directly involved in extreme drinking but may nonetheless be harmed by it.

A first step in policies targeted at drinking settings is the implementation of responsible practice codes for venue management and proper sale and service of beverage alcohol. Codes in this area ensure proper training for staff on a number of issues to help discourage extreme drinking and manage its potentially harmful outcomes. Management and staff training in techniques to prevent and deal with intoxicated patrons and alcohol-impaired driving, as well as attention to the quality of beverages served, are necessary components of any responsible hospitality initiative (for instance, Alcohol Focus Scotland's ServeWise and the TIPS program in the United States). Similarly, a requirement for customers to show proof of age can help avoid sales to underage drinkers, and liability laws can help ensure compliance. Addressing the clientele of drinking venues is also an important contributor to minimizing potential harm. Some establishments in the United Kingdom, for example, have implemented policies banning "hen" or "stag" nights, at which extreme drinking is more likely to occur. Finally, last calls before closing in many drinking establishments often mean that patrons will purchase several drinks at once and drink them quickly before leaving. Responsible service codes may choose to stop the use of last calls or restrict the number of drinks permitted per customer.

An increasing trend reported among some young people has been to drink at home before going out, because it is far less expensive than drinking in bars and nightclubs. As a result, preparty extreme drinking is becoming more common (e.g., Forsyth, 2006; Galloway, Forsyth, & Shewan, 2007). Screening for already intoxicated patrons can therefore be effective in reducing the potential for harm among young people trying to enter alcohol-serving venues. Safe rides can be offered to make sure that intoxicated patrons are delivered safely to their doorsteps.

Another more immediate concern, namely commercial practices at the retail level, can be more difficult to address due to the sheer number and diffusion of small retailers. Certain promotions, such as happy hours, "two-fers," and various other gimmicks intended to draw patrons, may encourage extreme alcohol consumption. Although most retail alcohol sales are not promoted in this fashion and most retailers have responsible practices, some outlets make beverage alcohol accessible in large amounts and at relatively low cost in a very visible way. In some areas, notably where many of the individuals frequenting alcohol-serving venues are students and other young people, local governments place restrictions on such promotions, and advertisements for them may also be banned from youth publications such as university newspapers. In addition, while nonalcohol beverages are available in most on-premise establishments, they are often priced above or at least on a par with beverage alcohol, making them less desirable. Consideration could be given to lower-cost pricing of nonalcohol beverages, at least where beverage price is not used in lieu of a "cover charge" for the entertainment; other measures might include stocking a wide and appealing selection of nonalcohol beverages, advertised along with alcohol options. In general, self- or co-regulation of retail practices (e.g., with the involvement of local governments) should be encouraged.

For policies on responsible retail service to work, enforcement is important. Increased and more stringent self-regulation of serving establishments in the United Kingdom, for example, is a direct result of increased scrutiny of serving and retail practices (Portman Group, 2007). Licensing can be made contingent on the implementation of service and sales codes, as is the case in New Zealand (ALAC, 2005). Other incentives, such as diminished legal liability for any adverse outcomes provided that responsible retail and server practices are in effect, can also be useful (reviewed in Sloan, Stout, Whetten-Goldstein, & Liang, 2000). The community too has an important role to play in the enforcement of compliance and requirements for server codes; its involvement can ensure that broader concerns, such as issues of safety and public order, are addressed. It is important to view such measures within the context of the infrastructure and urban planning in general. The availability of safe public transportation, for example, is a crucial component of minimizing potential harm.

Advertising and marketing of beverage alcohol should not encourage irresponsible or extreme drinking behavior. Although the evidence is weak in support of such an influence on the part of commercial communications and even shows no impact on the levels of alcohol consumed (e.g., Grube, 2000; Wilcox & Gangadharbatla, 2006), it is fair to say that commercial communications are closely tied to prevailing cultural attitudes and societal norms regarding drinking. It is generally agreed upon, however, that advertising should not condone or depict inappropriate drinking patterns.

By and large, producers of beverage alcohol have developed voluntary standards or codes that guide their advertising and other commercial communications. Table 7.2 offers a summary of policies implemented and upheld by some of the leading producers and various trade associations. Many producers have their own individual responsible advertising and marketing policies, while in many countries there are industry-wide responsible marketing codes applicable to all producers. The codes are often enforced by third-party complaints panels. Most codes on advertising and marketing include provisions against targeting underage people in word or spirit, and prohibit the endorsement of extreme drinking practices. Advertising and marketing of beverage alcohol is regulated by governments in some countries, while it is devolved to various degrees of self-regulation by producers in others (ICAP, 2001; WHO,

TABLE 7.2 Provisions of Codes on Commercial Communications Developed by Leading Beverage Alcohol Producers, Trade Associations, and Social Aspects Organizations (with Particular Relevance to Extreme Drinking)

Provisions, in codes, against specific undesirable practices	Company or Organization															
	SABMiller	Allied Domecq	Brown-Forman	Molson Coors	Diageo	Foster's	Heineken	Brewers of Europe	AAB, DSICA, WFA & LMAA*	Beer Institute USA	Wine Institute USA	DISCUS	Portman Group	EFRD	ARA/ASA, S. Africa	MEAS Ireland
Encouragement of immoderate/excessive drinking	✓	✓	✓	✓	✓	✓	✓	✓	✓	✓	✓	✓	✓	✓	✓	✓
Targeting minors	✓	✓	✓	✓	✓	✓	✓	✓	✓	✓	✓	✓	✓	✓	✓	✓
Placement at events where audience majority is under age	✓	✓	✓	✓	✓	✗	✓	✓	✓	✓	✓	✓	✓	✓	✓	✓
Subjects in adverts aged under 25 years	✓	✓	✓	✓	✓	✓	✓	✗	✓	✓	✓	✓	✓	✗	✓	✓
Implication of enhanced physical ability	✓	✓	✓	✓	✓	✓	✓	✓	✓	✓	✓	✓	✓	✓	✓	✓
Implication of enhanced sexual ability	✓	✓	✓	✓	✓	✓	✓	✓	✓	✓	✗	✓	✓	✓	✓	✓
Implication of enhanced social ability	✓	✓	✓	✓	✓	✓	✓	✓	✓	✓	✓	✓	✓	✓	✓	✓
Depiction of unsafe conditions (drinking and driving)	✓	✓	✓	✓	✓	✓	✓	✓	✓	✓	✓	✓	✓	✓	✓	✓
Depiction of intoxication	✓	✓	✓	✓	✓	✓	✓	✓	✓	✓	✓	✓	✗	✗	✓	✓
Association with violence	✓	✓	✓	✓	✓	✓	✓	✓	✓	✗	✓	✓	✓	✓	✓	✓
Association with illegal activity/drugs	✓	✓	✓	✓	✓	✓	✓	✗	✗	✓	✗	✓	✓	✗	✗	✓
Emphasis on high alcohol content	✓	✓	✓	✓	✓	✓	✓	✓	✓	✗	✓	✓	✓	✓	✓	✓
Negative portrayal of abstinence	✓	✓	✗	✓	✓	✓	✓	✓	✗	✓	✗	✓	✗	✓	✗	✗

*Australian Associated Brewers (AAB), Distilled Spirits Industry Council of Australia Inc. (DSICA), Winemakers Federation of Australia (WFA), Liquor Merchants Association of Australia (LMAA)

2004). A mix of regulation and self-regulation, despite its detractors, has a proven track record and is reasonably well enforced (e.g., Evans & Kelly, 1999; Evans et al., 2003; European Advertising Standards Alliance, 2007).

Community Initiatives

As discussed in this chapter, alcohol policy should not be viewed exclusively within the context of government, legislation, and structural change. Policy can also be made and implemented at the community level, involving a range of stakeholders (e.g., Wallin, Norström, & Andreasson, 2003). Such policy partnerships have shown considerable promise in the guise of community "accords" (Auckland City Council, 2007b; Crime Prevention Unit, Department of the Prime Minister and Cabinet, Alcohol Advisory Council of New Zealand, & New Zealand Police, 2000; Felson, Berends, Richardson, & Veno, 1997; New South Wales Department of Gaming and Racing, 2004). These accords, while not formal policy, ensure that the crucial stakeholders are involved in the implementation of various measures to promote safety and public order in relation to licensed premises. Accords are largely voluntary and rely on the stakeholders to implement and uphold them. They involve local police, business owners, community leaders, media, local government, and others who have a part to play (Stimson, Grant, Choquet, & Garrison, 2007).

Local approaches to alcohol policy generally rely on two components: modifying the drinking environment, and educating all stakeholders and the targets of the different measures. The process involves several elements (reviewed in ICAP, 2005):

- encouraging dialogue with the community and being responsive to its needs;
- achieving a general agreement on simple and easy-to-understand rules and codes of practice for serving establishments and their patrons;
- providing businesses with financial incentives for compliance with codes, such as making licensing contingent on good practice;
- encouraging responsibility among retailers, managers, and servers in establishments by educating them on social and community issues;
- implementing interventions and training for servers, even making them a requirement for licensing;
- forming alliances with policing and enforcement authorities where intervention may be needed;
- providing adequate public transportation and accessibility;
- avoiding the imposition of undue restrictions on the availability of alcohol beverages;
- recognizing the role of alcohol in entertainment and within social settings and acknowledging the need to address it within a larger policy context.

CONCLUSIONS

Concerns about extreme drinking are greatest at the community level, where they focus largely on issues of safety and public order. Policy measures are therefore needed that can actually respond to the most immediate issues, in a way that addresses the particular needs or constraints within a given context. While policy measures are generally thought of as originating with government at national level, filtering down for implementation at the local level, it may be worth reexamining this premise. Policy should perhaps be regarded as the domain of a number of different stakeholders, many of them within the local community and directly in touch with the key concerns at hand.

Set against the backdrop of a broad structural framework developed at national level, policies can also be crafted in a more focused way, tailored to culture, local priorities, and specific needs. This allows policy to be realistic and more feasible to implement, while flexible enough to respond to the immediacy of concerns and priorities. Using what is available and proven and sharing ownership of problems and their solutions may be a more effective way of introducing the cultural shifts that are needed to address extreme drinking and the potential harms caused by its outcomes.

REFERENCES

Aertgeerts, B., Buntinx, F., Bande-Knops, J., Vandermeulen, C., Roelants, M., Ansoms, S., et al. (2000). The value of CAGE, CUGE, and AUDIT in screening for alcohol abuse and dependence among college freshmen. *Alcoholism: Clinical and Experimental Research, 24,* 53–57.

Alcohol Advisory Council of New Zealand (ALAC). (2005). *Host responsibility: Guidelines for licensed premises.* Auckland, New Zealand: Author.

Antalova, L., & Martinic, M. (2005). *Beverage alcohol availability controls.* ICAP Review 1. Washington, D.C.: International Center for Alcohol Policies.

Auckland City Council. (2007a). *Alcohol bans: Permanent alcohol ban areas.* Retrieved February 17, 2007, from http://www.aucklandcity.govt.nz/council/documents/liquorban/areas.asp.

Auckland City Council. (2007b). *Alcohol strategy.* Retrieved February 17, 2007, from http://www.aucklandcity.govt.nz/council/documents/alcoholstrategy/contents.asp.

Australian Institute of Criminology. (2006). Gove peninsula community patrol (Northern Territory). In *Winning projects 2006: Australian crime and violence prevention awards* (pp. 3–4). Canberra, Australia: Author.

Babor, T. F., Caetano, R., Casswell, S., Edwards, G., Giesbrecht, N., Graham, K., et al. (2003). *Alcohol: No ordinary commodity.* Oxford, U.K.: Oxford University Press.

Babor, T. F., De La Fuente, J. R., Saunders, J., & Grant, M. (1992). *AUDIT—The Alcohol Use Disorder Identification Test: Guidelines for use in primary health care.* Geneva, Switzerland: World Health Organization.

Babor, T. F., Higgins-Biddle, J., Saunders, J. B., & Monteiro, M. G. (2001). *AUDIT—The Alcohol Use Disorders Identification Test: Guidelines for use in primary care* (2nd ed.). Geneva, Switzerland: World Health Organization.

Baigorri, A., & Fernández, R. (2004). *Botellón: Un conflicto posmoderno.* Barcelona, Spain: Acaria Editorial.

Baker, T. K., Johnson, M. B., Voas, R. B., & Lange, J. E. (2000). Reduce youthful binge drinking: Call an election in Mexico. *Journal of Safety Research, 31*, 61–69.

Benton, S. L., Benton, S. A., & Downey, R. G. (2006). College student drinking, attitudes toward risks, and drinking consequences. *Journal of Studies on Alcohol, 67*, 543–551.

Benton, S. L., Downey, R. G., Glider, P. S., Benton, S. A., Shin, K., Newton, D. W., et al. (2006). Predicting negative drinking consequences: Examining descriptive norm perception. *Journal of Studies on Alcohol, 67*, 399–405.

Benton, S. L., Schmidt, J. L., Newton, F. B., Shin, K., Benton, S. A., & Newton, D. W. (2004). College student protective strategies and drinking consequences. *Journal of Studies on Alcohol, 65*, 115–121.

Berkowitz, A. D. (2005). An overview of the social norms approach. In L. C. Lederman & L. P. Stewarts (Eds.), *Changing the culture of college drinking: A socially situated health communication campaign* (pp. 193–214). Creskill, NJ: Hampton Press.

Brady, M., Nicholls, R., Henderson, G., & Byrne, J. (2006). The role of rural sobering-up centre in managing alcohol-related harm to Aboriginal people in South Australia. *Drug and Alcohol Review, 25*, 201–206.

Brugal, M. T., Rodríguez-Martos, A., & Villalba, J. R. (2006). Nuevas y viejas adicciones: Implicaciones para la salud pública [New and old addictions: Implications for public health]. *Informe Sociedad Española de Salud Pública y Administración Sanitaria (SESPAS) 2006: Los desajustes de la salud en el mundo desarrollado, 20*(Suppl.1), 55–62.

Chaloupka, F. J., Grossman, M., & Saffer, H. (1998). The effects of price on the consequences of alcohol use and abuse. *Recent Developments in Alcoholism, 14*, 331–346.

Chaloupka, F. J., Grossman, M., & Saffer, H. (2002). The effects of price on alcohol consumption and alcohol-related problems. *Alcohol Research & Health, 26*, 22–34.

Chen, M. J., Paschall, M. J., & Grube, J. W. (2006). Motives for malt liquor consumption in a sample of community college students. *Addictive Behaviors, 31*, 1295–1307.

Chiauzzi, E., Green, T. C., Lord, S., Thum, C., & Goldstein, M. (2005). My student body: A high-risk drinking prevention web site for college students. *Journal of American College Health, 53*, 263–274.

Chikritzhs, T., & Stockwell, T. R. (2002). The impact of later trading hours for Australian public houses (hotels) on levels of violence. *Journal of Studies on Alcohol, 63*, 591–599.

Coate, D., & Grossman, M. (1988). Effects of alcoholic beverage prices and legal drinking age on youth alcohol use. *Journal of Law and Economics, 31*, 145–171.

Comas, D. (2004). *Las experiencias de la vida: Aprendizajes y riesgos* [Life experiences: Apprenticeships and responsibilities]. Informe Juventud en España, Parte 3. Madrid, Spain: INJUVE.

Consejería de Gobernación. (2006). *Estudio sobre la repercusión de la futura ley sobre potestades administrativas en materia de actividades de ocio en los espacios abiertos de los municipios de Andalucía* [Study of the repercussions of the future law regarding administrative powers on the nature of outdoor leisure activities in Andalucian municipalities]. Sevilla, Spain: Junta de Andalucía.

Cook, R. L., Chung, T., Kelly, T. M., & Clark, D. B. (2005). Alcohol screening in young persons attending a sexually transmitted disease clinic: Comparison of AUDIT, CRAFFT, and CAGE instruments. *Journal of General Internal Medicine, 20*, 1–6.

Crime Prevention Unit, Department of the Prime Minister and Cabinet, Alcohol Advisory Council of New Zealand (ALAC), & New Zealand Police. (2000). *Alcohol accords: Getting results. A practical guide for accord partners.* Retrieved March 4, 2007, from http://www.ndp.govt.nz/alcohol/alcoholaccords-gettingresults.pdf.

Cunningham, J. A., Humphreys, K., Kypri, K., & van Mierlo, T. (2006). Formative evaluation and three-month follow-up of an online personalized assessment feedback intervention for problem drinkers. *Journal of Medical Internet Research*, 8, e5.

Currie, C., Roberts, C., Morgan, A., Smith, R., Settertobulte, W., Samdal, O., et al. (Eds.).
(2004). *Young people's health in context. Health Behaviour in School-aged Children
(HBSC) study: International report from the 2001/2002 survey.* Health Policy for
Children and Adolescents No. 4. Copenhagen, Denmark: WHO Regional Office for
Europe.

Dahlgren, G., & Whitehead, M. (2006). *Levelling up (Part 2): A discussion paper on
European strategies for tackling social inequities in health.* Copenhagen, Denmark:
WHO Regional Office for Europe.

DeJong, W., Schneider, S. K., Towvim, L. G., Murphy, M. J., Doerr, E. E., Simonsen, N. R.,
et al. (2006). A multisite randomized trial of social norms marketing campaigns to
reduce college student drinking. *Journal of Studies on Alcohol*, 67, 868–879.

Elzo, J., Laespada, M. T., & Pallarés, J. (2003). *Más allá del botellón: Análisis socio-
antropológico del consumo de alcohol en los adolescentes y jóvenes [Beyond the
botellón: Socioanthropological analysis of adolescent and juvenile alcohol con-
sumption].* Madrid, Spain: Agencia Antidroga.

Evans, J. M., Dash, J. F., Blickman, N., Peeler, C. L., Engle, M. K., Mulholland, J., et
al. (2003). *Alcohol marketing and advertising: A report to Congress.* Retrieved
August 14, 2007, from the Federal Trade Commission Web site: http://www.ftc.gov/
os/2003/09/alcohol08report.pdf.

Evans, J. M., & Kelly, R. F. (1999). *Self-regulation in the alcohol industry: A review of
industry efforts to avoid promoting alcohol to underage consumers.* Retrieved August
14, 2007, from the Federal Trade Commission Web site: http://www.ftc.gov/reports/
alcohol/alcoholreport.htm.

European Advertising Standards Alliance (EASA). (2007). *Advertising self-regulation in
Europe* (5th ed.). Brussels, Belgium: Author.

European Commission. (2007). *Attitudes towards alcohol.* Special Eurobarometer 272b.
Retrieved March 14, 2007, from http://ec.europa.eu/health/ph_determinants/
life_style/alcohol/documents/ebs272_en.pdf.

Fell, J. C., Lacey, J. H., & Voas, R. B. (2004). Sobriety checkpoints: Evidence of effectiveness is strong, but use is limited. *Traffic Injury Prevention*, 5, 220–227.

Felson, M., Berends, R., Richardson, B., & Veno, A. (1997). Reducing pub hopping and
related crime. In R. Homel (Ed.), *Policing for prevention: Reducing crime, public
intoxication, and injury* (pp. 115–132). Crime Prevention Studies, No. 7. Monsey,
NY: Criminal Justice Press.

Forsyth, A. J. M. (2006, October). *Assessing the relationships between late night drinks
marketing and alcohol-related disorder in public space.* Retrieved May 28, 2007,
from Alcohol Education and Research Council (AERC) Web site: http://www.aerc.
org.uk.

Foxcroft, D., Ireland, D., Lowe, G., & Breen, R. (2002). Primary prevention for alcohol misuse in young people. *Cochrane Database of Systematic Reviews 2002, 3.*
Retrieved March 14, 2007, from http://www.mrw.interscience.wiley.com/cochrane/
clsysrev/articles/CD003024/frame.html.

Galloway, J., Forsyth, A. J. M., & Shewan, D. (2007, February). *Young people's street drinking behaviour: Investigating the influence of marketing and subculture.* Retrieved
May 28, 2007, from the Alcohol Education and Research Council (AERC) Web site:
http://www.aerc.org.uk/documents/pdf/finalReports/044Steet_Drinking.pdf.

Goddard, E. (2006). *General Household Survey 2005: Smoking and drinking among adults,
2005.* London: Office for National Statistics.

Grabowsky, P., & James, M. (Eds.). (1997). *The promise of crime prevention: Leading crime prevention programs.* Australian Institute of Criminology Research and Public Policy Series. Griffith, Australia: Australian Institute of Criminology. (Original work published 1995)

Greenfield, T. K., & Rogers, J. D. (1999). Who drinks most of the alcohol in the U.S.? The policy implications. *Journal of Studies on Alcohol, 60,* 78–89.

Grossman, M., Chaloupka, F. J., Saffer, H., & Laixuthai, A. (1995). Effects of alcohol price policy on youth: A summary of economic research. In G. M. Boyd, J. Howard, & R. A. Zucker (Eds.), *Alcohol problems among adolescents: Current directions in prevention research* (pp. 225–242). Hillsdale, NJ: Erlbaum.

Grube, J. W. (2000, June). Alcohol advertising: What are the effects? In *10th special report to the U.S. Congress on alcohol and health: Highlights from current research* (pp. 412–426). Bethesda, MD: National Institute on Alcohol Abuse and Alcoholism.

Gruenewald, P. J., Ponicki, W. R., Holder, H., & Romelsjö, A. (2006). Alcohol prices, beverage quality, and the demand for alcohol: Quality substitutions and price elasticities. *Alcoholism: Clinical and Experimental Research, 30,* 96–105.

Härstedt, K. (2004). *Vår gar gränsen?* [Where do we set the limit?]. Stockholm: Statens Offentliga Utredningar.

Haworth, A., & Simpson, R. (Eds.). (2004). *Moonshine markets: Issues in unrecorded alcohol beverage production and consumption.* New York: Brunner-Routledge.

Hester, R. K., & Miller, J. H. (2006). Computer-based tools for diagnosis and treatment of alcohol problems. *Alcohol Research and Health, 29,* 36–40.

Hibell, B., Andersson, B., Bjarnason, T., Ahlström, S., Balakireva, O., Kokkevi, A., et al. (2004). *The ESPAD Report 2003: Alcohol and other drug use among students in 35 European countries.* Stockholm: Swedish Council for Information on Alcohol and Other Drugs (CAN) and the Pompidou Group at the Council of Europe.

Hill, L., & Stewart, L. (1996). The Sale of Liquor Act, 1989: Reviewing regulatory practices. *Social Policy Journal of New Zealand, 7,* 174–190.

Houlahan, M. (2006, November 9). Drinking age stays at 18, review announced. *The New Zealand Herald* [Online]. Retrieved May 12, 2007, from http://www.nzherald.co.nz.

Hungerford, D. W., & Pollock, D. A. (2003). Emergency department services for patients with alcohol problems: Research directions. *Academic Emergency Medicine, 10,* 79–84.

International Center for Alcohol Policies (ICAP). (2001). *Self-regulation of beverage alcohol advertising.* ICAP Report 9. Washington, D.C.: Author.

International Center for Alcohol Policies (ICAP). (2003). *International drinking guidelines.* ICAP Report 14. Washington, D.C.: Author.

International Center for Alcohol Policies (ICAP). (2004). *Alcohol education and its effectiveness.* ICAP Report 16. Washington, D.C.: Author.

International Center for Alcohol Policies (ICAP). (2005). Module 4: Responsible hospitality. In *ICAP Blue Book: Practical guides to alcohol policy and prevention.* Retrieved April 9, 2007, from http://www.icap.org/portals/0/download/all_pdfs/blue_book/Module_04_Responsible_Hospitality.pd.

International Center for Alcohol Policies (ICAP). (2006). *Alcohol taxation.* ICAP Report 18. Washington, D.C.: Author.

International Center for Alcohol Policies (ICAP). (2007). *Table: International drinking guidelines.* Retrieved March 27, 2007, from http://icap.org/PolicyIssues/DrinkingGuidelines/GuidelinesTable/tabid/204/Default.aspx.

International Center for Alcohol Policies (ICAP). (2008a). *Informing consumers about beverage control.* ICAP Report 20. Washington, D.C.: Author.

International Center for Alcohol Policies (ICAP). (2008b). *Table: Minimum age limits worldwide*. Retrieved February 3, 2008, from http://www.icap.org/PolicyIssues/YoungPeoplesDrinking/AgeLawsTable/tabid/219/Default.aspx.

Jessor, R., Costa, F. M., Krueger, P. M., & Turbin, M. S. (2006). A developmental study of heavy episodic drinking among college students: The role of psychosocial and behavioral protective and risk factors. *Journal of Studies on Alcohol, 67*, 86–94.

Johnston, L. D., O'Malley, P. M., Bachman, J. G., & Schulenberg, J. E. (2006). *Monitoring the future national survey results on drug use, 1975–2005: Vol. 1. Secondary school students*. Bethesda, MD: National Institute on Drug Abuse.

Kelly, T. M., Donovan, J. E., Chung, T., Cook, R. L., & Delbridge, T. R. (2004). Alcohol use disorders among emergency department-treated older adolescents: A new brief screen (RUFT-Cut) using the AUDIT, CAGE, CRAFFT, and RAPS-QF. *Alcoholism: Clinical and Experimental Research, 28*, 746–753.

Landry, M., Guyon, L., Bergeron, J., & Provost, G. (2002). Évaluation de la toxicomanie chez les adolescents: Développement et validation d'un instrument [Development and validation of an evaluation tool for drug addiction in adolescents]. *Alcoologie et Addictologie, 24*, 7–13.

Lange, J. E., Lauer, E. M., & Voas, R. B. (1999). Survey of the San Diego-Tijuana cross-border binging: Methods and analysis. *Evaluation Review, 23*, 378–398.

Lee, C. M., Maggs, J. L., & Rankin, L. A. (2006). Spring break trips as a risk factor for heavy alcohol use among first-year college students. *Journal of Studies on Alcohol, 67*, 911–916.

Lundborg, P. (2002). Young people and alcohol: An econometric analysis. *Addiction, 97*, 1573–1582.

Mackenbach, J. P. (2006). *Health inequalities: Europe in profile*. An independent, expert report commissioned by the United Kingdom Presidency of the European Union. London: Central Office of Information.

Manning, W. G., Blumberg, L., & Moulton, L. H. (1995). The demand for alcohol: The differential response to price. *Journal of Health Economics, 14*, 123–148.

Measham, F., Aldridge, J., & Parker, H. (2001). *Dancing on drugs: Risk, health and hedonism in the British club scene*. London: Free Association Books.

McKee, M., Sűzcs, S., Sárváry, A., Adany, R., Kiryanov, N., Saburova, L., et al. (2005). The composition of surrogate alcohols consumed in Russia. *Alcoholism: Clinical and Experimental Research, 29*, 1884–1888.

Ministerial Council on Drug Strategy. (2006). *National alcohol strategy 2006–2009. Towards safer drinking cultures*. Canberra, Australia: Commonwealth of Australia.

Musitu, G., & Bascones, A. (2006). *Botellón en Málaga: Realidades y propuestas [Botellón in Malaga: Realities and proposals]*. Madrid, Spain: Fundación Alcohol y Sociedad.

National Health and Medical Research Council (NHMRC). (2001). *Australian alcohol guidelines: Health risks and benefits*. Canberra, Australia: Commonwealth of Australia.

National Institute on Alcohol Abuse and Alcoholism (NIAAA). (1997). *NIAAA Director's report on Institute activities to the National Advisory Council on Alcohol Abuse and Alcoholism, June 5, 1997*. Retrieved February 12, 2007, from http://www.niaaa.nih.gov/AboutNIAAA/AdvisoryCouncil/DirectorsReports/.

National Research Council & Institute of Medicine. (2004). *Reducing underage drinking: A collective responsibility*. Washington, D.C.: National Academies Press.

Navarrete, L. (2002). *El fenómeno del botellón en la Comunidad de Madrid [The botellón phenomenon in the Madrid community]*. Madrid, Spain: Colegio de Politólogos y Sociólogos de Madrid, Colegio Oficial de Psicólogos de Madrid, Colegio Oficial de Médicos de Madrid.

New South Wales Department of Gaming and Racing. (2004). *Liquor accords: Local solutions for local problems.* Sydney, Australia: Author.

Nordlund, S., & Österberg, E. (2000). Unrecorded alcohol consumption: Economics and its effects on alcohol control in the Nordic countries. *Addiction, 95*(Suppl. 14), 23–29.

Peek-Asa, C. (1999). The effect of random alcohol screening in reducing motor vehicle crash injuries. *American Journal of Preventive Medicine, 16*(Suppl. 1), 57–67.

Plant, E., & Plant, M. (2005). A "leap in the dark?" Lessons for the United Kingdom from past extensions of bar opening hours. *International Journal of Drug Policy, 16*, 363–368.

Portman Group. (2007). *The code of practice on the naming, packaging and promotion of alcoholic drinks* (4th ed.). London: Author.

Positive impact of screening testing in Austria. (2007, March). *Drink Driving Monitor*, No. 1. Retrieved June 27, 2007, from http://www.etsc.be/documents/DDMonitor1_Final.pdf.

Report: Zero tolerance no solution for school. (2001, March 17). *Join Together Research News*. Retrieved March 27, 2007, from http://www.jointogether.org/news/research/summaries/2001/report-zero-tolerance-no-for.html.

Schulenberg, J., & Maggs, J. L. (2002). A developmental perspective on alcohol use and heavy drinking during adolescence and the transition to young adulthood. *Journal of Studies on Alcohol, Supplement 14*, 54–70.

Schulenberg, J., O'Malley, P.M., Bachman, J. G., Wadsworth, K. N., & Johnston, L. D. (1996). Getting drunk and growing up: Trajectories of frequent binge drinking during the transition to young adulthood. *Journal of Studies on Alcohol, 57*, 289–304.

Scottish Executive. (2002). *Plan for action on alcohol problems.* Edinburgh, U.K.: Author.

Servicio de Atención a la Movida (SAM). (2004). *Estudio sobre la movida malagueña [A study of the Malaga scene].* Málaga, Spain: Author.

Single, E. (1993). Recent developments in alcoholism: Public drinking. *Recent Developments in Alcoholism, 11*, 143–152.

Skiba, R. J. (2000). *Zero tolerance, zero evidence: An analysis of school disciplinary practice.* Policy Research Report No. SRS2. Bloomington, IN: Indiana Education Policy Center.

Sloan, F. A., Stout, E. M., Whetten-Goldstein, K., & Liang, L. (2000). *Drinkers, drivers and bartenders: Balancing private choices and public accountability.* Chicago: University of Chicago Press.

Stimson, G., Grant, M., Choquet, M., & Garrison, P. (Eds.). (2007). *Drinking in context. Patterns, interventions, and partnerships.* New York: Routledge.

Stockwell, T. (2006). Alcohol supply, demand and harm reduction: What is the strongest cocktail? *International Journal of Drug Policy, 17*, 269–277.

Talbot, D. (2006). The Licensing Act 2003 and the problematization of the night-time economy: Planning, licensing and subcultural closure in the U.K. *International Journal of Urban & Regional Research, 30*, 159–171.

Treno, A. J., Gruenewald, P. J., Wood, D. S., & Ponicki, W. R. (2006). The price of alcohol: A consideration of contextual factors. *Alcoholism: Clinical and Experimental Research, 30*, 1734–1742.

Turbin, M. S., Jessor, R., Costa, F. M., Dong, Q., Zhang, H., & Wang, C. (2006). Protective and risk factors in health-enhancing behavior among adolescents in China and the United States: Does social context matter? *Health Psychology, 25*, 445–454.

U.K. Prime Minister's Strategy Unit, Cabinet Office. (2004). *Alcohol harm reduction: A strategy for England.* Retrieved August 14, 2007, from http://www/strategy.gov.uk/work_areas/alcohol_misuse/index.asp.

U.S. Government Printing Office. (n.d.). Sec. 158: National minimum drinking age. In *Title 23: Highways, United States Code, 2000 edition*. Retrieved February 14, 2007, from http://www.gpoaccess.gov/uscode/browse.html.

Voas, R. B., Lange, J. E., & Johnson, M. B. (2002). Reducing high-risk drinking by young Americans south of the border: The impact of a partial ban on sales of alcohol. *Journal of Studies on Alcohol, 63*, 286–292.

Voas, R. B., Romano, E., Kelley-Baker, T., & Tippetts, A. S. (2006). A partial ban on sales to reduce high-risk drinking south of the border: Seven years later. *Journal of Studies on Alcohol, 67*, 745–753.

Wallin, E., Norström, T., & Andreasson, S. (2003). Alcohol prevention targeting licensed premises: A study of effects on violence. *Journal of Studies on Alcohol, 64*, 270–277.

Wang, Y. C., Lee, C. M., Lew-Ting, C. Y., Hsiao, C. K., Chen, D. R., & Chen, W. J. (2005). Survey of substance use among high school students in Taipei: Web-based questionnaire versus paper-and-pencil questionnaire. *Journal of Adolescent Health, 37*, 289–295.

Werner, M. J., Joffe, A., & Graham, A. V. (1999). Screening, early identification, and office-based intervention with children and youth living in substance-abusing families. *Pediatrics, 103*, 1099–1112.

Wilcox, G. B., & Gangadharbatla, H. (2006). What's changed? Does beer advertising affect consumption in the United States? *International Journal of Advertising, 25*, 35–50.

World Health Organization (WHO). (1986). *Young people's health—A challenge for society: Report of a WHO Study Group on young people and "Health for All by the Year 2000."* Technical Report Series No.731. Geneva, Switzerland: Author.

World Health Organization (WHO). (2004). *Global status report: Alcohol policy*. Geneva, Switzerland: Author.

Yanovitzky, I., Stewart, L. P., & Lederman, L. C. (2006). Social distance, perceived drinking by peers, and alcohol use by college students. *Health Communication, 19*, 1–10.

Chapter 8

Feasible Interventions
Tackling Extreme Drinking in Young People

Mônica Gorgulho and Daniya Tamendarova

This chapter reviews the wide range of interventions aimed at countering extreme drinking among adolescents and young adults. Many such approaches target the individual by attempting to raise awareness and modify perceptions of accepted norms or expectancies related to alcohol, and aim to change behavior by teaching skills for responsible decision-making about drinking and certain other activities, such as driving. Others focus on the physical and legal environments that surround alcohol consumption, for instance venues in which young people can have access to alcohol.

The sections below focus on three key settings that have been utilized to reach this population: educational institutions, the workplace, and the broader community. Within these contexts, special attention must be paid to young people at an increased risk for extreme drinking and harm—for instance, current heavy drinkers, youths with a family history of alcohol dependence and problems, and those with an experience of alcohol-related emergencies. Particular attention should also be paid to marginalized groups, who may not be reachable through mainstream interventions.

Although an effort has been made to provide a global view of the topic, the majority of approaches presented here have been developed and implemented in Western countries. The bulk of research on tackling risky alcohol consumption among young people comes from North America (the United States and Canada), several European countries (in particular, the United

Kingdom), Australia, and New Zealand (e.g., for an international review of research on college students, see Karam, Kypri, & Salamoun, 2007). Readers should keep in mind that the relevance of this work beyond these regions— whether or not particular approaches and programs are transportable for use in other countries and cultures—may be limited because of the variance in resources, expertise, and realities that surround young people in a particular society (the prevalent drinking culture, public health and education systems, and income disparities, to name a few). For example, the relatively high minimum drinking age in the United States (21 years) creates a distinct drinking context for young people in U.S. schools, resulting in priorities and means for prevention unlike those in the majority of countries that legislate for legal age limits, which normally range between 16 and 18 years (see chapter 7). School attrition rates in many developing countries may diminish the reach of prevention programs targeted at older students; interventions aimed at parents or children at early stages of education and young adults in the workplace and other community settings would appear more relevant in this context. To respond to a variety of local conditions, this chapter includes both the complex approaches that may call for extensive planning, existing infrastructure, and resources and those likely to require minimal preparation and funds in their development, implementation, and delivery (see also International Center for Alcohol Policies [ICAP], 2005c).

A prerequisite for selecting appropriate initiatives and evaluating their outcomes is having a clear notion of what is needed and available within a particular setting and what is to be achieved by a given intervention, be it simply providing the information, raising awareness, or triggering behavior change (for discussion, see Stimson, Grant, Choquet, & Garrison, 2007, pp. 173–191). It should be borne in mind that no one program or strategy described here can *alone* be sufficient to address extreme drinking. Rather, a mix of approaches applied in a number of youth contexts—and supported by a range of stakeholders (chapter 6) and policy measures (chapter 7)—should be implemented, guided by the needs, attitudes, and resources within a given community.

EDUCATIONAL SETTINGS

Directed either at the general student body, high-risk groups within it, or both, school programs against extreme drinking primarily take the form of *alcohol education* and *skills training*. Notable among alcohol education initiatives is the *social norms marketing* approach, which tackles students' misperceptions about peer behavior related to alcohol. Another approach, developed specifically for individuals with risky drinking patterns, involves *brief interventions* that employ a range of harm reduction strategies, from motivational interviewing and personalized feedback to normative re-education and moderate drinking skills. Finally, interventions aimed at the school and the nearby communities target the *drinking contexts*, structures and dynamics that may surround student drinking. Each of these approaches is examined below, but not all will suit every setting. In general, multi-component programs appear to be more likely to bring positive results (e.g., National Research Council & Institute of Medicine, 2004; Task Force of the National Advisory Council on Alcohol Abuse and Alcoholism, 2002; Ziemelis, Bucknam, & Elfessi, 2002). Importantly, in order to be accepted by young people, any such program would need to acknowledge the positive attributes and ritual benefits many young people tend to assign to alcohol and offer attractive safer alternatives to extreme consumption (Broadbear, O'Toole, & Angermeier-Howard, 2000; Lederman, Stewart, Goodhart, & Laitman, 2003; Treise, Wolburg, & Otnes, 1999; see also chapter 4).

Alcohol Education and Skills Training

Traditional education campaigns provide information about alcohol and its effects. Delivered through a range of channels—both formal and informal—these primarily aim to raise awareness and provide recommendations on alcohol-related risks and benefits for the general public or its subgroups (for review, see Foxcroft, Ireland, Lowe, & Breen, 2002; ICAP, 2005a; Jones et al., 2007; National Research Council & Institute of Medicine, 2004). A secondary goal of alcohol education is to encourage individuals to make informed and responsible drinking choices and, in the case of extreme drinkers, to reconsider and change their behavior. To aid decision-making with regards to extreme drinking, many education programs go beyond simply providing information and incorporate a skills-building component that aims to train the target audience in responding effectively to various life situations.

A captive audience, young people in primary and secondary schools, colleges, and universities have been the obvious targets of alcohol education and skills training (Karam et al., 2007). Incorporated into the curricula and some school or student services, such as health centers and student organizations, alcohol education employs an arsenal of "negative" and "positive" messaging (Ott & Haertlein, 2002). The former informs young people of the negative physical and social outcomes of problem drinking and any potential disciplinary sanctions under school or community ordinances. "Positive" messaging focuses on techniques aimed at minimizing harm, either through moderating drinking patterns or a recommendation of abstinence from alcohol for all under the legal drinking age. Thus, many alcohol education and skills training campaigns do not focus specifically on extreme drinking, but may address it indirectly by providing information about negative outcomes and alcohol-related laws, encouraging moderate consumption, or discouraging underage drinking.

The duration and intensity of classroom-based education and skills training programs vary from extensive intervention over a number of years to several lessons that may be followed by one or two waves of booster sessions. Implemented in many developing and developed countries (e.g., Bils, 1999; Botvin, Griffin, Diaz, & Ifill-Williams, 2001; Department of Education,

Republic of South Africa, 1997; ICAP, 2000; Jones et al., 2007; Smith et al., 2004), these programs may address alcohol within the broader context of health, wellbeing, and social skills by focusing on students' self-esteem, stress- and time-management, or generic risk-reduction, and can involve educational components for parents, teachers, and school administrators (e.g., Turrisi, Jaccard, Taki, Dunnam, & Grimes, 2001). General skills training, or *life skills*, can begin at a very young age, facilitating behaviors that would act as protective factors when students grow older and begin to explore alcohol (e.g., ICAP, 2000; Schinke, Tepavac, & Cole, 2000). When working with diverse student populations, some programs incorporate local cultural values, legends, and stories into the lesson format and utilize existing traditional support structures in order to engage indigenous students and minority groups (Hawkins, Cummins, & Marlatt, 2004; Schinke et al., 2000).

The way alcohol education and skills training programs address extreme drinking depends on a given project's end goal. Thus, programs may emphasize moderate drinking skills through fostering self-control and self-assessment, responsible decision-making, social resistance skills, and coping mechanisms that do not involve substance abuse (e.g., McBride, Farrington, Midford, Meuleners, & Phillips, 2004; McBride, Midford, Farrington, & Phillips, 2000). Programs may also teach young people to manage the potential effects of extreme drinking and minimize harm by, for instance, teaching them to recognize and respond to signs of intoxication or alcohol poisoning in friends (Caudill, Luckey, Crosse, Blane, Ginexi, & Campbell, 2007; Coleman & Catar, 2005) or by attempting to modify young people's expectancies about the likely outcomes of their drinking choices (see Example of Intervention, "Expectancy Challenge"). Alternatively, programs may deliver information and skills training within abstinence-oriented initiatives, emphasizing social resistance skills—resisting not only the peer pressure to drink heavily, but to drink at all.

Example of Intervention: Expectancy Challenge

The role of expectancies in motivating extreme drinking and shaping behavior during intoxication has been discussed in chapter 4. Research suggests that "reducing positive expectancies may be a[n]…appropriate goal for preventing problem drinking, whereas enhancing negative expectancies may be a more appropriate goal for changing problem drinking" (McNally & Palfai, 2001, p. 729). A promising approach to reducing risky patterns of alcohol consumption among young people, especially when directed at heavy-drinking students, involves an effort to *modify* alcohol expectancies (for review, see Larimer & Cronce, 2007). In addition to providing information on the link between alcohol expectancies and drinking outcomes (including alcohol-related sexual expectations), *expectancy challenge programs* often include several sessions of direct experience, where a group of young people are administered either alcohol or placebo, asked to perform various social tasks, and then guess which participants (including themselves) received alcohol based on their behavior. In such programs, students' ability to successfully identify alcohol-receiving peers is normally no better than chance, which increases participants' understanding

of the role that the environment and expectations about alcohol play in producing social outcomes of drinking and encourages self-control in response to
alcohol-related cues in the environment (Darkes & Goldman, 1993, 1998; Wiers
& Kummeling, 2004; van de Luitgaarden, van den Wildenberg, & Smulders,
2005). Multi-session alcohol expectancy challenges, including those with direct
alcohol/placebo experience, have been promising in reducing consumption—
at least in the short term—among heavy-drinking male students and, within
a mixed-gender setting, among heavy-drinking female students (Darkes &
Goldman, 1993, 1998; Wiers & Kummeling, 2004; Wiers, van de Luitgaarden,
van der Wildenberg, & Smulders, 2005), but the logistic difficulty of implementing multiple sessions, recruiting participants, and adapting the program to
real-life situations remains a challenge (Musher-Eizenman & Kulick, 2003; van
de Luitgaarden, Wiers, Knibbe, & Boon, 2006; Wiers & Kummeling, 2004).

The effectiveness of alcohol education and skills training has been questioned (e.g., Babor et al., 2003), although lack of rigorous evaluation has been
a notable obstacle (Foxcroft et al., 2002) and does not in itself imply ineffec-
tiveness. Found to raise awareness about alcohol in general, education initiatives have been deemed less successful—on their own—in changing behavior,
particularly in the long term (e.g., Walters, Bennett, & Noto, 2000). It should
be noted, however, that thorough traditional education and skills training programs often require extensive funding and outside professional involvement
(e.g., Williams, Perry, Farbakhsh, & Veblen-Mortenson, 1999), thus making
their development, implementation, and assessment difficult in the context of
limited resources, time, and experience. Moreover, the multi-session format
of many programs may further complicate program delivery and recruitment
and raise attrition rates.

In terms of addressing extreme drinking, abstinence-oriented initiatives
and strategies focused solely on negative messaging have been found to have
little effect on young people who are already consuming alcohol and who have
an experience of extreme drinking. Particularly for these youths, extending
the goal of alcohol education from exclusive stress on abstinence and delayed
or reduced drinking to harm minimization techniques has been suggested as
a more viable approach (e.g., McBride et al., 2004; Walters & Bennett, 2000).
In addition, top-down programs that rely on coercive tactics, emphasize only
negative outcomes, and allow little interaction with young people—interventions delivered unilaterally by teachers, health workers, or others in a position
of authority, with little student involvement—have been criticized for failing
to engage and resonate with the target audience, especially young drinkers
prone to high-risk behaviors (Centre for Addiction and Mental Health, 1999;
Ennett, Tobler, Ringwalt, & Flewelling, 1994; Marlatt, 1998).

At the same time, research indicates that traditional alcohol education
and skills training can be useful components within broader prevention initiatives (e.g., DeJong & Hingson, 1998). Moreover, social norms marketing,
a relatively new approach falling under the heading "alcohol education" and
focusing on peer norms and pressures, appears useful in reducing extreme
drinking. In addition, brief interventions for high-risk students that incorporate

several harm reduction strategies, including the provision of information on alcohol and drinking patterns and skills training, have been effective, particularly when funds, time, and access to students are limited. These strategies are discussed next.

Social Norms Marketing

The social norms marketing (SNM) approach builds on the notion that young people's drinking behavior is influenced by their perceptions of peer norms and practices (for an overview, see Berkowitz, 2005; ICAP, 2005b; Perkins, 2002, 2003). Research from different countries has shown that young people regularly overestimate the prevalence of heavy drinking among their peers (Kypri & Langley, 2003; McAlaney & McMahon, 2007; Perkins, 2007; Perkins & Berkowitz, 1986; Perkins, Haines, & Rice, 2005). This misperception often leads to actual increases in alcohol consumption among initially low-risk drinkers and nondrinkers or, in the case of heavy drinkers, to a persistence of this behavior (Borsari & Carey, 2001; Carey, Borsari, Carey, & Maisto, 2006; Perkins et al., 2005). Social norms marking campaigns use a variety of formal and informal channels to provide accurate information about actual drinking patterns among young people, arguing that dispelling misperceptions would decrease risky drinking. Thus, the emphasis of such programs is on the positive behavior of the majority, rather than the negative conduct of a highly visible minority (Ott & Haertlein, 2002).

This approach has been primarily used on college and university campuses, though several programs have been adapted for the secondary school environment (e.g., Christensen, 2005; Haines, Barker, & Rice, 2003; Ott & Doyle, 2005). A key aspect of social norms marketing is that each school develops messages based on data from its own student body; this aims to increase the believability and relevance of a given campaign for students. Thus, preliminary research is necessary to establish campus norms, actual drinking patterns, popular media outlets (student newspaper, fliers, posters, Web sites, satellite television), credible and respected local information sources or sponsors (school health center, a research institute, a youth organization), and images and messages that would resonate with the target audience. Schools may engage students in developing parts of the campaign as class projects and train teachers in incorporating alcohol-related topics into the curriculum (e.g., Perkins & Craig, 2002).

Whereas many SNM programs are broad in scope, presenting "average" or "typical" behaviors and attitudes, the influence of these messages is not uniform across the entire student body (Borsari & Carey, 2003; Cho, 2006). Networks of friends or peers within certain student subpopulations are often more important reference groups than the school as a whole; and misperceptions about these small-group norms are highly correlated to behavior (e.g., Yanovitzky, Stewart, & Lederman, 2006). Thus, a growing number of SNM interventions focus on members of particular groups, normally seen to be at high risk of extreme drinking, for instance first-year college students, student-athletes, fraternity and sorority members (see Case Study, "Drinking among Sorority and Fraternity Students in the United States," below), and student dormitory residents, or are used as part of individual counseling for young people already exhibiting problem behavior (see the section on *Brief Interventions* below).

Targeted SNM programs can also be useful in engaging marginalized populations. For instance, an SNM campaign that aimed to reduce the incidence of sexual assault developed a set of communication styles that were inclusive of deaf and hard-of-hearing students (White, Williams, & Cho, 2003). Ultimately, such programs will inform and reformat the communication styles of campus-wide campaigns to reach a broader audience. Unlike campus-wide efforts that normally rely on electronic or print media, targeted SNM programs are usually delivered as part of peer training, academic classes, small-group discussions, or workshops and may run within the context of campus-wide campaigns.

In the United States, one in nine colleges has implemented a social norms program of some kind (Wechsler, Kelley, Weitzman, San Giovanni, & Seibring, 2000), and this approach is being adapted for other countries (Hughes, 2006; Kypri & Langley, 2003; McAlaney & McMahon, 2007).[1] A literature review of interventions to reduce high-risk college drinking by the Task Force of the U.S. National Advisory Council on Alcohol Abuse and Alcoholism (2002) found the intensive social norms approach to be "promising," (see also Berkowitz, 1997; DeJong & Linkenbach, 1999; Haines, 1996, 1998; Haines & Spear, 1996; Johannessen, Collins, Mills-Novoa, & Glider, 1999). A number of studies since the Task Force report have found that school-wide SNM campaigns were successful, with students reporting more accurate perceptions of peer drinking and related decreases in heavy drinking (of 20% or more) and alcohol-related problems (e.g., Fabiano, 2003; Haines & Barker, 2003; Perkins & Craig, 2002; Perkins et al., 2005). Haines, Barker, and Rice (2003) reported similar results among high school students, following a media-led SNM campaign on both alcohol and tobacco use that also targeted parents and teachers. Well-implemented programs utilized a combination of channels to deliver simple, clear-cut messages in unison—from poster and electronic media efforts to class projects (Berkowitz, 2005).

Targeted SNM interventions have been successful in high-risk samples (e.g., *first-year college students:* Cimini, Page, & Trujillo, 2002; Schroeder

---

[1] Although the social norms approach is best known for programs focused on reducing extreme drinking among young people, it is being implemented in other areas, for instance: reducing tobacco use; promoting various aspects of traffic safety—such as seat belt use and prevention of alcohol-impaired driving; increasing tax compliance and motivation for academic success; developing a healthy body image; preventing HIV/AIDS risk behaviors (lack of condom use and having multiple sexual partners); delaying of sexual initiation among adolescents; and preventing sexual assault. For more information, see the Web site of the Social Norms Resource Center (SNRC): http://www.socialnorms.org/CaseStudies/casestudies.php.

& Prentice, 1998; *fraternities and sororities:* Bonday & Bruce, 2003;
Johannessen, 2004; *several high-risk groups at once:* Far & Miller, 2003;
Peeler, Far, Miller, & Brigham, 2000). For instance, a comprehensive social
norms campaign in the United States, designed to reduce harmful misconcep-
tions of drinking among student-athletes—a subpopulation with consistently
higher rates of extreme drinking than the general student population in the
U.S.—reported that

> having an estimated peak blood alcohol concentration (BAC) of 0.8% or higher
> based on typical drinking at parties and bars was 30% less likely in the post-
> intervention group, the likelihood of consuming 10 or more drinks at parties
> or bars was cut by more than one third, and the likelihood of experiencing fre-
> quent negative consequences of drinking was cut by one third. (Perkins & Craig,
> 2006, p. 886)[2]

This program employed a variety of intervention techniques, including
posters and school newspaper advertisements, electronic mail messages to all
student athletes, computers in the athletic facilities displaying program information, and training of student-athletes in being peer educators.

Other targeted SNM programs that reported decreases in college extreme
drinking used interactive peer theater to deliver messages (Cimini et al., 2002;
see also BACCHUS, 2002) or combined delivery of focused normative information with other strategies, such as personalized feedback (e.g., Mattern &
Neighbors, 2004), environmental management (Bauerle, Burwell, & Turner,
2002), and moderate drinking skills training (Johannessen, 2004). Working
with secondary school students, an initiative that incorporated aspects of normative programming with education on alcohol effects (particularly in the
context of alcohol-impaired driving) and skills training in minimizing alcohol-related risks and resisting peer pressure was associated with reductions
in extreme drinking and related consequences (Shope, Copeland, Maharg,
Dielman, & Butchart, 1993; Shope, Copeland, Marcoux, & Kamp, 1996). In
addition to adapting SNM programming to various groups at risk of extreme
drinking, researchers have proposed to tailor this approach to address misperceptions about so-called "celebration drinking," or drinking during special
occasions (such as vacations, birthdays, end-of-semester parties, certain holidays, and sports events) when "even those who may not typically drink will do
so, and those who are drinkers see these as occasions to drink more than usual
or to get drunk" (Martell, Atkin et al., 2006, p. 14; see also Neighbors, Oster-
Aaland, Bergstrom, & Lewis, 2006). Young people appear to overestimate
the percentage of their peers who drink heavily during such events, indicating
that the SNM approach may be useful; further research is needed to explore
appropriate ways to intervene.

---

[2] Reprinted with permission from the *Journal of Studies on Alcohol*, vol. 67, pp. 880–889,
2006. Copyright by Alcohol Research Documentation, Inc., Rutgers Center of Alcohol
Studies, Piscataway, NJ 08854.

FIGURE 8.1 Spring break hits Florida's beaches (2007). © Joe Raedle/Getty Images.

Overall, it must be recognized that, "[S]ocial norms campaigns may not affect all groups equally (especially at first) and—sustained effort is required over a period of years to normalize improvements and extend them to all students" (Berkowitz, 2005). Importantly, reports of unsuccessful social norms campaigns outline some potential pitfalls during the multiple stages of SNM program development and implementation (Clapp, Lange, Russell, Shillington, & Voas, 2003; Granfield, 2002; Russell, Clapp, & DeJong, 2005; Werch, Pappas, Carlson, DiClemente, Chally, & Sinder, 2000)—for instance, insufficient duration, intensity, or reach of the program; use of confusing and unpersuasive messages; incongruence between messages and images illustrating them; and use of information sources that are not perceived as credible by the target audience (see discussion in Berkowitz, 2005; DeJong, 2003; Rice, 2002). Methodological difficulties in study design, implementation, and evaluation may further obscure positive effects or weaken researchers' claims of success (e.g., Gomberg, Schneider, & DeJong, 2001). Finally, in evaluating initiatives, it is important to ensure the appropriateness of the chosen sample and measures of effectiveness.

Despite the wide acceptance of SNM programming in the research and prevention community, several studies questioned the overall validity and effectiveness of this approach. Critics note that, while it may be appropriate for frequent extreme drinkers, SNM messaging may actually lead to drinking among abstainers and increase consumption among infrequent extreme drinkers (Wechsler, Nelson, Lee, Seibring, Lewis, & Keeling, 2003; Wechsler & Kuo, 2000; Werch et al., 2000). Moreover, a recent national study by Wechsler, and colleagues (2003) criticized studies in favor of the approach on methodological grounds, cited the failed initiatives listed above, and reported that the authors' own inquiry "did not detect a decrease in alcohol consumption at schools that implemented a social norms marketing program on measures of the quantity, frequency, or volume of student alcohol use, or in measures of drunkenness and heavy episodic drinking" (p. 491). The study surveyed senior administrators of 98 tertiary institutions in the United States on whether or not their school employed an SNM program and then compared changes in student drinking for schools with and without the intervention. It did not, however, examine the scope, intensity, or quality of the SNM programs reported by administrators and was criticized for poor sample sizes and a weak definition of the experimental group (e.g., Perkins & Linkenbach, 2003).

In response to the critics' call for more rigorous research on the effectiveness of social norms marketing, multi-site randomized trials are being conducted across the United States. As an initial result, an analysis by DeJong and colleagues (2006), although revealing more modest changes in behavior than earlier studies in support of the approach, reported that SNM campaigns appeared to have a strong protective effect on several important heavy-drinking measures. Further large-scale studies will evaluate the role of external factors that may influence students' response to SNM programming—for instance, other prevention programs and campus or community alcohol policies. Reviews of SNM campaigns as a single strategy aside, normative re-education has been an important component of many successful brief interventions targeted at heavy-drinking youth.

Case Study: Drinking among Sorority and Fraternity Students in the United States

Jason Kilmer and Mary Larimer

Fraternities and sororities comprise what is known as the "Greek system" on U.S. college campuses, a collection of social organizations and living groups identified, with few exceptions, by names consisting of two to three Greek letters. Hence, members of fraternities and sororities are often referred to as "Greeks," and many events affiliated with these organizations maintain the "Greek" label (for instance, "Greek Week"). These organizations are recognized on each campus as a "chapter" of the national or international "Greek" organization. In many settings, members of fraternities or sororities actually live in a house with their fellow members, referred to as their "brothers" or "sisters." Active members may move out of the house while staying affiliated with the chapter's social events or, at colleges where the chapter does not own a house, may reside in a student dormitory or an off-campus setting while still coming together for social events. As part of their regular practices, fraternities and sororities routinely engage in and promote philanthropic or charitable activities. These events are frequently very visible on campus and, at times, are recognized by the college, university, or local media.

Over 80% of college students in the United States report alcohol consumption in the past year, and almost 50% report that they have been drunk at least once in the past 12 months (Johnston, O'Malley, Bachman, & Schulenberg, 2006). Within this population of college students, research has long suggested that students residing in fraternities and sororities drink alcohol at rates higher

FIGURE 8.2 Drinking with fraternity brothers. © Tore Bergsaker/Sygma/Corbis.

than their peers living in on-campus dormitories or in a range of off-campus settings (Larimer, Irvine, Kilmer, & Marlott, 1997). Consequently, images of fraternity and sorority members drinking heavily are pervasive in both the scientific and entertainment realms.

Although it is not the case that all students living in "Greek system" settings drink or are heavy drinkers, elevated rates of heavy alcohol consumption in fraternities and sororities have been documented for decades (Caudill, Crosse, Campbell, Howard, Luckey, & Blane, 2006; Larimer, Anderson, Baer, & Marlatt, 2000; Lee, Maggs, & Rankin, 2006; Wilke, Siebert, Delva, Smith, & Howell, 2005). Simons and colleagues (2005) found that fraternity and sorority members had higher alcohol severity scores (measured by the Addiction Severity Index) and higher drug scores than did their peers who were not members. Even when prior drinking is accounted for, "Greek system" membership seems to be significantly associated with prospective heavy drinking (Sher, Bartholow, & Nanda, 2001).

Differences in alcohol consumption between "Greek system" and "non-Greek" students could exist prior to attending college (Larimer et al., 2000). Research indicates that students living in fraternities and sororities reported more drinking in high school than their fellow students residing in residence halls, suggesting that, to some degree, students may self-select into heavier drinking settings. Once in college, however, being in a fraternity or sorority is associated with increased risks even when other factors are accounted for (Larimer et al., 2000). In the study by Larimer and colleagues (2000), fraternity residence was associated with more drinking-related consequences. "Greek system" members also had a greater likelihood of attributing sexual and aggressive outcomes (including feeling sexier and more sexually aggressive) to alcohol than did students living in a residence hall setting. There is also variability in drinking between different chapters or "houses" within the "Greek system." One study (Larimer, 1992) found that fraternity members in the house with the top "party house" reputation on campus drank almost 42 standard drinks per week, as compared to approximately 12 standard drinks per week in the chapter with the lowest reputation for partying (one standard drink in the United States contains 14 grams of ethanol). Thus, while overall fraternity or sorority membership is associated with increased risks, members of some organizations are engaging in particularly extreme drinking behaviors.

As has been demonstrated in most research with fraternities and sororities, most students living in those settings are younger than the legal U.S. drinking age (younger than 21 years of age). Within the population of college students, youths under the legal drinking age may be a particularly risky group based on their behavior, and fraternities/sororities could provide the setting for this risky behavior. Wechsler, Kuo, Lee, and Dowdall (2000) found that students under the 21-year legal drinking age were more likely to attend off-campus parties, social events/parties in residence halls, on-campus dances, and fraternity parties (attended by 45% of underage students in the past 30 days, compared to 26% of students over the legal drinking age). Additionally, these underage students more often reported heavy drinking episodes (defined by the researchers in this study as instances in which five or more drinks were consumed at least once in the past two weeks) at off-campus parties and fraternity parties than did those of the legal age. Of individuals who attended fraternity parties, 47% of underage students engaged in episodes of consuming five or more drinks, compared to 39% of students 21 or older. Interestingly, even when students residing in fraternities and sororities have been excluded from analyses, fraternity parties remain the setting in which the greatest proportion of students in attendance report consumption of alcohol (Harford, Wechsler, & Seibring, 2002).

Regardless of where students attend parties, affiliation with a fraternity or sorority seems to be associated with heavier drinking episodes by students under age 21. Wechsler, Kuo, and colleagues (2000) determined that underage fraternity or sorority members were three times more likely to drink five or more drinks than their nonmember peers, and those underage students actually residing in a sorority or fraternity house were more than six times as likely to endorse this behavior. Only 2.9% of the sample of 7,061 underage students lived in the "Greek system," so data should be interpreted with caution; however, it does seem that the fraternity and sorority setting is associated with heavier drinking, and that the prevalence of drinking for underage students is higher in this environment.

Fraternity and sorority members over the age of 21 are also not without risk. Glindemann, Ehrhart, Maynard, and Geller (2006) described the concept of "front-loading," drinking before arriving at a party environment, and specifically studied drinking prior to arriving in a downtown bar setting. The authors sampled every third group of one to five people, and found that fraternity men were significantly more intoxicated than male "non-Greeks," sorority women, and female "non-Greeks." The authors noted that a selection bias could exist in the event that abstainers declined to participate (which would have oversampled drinkers), but highlighted the importance of assessing drinking and related risks across multiple settings when working with fraternity and sorority members.

Several studies have highlighted the role that perception of one's peers plays in impacting a student's drinking (Borsari & Carey, 2003; Perkins, 2002). Research indicates that students typically overestimate the acceptability of excessive drinking, the prevalence of drinking among their peers, and the amount of alcohol consumed by their peers. In a discussion of stereotypes about alcohol consumption, fraternity and sorority members were consistently identified by their peers as students who drink heavily (Ashmore, Del Boca, & Beebe, 2002). However, within the "Greek system" setting, analyses examining possible mediators of the link between "Greek" membership and heavy drinking suggest that this relationship could at least be partially accounted for by perceived norms of peer alcohol use. More than their "non-Greek" peers, fraternity and sorority members perceive higher levels of alcohol use as normative and exhibit higher levels of acceptability and support of heavy drinking practices (Sher et al., 2001). Further, perceived amount of drinking (*descriptive norms*) predicted concurrent drinking, and perceived approval of heavy drinking (*injunctive norms*) predicted both concurrent and future alcohol use and problems over a one-year period for fraternity and sorority members (Larimer, Turner, Mallett, & Geisner, 2004).

Despite clear findings that "Greeks" drank more heavily than "non-Greeks" during their college years, Sher and colleagues (2001) found that the difference was no longer apparent three years after graduation. That outcome highlights the importance of prevention and intervention efforts to reduce risks and harm during the college years, as such drinking appears to represent a developmental window of risk. Several studies indicate fraternity and sorority members are responsive to preventive approaches based on motivational feedback and skills training (Larimer & Cronce, 2002, 2007). However, research also suggests fraternity and to some extent sorority members continue to drink more heavily than their nonmember peers even after participating in an efficacious motivational intervention and after reducing their drinking in response to intervention (Marlatt et al., 1998). This suggests that environmental or systems-level interventions may need to be integrated with efficacious individual interventions to further reduce drinking in these organizations. One novel approach to prevention was documented by Glindemann and colleagues (2007), describing a creative intervention in which the opportunity to win a financial reward through a raffle was offered to fraternity students drinking up to but not exceeding a BAC level of .05%. At intervention parties, the percentage of students below the BAC level associated with being legally intoxicated (.08% in the United States) increased while rates in the control condition actually decreased. Although there are limitations to the study (a total of six fraternities at one college were observed at parties until 1:00 a.m., after which experimenters left the premises), the authors suggest that an incentive-based intervention could be self-sustaining if, for example, entrance to the party required a cover charge that could be used in part for the incentive. In the light of finding so far, additional research on the use of incentives to impact behaviors seems warranted.

Interestingly, membership in a "Greek" organization may provide some degree of reduced risk for frequent drinkers. For example, Larimer and colleagues (2000) showed that high- and low-frequency drinkers in sororities did not differ in the negative consequences they reported; meanwhile, for women in residence halls, high-frequency drinkers reported significantly more negative consequences than did low-frequency drinkers. The authors suggested that, although living in the "Greek system" may carry an overall increased risk for women, it may actually serve as a protective factor for women who are heavier drinkers (Larimer et al., 2000). Future research could examine the reasons behind this to consider specific factors impacting student health and wellbeing.

Research suggests that, while rates of alcohol consumption remain high in "Greek system" settings compared to their "non-Greek" equivalents, fraternities and sororities may be making important progress toward being a "more responsible group" (Caron, Moskey, & Hovey, 2004, p. 64). Further, with concerns about liability on college campuses becoming more and more prominent in an increasingly litigious society, colleges and universities have been encouraged to partner with "Greek" chapters as students and administrators alike look to the future of alcohol prevention (Elkins, Helms, & Pierson, 2003). The quest for "what works" in responding to risky drinking by members of sorority and fraternity organizations continues, and recent studies suggest reason for optimism in this pursuit (Larimer & Cronce, 2007).

Brief Interventions

An approach used specifically to target individuals who have developed problematic drinking patterns but are not alcohol-dependent involves brief interventions that employ a range of harm reduction strategies. Normally relying on short sessions with counselor, peer educator, or health professional that range from several minutes to several longer sessions, brief interventions are relatively easy to implement, since they do not require extensive planning and training. Originally developed for adults within the treatment setting, brief interventions are especially appropriate for young extreme drinkers because these young people tend to see their alcohol consumption as unproblematic and do not seek help. The use of this approach to target adolescents and young adults has been particularly studied in educational institutions (D'Amico & Fromme, 2002; Marlatt, 1998), but has also been employed by medical and law enforcement services (see chapter 7).

Brief interventions may utilize a number of the techniques described above—social norms reeducation, alcohol expectancy challenge, skills training (particularly self-monitoring and self-assessment), and the provision of information—but also add elements of motivational interviewing and personalized feedback. Motivational interviewing relies on the notion that it is ultimately up to individuals to modify their drinking, develop a strategy for change, and commit to this decision; the technique aims to minimize participants' ambivalence about reconsidering their behavior (Miller, Zweben, Diclemente, & Rychtarik, 1992; Miller & Rollnick, 2002). Personalized feedback—delivered in person, by mail, or electronically—is based on either a self-reported questionnaire or a formal screening instrument, developed to help detect problematic alcohol consumption; it is nonconfrontational and nonjudgmental, designed "to heighten the participant's awareness of personal patterns of use, peer norms, risks related to use, and the experience of negative consequences under certain drinking conditions" (White, 2006, p. 312). The end goal of brief interventions is decided jointly by participants and practitioner and may range from abstinence to modified drinking patterns. The emphasis, however, is on motivating clients to reduce risky behaviors and avoid harmful outcomes rather than on achieving a specific drinking target (for discussion, see White, 2006).

Students may receive brief interventions voluntarily, as part of school sanctions for infringement of alcohol-related rules, as a follow-up to a medical or academic emergency related to drinking, or as part of outreach for young people in heavy-drinking settings (for instance, residents of student dormitories or fraternities and first-year university students; see Case Study, "Drinking among Sorority and Fraternity Students in the United States," above). Although not meant for alcohol-dependent youth, brief interventions can be an important first step in delivering treatment by offering assessment, advice, and referral to professional care.

Brief interventions may be delivered individually or as part of a group session (Neighbors, Larimer, Lostutter, & Woods, 2006; see examples of brief interventions below). Some researchers discourage the use of the group format for the delivery of brief interventions because it may normalize heavy consumption among participants by exposing them to other extreme-drinking peers, and suggest that individually administered feedback may be more likely to change students' perceptions of norms (e.g., Walters, Bennett, & Noto, 2000). Whatever the format, research from different countries indicates that this approach is most effective for young people already engaging in high-risk drinking, rather than for the general student population (e.g., Larimer et al., 2001; Ståhlbrandt, Johnsson, & Berglund, 2007).

Examples of Intervention: Brief Intervention Programs

Group-Focused Approach: ASTP

The Alcohol Skills Training Program (ASTP), from which many brief interventions derive, is a group initiative developed specifically for young extreme drinkers who have experienced or are at risk of experiencing alcohol-related problems (Fromme, Marlatt, Baer, & Kivlahan, 1994; Hernandez, Skewes, Resor, Villaneuva, Hanson, & Blume, 2006; Kivlahan, Marlatt, Fromme, Coppel, & Williams, 1990). ASTP teaches young people alcohol moderation skills—for example, assessing their own BAC levels and avoiding alcohol when performing certain tasks, such as driving or taking medication. In addition, it employs motivational interviewing to encourage students to come up with personally relevant reasons for reducing their drinking, provides accurate information about alcohol effects and peer norms, and dispels common myths about alcohol. The intervention, delivered in eight, six, and two sessions, has been associated with reductions in alcohol consumption (reflected in participants' peak blood alcohol levels and the average amounts of alcohol consumed weekly, monthly, or during a heavy drinking situation) and related problems, though the strongest effect was attributed to the longest, eight-session format (Baer, Marlatt, Kivlahan, Fromme, Larimer, & Williams, 1992; Kivlahan et al., 1990; Miller, Kilmer, Kim, Weingardt, & Marlatt, 2001). The program has been recently adapted for Mexican-American college students in the United States with promising results, indicating that it can be successfully transferred to other cultures and can appeal to minority students within diverse student populations (Hernandez et al., 2006).

Individual-Focused Approach: BASICS

Many brief interventions delivered individually are modeled on the Brief Alcohol Screening and Intervention for College Students (BASICS). Derived from ASTP, BASICS relies on two short individualized sessions with a counselor (Dimeff, Baer, Kivlahan, & Marlatt, 1999; Murphy et al., 2001). The first session provides factual information about alcohol and assesses the participant's current drinking patterns and perceptions about alcohol. The second session—normally

taking place within the next two weeks—provides nonconfrontational, nonjudgmental feedback about the participant's drinking in comparison to his or her
peers (for instance, peak BAC level, alcohol-related problems, and personal
risk factors) and discusses some of the strategies to reduce risk and make safer
drinking choices. Research indicates that students who receive BASICS report
lower levels of alcohol consumption and related negative outcomes than their
counterparts not exposed to the program (Baer, Kivlahan, Blume, McKnight,
& Marlatt, 2001; Marlatt et al., 1998); reductions in drinking appear to persist
months and even years after participating in BASICS (Baer et al., 2001; Borsari
& Carey, 2000). Moreover, many postintervention students report that they
react differently to their friends' drinking after the program, thus broadening
the reach of the intervention when implemented in densely populated settings
where drinking levels are traditionally high (for instance, student dormitories or
fraternities and sororities).

Some new brief interventions have replaced in-person assessment or
delivery of personalized feedback with written or Web-based contact, further reducing the costs of implementation. Research in the United States
(Neighbors, Lewis, Bergstrom, & Larimer, 2006; Saitz et al., 2007) and New
Zealand (Kypri, 2004) indicates that feedback delivered by mail or the Web
is no less likely to produce reductions in extreme drinking than interventions
relying on interpersonal interaction. Thus, it appears that "the efficacy of
[brief interventions] for—students may not depend on personal contact, but
instead may be the result of the feedback provided" (White, 2006, p. 316; see
also Larimer & Cronce, 2002). Furthermore, written personalized feedback
may in fact be particularly effective with participants feeling ambivalent about
change, whose resistance could be exacerbated in the presence of a counselor (Murphy et al., 2004). Surveys of young heavy drinkers in the United
States (Chiauzzi, Green, Lord, Thum, & Goldstein, 2005) and New Zealand
(Kypri, 2004) revealed an interest among these young people in accessing
both assessment and feedback electronically and a reluctance to discuss their
drinking habits with health professionals. Thus, Web-based interventions
provide a promising channel for reaching extreme-drinking students within
an anonymous, nonintrusive setting, although further study is necessary to
determine components of feedback that would make it appealing to different
groups of students (Saitz et al., 2007; White, 2006). For instance, personalized
feedback using gender-specific terms and including gender-specific drinking
norms appears to be more effective for female participants in comparison to
their male counterparts, who respond well to gender-neutral feedback (Lewis
& Neighbors, 2007).

Drinking Contexts: Reshaping the Environment

In addition to the approaches focused on the individual, many schools implement a number of interventions aimed to shape the social, physical, and regulatory contexts surrounding student extreme drinking. The tenor of these

efforts ranges from a complete ban on alcohol on school property and strict enforcement of alcohol-related sanctions to various harm reduction strategies intended to change the actual student norms, provide safer alternatives to extreme drinking, or offer safer drinking environments (for review, see Alberta Alcohol and Drug Abuse Commission [AADAC], 2005; Coleman & Cater, 2005; Karam et al., 2007; Toomey, Lenk, & Wagenaar, 2007).

Issues involved in developing local alcohol policy, its enforcement, and formal monitoring of young people's social and commercial access to alcohol are described in chapter 7. Overall, as Ziemelis et al. (2002) concluded:

> [S]trategies that focus on discouraging or deglamorizing substance use [within school settings] were associated with better program outcomes than those merely banning or restricting such use—students were most amenable to regulatory prevention efforts when program personnel solicited their input, when such efforts were part of a comprehensive program that also included educational and informational components, and when the institution encouraged active student participation and involvement in prevention. (pp. 248–249)

Many schools employ multiple strategies targeting the drinking environment, often in unison with programs aimed at the individual. Figure 8.3 offers an example of the many elements involved in one campus-wide initiative against extreme drinking, NU Directions, developed and implemented at a U.S. college (Newman, Shell, Major, & Workman, 2006).

FIGURE 8.3 Model of comprehensive strategy for NU Directions. Reprinted from the *International Journal of Drug Policy*, Vol. 17, I. M. Newman, D. F. Shell, L. J. Major, & T. A. Workman, "Use of policy, education, and enforcement to reduce binge drinking among university students: The NU Directions project," pp. 339–349. Copyright 2006, with permission from Elsevier.

Although imposing alcohol-free environments confers certain protective effects to some students, such initiatives appear to reduce *casual* rather than extreme drinking (Odo, McQuiller, & Stretesky, 1999). For many young people, heavy alcohol consumption plays a significant ritual role in ensuring positive social interaction, coping with the stress of academic life, and reaching maturity (see chapters 2, 4, and 5). Entertainment options that would provide alternatives to extreme drinking as the staple of recreational activities include the promotion of school-sponsored events or meeting venues that do not center around alcohol, such as art performances, discussion groups, and student coffee houses.

It should be noted that alcohol-free occasions and contexts are initially unlikely to attract risky drinkers. Skills deficits often "limit the ability of [these youths] to derive reinforcement from certain types of substance-free activities" (Correia, Carey, Simons, & Borsari, 2003, p. 367). Providing social occasions where moderate drinking is the norm may be a viable option for reaching these young people. For instance, Ohaeri and colleagues (1996) described alcohol consumption among a nationwide university student club in Nigeria, "The Kegites" (see also chapter 5, "Nigeria"). The club promotes pleasurable uses of a traditional alcohol brew, palm wine, within a regulated drinking setting that discourages heavy consumption and promotes a climate of mutual support among participants. This further underscores the importance of building social, as well as regulatory, safeguards against student extreme drinking.

In this context, studies on the role of *social capital* in educational institutions provide further insight to approaching drinking contexts (Weitzman & Chen, 2005). Social capital is "a contextual characteristic describing patterns of civic engagement, trust, and mutual obligation among persons" (Weitzman & Kawachi, 2000, p. 1936; see also Lochner, Kawachi, & Kennedy, 1999). Within educational settings, a sense of community among students (Spitzberg & Thorndike, 1992), strengthened through civic involvement and voluntary activities, has been linked to lower rates of risky drinking; this applied also to high-risk students (Weitzman & Chen, 2005; Weitzman & Kawachi, 2000). According to Weitzman and Kawachi (2000):

> Campuses with high levels of social capital may provide the patterns of interconnectedness and mutual obligation required for collective regulation of deviancy in a group. Although social capital may have little effect on (or even encourage) light drinking, it may protect against binge and problem drinking. (p. 1936)

Finally, working with communities that surround schools, colleges, and universities is an important component of tackling student drinking environments. Parents (see Example of Intervention, "School–Family Programs"), servers and sellers of beverage alcohol, and local leaders provide additional channels for influencing adolescents and young adults beyond the walls of secondary and tertiary institutions. For example, schools may partner with tribal organizations in shaping messages for, changing norms among, and delivering services to indigenous young people and their families (Hawkins et al., 2004). Reciprocity between school and community policies, programs, campaigns, and services can strengthen school-based interventions and help reduce acute problems linked to student extreme drinking, such as alcohol-impaired driving, public disorder, and injuries (see chapters 6 and 7; and the section on *Community Settings* below).

Example of Intervention: School–Family Programs

Since many risk factors associated with problem drinking in young people originate in families, schools can work with local community organizations to provide outreach, alcohol education, and skills training to parents and caretakers of students deemed to be at high risk for delinquency and substance abuse. Programs focus on enhancing family functioning, preventing or intervening in problem drinking by youth or family members, and coping with stress. One such intervention is the Strengthening Families Program (SFP), a behavioral skills training initiative for parents and schoolchildren that consists of fourteen 2-hour sessions. SFP has shown considerable promise in producing long-term positive change in alcohol consumption among participants from diverse backgrounds (Foxcroft et al., 2003) and has led to reductions in high-risk factors (family conflict and stress, child depression and aggression, and substance use among parents and children) and a rise in protective factors (prosocial behaviors in children, better parenting skills, and improved family environment).

WORKPLACE

Many young people are not enrolled in academic institutions. In developed countries, a number of young adults leave after some level of secondary education and enter the workforce; in developing countries, school attrition often occurs even earlier. Reaching young extreme drinkers not enrolled in secondary or tertiary institutions is a challenge. The workplace offers a promising venue to access them, since it serves as an organized setting where young people gather for a defined period of time. Moreover, the number and proportion of young people in the workforce are rising in many countries, further underscoring the need to modify existing workplace programs to engage this population (Batts, Grabill, Galvin, & Schlenger, 2005).

Research shows that young adults often constitute the heaviest-drinking segments within the workforce. For instance, in a study of Australian police officers, 18- to 25-year-olds reported the highest levels of heavy alcohol consumption and related problems among all age groups in the sample (Davey, Obst, & Sheehan, 2000). In the United States, employed individuals aged 16–25 years were found to be twice as likely to engage in excessive drinking as their older counterparts (U.S. Department of Labor, Bureau of Labor Statistics, 2005). And in the United Kingdom, the workplace was identified as a major location that "captures" important heavier-drinking groups, including 16- to 24-year-olds (Mulvihill, Taylor, Waller, Naidoo, & Thom, 2005).

In general, research links employee problem drinking with a number of negative worksite outcomes, including poor performance, social and interpersonal problems, absenteeism, high employee turnover, and accidents that may affect not only drinkers themselves, but their colleagues, employers, and the broader community (e.g., Hoffman & Larison, 1999; Mangili, 2004; Silva, Gaunekar, Patel, Kukalekar, & Fernandes, 2003; World Health Organization, 2004). Several factors appear to influence employee drinking and the likelihood of problems, such as prevailing workplace culture and norms with regard to alcohol, levels of alienation and stress, and the existence of company alcohol policy and enforcement (Ames & Grube, 1999; Ames, Grube, & Moore, 2000; Ames & Janes, 1992; Bacharach, Bamberger, & Sonnenstuhl, 2002; Bennett & Lehman, 1998; Greenberg & Grunberg, 1995; Trice, 1992; Yang, Yang, & Kawachi, 2001). In addition, drinking patterns of individuals in certain occupations and sectors—such as transportation, aviation, construction, public safety, military, the beverage alcohol industry, and hospitality—tend to be more risky and are of particular concern because of the high physical or mental concentration required in their job performance, a high level of danger, or alcohol's prominent place within the workplace environment (Davey et al., 2000; ICAP, 2003; Richmond, Wodak, Kehoe, & Heather, 1998). Young adults are often among these heavy drinkers. For instance, in a study of mine employees, younger males reported the highest rates of problem drinking and adverse alcohol-related outcomes within an already heavy-drinking workforce sample (Lennings, Feeney, Sheehan, Young, McPherson, & Tucker, 1997). Young military recruits aged 18 to 25 years in the United States exhibit significantly higher levels of excessive alcohol consumption than both their civilian counterparts and older coworkers (Ames & Cunradi, 2004/2005; see also Bray et al., 2003; Substance Abuse and Mental Health Services Administration [SAMHSA], 2002), and recent data on the United Kingdom's armed forces indicate that "heavy drinking is more common in young, single personnel," both male and female (Fear et al., 2007, p. 1756).

Many organizations, particularly in the safety-sensitive sectors, establish a formal alcohol policy that prohibits drinking at or before work and set a range of disciplinary actions for noncompliance (for review, see ICAP, 2003). The effectiveness of a workplace alcohol policy, however, depends on enforcement and does not address off-the-job drinking, which still has an impact on work performance, employee health, and job retention. Thus, businesses have implemented a number of interventions to address problem drinking in the workforce that extend beyond stated company policy, but the prevalence and structure of these programs vary across developed and developing countries, sectors, and organization types and sizes. Where they exist, workplace programs may include health promotion, alcohol education and skills training, counseling and brief interventions for risky drinkers, and referral to treatment. Many of these programs focus on early identification and reduction of existing problems and aim to help employees maintain their jobs and productivity (for review, see Cook & Schlenger, 2002; Roman & Blum, 2002).

Worksite interventions are normally directed at the mainstream worker, and their relevance to young people remains to be fully determined (Batts et al., 2005). However, certain promising approaches that either target the individual, groups, or the workplace environment should be recognized as potential avenues for youth interventions.

Employee Assistance Programs and Drug Testing

Particularly in developed countries, worksite identification of problem drinkers and intervention are traditionally carried out through employee assistance programs (EAPs) and drug testing (Roman & Blum, 1999, 2002). Derived from occupational alcoholism initiatives, these approaches have shown limited ability to capture individuals in the lower spectrums of problem drinking, which is where young extreme drinkers are mostly found. Moreover, drug testing has been a sensitive issue, raising a number of privacy and cost concerns (e.g., Bennett & Lehman, 2003; Building Trades Group Drug and Alcohol Program, n.d.). Greater emphasis on supportive rather than disciplinary action has been suggested as a more appropriate and long-term solution to workforce substance abuse issues. Thus, efforts have been made to increase EAP's inclusiveness of a diverse workforce and drinking trajectories. These modifications could prove successful in engaging young adults.

Offered by companies or labor unions, or through management-union collaboration, EAPs generally provide substance abuse and mental health assessment, diagnosis, and treatment, and depend on self-referral or referral by supervisors. The ability of EAPs to act as an early identification tool for risky drinking hinges on the degree of employee awareness about alcohol issues and the services offered, a guarantee of confidentiality, and supervisor training in recognizing and addressing problems. The key challenge in increasing the sensitivity of EAPs to employee needs is to boost self-referrals across the entire workforce rather than relying on formal action by supervisors. Lessons from efforts to encourage voluntary utilization of EAP services may benefit young people. For instance, in a U.S. study of an EAP updated to be more inclusive of women and minorities (Zarkin, Bray, Karuntzos, & Demiralp, 2001), the authors cautioned against explicitly targeting or representing particular subgroups in worksite outreach efforts, since this would risk portraying them as problem workers and create further barriers to their willingness to utilize services. The end result was an enhanced standard EAP package with potential to reach a broad audience but also to appeal to specific segments of the population. Utilization of the new program increased across the entire sample workforce (Zarkin et al., 2001). Young employees— young women and minority and indigenous youth among them—may be another group that could similarly be included in enhanced EAP materials and outreach.

Health Promotion and Wellness Programs: Skills Training

The availability and delivery of EAP services relies on resources, the existence of the right infrastructure, and experience. In addition, many extreme drinkers resist recognizing their behavior as problematic and their off-the-job drinking may not be easily detected through formal worksite channels. To reach these workers, broader awareness and skills training are in order. Embedding alcohol misuse issues into general health and wellness promotion—for instance, by incorporating them into stress management education and brief small-group training offered to all employees—has been linked to declines in risky drinking (Buning, Gorgulho, Melcop, & O'Hare, 2003; Cook, Back, Trudeau, & McPherson, 2003; Heirich & Sieck, 2003; Snow, Swan, & Wilton, 2002). Moreover, addressing alcohol-related topics within the positive context of healthy lifestyle avoids the stigma typically attached to substance abuse, thus increasing the willingness of both employers and employees to approach the issue (Deitz, Cook, & Hersch, 2005). To further encourage help-seeking and behavior change, programs can include information on self-assessment, specific techniques to reduce heath risks (including risks from problem drinking), and available substance use and mental health services. In a study of a worksite wellness program that focused on stress reduction, the utilization of substance abuse and mental health services increased, particularly among employees aged 20–29 years (Deitz et al., 2005).

Peer Interventions and Team Training

Targeting individual perceptions and behaviors, however, may not be enough in all workplace settings. Research has shown that sustainable success of health promotion programs relies on the actual social norms and culture prevalent within the worksite (Allen & Allen, 1990; Barrientos-Gutierrez, Gimeno, Mangione, Harrist, & Amick, 2007). An approach that successfully targets these aspects of the work environment emphasizes peer intervention. The main goal of such programs is to change drinking norms that are conducive to extreme consumption, whether as a means of socializing or of coping with problems. These initiatives appear to be particularly appropriate for occupations that depend on a high level of teamwork and are physically risky or safety-sensitive. Individuals employed in such settings—including many young people—tend to report higher levels of alcohol consumption and peer acceptance of their drinking than other workers (Holcom, Lehman, & Simpson, 1993; Lehman & Bennett, 2002). Peer interventions involve several interactive team sessions that focus on increasing the sense of personal responsibility for group safety and wellbeing, address permissive drinking cultures as a potential risk factor for harm, and train individuals in identifying problems, coping with stress, and developing appropriate help-seeking and help-giving behaviors. Special training sessions have been developed for employees and supervisors. Such training appears to enhance positive health behavior, reduce extreme consumption in both moderate- and high-risk drinking samples, and boost peer responsiveness to and referral of problem coworkers. Importantly, team training can be successfully implemented within the context of small- and medium-sized organizations and adapted to respond to various drinking cultures and norms. Young males in the blue-collar workforce have been one of the main target groups of one such intervention (see Cook, Back, & Trudeau, 1996).

Workplace Brief Interventions

For many workplace interventions, the existence of referral and support resources is an important prerequisite. Where these are absent, brief interventions with motivational interviewing and personalized feedback, currently employed in educational and medical settings, appear promising when transferred to the workplace, particularly among women (Anderson & Larimer, 2002). The ability of these initiatives to engage extreme drinkers who do not perceive themselves as at risk for harm is particularly noteworthy. When such initiatives are adapted to the workplace environment, it is suggested that they should take the form of individualized sessions that include alcohol education, assessment, and skills training within the broader health and wellness context to encourage self-selection among participants (Anderson & Larimer, 2002; Richmond, Kehoe, Heather, & Wodak, 2000).

It has been suggested that assessment of participants' drinking patterns and an individualized response provided during workplace brief interventions may be the main factors in motivating behavior change (Richmond, Heather, Wodak, Kehoe, & Webster, 1995; Scott & Anderson, 1991). To that end, studies have explored the possibility of delivering comprehensive but brief alcohol education, skills training, assessment (of drinking, as well as stress levels and coping styles), and feedback electronically, with promising results. Young people may be particularly responsive to this approach. Although basic computer skills are a prerequisite for individuals to benefit from the program, organizations where computers are not part of the everyday activity could encourage access by making several computers available to all employees in private and easily accessible areas (Matano, Futa, Wanat, Mussman, & Leung, 2000).

Event-Specific Campaigns

Finally, extreme drinking can be addressed within broad awareness programs offered during particular times in the work cycle (for instance during high-stress deadline periods) or around holidays. In Brazil, a computerized program delivered before the Carnival, a time when risky drinking is a salient feature, encouraged employees to access health-related information and provided advice on minimizing harm through responsible decision-making

(Gorgulho & Da Ros, 2006). Some companies offer a confidential free ride service to employees after a night out during the winter holiday season, aimed at avoiding alcohol-impaired driving (National Highway Traffic Safety Administration, n.d.). Although these programs do not specifically target extreme drinking, they seek to minimize any potential harm. Creating a convivial work environment where employees' behavior is treated as an asset rather than being policed appears to be key in encouraging safer behaviors both on and off the job.

COMMUNITY SETTINGS

Settings surrounding young people outside school and the workplace can be broadly described as "community settings." A wide range of stakeholders are involved in addressing young people's drinking within this general environment. The diverse interventions they implement include media campaigns; responsible hospitality programs in bars, pubs, and nightclubs; efforts against particular alcohol-related outcomes, such as traffic crashes and public disorder; programs for marginalized youths; and comprehensive community initiatives that address several aspects of the drinking context (for an overview of targeted community interventions aimed at young people, alcohol-related behaviors, and drinking environments, see Stimson et al., 2007).

Media Campaigns

Media-based public health campaigns against extreme drinking often target the younger segments of society. Aimed to raise awareness about alcohol, potential risks, sensible drinking levels, and available services, these programs may also attempt to shift drinking norms, expectancies, and attitudes toward certain behaviors by dispelling alcohol myths and publicizing the antisocial aspects of intoxication and drunkenness. For example, "Alcohol: Know Your Limits," the first national campaign to target 18- to 24-year-olds in the United Kingdom, uses television, radio and cinema advertisements, posters, and online tools to underscore the disconnect between an intoxicated person's feeling of invincibility and his or her actual vulnerability to physical and social harm ("Too much alcohol makes you feel invincible when you're most vulnerable"). According to the U.K. Department of Health, the initial evaluation of the campaign demonstrated that it was "highly effective in raising awareness and had a high level of recall among young people" (Department of Health, Home Office, Department for Education and Skills, & Department for Culture, Media and Sport, 2007, p. 34).

Without focusing specifically on extreme drinking or its negative consequences, media campaigns can also impart information on avoiding particular activities after drinking and offer advice on self-management and peer support. Awareness outreach can also target adults who may have an influence over young people's behaviors, including parents. Thus, "100% Cool," a drink–drive campaign designd to popularize the concept of a designated driver in Portugal, targeted 18- to 26-year-olds, but also parents and other adults whose behaviors and views have an impact on young people. The campaign, which stressed the positive social aspects of responsible drinking, was favorably received by the target groups, and its concept has been integrated into popular youth culture (Amsterdam Group, Institut Belge pour la Sécurité Routière, & Arnoldus, 2003).

Drinking Establishments

Drinking establishments that tend to attract a younger clientele are useful forums for popularizing the images and messages of health media campaigns. Outreach materials placed in such venues can focus on self-assessment tools and provide personal safety tips, especially for women. In addition to imparting information, these settings can offer fertile ground for screening and individual brief interventions like those targeting young people in educational, medical, and workplace contexts. An initial study of one such program, Operation DrinkSafe in Australia, concluded that "brief interventions which include both a personal health risk assessment and BAC drink/drive education may be effective in hotels, clubs, bars, and taverns" (van Beurden, Reilly, Dight, Mitchell, & Beard, 2000, p. 301). An important feature of Operation DrinkSafe was a partnership between local police and health services, which "helped to facilitate a high degree of co-operation and acceptance by licensees and their customers" (p. 301).

Responsible hospitality training of managers, servers, and security personnel in drinking establishments can help further reduce the prevalence and negative consequences of extreme drinking (e.g., Graham, Jelley, & Purcell, 2005; Graham, Schmidt, & Gillis, 1995; Holder & Wagenaar, 1994). The ServerWise initiative in Scotland, TIPS in the United States, and the Safer Bars program in Canada (which was specifically designed to reduce alcohol-related aggression in licensed premises) are examples of such interventions. In addition to educating staff in their responsibilities under licensing law, the emphasis is placed on refusing to serve intoxicated patrons and individuals under the legal drinking age, preventing alcohol-impaired driving through designated driver programs or safe ride services, and resolving potential conflict situations peacefully. Physical modifications to the drinking environment—ensuring easy access to the bar, restrooms, and seating areas; better lighting; and use of safety glass or plastic cups for drinks—may accompany server training in creating secure and enjoyable drinking settings for all customers (Graham & Homel, 1997). Other options include the provision of non- and low-alcohol drinks, snacks, and entertainment and limiting promotions that could encourage overconsumption, such as "Happy Hours" (see discussion in Stimson et al., 2007). In addition to policy measures and enforcement (chapter 7), the compliance of venues with responsible hospitality practices can be encouraged through informal local monitoring and best practice award schemes, such as PubWatch and Best Bar None in the U.K., run in partnership by local authorities, law enforcement agencies, and businesses (Department of Health, Home Office, Department for Education and Skills, & Department for Culture, Media and Sport, 2007).

Street-Based Interventions: Marginalized Youth and Street Drinking

Accessing marginalized young people, who cannot be easily reached through mainstream public campaigns and venues, schools, and the workplace, is a challenge. Street-based youth interventions that draw on informal channels of communication have been growing in number. Research indicates that long-term, area-based projects are giving way to short-term initiatives targeted at high-risk groups on specific issues (Crimmens et al., 2004). These initiatives play a key role in connecting many socially excluded young people to services, education, and employment opportunities, which are otherwise out of their reach. Further research is needed to evaluate the responsiveness of these programs to extreme drinking. However, it appears that emphasis on voluntary involvement and individual-focused interventions is the most realistic approach. Targeting both high-risk/need youth and their less problematic peers has been suggested, since "these young people often constitute potentially powerful influence and support systems" (Crimmens et al., 2004).

When appropriate, family functioning and training efforts such as the one described above (see Example of Intervention, "School–Family Programs")—delivered through, for example, faith-based and shelter organizations—can be an option for enhancing self-efficacy and risk management among socially excluded youth. Some researchers have proposed attracting indigenous or minority service providers as a means to improve delivery of services to clients from diverse backgrounds (Robertson, Haitana, Pitama, & Huriwai, 2006). And brief interventions are increasingly implemented within the contexts of law enforcement and social services to respond to young people (see chapter 7).

Some young people's drinking is outside the mainstream and viewed as risky because of *where* they choose to drink. Thus, in some countries, street drinking is a concern, associated with an elevated risk for harm and public order issues (e.g., Case Study, "*Botellón* in Spain" in chapter 7; United Kingdom—Coleman & Cater, 2005; Galloway, Forsyth, & Shewan, 2007). Surveys of young street drinkers in Scotland and Spain revealed that, while carrying strong social significance, street drinking may be a "forced option," motivated by high prices at licensed alcohol-serving establishments (Scotland, Spain), refused access to these venues by young people under the drinking age (Scotland), and lack of alternative free indoor settings where young people can socialize (Baigorri & Fernández, 2004; Consejer'a de Gobernación, 2006; Galloway et al., 2007; Musitu & Bascones, 2006; Navarrete, 2002).

Efforts to address this social phenomenon are often directed at controlling the spectacle of street drinking through increased policing and limits on alcohol consumption in certain public areas. However, these measures appear to simply disperse and move such activity elsewhere, often to more secluded locations that present additional environmental hazards to young people, whether or not they engage in heavy drinking (Galloway et al., 2007). A comprehensive set of targeted interventions aimed at minimizing harm and involving a wide range of actors may be better suited to tackle the issue. Education outreach—delivered, for instance, through street-based workers and organizations, retailers likely to be frequented by street drinkers, and/or public media channels—could provide practical information about the physical effects of rapid alcohol consumption, assessment of intoxication in self and others, and ways to respond to alcohol-related emergencies in friends. Where appropriate, such outreach could also address certain high-risk behaviors that may accompany street drinking—for instance, risky sexual practices (Galloway et al., 2007). As discussed above, physical modifications to the drinking environment have proven effective in minimizing harm inside alcohol-serving establishments. Similarly, modifying the physical environment in "known" public drinking spots and replacing glass bottles used to contain alcohol with safety glass or plastic may help reduce some of the physical dangers associated with street drinking. Finally, providing free venues and entertainment options for young people could give them a safe, comfortable alternative to meeting and drinking on the street (Case Study, "*Botellón* in Spain" in chapter 7; Galloway et al., 2007).

Involving young people themselves in the dialogue with communities and other stakeholders can help find additional practical and mutually acceptable ways to address street drinking (Musitu & Bascones, 2006). It should be noted, however, that alcohol consumption may be perceived by these young people as an important, positive ingredient of their social life, a reality that must be at least acknowledged. Thus, a survey of Scottish street drinkers, aged between 16 and 25 years and belonging to several youth subcultures, revealed the following:

> Suggestions made by underage drinkers were typically for activities which would "keep them off the streets." However, it was clear that these activities were ones which did not rule out drinking but instead made drinking more comfortable and safer for those involved by providing a more secure indoor location (or at least a location which kept young people out of harm's way). Equally, when it came to the question of outdoor drinking, it was clear that the blanket ban currently in place in many areas was inappropriate as not only did this prevent "social" drinkers from enjoying themselves safely but also displaced those with more antisocial tendencies to places where they might be more likely to cause trouble. Providing designated drinking areas where drinking could be contained but where drinkers could relax and feel safe (e.g., well-lit "tolerance zones" monitored by CCTV or near a police station) might be considered. (Galloway et al., 2007, p. 108)

In Scotland or any other country with a legal drinking age, however, creating such "tolerance zones" presents an important problem: Many street drinkers are under the drinking age limit (18 years in the United Kingdom), and their alcohol consumption is illegal. Targeted interventions must be balanced with the existing legislation. In this context, encouraging responsible sales practices in local alcohol retail outlets, including the small independent off-licenses—the preferred sources of alcohol for many street drinkers—should be part of community action.

Multi-Component, Multi-Stakeholder Initiatives

Given the multitude of local needs, channels for intervention, and stakeholders, a comprehensive set of multi-component, partner initiatives has been implemented in many communities (e.g., Mistrall, Velleman, Templeton, & Mastache, 2006; Stafström, Östergren, Larsson, Lindgren, & Lundborg, 2006; Thom & Bayley, 2007). Often delivered to the community as a whole, such efforts address young people's drinking within the broader context of culture change, public order, or injury prevention (Thom & Bayley, 2007). For example, community accords, implemented in different countries and described in chapter 7, serve as the framework for targeted interventions in drinking establishments and public settings. At the same time, awareness campaigns to reduce alcohol-related harm during holidays, fiestas, and festivals have been backed by contributions from the police, public transport administration, and the beverage alcohol industry (e.g., Gorgulho & Da Ros, 2006; see also Stimson et al., 2007, pp. 63–64, 118).

Communities can also come together through international cooperation. Thus, the Border Binge-Drinking Reduction Program in the United States and Mexico involves stakeholders from both countries, working together to reduce harm from cross-border underage and extreme drinking (Voas, Tippetts, Johnson, Lange, & Baker, 2002; see chapter 7). Many young people travel from the United States to Mexico to drink so that they can take advantage of the latter's lower drinking age and alcohol prices. These trips have resulted in high rates of alcohol-impaired driving and disorder in border communities. Supported by increased law enforcement, the program's many components resulted in reductions in alcohol-impaired driving, BAC levels of returning drinkers, and negative consequences (SAMHSA, n.d.). These and other initiatives illustrate the importance of engaging a variety of community actors—including the young people themselves—and relying on flexible, comprehensive interventions that address local concerns within the context of available resources and public approval.

CONCLUSIONS

Reducing the prevalence of extreme drinking by young people and minimizing harm requires intervention in a range of youth settings. Three were examined here: educational institutions, the workplace, and the broader community.

A wide range of approaches have been developed and implemented to affect both the individual and the environment within these settings. Overall, it appears that interactive, multi-component programs are more likely to produce sustained, positive results. The reality is that, for many young people, the pattern of extreme drinking carries important social connotations and ritual significance. To truly engage this segment of the population and reduce the harms associated with their behavior, this reality cannot be ignored as programs attempt to modify perceptions, enable informed decision-making, and change the social and physical structures and dynamics surrounding the young in different facets of their lives.

REFERENCES

Alberta Alcohol and Drug Abuse Commission. (2005). *Preventing heavy episodic drinking among youth and young adults: A literature review*. Edmonton, Canada: Author.

Allen, J., & Allen, R. F. (1990). *A sense of community, a shared vision and a positive culture: Core enabling factors in successful culture-based change*. Retrieved January 5, 2008, from http://healthyculture.com/Articles/Triangle.html.

Ames, G. M., & Cunradi, C. (2004/2005). Alcohol use and preventing alcohol-related problems among young adults in the military. *Alcohol Research and Health, 28*, 252–257.

Ames, G. M., & Grube, J. W. (1999). Alcohol availability and workplace drinking: Mixed method analyses. *Journal of Studies on Alcohol, 60*, 383–393.

Ames, G. M., Grube, J. W., & Moore, R. S. (2000). Social control and workplace drinking norms: A comparison of two organizational cultures. *Journal of Studies on Alcohol, 61*, 203–219.

Ames, G. M., & Janes, C. A. (1992). A cultural approach to conceptualizing alcohol and the workplace. *Alcohol Health and Research World, 16*, 112–119.

Amsterdam Group, Institut Belge pour la Sécurité Routière, & Arnoldus. (2003). *Designated driver campaigns against drink-driving in Europe 2003*. Brussels: Amsterdam Group (now European Forum for Responsible Drinking).

Anderson, B. K., & Larimer, M. E. (2002). Problem drinking and the workplace: An individualized approach to prevention. *Psychology of Addictive Behavior, 16*, 243–251.

Ashmore, R. D., Del Boca, F. K., & Beebe, M. (2002). Alkie, "frat brother," and "jock": Perceived types of college students and stereotypes about drinking. *Journal of Applied Social Psychology, 32*, 895–907.

Babor, T. F., Caetano, R., Caswell, S., Edwards, G., Giesbrecht, N., Graham, K., et al. (2003). *Alcohol: No ordinary commodity. Research and public policy*. Oxford, U.K.: Oxford University Press.

BACCHUS. (2002). *Customized health education materials*. Minneapolis, MN: Author.

Bacharach, S. B., Bamberger, P. A., & Sonnenstuhl, W. J. (2002). Driven to drink: Managerial control, work-related risk factors, and employee problem drinking. *Academy of Management Journal, 45*, 637–658.

Baer, J. S., Kivlahan, D. R., Blume, A. W., McKnight, P., & Marlatt, G. A. (2001). Brief intervention for heavy-drinking college students: 4-year follow-up and natural history. *American Journal of Public Health, 91*, 1310–1316.

Baer, J. S., Marlatt, G. A., Kivlahan, D. R., Fromme, K., Larimer, M. E., & Williams, E. (1992). An experimental test of three methods of alcohol risk reduction with young adults. *Journal of Consulting and Clinical Psychology, 60*, 974–979.

Baigorri, A., & Fernández, R. (2004). *Botellón: Un conflicto posmoderno* [*Botellón: A postmodern conflict*]. Barcelona, Spain: Acaria Editorial.

Barrientos-Gutierrez, T., Gimeno, D., Mangione, T. W., Harrist, R. B., & Amick, B. C. (2007). Drinking social norms and drinking behaviors: A multilevel analysis of 137 workgroups in 16 worksites. *Occupational and Environmental Medicine, 64,* 602–608.

Batts, K. R., Grabill, T. C., Galvin, D. M., & Schlenger, W. E. (2005). *Contextual and other factors related to workplace-based substance abuse prevention and early intervention for adolescents and young adults.* Rockville, MD: Substance Abuse and Mental Health Services Administration.

Bauerle, J., Burwell, C., & Turner, J. C. (2002, May 23). *Social norms marketing at the University of Virginia.* Paper presented at the Annual Meeting of the American College Health Association, Washington, D.C.

Bennett, J. B., & Lehman, W. E. K. (1998). Workplace drinking climate, stress, and problem indicators: Assessing the influence of teamwork (group cohesion). *Journal of Studies on Alcohol, 59,* 608–618.

Bennett, J. B., & Lehman, W. E. K. (Eds.). (2003). *Preventing workplace substance abuse: Beyond drug testing to wellness.* Washington, D.C.: American Psychological Association.

Bennett, M. E., Miller, J. H., & Woodall, W. G. (1999). Drinking, binge drinking, and other drug use among southwestern undergraduates: Three-year trends. *American Journal of Drug and Alcohol Abuse, 25,* 331–350.

Berkowitz, A. D. (1997). From reactive to proactive prevention: Promoting an ecology of health on campus. In P. C. Rivers & E. R. Shore (Eds.), *Substance abuse on campus: A handbook for college and university personnel* (pp. 119–139). Westport, CT: Greenwood Press.

Berkowitz, A. D. (2005). An overview of the social norms approach. In L. C. Lederman & L. P. Stewarts (Eds.), *Changing the culture of college drinking: A socially situated health communication campaign* (pp. 193–214). Creskill, NJ: Hampton Press.

Bils, L. (1999). Prévention primaire en Belgique francophone [Primary prevention in French-speaking Belgium]. *Alcoologie, 21*(HS), 187–192.

Bonday, M., & Bruce, S. (2003). Small group norms interventions with Greeks at the University of Virginia. *Report on Social Norms, 3,* 3–6.

Borsari, B., & Carey, K. B. (2000). Effects of a brief motivational intervention with college student drinkers. *Journal of Consulting and Clinical Psychology, 68,* 728–733.

Borsari, B., & Carey, K. B. (2001). Peer influences on college drinking: A review of the research. *Journal of Substance Abuse, 13,* 391–424.

Borsari, B., & Carey, K. B. (2003). Descriptive and injunctive norms in college drinking: A meta-analytic integration. *Journal of Studies on Alcohol, 64,* 331–341.

Botvin, G. J., Griffin, K. W., Diaz, T., & Ifill-Williams, M. (2001). Preventing binge drinking during early adolescence: One- and two-year follow-up of a school-based preventive intervention. *Psychology of Addictive Behaviors, 15,* 360–365.

Bray, R. M., Hourani, L. L., Rae, K. L., Dever, J. A., Brown, J. M., Vincus, A. A., et al. (2003). *2002 Department of defense survey of health related behaviors among military personnel.* Triangle Park, NC: Research Triangle Institute.

Broadbear, J. T., O'Toole, T. P., & Angermeier-Howard, L. K. (2000). Focus group interviews with college students about binge drinking. *International Electronic Journal of Health Education, 3,* 89–96.

Building Trades Group Drug and Alcohol Program. (n.d.). *Policy on alcohol and other drug testing in the workplace.* Sydney, Australia: Author.

Buning, E., Gorgulho, M., Melcop, A. G., & O'Hare, P. (Eds.). (2003). *Alcohol and harm reduction: An innovative approach for countries in transition.* Amsterdam, Netherlands: International Coalition on Alcohol and Harm Reduction.

Carey, K. B., Borsari, B., Carey, M. P., & Maisto, S. A. (2006). Patterns and importance of self-other differences in college drinking norms. *Psychology of Addictive Behaviors, 20,* 385–393.

Caron, S. L., Moskey, E. G., & Hovey, C. A. (2004). Alcohol use among fraternity and sorority members: Looking at change over time. *Journal of Alcohol and Drug Education, 47,* 51–66.

Caudill, B. D., Crosse, S. B., Campbell, B., Howard, J., Luckey, B., & Blane, H. T. (2006). High-risk drinking among college fraternity members: A national perspective. *Journal of American College Health, 55,* 141–155.

Caudill, B. D., Luckey, B. S., Crosse, B., Blane, H. T., Ginexi, E. M., & Campbell, B. (2007). Alcohol risk-reduction skills training in a national fraternity: A randomized intervention trial with longitudinal intent-to-treat analysis. *Journal of Studies on Alcohol and Drugs, 68,* 399–409.

Centre for Addiction and Mental Health. (1999). *Alcohol and drug prevention programs for youth: What works?* Toronto, Canada: Author.

Chiauzzi, E., Green, T. C., Lord, S., Thum, C., & Goldstein, M. (2005). My student body: A high-risk drinking prevention web site for college students. *Journal of American College Health, 53,* 263–274.

Cho, H. (2006). Readiness to change, norms, and self-efficacy among heavy-drinking college students. *Journal of Studies on Alcohol, 67,* 131–138.

Christensen, S. (2005). The snowball survey as a component of a high school social norms marketing intervention: A pilot study. *Social Norms Review, 1,* 3–9.

Cimini, M. D., Page, J. C., & Trujillo, D. (2002). Using peer theater to deliver social norm information: The Middle Earth Players program. *Report on Social Norms, 2,* 1–8.

Clapp, J. D., Lange, J. E., Russell, C., Shillington, A., & Voas, R. B. (2003). A failed social marketing campaign. *Journal of Studies on Alcohol, 64,* 409–414.

Coleman, L., & Cater, S. (2005). *Underage "risky" drinking: Motivations and outcomes.* York, U.K.: Joseph Rowntree Foundation.

Consejería de Gobernación. (2006). *Estudio sobre la repercusión de la futura ley sobre potestades administrativas en materia de actividades de ocio en los espacios abiertos de los municipios de Andalucía* [*Study of the repercussions of the future law on administrative legal authorities regarding open air leisure activities in Andalucían municipalities*]. Sevilla, Spain: Junta de Andalucía.

Cook, R., Back, A. S., & Trudeau, J. (1996). Preventing alcohol use problems among blue-collar workers: A field test of the Working People Program. *Substance Use and Misuse, 31,* 255–275.

Cook, R., Back, A. S., Trudeau, J., & McPherson, T. L (2003). Integrating substance abuse prevention into health promotion programs in the workplace. In J. B. Bennett & W. E. K. Lehman (Eds.), *Preventing workplace substance abuse: Beyond drug testing to wellness* (pp. 97–133). Washington, D.C.: American Psychological Association.

Cook, R., & Schlenger, W. (2002). Prevention of substance abuse in the workplace: Review of research on the delivery of services. *Journal of Primary Prevention, 23,* 115–141.

Correia, C. J., Carey, K. B., Simons, J., & Borsari, B. E. (2003). Relationships between binge drinking and substance-free reinforcement in a sample of college students: A preliminary investigation. *Addictive Behaviors, 28,* 361–368.

Crimmens, D., Factor, F., Jeffs, T., Pitts, J., Pugh, C., Spence, J., et al. (2004). *Reaching socially excluded young people: A national study of street-based youth work.* Leicester, U.K.: National Youth Agency & Joseph Rowntree Foundation.

D'Amico, E. J., & Fromme, K. (2002). Brief prevention for adolescent risk-taking behavior. *Addiction, 97*, 563–574.

Darkes, J., & Goldman, M. S. (1993). Expectancy challenge and drinking reduction: Experimental evidence for a mediational process. *Journal of Consulting and Clinical Psychology, 61*, 344–353.

Darkes, J., & Goldman, M. S. (1998). Expectancy challenge and drinking reduction: Process and structure in the alcohol expectancy network. *Experimental and Clinical Psychopharmacology, 6*, 64–76.

Davey, J. D., Obst, P. L., & Sheehan, M. C. (2000). Developing a profile of alcohol consumption patterns of police officers in a large scale sample of an Australian police service. *European Addiction Research, 6*, 205–212.

Deitz, D., Cook, R., & Hersch, R. (2005). Workplace health promotion and utilization of health services. *Journal of Behavioral Health Services and Research, 32*, 306–319.

DeJong, W. (2003). The social norms approach to building campus support for policy change. In H. W. Perkins (Ed.), *The social norms approach to preventing school and college age substance abuse: A handbook for educators, counselors, and clinicians* (pp. 154–169). San Francisco, CA: Jossey-Bass.

DeJong, W., & Hingson, R. (1998). Strategies to reduce driving under the influence of alcohol. *Annual Review of Public Health, 19*, 359–378.

DeJong, W., & Linkenbach, J. (1999). Telling it like it is: Using social norms marketing campaigns to reduce student drinking. *American Association Higher Education Bulletin, 52*, 11–13.

DeJong, W., Schneider, S. K., Towvim, L. G., Murphy, M. J., Doerr, E. E., Simonsen, N. R., et al. (2006). A multisite randomized trial of social norms marketing campaigns to reduce college student drinking. *Journal of Studies on Alcohol, 67*, 868–879.

Department of Education, Republic of South Africa. (1997). *Curriculum 2005: Grades 1–9.* Pretoria, South Africa: Author.

Department of Health, Home Office, Department for Education and Skills, & Department for Culture, Media and Sport. (2007). *Safe. Sensible. Social. The next steps in the National Alcohol Strategy.* London: Department of Health & Home Office.

Dimeff, L. A., Baer, J. S., Kivlahan, D. R., & Marlatt, G. A. (1999). *Brief alcohol screening and intervention for college students.* New York: Guilford.

Elkins, B., Helms, L. B., & Pierson, C. T. (2003). Greek-letter organizations, alcohol, and the courts: A risky mix? *Journal of College Student Development, 44*, 67–80.

Ennett, S. T., Tobler, N. S., Ringwalt, C. L., & Flewelling, R. L. (1994). How effective is drug abuse resistance education? A meta-analysis of Project DARE outcome evaluations. *American Journal of Public Health, 84*, 1394–1401.

Fabiano, P. M. (2003). Applying the social norms model to universal and indicated alcohol interventions at Western Washington University. In H. W. Perkins (Ed.), *The social norms approach to preventing school and college age substance abuse: A handbook for educators, counselors, and clinicians* (pp. 83–99). San Francisco, CA: Jossey-Bass.

Far, J. M., & Miller, J. A. (2003). Small groups norms-challenging model: Social norms interventions with targeted high-risk groups. In H. W. Perkins (Ed.), *The social norms approach to preventing school and college age substance abuse: A handbook for educators, counselors, and clinicians* (pp. 111–132). San Francisco, CA: Jossey-Bass.

Fear, N. T., Iversen, A., Meltzer, H., Workman, L., Hull, L., Greenberg, N., et al. (2007). Patterns of drinking in the U.K. Armed Forces. *Addiction, 102*, 1749–1759.

Foxcroft, D., Ireland, D., Lister-Sharp, D. J., Lowe, G., & Breen, R. (2003). Longer-term primary prevention for alcohol misuse in young people: A systematic review. *Addiction, 98*, 397–411.

Foxcroft, D., Ireland, D., Lowe, G., & Breen, R. (2002). Primary prevention for alcohol misuse in young people. *Cochrane Database of Systematic Reviews 2002, 3.* Retrieved March 14, 2007, from http://www.mrw.interscience.wiley.com/cochrane/clsysrev/articles/CD003024/frame.htm.

Fromme, K., Marlatt, G. A., Baer, J. S., & Kivlahan, D. R. (1994). The Alcohol Skills Training Program: A group intervention for young adults. *Journal of Substance Abuse Treatment, 11,* 143–154.

Galloway, J., Forsyth, A., & Shewan, D. (2007). *Young people's street drinking behaviour: Investigating the influence of marketing and subculture.* Retrieved May 19, 2007, from http://www.aerc.org.uk/publicationsFinalRep.htm.

Glindemann, K. E., Ehrhart, I. J., Drake, E. A., & Geller, E. S. (2007). Reducing excessive alcohol consumption at university fraternity parties: A cost-effective incentive/reward intervention. *Addictive Behaviors, 32,* 39–48.

Glindemann, K. E., Ehrhart, I. J., Maynard, M. L., & Geller, E. S. (2006). Alcohol frontloading among college students: Exploring the need for prevention intervention. *Journal of Alcohol and Drug Education, 50,* 5–13.

Gomberg, L., Schneider, S. K., & DeJong, W. (2001). Evaluation of a social norms marketing campaign to reduce high-risk drinking at the University of Mississippi. *American Journal of Drug and Alcohol Abuse, 27,* 375–389.

Gorgulho, M., & Da Ros, V. (2006). Alcohol harm reduction in Brazil. *International Journal of Drug Policy, 17,* 350–357.

Graham, K., & Homel, R. (1997). Creating safer bars. In M. Plant, E. Single, & T. Stockwell (Eds.), *Alcohol: Minimizing the harm. What works?* (pp. 171–192). London: Free Association Books.

Graham, K., Jelley, J., & Purcell, J. (2005). Training bar staff in preventing and managing aggression in licensed premises. *Journal of Substance Use, 10,* 48–61.

Graham, K., Schmidt, G., & Gillis, K. (1995). Circumstances when drinking leads to aggression: An overview of research findings. *Contemporary Drug Problems, 23,* 493–557.

Granfield, R. (2002). Can you believe it? Assessing the credibility of a social norms campaign. *Report on Social Norms. 2,* 1–8.

Greenberg, E. S., & Grunberg, L. (1995). Work alienation and problem alcohol behavior. *Journal of Health and Social Behavior, 36,* 83–102.

Haines, M. (1996). *Social norms approach to preventing binge drinking at colleges and universities.* Newton, MA: Higher Education Center for Alcohol and Other Drug Prevention.

Haines, M. (1998). Social norms: A wellness model for health promotion in higher education. *Wellness Management, 14,* 1, 8.

Haines, M., & Barker, G. (2003). The NIU experiment: A case study of the social norms approach. In H. W. Perkins (Ed.), *The social norms approach to preventing school and college age substance abuse: A handbook for educators, counselors, and clinicians* (pp. 21–34). San Francisco, CA: Jossey-Bass.

Haines, M., Barker, G., & Rice, R. (2003). Using social norms to reduce alcohol and tobacco use in two Midwestern high schools. In H. W. Perkins (Ed.), *The social norms approach to preventing school and college age substance abuse: A handbook for educators, counselors, and clinicians* (pp. 235–244). San Francisco, CA: Jossey-Bass.

Haines, M., & Spear, S. F. (1996). Changing the perception of the norm: A strategy to decrease binge drinking among college students. *Journal of American College Health, 45,* 134–140.

Harford, T. C., Wechsler, H., & Muthén, B. O. (2003). Alcohol-related aggression and drinking at off-campus parties and bars: A national survey of current drinkers in college. *Journal of Studies on Alcohol, 64,* 704–711.

Harford, T. C., Wechsler, H., & Seibring, M. (2002). Attendance and alcohol use at parties and bars in college: A national survey of current drinkers. *Journal of Studies on Alcohol, 63,* 726–733.

Hawkins, E. H., Cummins, L. H., & Marlatt, G. A. (2004). Preventing substance abuse in American Indian and Alaska native youth: Promising strategies for healthier communities. *Psychological Bulletin, 130,* 304–323.

Heirich, M., & Sieck, C. J. (2003). Helping at-risk drinkers reduce their drinking: Cardiovascular wellness outreach at work. In J. B. Bennett & W. E. K. Lehman (Eds.), *Preventing workplace substance abuse: Beyond drug testing to wellness* (pp. 135–164). Washington, D.C.: American Psychological Association.

Hernandez, D. V., Skewes, M. C., Resor, M. R., Villanueva, M. R., Hanson, B. S., & Blume, A. W. (2006). A pilot test of an alcohol skills training programme for Mexican-American college students. *International Journal of Drug Policy, 17,* 320–328.

Hoffman, J., & Larison, C. (1999). Drug use, workplace accidents and employee turnover. *Journal of Drug Issues, 29,* 341–364.

Holcom, M. L., Lehman, W. E. K., & Simpson, D. D. (1993). Employee accidents: Influences of personal characteristics, job characteristics, and substance use. *Journal of Safety Research, 24,* 205–221.

Holder, H. D., & Wagenaar, A. C. (1994). Mandated server training and reduced alcohol-involved traffic crashes: A time series analysis of the Oregon experience. *Accident Analysis and Prevention, 26,* 89–97.

Hughes, C. (2006). Preventing alcohol-related harm among Australian rural youth: Investigating the social norms approach. *Social Norms Review, 1,* 3–14.

International Center for Alcohol Policies (ICAP). (2000). *Life skills education in South Africa and Botswana*. Washington, D.C.: Author.

International Center for Alcohol Policies (ICAP). (2003). *Alcohol and the workplace*. ICAP Report 13. Washington, D.C.: Author.

International Center for Alcohol Policies (ICAP). (2005a). *Alcohol education and its effectiveness*. ICAP Report 16. Washington, D.C.: Author.

International Center for Alcohol Policies (ICAP). (2005b). Module 3: Social norms marketing. In *ICAP Blue Book: Practical guides for alcohol policy and prevention approaches*. Retrieved August 12, 2007, from www.icap.org.

International Center for Alcohol Policies (ICAP). (2005c). *ICAP Blue Book: Practical guides for alcohol policy and prevention approaches*. Retrieved August 12, 2007, from www.icap.org.

Johannessen, K. (2004). *Reducing high-risk drinking in sorority women using a social norms approach*. Little Falls, NJ: PaperClip Communications.

Johannessen, K., Collins, C., Mills-Novoa, B., & Glider, P. (1999). *A practical guide to alcohol abuse prevention: A campus case study in implementing social norms and environmental management approaches*. Tucson, AZ: Campus Health Service, University of Arizona.

Johnston, L. D., O'Malley, P. M., Bachman, J. G., & Schulenberg, J. E. (2006). *Monitoring the future national survey results on drug use, 1975–2005: Vol. 2. College students and adults ages 19–45*. Bethesda, MD: National Institute on Drug Abuse.

Jones, L., James, M., Jefferson, T., Lushey, C., Morleo, M., Stokes, E., et al. (2007, April). *A review of the effectiveness and cost-effectiveness of interventions delivered in primary and secondary schools to prevent and/or reduce alcohol use by young people under 18 years old*. London: National Institute for Health and Clinical Excellence.

Karam, E., Kypri, K., & Salamoun, M. (2007). Alcohol use among college students: An international perspective. *Current Opinion in Psychiatry, 20,* 213–221.

Kivlahan, D. R., Marlatt, G. A., Fromme, K., Coppel, D. B., & Williams, E. (1990). Secondary prevention with college drinkers: Evaluation of an alcohol skills training program. *Journal of Consulting and Clinical Psychology, 58,* 805–810.

Kypri, K. (2004). College student hazardous drinking in New Zealand, the USA, UK, and Australia: Implications for research, policy, and intervention (pp. 324–325). In J. B. Saunders, K. Kypri, S. T. Walters, R. G. Laforge, & M. E. Larimer, Approaches to brief intervention for hazardous drinking in young people. *Alcoholism: Clinical and Experimental Research, 28,* 322–329.

Kypri, K., & Langley, J. D. (2003). Perceived social norms and their relation to university student drinking. *Journal of Studies on Alcohol, 64,* 829–834.

Larimer, M. E. (1992). *Alcohol abuse and the Greek system: An exploration of fraternity and sorority drinking.* Unpublished doctoral dissertation, University of Washington, Seattle.

Larimer, M. E., Anderson, B. K., Baer, J. S., & Marlatt, G. A. (2000). An individual in context: Predictors of alcohol use and drinking problems among Greek and residence hall students. *Journal of Substance Abuse, 11,* 53–68.

Larimer, M. E., & Cronce, J. M. (2002). Identification, prevention, and treatment: A review of individual-focused strategies to reduce problematic alcohol consumption by college students. *Journal of Studies on Alcohol Supplement, 14,* 148–163.

Larimer, M. E., & Cronce, J. M. (2007). Identification, prevention, and treatment revisited: Individual-focused college drinking prevention strategies, 1999–2006. *Addictive Behaviors, 32,* 2439–2468.

Larimer, M. E., Irvine, D., Kilmer, J., & Marlatt, G. A. (1997). College drinking and the Greek system: Examining the role of perceived norms for high-risk behavior. *Journal of College Student Development, 38,* 587–598.

Larimer, M. E., Turner, A. P., Anderson, B. K., Fader, J. S., Kilmer, J. R., Palmer, R. S., et al. (2001). Evaluating a brief alcohol intervention with fraternities. *Journal of Studies on Alcohol, Special Issue, 62,* 370–380.

Larimer, M.E., Turner, A. P., Mallett, K. A., & Geisner, I. M. (2004). Predicting drinking behavior and alcohol-related problems among fraternity and sorority members: Examining the role of descriptive and injunctive norms. *Psychology of Addictive Behaviors, 18,* 203–212.

Lederman, L. C., Stewart, L. P., Goodhart, F. W., & Laitman, L. (2003). A case against "binge" as the term of choice: Convincing college students to personalize messages about dangerous drinking. *Journal of Health Communication, 8,* 79–91.

Lee, C. M., Maggs, J. L., & Rankin, L. A. (2006). Spring break trips as a risk factor for heavy alcohol use among first-year college students. *Journal of Studies on Alcohol, 67,* 911–916.

Lehman, W. E. K., & Bennett, J. B. (2002). Job risk and employee substance use: The influence of personal background and work environment factors. *American Journal of Drug and Alcohol Abuse, 28,* 263–286.

Lennings, C. J., Feeney, G. F., Sheehan, M., Young, R. M., McPherson, A., & Tucker, J. (1997). Work-place screening of mine employees using the alcohol use disorders identification test (AUDIT) and alcohol breathalyzation. *Drug and Alcohol Review, 16,* 357–363.

Lewis, M. A., & Neighbors, C. (2007). Optimizing personalized normative feedback: The use of gender-specific referents. *Journal of Studies on Alcohol and Drugs, 68,* 228–237.

Lochner, K., Kawachi, I., Kennedy, B. P. (1999). Social capital: A guide to measurement. *Health & Place, 5,* 259–270.

Mangili, A. (2004). Il alcol e lavoro [Alcohol and work]. *Giornale Italiano di Medicina del Lavoro ed Ergonomia, 26,* 255–258.

Marlatt, G. A. (Ed.). (1998). *Harm reduction: Pragmatic strategies for managing high-risk behaviors.* New York: Guilford.

Marlatt, G. A., Baer, J. S., Kivlahan, D. R., Dimeff, L. A., Larimer, M. E., Quigley, L. A., et al. (1998). Screening and brief intervention for high-risk college student drinkers: Results from a two-year follow-up assessment. *Journal of Consulting and Clinical Psychology, 66,* 604–615.

Martell, D., Atkin, C. K., Hembroff, L. A., Smith, S. W., Baumer, A. J., & Greenamayer, J. (2006). College students and "celebration drinking." *Social Norms Review, 1,* 10–17.

Matano, R. A., Futa, K. T., Wanat, S. F., Mussman, L. M., & Leung, C. W. (2000). The employee stress and alcohol project: The development of a computer-based alcohol abuse prevention program for employees. *Journal of Behavioral Health Services and Research, 27,* 152–165.

Mattern, J. L., & Neighbors, C. (2004). Social norms campaigns: Examining the relationship between changes in perceived norms and changes in drinking levels. *Journal of Studies on Alcohol, 65,* 489–493.

McAlaney, J., & McMahon, J. (2007). Normative beliefs, misperceptions, and heavy episodic drinking in a British student sample. *Journal of Studies on Alcohol and Drugs, 68,* 385–392.

McBride, N., Farrington, F., Midford, R., Meuleners, L., & Phillips, M. (2004). Harm minimization in school drug education: Final results of the School Health and Alcohol Harm Reduction Project (SHAHRP). *Addiction, 99,* 278–291.

McBride, N., Midford, R., Farrington, F., & Phillips, M. (2000). Early results from a school alcohol harm minimization study: School Health and Alcohol Harm Reduction Project. *Addiction, 95,* 1021–1042.

McNally, A. M., & Palfai, T. P. (2001). Negative emotional expectancies and readiness to change among college student binge drinkers. *Addictive Behaviors, 26,* 721–734.

Miller, E. T., Kilmer, J. R., Kim, E. L., Weingardt, K. R., & Marlatt, G. A. (2001). Alcohol skills training for college students. In P. M. Monti, S. M. Colby, & T. A. O'Leary (Eds.), *Adolescents, alcohol, and substance abuse: Reaching teens through brief interventions* (pp. 58–79). New York: Guilford.

Miller, W. R. (1996). *Form 90: A structured assessment interview for drinking and related behaviors. Test manual.* Project MATCH Monograph Series (Vol. 5). Rockville, MD: National Institute on Alcohol Abuse and Alcoholism.

Miller, W. R., & Rollnick, S. (2002). *Motivational interviewing: Preparing people for change.* New York: Guilford.

Miller, W. R., Zweben, A., Diclemente, C. C., & Rychtarik, R. G. (1992). *Motivational enhancement therapy manual: A clinical research guide for therapists treating individuals with alcohol abuse and dependence. NIAAA Project MATCH Monograph Series Volume 2.* Rockville, MD: National Institute on Alcohol Abuse and Alcoholism.

Mistral, M., Velleman, R., Templeton, L., & Mastache, C. (2006). Local action to prevent alcohol problems: Is the UK Community Alcohol Prevention Programme the best solution? *International Journal of Drug Policy, 17,* 278–284.

Mulvihill, C., Taylor, L., Waller, S., Naidoo, B., & Thom, B. (2005, March). *Prevention and reduction of alcohol misuse: Evidence briefing* (2nd ed.). London: Health Development Agency.

Murphy, J. G., Duchnick, J. J., Vuchinich, R. E., Davison, J. W., Karg, R. S., Olson, A. M., et al. (2001). Relative efficacy of a brief motivational intervention for college student drinkers. *Psychology of Addictive Behaviors, 15,* 373–379.

Murphy, J. G., Benson, T. A., Vuchinich, R. E., Deskins, M. M., Eakin, D., Flood, A. M., et al. (2004). A comparison of personalized feedback for college student drinkers delivered with and without a motivational interview. *Journal of Studies on Alcohol, 65,* 200–203.

Musher-Eizenman, D., & Kulick, A. (2003). An alcohol expectancy-challenge prevention program for at-risk college women. *Psychology of Addictive Behaviors, 17,* 163–166.

Musitu, G., & Bascones, A. (2006). *Botellón en Málaga: Realidades y propuestas* [*Botellón in Malaga: Realities and proposals*]. Madrid, Spain: Fundación Alcohol y Sociedad.

National Highway Traffic Safety Administration. (n.d.). *Success story: GEICO insurance's Project LIFT helps make the holidays safer for its employees.* Retrieved May 2, 2007, from http://www.nhtsa.dot.gov/people/injury/alcohol/DesignatedDriver/employers2.html.

National Research Council & Institute of Medicine. (2004). Youth-oriented interventions. In *Reducing underage drinking: A collective responsibility* (pp. 185–215). Washington, DC: National Academies Press.

Navarrete, L. (2002). *El fenómeno del botellón en la Comunidad de Madrid* [*The botellón phenomenon and the Madrid community*]. Madrid, Spain: Colegio de Politólogos y Sociólogos de Madrid, Colegio Oficial de Psicólogos de Madrid, Colegio Oficial de Médicos de Madrid.

Neighbors, C., Larimer, M. E., Lostutter, T. W., & Woods, B. A. (2006). Harm reduction and individually focused alcohol prevention. *International Journal of Drug Policy, 17,* 304–309.

Neighbors, C., Lewis, M. A., Bergstrom, R. L., & Larimer, M. E. (2006). Being controlled by normative influences: Self-determination as a moderator of a normative feedback alcohol intervention. *Health Psychology, 25,* 571–579.

Neighbors, C., Oster-Aaland, L., Bergstrom, R. L., & Lewis, M. A. (2006). Event- and context-specific normative misperceptions and high-risk drinking: 21st birthday celebrations and football tailgating. *Journal of Studies on Alcohol, 67,* 282–289.

Newman, I. M., Shell, D. F., Major, L. J., & Workman, T. A. (2006). Use of policy, education, and enforcement to reduce binge drinking among university students: The NU Directions project. *International Journal of Drug Policy, 17,* 339–349.

Odo, J., McQuiller, L., & Stretesky, P. (1999). An empirical assessment of the impact of RIT's student alcohol policy on drinking and binge drinking behaviour. *Journal of Alcohol and Drug Education, 44,* 49–67.

Ohaeri, J. U, Oduyela, S. O., Odejide, A. O., Dipe, T. M, Ikwuagwu, P. U., & Zamani, A. (1996). The history and drinking behaviour of the Nigerian students' palm wine drinkers club. *Drugs: Education, Prevention and Policy, 3,* 171–183.

Ott, C. H., & Doyle, L. H. (2005). An evaluation of the Small Group Norms Challenging Model: Changing substance use misperceptions in five urban high schools. *High School Journal, 88,* 45–55.

Ott, C. H., & Haertlein, C. (2002). Social norms marketing: A prevention strategy to decrease high-risk drinking among college students. *Nursing Clinics of North America, 37,* 351–364.

Peeler, C. M., Far, J., Miller, J., & Brigham, T. A. (2000). Analysis of the effects of a program to reduce heavy drinking among college students. *Journal of Alcohol and Drug Education, 45,* 39–54.

Perkins, W. (2002). Social norms and the prevention of alcohol misuse in collegiate contexts. *Journal of Studies on Alcohol Supplement, 14,* 164–172.

Perkins, H. W. (Ed.). (2003). *Social norms approach to preventing school and college age substance abuse: A handbook for educators, counselors, and clinicians.* San Francisco, CA: Jossey-Bass.

Perkins, H. W. (2007). Misperceptions of peer drinking norms in Canada: Another look at the "reign of error" and its consequences among college students. *Addictive Behaviors, 32,* 2645–2656.

Perkins, H. W., & Berkowitz, A. D. (1986). Perceiving the community norms of alcohol use among students: Some research implications for campus alcohol education programming. *International Journal of the Addictions, 21,* 961–976.

Perkins, H. W., & Craig, D. W. (2002). *Multifaceted social norms approach to reduce high-risk drinking: Lessons from Hobart and William Smith Colleges.* Newton, MA: Higher Education Center for Alcohol and Other Drug Prevention.

Perkins, H. W., & Craig, D. W. (2006). A successful social norms campaign to reduce alcohol misuse among college student-athletes. *Journal of Studies on Alcohol, 67,* 880–889.

Perkins, H. W., Haines, M. P., Rice, R. (2005). Misperceiving the college drinking norm and related problems: A nationwide study of exposure to prevention information, perceived norms and student alcohol misuse. *Journal of Studies on Alcohol, 66,* 470–478.

Perkins, H. W., & Linkenbach, J. (2003). *Harvard study of social norms deserves an "F" grade for flawed research design.* Retrieved August 19, 2007, from http://www.socialnorms.org/pdf/PerkinsLinkenbachOpinion2.pdf.

Perry, C. L., Williams, C. L., Veblen-Mortenson, S., Toomey, T. L., Komro, K. A., Anstine, P. S., et al. (1996). Project Northland: Outcomes of a communitywide alcohol use prevention program during early adolescence. *American Journal of Public Health, 86,* 956–965.

Rice, R. (2002). Some notes on methodological and other issues. In A. Berkowitz (Ed.), *Responding to the critics: Answers to some common questions and concerns about the social norms approach.* Little Falls, NJ: PaperClip Communications.

Richmond, R., Heather, N., Wodak, A., Kehoe, L, & Webster, I. (1995). Controlled evaluation of a general practice-based brief intervention for excessive drinking. *Addiction, 90,* 119–132.

Richmond, R., Kehoe, L., Heather, N., & Wodak, A. (2000). Evaluation of a workplace brief intervention for excessive alcohol consumption: The workscreen project. *Preventive Medicine, 30,* 51–63.

Richmond, R., Wodak, A., Kehoe, L., & Heather, N. (1998). How healthy are the police? A survey of life-style factors. *Addiction, 93,* 1729–1737.

Robertson, P. J., Haitana, T., Pitama, S., & Huriwai, T. T. (2006). A review of the workforce development literature for the Maori addiction treatment field in Aotearoa/New Zealand. *Drug and Alcohol Review, 25,* 233–239.

Roman, P., & Blum, T. (1999). Employee assistance programs and other workplace interventions. In M. Galanter & H. Kleber (Eds.), *Textbook of substance abuse treatment* (2nd ed., pp. 423–435). Washington, D.C.: American Psychiatric Press.

Roman, P., & Blum, T. (2002). The workplace and alcohol prevention. *Alcohol Research and Health, 26,* 49–57.

Russell, C. A., Clapp, J. D., & DeJong, W. (2005). Done 4: Analysis of a failed social norms marketing campaign. *Health Communication, 17,* 57–65.

Saitz, R., Palfai, T. P., Freedner, N., Winter, M. R., Macdonald, A., Lu, J., et al. (2007). Screening and brief intervention online for college students: The iHealth study. *Alcohol and Alcoholism, 42,* 28–36.

Schinke, S. P., Tepavac, L., & Cole, K. C. (2000). Preventing substance use among native American youth: Three-year results. *Addictive Behaviors, 25,* 387–397.

Schroeder, C. M., & Prentice, D. A. (1998). Exposing pluralistic ignorance to reduce alcohol use among college students. *Journal of Applied Social Psychology*, *28*, 2150–2180.

Scott, E., & Anderson, P. (1991). Randomized controlled trial of general practitioner intervention in women with excessive alcohol consumption. *Drug and Alcohol Review*, *10*, 313–321.

Sher, K. J., Bartholow, B. D., & Nanda, S. (2001). Short- and long-term effects of fraternity and sorority membership on heavy drinking: A social norms perspective. *Psychology of Addictive Behaviors, 15,* 42–51.

Shope, J. T., Copeland, L. A., Maharg, R., Dielman, T. E., & Butchart, A. T. (1993). Assessment of adolescent refusal skills in an alcohol misuse prevention study. *Health Education Quarterly*, *20*, 373–390.

Shope, J. T., Copeland, L. A., Marcoux, B. C., & Kamp, M. E. (1996). Effectiveness of a school-based substance abuse prevention program. *Journal of Drug Education*, *26*, 323–337.

Silva, M. C., Gaunekar, G., Patel, V., Kukalekar, D. S., & Fernandes, J. (2003). The prevalence and correlates of hazardous drinking in industrial workers: A study from Goa, India. *Alcohol and Alcoholism*, *38*, 79–85.

Simons, L., Klichine, S., Lantz, V., Ascolese, L., Deihl, S., Schatz, B., & Wright, L. (2005). The relationship between social-contextual factors and alcohol and polydrug use among college freshmen. *Journal of Psychoactive Drugs, 37,* 415–424.

Smith, E. A., Swisher, J. D., Vicary, J. R., Bechtel, L. J., Minner, D., Henry, K. L., et al. (2004). Evaluation of life skills training and infused-life skills training in a rural setting: Outcomes at two years. *Journal of Alcohol and Drug Education, 48*, 51-70.

Snow, D. L., Swan, S. C., & Wilton, L. (2003). Workplace coping-skills intervention to prevent alcohol abuse. In J. B. Bennett & W. E. K. Lehman (Eds.), *Preventing workplace substance abuse: Beyond drug testing to wellness* (pp. 57–96). Washington, D.C.: American Psychological Association.

Spitzberg, I. J., & Thorndike, V. V. (1992). *Creating community on college campuses.* Albany, NY: State University of New York Press.

Stafström, M., Östergren, P. O., Larsson, S., Lindgren, B., & Lundborg, P. (2006). A community action programme for reducing harmful drinking behaviour among adolescents: The Trelleborg Project. *Addiction*, *101*, 813–823.

Ståhlbrandt, H., Johnsson, K.O., & Berglund, M. (2007). Two-year outcome of alcohol interventions in Swedish university Halls of Residence. *Alcoholism: Clinical and Experimental Research*, *31*, 458–466.

Stimson, G., Grant, M., Choquet, M., & Garrison, P. (Eds.). (2007). *Drinking in context: Patterns, interventions, and partnerships.* New York: Routledge.

Substance Abuse and Mental Health Services Administration (SAMHSA). (n.d.). *Border Binge-drinking Reduction program.* Retrieved August 28, 2007, from http://www.publicstrategies.org/newborder/pdf/BorderBinge.pdf.

Substance Abuse and Mental Health Services Administration (SAMHSA). (2002). *Findings from the 2001 National Household Survey on Drug Abuse: Vol. 1. Summary of national findings.* Rockville, MD: SAMHSA Office of Applied Studies.

Task Force of the National Advisory Council on Alcohol Abuse and Alcoholism. (2002). *How to reduce high-risk college drinking: Use proven strategies, fill research gaps.* Bethesda, MD: National Institutes of Health.

Thom, B., & Bayley, M. (2007). *Multi-component programmes: An approach to prevent and reduce alcohol-related harm.* York, U.K.: Joseph Rowntree Foundation.

Toomey, T. L., Lenk, K. M., & Wagenaar, A. C. (2007). Environmental policies to reduce college drinking: An update of research findings. *Journal of Studies on Alcohol and Drugs*, *68*, 208–219.

Treise, D., Wolburg, J. M., & Otnes, C. C. (1999). Understanding the "social gifts" of drinking rituals: An alternative framework for PSA development. *Journal of Advertising, 28,* 17–31.

Trice, H. M. (1992). Work-related risk factors associated with alcohol abuse. *Alcohol Health and Research World, 16,* 106–111.

Turrisi, R., Jaccard, J., Taki, R., Dunnam, H., & Grimes, J. (2001). Examination of the short-term efficacy of a parent intervention to reduce college student drinking tendencies. *Psychology of Addictive Behaviors, 15,* 366–372.

U.S. Department of Labor, Bureau of Labor Statistics. (2005). *Current population survey 2005.* Retrieved May 1, 2007, from http://www.bls.gov.

van Beurden, E., Reilly, D., Dight, R., Mitchell, E., & Beard, J. (2000). Alcohol brief intervention in bars and taverns: A 12-month follow-up study of Operation DrinkSafe in Australia. *Health Promotion International, 15,* 293–302.

van de Luitgaarden, J., Wiers, R. W., Knibbe, R. A., & Boon, B. J. (2006). From the laboratory to real life: A pilot study of an expectancy challenge with "heavy drinking" young people on holiday. *Substance Use and Misuse, 41,* 353–368.

Voas, R. B., Tippetts, A. S., Johnson, M. B., Lange, J. E., & Baker, J. (2002). Operation safe crossing: Using science within a community intervention. *Addiction, 97,* 1205–1214.

Walters, S. T., & Bennett, M. E. (2000). Addressing drinking among college students: Review of the empirical literature. *Alcoholism Treatment Quarterly, 18,* 61–77.

Walters, S. T., Bennett, M. E., & Noto, J. V. (2000). Drinking on campus: What do we know about reducing alcohol use among college students? *Journal of Substance Abuse Treatment, 19,* 223–228.

Wechsler, H., Kelley, K., Weitzman, E. R., San Giovanni, J. P., & Seibring, M. (2000). What colleges are doing about student binge drinking: A survey of college administrators. *Journal of American College Health, 48,* 219–226.

Wechsler, H., & Kuo, M. (2000). College students define binge drinking and estimate its prevalence: Results of a national survey. *Journal of American College Health, 49,* 57–64.

Wechsler, H., Kuo, M., Lee, H., & Dowdall, G. W. (2000). Environmental correlates of underage alcohol use and related problems of college students. *American Journal of Preventive Medicine, 19,* 24–29.

Wechsler, H., Nelson, T. F., Lee, J. E., Seibring, M., Lewis, C., & Keeling, R. P. (2003). Perception and reality: A national evaluation of social norms marketing interventions to reduce college students' heavy alcohol use. *Journal of Studies on Alcohol, 64,* 484–494.

Weitzman, E. R., & Chen, Y. Y. (2005). Risk modifying effect of social capital on measures of heavy alcohol consumption, alcohol abuse, harms, and secondhand effects: National survey findings. *Journal of Epidemiology and Community Health, 59,* 303–309.

Weitzman, E. R., & Kawachi, I. (2000). Giving means receiving: The protective effect of social capital on binge drinking on college campuses. *American Journal of Public Health, 90,* 1936–1939.

Werch, C. E., Pappas, D. M., Carlson, J. M., DiClemente, C. C., Chally, P. S., & Sinder, J. A. (2000). Results of a social norm intervention to prevent binge drinking among first-year residential college students. *Journal of American College Health, 49,* 85–92.

White, H. R. (2006). Reduction of alcohol-related harm on United States campuses: The use of personal feedback interventions. *International Journal of Drug Policy, 17,* 310–319.

White, J., Williams, L. V., & Cho, D. (2003). *A social norms intervention to reduce coercive behaviors among deaf and hard-of-hearing college students.* Little Falls, NJ: PaperClip Communications.

Wiers, R. W., & Kummeling, R. H. (2004). An experimental test of an alcohol expectancy challenge in mixed gender groups of young heavy drinkers. *Addictive Behaviors, 29,* 215–220.

Wiers, R. W., van de Luitgaarden, van den Wildenberg, E., & Smulders, F. T. (2005). Challenging implicit and explicit alcohol-related cognitions in young heavy drinkers. *Addiction, 100,* 806–819.

Wilke, D. J., Siebert, D. C., Delva, J., Smith, M. P., & Howell, R. L. (2005). Gender differences in predicting high-risk drinking among undergraduate students. *Journal of Drug Education, 35,* 79–94.

Williams, C. L., Perry, C. L., Farbakhsh, K., & Veblen-Mortenson, S. (1999). Project Northland: Comprehensive alcohol use prevention for young adolescents, their parents, schools, peers and communities. *Journal of Studies on Alcohol, Supplement 13,* 112–124.

World Health Organization (WHO). (2004). *Global status report: Alcohol policy.* Geneva, Switzerland: Author.

Yang, M. J., Yang, M. S., & Kawachi, I. (2001). Work experience and drinking behavior: Alienation, occupational status, workplace drinking subculture and problem drinking. *Public Health, 115,* 265–271.

Yanovitzky, I., Stewart, L. P., & Lederman, L. C. (2006). Social distance, perceived drinking by peers, and alcohol use by college students. *Health Communication, 19,* 1–10.

Zarkin, G. A., Bray, J. W., Karuntzos, G. T., & Demiralp, B. (2001). The effect of an enhanced employee assistance program (EAP) intervention on EAP utilization. *Journal of Studies on Alcohol, 62,* 351–358.

Ziemelis, A., Bucknam, R. B., & Elfessi, A. M. (2002). Prevention efforts underlying decreases in binge drinking at institutions of higher education. *Journal of American College Health, 50,* 238–252.

Afterword

Marjana Martinic and Fiona Measham

There is evidence that a distinct pattern of alcohol consumption is increasingly a cause for concern in countries across the world because of its relationship with a range of health and social problems. Its visibility, particularly its high involvement of young people, makes this not only an issue for public safety and order in many countries, but also a highly contentious and politicized subject. We have argued in this book that the rapid and heavy drinking behavior under discussion is in need of a new term that fully encapsulates all of its facets, while attempting to sidestep the increasingly unproductive debate surrounding existing terminologies, their numeric definitions, clinical measurement and origin, and a highly charged media presence. We proposed that a useful alternative to terms like *binge* or *heavy episodic drinking* could be offered by *extreme drinking*.

As the preceding chapters have attempted to demonstrate, for better or worse, extreme drinking has always had a place in the historical, social, and cultural context of drinking. It has variously stood for social differences and for separating or stigmatizing those who engage in it from the mainstream of accepted behavior and social mores. In modern Western society, these distinctions continue. Extreme drinking is generally associated with the young, distinguishing them from older groups. Extreme drinking among the young is rarely condoned, though it is often recognized as the youth "sowing its wild oats," a means of experimenting with individual and societal boundaries. Drinking and drunkenness are often a central leisure activity, part of going out and the broader lifestyle of many young people in some cultures. Drinking may serve to facilitate social and sexual relationships and offer a way of exploring new freedoms, tensions, and responsibilities that come with the advent of adulthood.

Despite its apparent wantonness, extreme drinking seems to follow its own rules, adhering to certain conventions and constraints, circumscribed by cultural and societal norms. What may look like unbridled hedonism to the onlooker, may instead be a "controlled loss of control" for the drinkers themselves: Boundaries are, in fact, rarely entirely abandoned. There is a time and place for extreme drinking—usually outside the home environment, with friends, and frequently strategically planned around other activities or responsibilities. However, there is a dual goal to a night of extreme drinking: to get drunk, while at the same time remaining safe. We hope that our proposed term encapsulates all these aspects of this pattern of consumption, which, like extreme sports, can be a planned and purposeful pursuit of fun, excitement, and exhilaration, with varying degrees of actual and perceived risk involved.

Furthermore, this book has attempted to argue in favor of a new approach to addressing both the drinking pattern and its outcomes. Current discussions around extreme drinking focus on "binge drinking," particularly disagreements surrounding its quantifiable definition and measurement. Attempts to address it often include the regulation and criminalization of aspects of extreme drinking and of the young people who participate in it. A new approach is needed that takes into account motivations and the significant role of such drinking practices in contemporary youth and young adult lives, the exploration of limits and liminality, and an attempt to manage everyday constraints and pressures.

Growing rates of extreme drinking in some respects and in some cultures represent a significant change in drinking patterns, illustrating the shifting role that young people play in a changing modern world. Policy measures and interventions need to be specifically tailored to address these various issues. By raising awareness of the motivations, meanings, and consequences of this drinking pattern, it is hoped that a realistic reduction in the negative outcomes of extreme drinking can be achieved.

Procedures for Focus Groups on Extreme Drinking

The proposed focus groups are intended to examine the drinking behavior among young people in a number of countries around the world, focusing in particular on extreme drinking behavior, such as drunkenness and "binge drinking."

The purpose of conducting focus groups is to provide a basis for developing tools and approaches that could assist in reducing extreme drinking among young people and minimizing the risk for harm.

The suggested questions (see Annex 2) are intended to stimulate discussion and to elicit interaction, rather than to serve as a rigid framework for the session. They have been developed with a range of cultures in mind and are intended to assess the motivation and expectancies among young people in relation to extreme drinking behaviors, including drunkenness and "binge" drinking.

We would suggest convening groups of 12 to 20 young people who are over the legally mandated drinking age in your country. These young people should represent the demographic makeup of this group in your country and should be from a variety of socioeconomic and educational backgrounds. The groups should include young men as well as young women. If it is not possible to include both in one group, a separate session with young women should be held.

The results of the focus groups will be compiled and compared across cultures. They are intended to inform work on policy development and may be reported in upcoming ICAP publications, such as books or ICAP Reports.

ICAP does not collect and will not disseminate information from the focus groups for commercial purposes. The comments from the young people will not be attributed and will be used for comparative purposes and for analysis in the aggregate.

However, in producing the agreed report of the focus group sessions, we would encourage you to share with us as much information about the responses as possible, in the event that further analysis of the results is necessary.

All inquiries regarding these focus group discussions should be directed to Marjana Martinic, Vice President for Public Health, at ICAP.

Guiding Questions for Focus Groups[*]

PURPOSE

The purpose is to conduct focus groups in a number of countries where diverse drinking patterns are prevalent and to collect the views of young people on their drinking behavior. The focus is on extreme drinking, excessive drinking, so-called "binge" drinking, and intoxication. The focus groups will attempt to assess the degree to which young people engage in such drinking behavior, the role it plays in their lives and the lives of their peers, and their awareness of the potential risks involved. To the extent possible, the focus groups will examine the motivation behind "extreme drinking," and explore extreme drinking further within the context of young people's risk-taking behavior in general. Our hope would be to identify risk and protective factors, some of which may extend across cultures and others that might be culture-specific, but could be used to inform new approaches to policy, prevention, and education.

The individuals involved in the groups should draw upon their individual experiences and those prevailing in their particular society and culture. The questions below are intended to guide the discussion rather than elicit specific responses from the focus group participants. Please use them as you deem most appropriate.

DISCUSSION ON DRINKING IN GENERAL

1. *Please describe a typical drinking experience for you.* For example: when do you drink, what type of mood are you in, and how much do you typically drink?
   When do you drink alcohol? (weekends, after work, on holiday, etc.)

---

[*] Procedures for conducting the focus groups are set out in Annex 1.

When you drink, do you usually drink just a little, a moderate amount, or a lot?

Think about the last time you drank just a little bit:

    Where were you?

    Who else was there?

    How much did you drink?

Did you intend to drink about that amount before you started drinking?

How did you feel while you were drinking?

What was going on at the time?

Why did you drink a little rather than a lot?

What happened after you stopped drinking?

2. *What are the main influences in your decision to drink?* Your peers, your family? Other influences?

    Do you drink at home?

    Do members of your family drink? Could you describe how much, when, and where?

    Do your parents/family know and approve of your drinking?

    Do you drink primarily when you are with your friends?

    Do you (and your friends) drink because you are bored/there is nothing else to do?

    Do you drink when you feel sad, have problems?

    How old were you when you first began drinking?

    What was the occasion/circumstances when you had your first drink?

    Was it at home with your family, with friends, etc.? Outside the home?

3. *Please describe what a good drinking experience would be.* What would be considered a successful night out?

    Do you ever get together just to drink?

    Is drinking part of a broader social activity? Do you enjoy drinking while you are eating and talking?

    When you drink, are you usually out dancing or socializing with your friends?

    Do you get drunk when you are drinking?

    Do you plan to get drunk before you start drinking?

4. *What do you like about drinking?*

    Let's look at this list. If you had to pick the most important thing that you want to experience when you drink alcohol, what would it be?

        It's relaxing.

        It stimulates social interaction.

        It's what everyone else does.

        It makes me seem older and more sophisticated.

        I like the taste.

        I enjoy getting a "buzz."

        I enjoy getting drunk.

    (Any other answers?)

DISCUSSION ON EXTREME DRINKING

1. *Tell me what you think of this statement: "People your age like to drink to get drunk."* Do you agree with this statement, why or why not? Drinking to "get drunk"—is this what most young people do when they drink, or is this the behavior of just a few (for whatever reason)?

2. *What does it mean to get drunk?* How much would someone have to drink to be considered drunk or intoxicated, and how would they be acting? And who gets this way (everyone, everyone sometimes, men, women, older people, etc.)?

   What do you think when you see your friends drunk?

   Have you been drunk?

   How did that make you feel?

   How did you feel afterwards about your behavior when you were drunk?

   Is excessive drinking acceptable for people your age?

   Is excessive drinking more acceptable for older people or younger people (both, neither)?

   Is excessive drinking more common among men, women, or both the same?

   Do you think younger people drink more than older people?

   How do you think your drinking will change as you get older?

   When your parents were your age, did they drink in the same way as you? (Did they get drunk, not drink at all, etc.)

DESCRIBING CONTEXTS IN WHICH
PEOPLE DRINK TO EXCESS

1. *Do you think people intend to get drunk, or is it something that just happens?*
   Have you ever had more to drink on an occasion than you intended when you started out? If so, why did you drink more than you wanted to?

2. *Thinking about your own experiences, what is going on during these times when you or your friends drink too much?* Think about the last time you drank a lot:

   Where were you?

   Who else was there?

   How much did you drink?

   Did you expect or intend to drink that much before you started drinking?

   How did you feel while you were drinking?

   What was going on at the time?

   Why did you drink a lot rather than a little?

   What happened after you stopped drinking?

3. *What is your experience when you drink, but do not drink a lot?*
In which situations would you drink a little and in which would you drink a lot?
Was there a time you were in a similar situation (a community celebration, a party with friends, and so on) but didn't drink at all? What happened, what was the situation, how did you feel about not drinking?

DESCRIBING WHY PEOPLE DRINK TO EXCESS

1. *Why do you think people drink enough to become drunk?* What are some reasons you or your friends get drunk?
2. *Do you think that people who get drunk are more likely to use drugs? Or break the law?*
   Among people you know, are those who drink excessively also the ones who are more daring/likely to get into trouble?
   Have you been in trouble when you have been drinking? What happened? What were some of the outcomes?
3. *What do you like about getting drunk and what do you not like?*
   Tell me some reasons you and your friends drink to get drunk. What is it about being in that state that you like?
   Tell me some things you don't like about getting drunk: What do you dislike?
   If you were to drink enough to feel the effects of alcohol but not get drunk, would that be as much fun? Would that be considered a successful evening? Why or why not?
4. *We are very interested in how people think about the good and bad things that happen when they are drunk.* Can you tell us how you weigh the good and bad things that happen when drinking enough to be drunk?
   In your view, what are the positive and negative consequences of excessive drinking?
   How do you weigh the good and bad consequences of drinking?
   Is your view of what was good and what was bad the same when you are drinking as it is, for example, the following day?
5. *When bad things do happen, does it change your thinking about your drinking? What would be the one thing that would change how much you drink?*
   How much do you mind having the bad things happen? (These can include both social and physical outcomes, such as not feeling well, throwing up, safety, hangovers, etc.)
   Are there any consequences of drinking a lot that limit your drinking?
   Is there anything that might happen to you that would keep you from ever drinking again? Or that would cause you to drink less?

Index